WELLINGTON
A Military Life

WELLINGTON
A Military Life

GORDON CORRIGAN

Hambledon and London
London and New York

Hambledon and London

102 Gloucester Avenue
London, NW1 8HX

838 Broadway
New York
NY 10003-4812

First Published 2001

ISBN 1 85285 262 3

A description of this book is available from the
British Library and from the Library of Congress.

Typeset by John Saunders Design & Production, Reading

Printed on acid-free paper and bound in
Great Britain by Cambridge University Press

Contents

Plates

Illustration Acknowledgements

The author and the publishers are grateful to Malcolm MacGregor and the General Commanding the Household Division (nos 30 and 31), the National Army Museum (nos 7, 9, 17–20, 23 and 24), the National Portrait Gallery (nos 1, 4, 6, 11-13, 26–29 and 32) and Gale Scanlon (no. 2) for permission to reproduce illustrations.

Maps

Preface

Soldier, diplomat, statesman, university chancellor, Warden of the Cinque Ports, Lord Lieutenant of Hampshire, Knight of the Garter, confidant of monarchs and prime ministers: the first Duke of Wellington was all of these, but it is as a military commander that he is remembered. His campaigns and methods have been subjected to constant analysis, a process that started during his lifetime, and even 150 years after his death the flow of commentaries about the man and his army seems inexhaustible. Even the severest of later historians have rarely found fault, and when they have it has been but a minor part of the successful whole. Wellington was not a man who courted, or always received, public adulation. He was widely respected but rarely liked. He destroyed the majority of letters he received and never wrote for the public. Fortunately, much of his military and official correspondence does survive, as do private letters written by him in his later years. Unlike many great soldiers, before and since, he did not melt into genteel obscurity when his days of glory were over. Wellington fought his last battle – Waterloo – at the age of forty-six, and lived for another thirty-seven years during the whole of which period he held military, political or state offices. He is seen by many as a severe personage: the modern British public thinks of him as the Iron Duke, albeit that the phrase was coined in reference to a battleship after the Duke's death, but neither in politics nor as a commander of armies in the field was he by any means inflexible.[1] He was a genuine supporter of Catholic Emancipation; and he eventually acceded to the 1832 Reform Bill, not because he agreed with its principles, but because, unlike many of his fellow high Tories, he saw that what is inevitable is better given freely than extracted by force.

It may be asked why yet another study of Wellington should be added to the hundreds, perhaps thousands, of works devoted to the man and his battles. Glover and Weller have analysed the Duke's methods and battles, the Countess of Longford and Christopher Hibbert his life. The most recent work is by Peter Hofschröer, who has done historians an immense service by examining the relationship between Wellington and his German allies during the campaign of the Hundred Days in 1815. Hofschröer has attracted considerable attention by his suggestion that Wellington may have tricked the

Prussians into fighting at Ligny on 16 June 1815. I do not accept that this is proven, but even if it is true, so what? The British government was concerned about the extent of Prussian ambitions, with good reason, and Wellington was always a servant of the state: first, last and always. Hofschröer is not the first British historian to have questioned the Anglocentric view of the Prussians' contribution to Napoleon's Hundred Days; that accolade belongs to Colonel Charles Chesney, professor of military history at the cadet college at Sandhurst (later the Staff College, Camberley). Chesney, in a book first published in 1868, with further editions in 1869 and 1874, examined frankly and impartially the suggestion that Wellington failed to react in time to the French crossing of the frontier and was thus unable to support the Prussians at Ligny on 16 June 1815. Chesney's work and his conclusions had been all but forgotten until Hofschröer's recent books, but the publicity afforded to the latter is indicative of the interest Wellington and his campaigns still engender.

There are now few, if any, unexplored sources relating to Wellington, nor facts not already in the public domain, but I have personally examined the ground over which all the battles I describe were fought, and I have attempted to examine them afresh with an infantryman's eye. I have always been fascinated by Wellington – as many a subaltern, forced to listen to long dissertations late at night after a good dinner in the mess, will testify. Having often, when faced with a difficult matter of policy during my own modest military service, asked myself 'What would the Great Duke have done?', I make no apology for seeking to examine Wellington's greatness afresh and attempting to explain just how and why he was the great general that I believe him have been.

Some modern writers, when examining British wars, conclude that this or that was an unnecessary war. They arrive at their assessment by arguing that the expenditure in lives and specie was not commensurate with the situation post bellum. In other words, they argue, Britain was worse off after the war than it was before it, ergo the war should not have been fought. In my view these writers pose the wrong question. They should not ask 'Were we better off after the war than before it?' but rather 'Were we better off after the war than we would have been had we not fought at all?' If this latter question is addressed then a reasonable assessment of the necessity for the war, and thus of the competence of the government at the time, can be made. No judgement as to the abilities of the military commanders involved can be arrived at by the answer to this question, however, because in the Britain of the past three centuries the generals have had no hand in declaring war; only the responsibility for waging it once the political decision has been made. Whatever one's views now as to the merits of a Napoleonic Europe, it was certainly not in the contemporary British interest for France to dominate the

Continent. It was necessary for Britain to finance the anti-French coalitions and to contribute what it could in men and ships. This was a necessary war and Wellington, in India and later in the Peninsula, ensured that the British army played a vital role.

To be classified as 'great' a general must not only be successful but his success must have a lasting effect. It is not sufficient simply to win battles – many British generals have done that, even if more have not – he must win wars. While the winning need not necessarily place the country in a better position after the war than it was before, or even in a better position than it would have been had the war been lost, generals who win unpopular wars tend to be forgotten by the public at large. A general's reputation will only survive if he is seen by contemporaries and by subsequent historians as having been great, and this can often be out of proportion to the scale of his battles or wars. Wellington's army did not win all its battles (Burgos was a disaster and Albuhera only a victory in the sense that the French left the field). He commanded what was, by European standards, a tiny army in a peripheral theatre of the wars against Napoleonic France, yet not only his own countrymen but all Europe saw him as being great and deferred to his views, both after Napoleon's abdication in 1814 and after his final defeat in 1815.

Wellington's army never numbered more than 100,000 men, Spain was a subsidiary theatre, the Peninsular War was never a national war (although the waging of it was generally popular with the country at large), nor fought à l'outrance. The French were defeated in 1814 by the Austrians, Prussians and Russians when Wellington's army had only just reached the enemy homeland. Yet the combination of Trafalgar in 1805 and Waterloo in 1815 made Britain a world power - indeed the only world power – for nearly a century.

There were heroes before Agamemnon, and there had been able and successful British generals before Wellington. Stringer Lawrence (1697–1775), whose best work was done in India, was a brilliant trainer; Amherst (1717–1787) was successful in battle in his earlier days but declined as he got older and became a dead hand on military progress; Wolfe (1727–1759) might have achieved greatness had not a French bullet killed him before tuberculosis certainly would have; Abercromby (1734-1801), the captor of St Lucia and Trinidad and architect of the French defeat in Egypt, might have achieved lasting fame had he fought his battles in the European theatre; and Cornwallis (1738–1805) could have been great had he not been associated with a defeat not of his own making.

The most notable of Wellington's predecessors was Marlborough, who, like him, had to contend with difficult allies and keep one eye on his own government while commanding a small army a long way from home. Like

Arthur Wellesley, John Churchill won victory for the British against heavy odds, but his name is not still known to every schoolboy in the land, nor does he boast a railway station, two public schools, a village and innumerable closes, roads, streets and estates – in England alone - named after him or his battles. Nor, unlike Wellington, did Marlborough remain loyal to his political masters, his friends or his backers – he was largely driven by self-interest, and his behaviour prior to and during the 'Glorious Revolution' was by strict legal interpretation nothing less than treasonable. Finally, Marlborough lapsed into dotage in his old age, whilst Wellington remained mentally and physic-ally alert to the end of his days.

The weapons and tactics of the armies of Marlborough and Wellington were not very different: what was different was the method of managing them. While he did not fight a modern war, Wellington was in many ways the first of the modern generals. Unlike Marlborough, Wellington led a literate army whose doings were followed by a literate public. Marlborough's officers and soldiers did not keep diaries, nor write to the newspapers, and few published their memoirs. There is nothing from Marlborough's wars to compare with the personal accounts and letters written by participants in Wellington's wars, nor anything to compare with Gurwood's collection of Wellington's despatches, the latter being a model of clear, unambiguous and economical writing. One can imagine Wellington coping with the battles of the Great War, and even conducting the Normandy battles rather better than Montgomery, but it is difficult to imagine Marlborough making the same adjustment.

Wellington shines amongst his fellow generals. Sir John Moore might have achieved a comparable reputation – he was probably the only contemporary under whom Wellington would have been happy to serve – but his military life was cut short at Coruña. Black Bob Crauford was a thorough profes-sional, probably the best divisional commander in the Peninsula, if too inclined to seek battle without thought of the consequences to the rest of the army. He was killed at Ciudad Rodrigo in 1812. Beresford was a trusted subord-inate, a brilliant organiser and trainer with the ability to act independently. Wellington considered that Beresford should succeed to supreme command if he himself was killed or incapacitated, but his handling of troops in battle can only be described as adequate. Picton reached his ceiling, and met his death, as a divisional commander and Wellington kept Paget under a tight rein for very good reasons.

Wellington's very early days did not indicate his future greatness. A self-proclaimed sprig of the nobility (and very minor nobility at that), his early years were spent as an ADC, as a minor politician and as a lounge lizard in the making. It was not until he purchased a lieutenant colonelcy and command of the 33rd Foot at the age of twenty-four that he underwent an almost Pauline conversion and from then on devoted himself to his profession (not a noun applied to the military life in the late eighteenth century). He made his reputation in India, often thought of as a military backwater (although judging by the number of contemporary generals who had served there this view may be mistaken). He panicked at Seringapatam, for the only time in his life, then saved his army from potential massacre at Assaye, and planned and carried out the successful storming of Gawilghur. He returned to England as a major general, with his debts paid and in a position to enter into what turned out to be an unsatisfactory marriage, to which he remained loyal until it ended with his wife's death.

Wellington was successful and his victories made a difference to England's world position, but his reputation rests on far more than that. He had a natural assumption of command. He understood the political limits under which he operated. He had a happy knack of cooperating with allies, whatever he thought of them privately. He understood the importance of logistics in what we would now term third world countries. He appreciated the limitations of his subordinate commanders, using their talents and compensating for their weaknesses. He had a mastery of detail and was capable of prodigious amounts of work. He effectively ran the whole army himself. He had an astute feel for tactics and an ability to cut through the 'fog of war' and identify what was critical and what could be ignored or postponed. Finally, Wellington had that inherent and instinctive assumption of leadership and a confidence that communicated itself to those under him.

Argument still rages (at least in the military academies of the western world) as to whether leaders are born or made. Proponents of the functional theory of leadership aver that leadership can be defined by what a leader is required to do, and that those functions can be learned. If a man, or woman, carries out those quantifiable functions then he or she is by definition a leader. Advocates of what might be termed the genetic theory say that leaders are born with a natural ability to inspire others, and if this is lacking then the person can never be a leader. The answer, as so often, probably lies in the middle. However charismatic a personality may be, if he does not understand the principles of military management he cannot be a successful leader. Similarly, the most adept manager will not succeed if his personality traits are such that he does not inspire something above the call of mere duty. It is reasonable to assume that those who do not enjoy the practice of leadership do not aspire to it. Military officers will, if they are honest, admit that they obtain considerable satisfaction from directing the activities of others. If this could equally be said of the manager of a factory making tin boxes, the latter is not charged with persuading men to attempt something which may well lead to their own death or mutilation. Wellington was an instinctive leader, but he also knew how to manage military force to ensure that when he committed his troops they had all the material support they needed. They did not get paid very much, but they did get paid; they were often hungry, but they were fed; medical science was in its infancy, but the casualty evacuation system and the hospitals were as good as Wellington could make them.

The army that the young Arthur Wesley joined was not overconcerned with instruction in leadership. There was an assumption that officers were gentlemen and thus possessed of a natural superiority over those whom they commanded. Given the class structure of the time this was generally correct, but the only formal qualification for a commission was literacy; appointments in peace were obtained by patronage, assuming that the aspirant could obtain the funds needed to purchase his first commission. Many of the officers whom Wellington found in his Peninsular army were idle or incompetent, not because they lacked intelligence or education but because they lacked motivation. It is to Wellington's great credit that he provided that motivation, and by 1814 there were few officers left who were incapable of performing their duties. As he had received little if any formal education in leadership himself, he learned as he went along, and he also learned how to impart those lessons to others. As he said in relation to the Duke of York's less than satisfactory campaign in Flanders in 1794 and 1795: 'at least I learned how not to do it, which is always something'.

It has been said that the art of being a commanding officer is the art of commanding officers. The more senior the commander, the more remote from the rank and file he becomes. He must impress his will on those who have to carry out the 'business of the day', as Wellington put it, through his immediate subordinates. As a commander of an army Wellington rarely addressed the troops directly – he could not easily have done so – therefore he had to ensure that those who were the direct recipients of his orders understood what he wanted done and how he wanted it done. That he was able to motivate such diverse characters as the intellectual Le Marchant and the bloodthirsty Picton, and have the total respect of professionals such as Fletcher, his chief engineer, and McGrigor his chief medical officer, and control hotheads like Crauford and the young Prince of Orange, is indicative of his extraordinary qualities.

We are especially fortunate that so many eyewitness accounts survive, many published, others not. While many of the journals written by those who had served under Wellington are inaccurate or distorted, either due to the fog of war or in search of self-aggrandisement, in the absence of war diaries they are the nearest we can get to primary sources. Cavalié Mercer commanded a horse artillery troop (equivalent to a modern battery) at Waterloo, but saw

nothing of d'Erlon's attack on the Allied centre left, and despite being himself
positioned on Wellington's centre right saw little of the final attack by the
Imperial Guard – the smoke of war restricted his vision to a few yards.
Siborne's letters are increasingly viewed with suspicion, as cash on the nail
may have influenced what was published and what was not. Despite all this,
the contemporary accounts, taken in the round, do give an accurate picture
of what it must have been like to serve under the Great Duke and fight in his
battles.

As a soldier Wellington should be judged by what he did at the height of his
powers, as a commander of armies, rather than by his tenure as Commander-
in-Chief of the British army from 1842 to his death in 1852. By the time he was
ensconced in Horse Guards he was too old and too set in his ways to be the
effective reformer that he might have been in his younger days. The appalling
state of the British army in the Crimea has to be laid at Wellington's door - a
negation of everything that he strove for and insisted upon as a commander
in the field from 1794 to 1815 – even given that successive governments had
refused to spend money or pay much attention to the state of the army in
peace. It is from the confident, fit, alert commander at Assaye, Talavera and
Waterloo that Wellington's greatness derives; the disappointments of his
later years cannot detract from that.

I owe an enormous debt of thanks to those who have gone before, from those
who wrote of their own experiences in Wellington's army to modern authors.
In writing this book I have mined deeply in the seams of modern literature
about the man and his battles, and these sources are listed in the bibliog-
raphy. I have also been greatly encouraged by a number of historians far more
eminent than myself who have taken the trouble to read my endeavours and
advise upon them. In this context I am particularly grateful to Dr Gary
Sheffield, late of the Royal Military Academy Sandhurst and now of King's
College, London, whose help and guidance has been unflagging, and to my
fellow members of the British Commission for Military History, an extraordinary body which seems to contain at least one expert in any of the most
arcane aspects of historical scholarship.

In examining the mass of available material concerning my subject I have
tried to be guided by two principles. The first was enumerated by that great
scholar of the history of war, Colonel Charles Chesney, a professor and a
soldier. Quoting the early Victorian writer Cornewall Lewis, Chesney insisted
that 'historical evidence, like judicial evidence, is founded on the testimony of
credible witnesses'. For the second I follow the guidelines for judges
conducting a judicial review: 'Could a reasonable man, faced with the
evidence that he was faced with, have come to the conclusion that he did,

even if we, faced with the same evidence, might have come to a different conclusion?'

I also owe enormous thanks to those who have helped me in the preparation of this volume. The staffs of the Public Record Office, the British Library, the National Portrait Gallery and the Prince Consort's Library, Aldershot, have (as always), been unflaggingly courteous and informative. Having often been irritated by the standard of maps in some modern historical works, I am greatly indebted to my cartographer, Shelagh Lea. A combination of her own military service, a love of geography and inborn artistic talent has enabled her to take my scruffy first drafts of text and produce from them maps that are accurate, informative and easy to follow. I am grateful to Dr Tony Heathcote for his advice on the promotion system of the period; to John Hussey for his help with Bylandt's Brigade; and to Brigadier Douglas Wickenden, consultant psychiatrist to the British army, for his assessment of Field Marshal Prince Blücher. Malcolm MacGregor, an old friend from army days, has provided excellent photographs of Wellington's London house and office as they are today. Tony Morris and Martin Sheppard, of Hambledon and London, have been consistently encouraging during the preparation and editing of my work.

I must make particular reference to my wife Imogen, a veteran of twenty years in the Women's Royal Army Corps and no mean historian herself. That she was persuaded, in the early days of our marriage, to accompany me in a walk from Quatre Bras to Mont St-Jean in pouring rain in order to experience a little of what Wellington's men had to do, and that divorce was only mentioned once, says much. Despite it being her ruling at one stage of our married life that I was forbidden to mention the name Wellington at dinner parties, she has assisted me in the preparation of this book, proof-read it and compiled the index. Wellington is reputed to have ordered that his officers should not spend more than three days at a time on leave in Lisbon, this being the longest time that any man would wish to spend in bed with the same woman. I have spent sixteen years in bed with the same woman and I do not regret a moment of it.

1

Ireland

The year 1769 was not, in general, extraordinary. Austria occupied part of Poland, Russian troops entered Moldavia, the Privy Council in London decided to retain the duty on tea in the American colonies, the first steam road carriage was built, lightning conductors began to be placed on tall buildings, Joshua Reynolds was knighted, John Wilkes was expelled from Parliament and imprisoned, Pope Clement XIII died and Madame du Barry became the mistress of Louis XV. In Corsica, the wife of an obscure lawyer gave birth to a son whom the parents christened Napoleone; and, in Ireland, Anne Wesley, the Countess of Mornington, wife of a Professor of Music at Trinity College Dublin, produced a sixth child, who was named Arthur after a previous son who had died in infancy.

Nobody is absolutely certain where or when Arthur Wesley, the future Duke of Wellington, was born. At the time of his birth the family lived in what is now Upper Merrion Street, an expensive area of high-class residential property, not long built. Then it was plain Merrion Street, and local legend places the birth at number 24 (number 6 in 1769), others say number 21. The births column of the Dublin newspapers announced the birth of a son to the Countess of Mornington on 1 May 1769 in Merrion Street. Wellington himself, when filling in the return for the census of 1851, a year before his death, is said to have written 'Ireland, believed Athie' (in County Kildare), but the census returns were destroyed in 1913. The newspaper report seems the best evidence.[1]

The Wesleys were minor members of the Anglo-Irish nobility. The family had adopted the name Wesley as a result of Arthur's grandfather succeeding to the estate of his cousin, Garrett Wesley, whose family had taken the name on an advantageous marriage to a Wesley heiress. Previously the patronymic had been Colley, or Cowley, and their Irish antecedents are unclear, although they were certainly of the Protestant religion. They were said to have originated in Gloucestershire, but claimed to have been in Dublin for 400 years. Taken at face value, this would indicate that the Colleys arrived with Richard I's expedition in 1349, which succeeded in bringing the Gaelic and Anglo-Irish lords to heel, at least for a time.

The Wesleys, or Westleighs, whose blood was slighter bluer than that of the

Colleys, and into whom the Colleys married and whose estates they inherited, were said to have originated in Devon. They claimed to have been translated to Ireland with Henry II in 1169, where they settled in County Meath, but Anglo-Irish genealogy is notorious for the creation of unprovable links to a respectable English past (particularly if, like the Wesleys, the original bearers of the name had died out); and, given that they too were of the Protestant faith, they could equally well have come over with or shortly before Cromwell.

In 1728 Richard Colley, Arthur's grandfather, having inherited the estates of the last Wesley (a distant cousin), changed the family name to Wesley and was shortly afterwards created a baron in the Irish peerage, adopting the title of Baron Mornington after his recently acquired estates. His son, Garrett Wesley, succeeded him and in 1760 became Earl of Mornington and, as a junior title with yet another change of name, Viscount Wellesley, both titles in the Irish peerage. While the title became Wellesley, the family name did not. Although the eldest son, Richard, inherited both titles and changed his name to Wellesley on the death of their father in 1781, Arthur remained Wesley until both brothers were together in India, Richard as Governor-General and Arthur as a colonel in the army. Just why the spelling of the name was altered we do not know, although it does appear that the Wesleys had at some previous time been Wellesleys. Spelling was still fairly arbitrary in the 1760s, especially in Ireland; perhaps Garrett felt that Wellesley had a more aristocratic ring to it, or perhaps he wanted to distinguish his family from the Methodist preacher John Wesley. The Wellesleys always denied they were in any way related to John Wesley, despite the attempts of some contemporary writers to establish a link, and indeed it seems most unlikely that they were connected, other than by possibly having at some remote period a common ancestor. Presumably Arthur Wesley did not feel it was worth the trouble of changing his name until both brothers found themselves together in India, when different surnames might have caused confusion.

The position of the Anglo-Irish in the eighteenth century was anomalous. Like the Ulster loyalists of today, they professed attachment to an England which very largely ignored them, and treated their Parliament with disdain. They considered themselves to be English expatriates surrounded by a large and potentially hostile population, as indeed they were. Unlike their Norman and Angevin predecessors, they had not intermarried nor been absorbed into the Gaelic aristocracy. The males married each other's cousins and sisters and most had champagne tastes while living on beer incomes. Estates might be impressive – some ran to many thousand acres – but most were mortgaged several times over and rented to Irish tenant farmers, who were frequently unable to pay the rent demanded. Revolution, whether stirred by the French, the Spaniards or the papacy, was an ever-present fear. A large part of the tiny British army was stationed in Ireland – and with a nice irony 30 per cent of its recruits were Irish. The Yeomanry, the nearest equivalent to a police force, was almost exclusively Anglo-Irish. Both Catholic and Protestant families were large, but there was insufficient land to support all the sons. The outlets for younger sons were government or political service (either in England or at home), the church or the army.

Wellington always played down his Irish roots and in his later years was content to allow them to remain obscure. Amongst the many statements attributed to him, most of them apocryphal, is his reply to a query as to whether he was Irish: 'To be born in a stable does not make a man a horse.' Whether he actually said it does not matter: it was certainly his attitude and in this he was at one with the majority of the Anglo-Irish, who resolutely refused to identify with Ireland and the Irish, other than as the governing class. Minorities tend to exaggerate their purity of race, religion or culture, and the Protestant Irish clung to an identification with England at any cost, eschewing absorption into the mainstream of the despised natives.

Whatever the precise details of Arthur Wesley's genealogy, it is established that his father was an accomplished musician who composed numerous madrigals, catches and 'glees', as well as at least one march. He became a Doctor of Music and then, in 1764, Professor of Music at Trinity College, a short stroll from Mornington House in Merrion Street. It is said (notably by Fortescue) that Garrett owed his advancement in the peerage to the musical tastes of George III, although there is no evidence that the two ever met.

In 1760, at the age of twenty-three, Garrett Wesley married the sixteen-year-old Anne Hill, the progeny of a stout Ascendancy tradition. Her father had been plain Arthur Hill, a banker, before becoming Arthur Hill-Trevor and finally the first Viscount Dungannon. The Countess of Mornington's first son was born in the year of her marriage and in all she bore her husband nine children. Seven survived, Arthur being the sixth to be born, in 1769, but the fourth (behind Richard, William and Anne and before Gerald, Henry and Mary) to reach adulthood.

We do not know a great deal about Arthur Wesley's mother, although she appears to have been a woman of firm principles. It has been said that she had no great opinion of Arthur, considering him to be stupid, slow of speech and with a dull manner. She certainly never seems to have considered him a match for his eldest brother Richard, who from an early age showed an intellectual brilliance and a talent for administration that would take him, via Oxford and Parliament, to the Governor-Generalship of India. As Garrett died in 1781, when Arthur was only twelve years old, it is reasonable to assume that his mother was the major influence on the development of the future

Duke's character. While it may be going too far to suggest that the later propensity of her sons to contract unhappy, or at least unusual, marriages was due to their attitudes towards women having been formed by their relationship with their mother, in Arthur's lifelong habit of daily cold water bathing, his attention to detail, his strict interpretation of honour, his unshakeable integrity, his capacity for hard work, his temperate habits, his (usually disguised) craving for affection and his attention to household budgeting we can surely see the influence of the hard-headed Anglo-Irish Protestant ethic of his mother. Arthur Wesley may not consciously have set out to attract his mother's approval by success in the military sphere, but it must have been a factor which contributed to his determination to get to the top, and would appear to be a not uncommon driving force underlying the motivation of many great soldiers (Montgomery being the obvious example) whose relations with their mothers have been strained. He involved neither his mother, who died in 1831, nor his wife in his later greatness, and in family and sexual matters, as in his military life, he preferred to 'walk alone'. Many of the Great Duke's characteristics, however, are unlikely to have been the product of maternal genes. He was when young an accomplished player of the violin, and his religious tolerance, unconcern with sexual impropriety (except where his own family was concerned), a light-hearted view of the world outside soldiering and politics, and an ability to second guess both enemy and friend are more likely to have come from his talented, feckless father.

Long before his espousal of Catholic Emancipation, forced through Parliament for purely practical reasons, Arthur Wesley showed a toleration towards Romish practices wholly untypical of the Anglo-Irish Protestant. Much of this was harshly realistic: he served in an army in which around one third of the soldiers were Catholics, recruited from Ireland or Scotland, and which operated in, and was allied to, Catholic Spain and Portugal; yet his authorisation of the open attendance of soldiers at mass, and his friendship with Catholic clerics, went beyond the merely pragmatic. His own religious views seem to have been lightly held. On a number of occasions, notably after the battle of Sorauren in 1814 and the night after Waterloo, he said that he felt that the finger of God was upon him, but in this context it is clear that he used God as he might have said Providence or Fate. His introduction of chaplains into the army was a matter of discipline and welfare, rather than of theology, and a field sermon lasting more than twenty minutes would lead to an ostentatious examination of his watch at best and a rebuke at worst. He attended church when in England, more for form's sake than through any deeply held conviction, and often slept (and snored) throughout the proceedings. If he spoke about religion at all, he usually referred to Christianity rather than to any particular denomination, and said that it had the great advantage of requiring only that one lived without doing any harm to others. While his devotion appears to have increased in old age, this was probably the well-known tendency to back the horse both ways when mortality becomes imminent. His extraordinary relationship with the spiritualist Anna Maria Jenkins, which started in his sixties and only ceased shortly before his death, can surely be attributed to a lonely old man's fascination with a young and pretty girl who worshipped him. In religion, as in politics, he disliked party.[2]

When Arthur Wesley was seven his parents moved more or less permanently to London, one of the reasons given being the wish for the children not to grow up with Irish accents, which the Morningtons thought would be a disadvantage in later life. The family was in any case short of money and there was little left after Richard, the eldest, had been educated. Arthur first attended a school in the King's Road, Chelsea, where by his own admission he was a dreamy, shy boy who avoided the company of his outgoing, rougher fellow pupils. After the death of his father in 1781, and the mortgaging of the family's Irish estates, he was sent to Eton with his younger brother Gerald. At Eton in the 1780s the food was mediocre, bullying rife and scholastic achievement patchy. Arthur does not appear to have enjoyed being there, nor to have attained any honours. He was unable to master the classics, saying in later life that Eton had taught him never to take on anything about which he knew nothing, and never to speak in Latin. While he may have had a fight with a boy who threw a stone at him, he could not recall the incident years later. He also avoided football. It is most unlikely that he ever said that the battle of Waterloo was won on the playing fields of Eton, although he did send his two sons there and recommended it to those who asked his advice as to schooling.

In 1784 it was time for the youngest brother, Henry, to come to Eton, but the money did not run to the education of three sons there. After three largely unproductive years, Arthur was removed and, following a short period with a private tutor in Brighton, was taken to Brussels by his mother, who seems to have felt that if her dull son could not master Latin and Greek he might at least cope with French. Attending a local school, he managed to speak faltering French, with a Belgian accent, and was favourably reported on for his ability to play the violin, thus exhibiting at least one talent inherited from his father.

The question now facing Anne, dowager Countess of Mornington, was what to do with her ugly duckling. As the fourth child there would be no money or lands for him; there was little enough for his elder brother, now second Earl of Mornington, but at least making a career for himself in politics in Pitt the Younger's administration. Arthur's youngest brother, Henry, had showed some inclination to join the army and to the countess it seemed that this might do for poor Arthur – 'fit only for powder', as she put it. Before returning to England she installed her son in a private military academy in Angers in France, presided over by a M. de Pignerolle, where he was to remain until 1786.

The academy at Angers was far from being a Sandhurst, or even a St-Cyr. In many ways it typified the last days of the Ancien Régime, before the Revolution swept it away forever. The syllabus included the theory of fortifications, fencing and equitation, but more than anything else sought to inculcate the virtues of honour and nobility. The year's course does not appear to have been overly demanding, but it did smooth the rough edges off the young Wesley, and it did enable him to perfect his French, which he spoke and wrote simply but fluently thereafter. At a time when French, rather than English, was the language of diplomacy, and when it was often the only language which he had in common with his allies (notably Blücher and the Prussian high command), this would stand him in good stead in the future. He also mastered horsemanship, something he would pursue to the end of his days, whether as a means of transport round the battlefield or in pursuit of the fox on the hunting field. His riding was never stylish but, as he rarely seems to have fallen off, he was clearly competent enough. His mother was grudgingly impressed by his progress, considering him to have grown and to be much less ugly than he had been a year before. On leaving Angers in 1786, he was reported on by M. de Pignerolle as being an Irish lad of great promise. He had not yet shaken off the shackles of his birth.

The army that Arthur Wesley was to join was organisationally in a state of flux. Unlike the Prussians, the Austrians or the French, the British made no claim to military greatness on land. There had been no grand plan to create and maintain a British army. Expeditionary forces were cobbled together as and when needed, and speedily reduced to the bare minimum once no longer required. It was true that British arms had marched triumphantly across Europe under the great Marlborough, but after the Treaty of Utrecht in 1713 had brought the War of the Spanish Succession to an end little attention was paid to matters military until the Seven Years War of 1756 to 1763.

The English had long been suspicious of armies, seeing them as a threat to liberty and a drain on revenue. While no one alive in the mid eighteenth century could remember Cromwell's major generals, enough of a tradition had been passed down to imbue all classes with an antipathy to any power or independence of action being entrusted to the military. During the long peace after Marlborough's wars, there were many who thought that an army was an unnecessary irrelevance – England's defence was the sea, and was taken care of by the navy.

Originally the manning of garrisons and the conduct of operations on land were carried out by a collection of regiments raised for a specific purpose and then disbanded when the threat had passed. The reluctance of the government to spend money or to engage in active military management had given rise to the 'Regimental System', where the raising, equipping and command of regiments was effectively contracted out to an individual, known as the colonel of the regiment, not to be confused with the more generally understood rank of colonel. A colonel of a regiment might have military experience, but not necessarily, and received a lump sum from the government in return for an undertaking to produce a regiment manned, trained and equipped for the business of war. The colonel was effectively the proprietor of the regiment, which wore uniforms designed by him, usually bore his name and was officered by men selected by him. The colonel might take the field with his regiment, but more often did not, so his surrogate, the lieutenant colonel, normally exercised day to day command. It was a system which gave rise to all manner of fraud and corruption but, given the antipathy to all things military in time of peace and a reluctance to spend, it would be a long time before this disparate collection of regiments would merge into a national army. Bad colonels lined their pockets by skimping on clothing and equipment, while good ones dug into their own funds to produce an effective body of men capable of taking the field. Tactics and drills were arbitrary and very much at the whim of the colonels or their representatives. Prior to 1714 there were hardly any barracks as such in England, troops being billeted in inns or in private houses. Even when a programme of barrack construction was begun, the government was accused of hiding troops away from the public gaze, so as to permit a covert increase in the size of the army. It was small wonder that the public disliked the army. The soldiers were poorly paid, were generally recruited from the lowest strata of society and were prone to indiscipline punctuated by occasional outbreaks of sobriety. In the absence of a police force, it was the army that put down rural unrest and controlled urban licence. While the navy won its battles and operated away from the public gaze, the soldiers, after Marlborough, generally lost their battles and were all too prominently in the public eye.[3]

Reform had to come. Eventually, and very slowly, it did. The process was begun by King George II, no doubt inspired by his own experiences under Marlborough at Oudenarde and his nominal command, as King, of the army at the battle of Dettingen. He may also have been inspired by the example of his continental neighbour, Frederick II ('the Great') of Prussia. In the same year as Dettingen, 1743, George issued the first of three royal warrants, the others following in 1747 and 1751, designed to regulate the structure of the army. These regulations dealt mainly with uniforms and colours, and transferred some of the powers of the colonels to the King and the government, but the army was still a collection of regiments rather than a corporate military body. The army fought well enough in the War of the Austrian Succession in 1740–48, but there had been little glory to be had in putting down rebellion at home in 1745 and 1746. In contrast, the Seven Years War brought gains in America, India and the Mediterranean, and led to the emergence of the Militia at home.

The Militia was a mixed blessing. Put on a proper organisational footing in 1757, the Militia came under the Home Department, rather than the Commander-in-Chief, and was originally intended as a substitute for the regular army, before evolving into a home defence force. Militia units were raised by parish authorities, under the direction of the Lords Lieutenant of the counties. Each county was to provide 1600 Protestant men to be selected by ballot. Men chosen were required to serve for three years, after which they would be exempt until all others liable had served. There were, inevitably, ways round the ballot. A man selected could pay a substitute to serve in his place, but the punishment for desertion from the Militia was compulsory enlistment into the regular army. By statute the Militia was subject to the Mutiny Acts, but it could not be required to serve outside the United Kingdom. Officers were not necessarily from the gentry, although many were, and as commissions were granted by the Lords Lieutenant without purchase, many sons of skilled artisans or small businessmen took this opportunity of experiencing some of the aspects of a military life, without its dangers. If the Royal Navy fulfilled its role of ensuring that an invasion of the British Isles was impossible, what then was the role of the Militia? Originally, and until well into the Napoleonic Wars, members of the Militia were forbidden to enlist in the regular army, thus depriving the latter of a large number of potential recruits. Militia service was in any case preferable to regular service, if only because the families of Militia soldiers who were killed or posted away from their home county became the responsibility of the parish, whereas those of regular soldiers were left to fend for themselves.[4]

Suspicion of military power had led to a system of checks and balances (mainly checks) to prevent the army from menacing the government. Theoretically the King was head of the army, but it was Parliament which provided the money to finance it. There was a Commander-in-Chief, although in peacetime the appointment was often left vacant. He was responsible for the training and discipline of the infantry and cavalry of the line, including the appointment, promotion and posting of their officers; also the finding of staff officers; the appointment of general officers at home; and the defence of Britain in time of war. He had no control over expeditionary forces or overseas garrisons. He also had no control over household troops, the Life Guards, the Royal Horse Guards and the Footguards, which came under the

King's prerogative. The Commander-in-Chief could only issue instructions to them via their colonels. From the end of the American and French wars in 1783 until the outbreak of the war with France in 1793 there was no Commander-in-Chief, a situation which did not enhance the prospects for reform.

Armies cannot move or operate without transport, arms, ammunition, and supplies, but these services were in the hands not of the Commander-in-Chief but of the Master General of the Ordnance. Unlike the Commander-in-Chief, the Master General of the Ordnance was a member of the government and its principal military adviser. The post was always filled and therefore acquired more influence than the often-vacant post of Commander-in-Chief. Under the Master General of the Ordnance came the Royal Artillery, the guns being under the command of the Master General but the drivers being civilians hired for the purpose when required, a situation which was not changed until the formation of the Corps of Artillery Drivers, composed of soldiers, in 1793. The Master General of the Ordnance also controlled the engineers, and had responsibility for the procurement of guns for the navy and for the provision of weapons, ammunition, maps, some items of clothing and various supply services for the army

Prior to 1794 there was no government minister responsible for the army, the senior figure being the Secretary at War, who was a political appointee responsible for all military management, including finance, the handling of commissions, controlling the budget and for movement of troops within the United Kingdom, but with no constitutional standing. Overseas, responsibility for military matters was shared between the Foreign Secretary and the Secretary of State for the Colonies. In 1751 Burke's Act for Economical Reform made the Secretary at War responsible to Parliament for the army and its finances, rather than being as previously merely the conduit between the King and the army. For the next thirty years the army underwent a series of reorganisations designed, on the one hand, to keep it firmly under civilian control and, on the other, to improve its efficiency. These included consecutive numbering of regiments, rather than the majority being known only by the name of their colonels, and a suggestion that regiments might take the name of, and recruit mainly from, designated counties. This latter proposal was promulgated to colonels in 1782. Some, a few, were in favour. The colonel of the 5th Foot replied that he could think of nothing better than having 'Northumberland' affixed to his regiment's title, but then the colonel was the Duke of Northumberland. Most were opposed and the proposal made little headway until Cardwell's reorganisation a century later. It was not until 1794 that a Secretary for War, a minister, was appointed. From 1801 the responsibilities for war and the colonies were combined into that of Secretary of State for War and the Colonies.

For the army of the late eighteenth century to undertake even the simplest of tasks it was necessary for the Commander-in-Chief (if one was appointed) to supply the infantry and cavalry (with royal concurrence if this involved household troops), the Master General of the Ordnance to provide artillery, supplies and ammunition, the Secretary at War to authorise movement, and the Treasury to agree the expenditure. It all meant that a military coup was almost impossible – and an operation of war very difficult.

The peacetime strength of the army was generally fixed at about 50,000. This, from a population of around 14,000,000, was regarded as tiny by European standards. Even at the height of the American war in 1781 the regular army was only 80,000 strong, with an annual budget of £3,609,532. The need to increase the size of the army in time of war created enormous organisational and recruiting difficulties, as did the government's propensity to reduce it again as quickly as possible once hostilities had ended. In 1783, with the American war over, mass desertions and mutiny led to an unseemly scramble to be rid of this pernicious instrument, leading to an surfeit of unemployed and unemployable soldiers.

Unlike the continental powers (notably the Prussians), whose armies had operated under unified military codes for years, the British army existed under a plethora of laws (including the Mutiny Act which had to be renewed by Parliament annually, else the army had no legal standing), general orders, royal warrants and the 'customs of the service'. There were no general instructions to regulate the tactical movement and deployment of troops in the field, which was left very much up to the commanding officers of the time. This did not matter very much when battalions were scattered around in colonial garrisons, often themselves split up into detachments, but it made the command of anything larger than a battalion in the field a matter of negotiation and persuasion. Thinking soldiers knew very well that this situation was untenable. In 1788 Colonel David Dundas, a future Commander-in-Chief, published his *Principles of Military Movements Chiefly Applicable to Infantry*. Intended to provide a standard system of deployment - into line, column, square and other formations – and words of command which would be understood throughout the army, Dundas's system was adopted by many regiments, but it was still only advisory and it was not until 1792 that *Regulations for Formations, Field Exercises and Movement of His Majesty's Forces* was issued under royal authority. Even then it took time for the regulations to be implemented throughout the army.[5]

Although there was a crisis increase of the army in 1787, the year Arthur Wesley joined, it was still officered under the peacetime system. Contrary to popular belief, army officers of the latter part of the eighteenth century were not from the aristocracy, although many of the colonels of regiments were.

Rather they were sons of minor landed gentry (usually younger sons), of cler-
gymen, of prosperous tradesmen or of other army officers. A number were
the descendants of refugees from European persecution, such as Huguenots;
there was a disproportionate number of Scottish officers (25 per cent in 1792),
and a sprinkling of loyalist Americans who had decided not to remain in
America after independence. There were many Anglo-Irish officers but few
native Irish, not because of the legal prohibition on Catholics holding
commissions, which had largely been ignored for generations, but because of
the low standard of Irish education. The only formal educational qualification required by officers was literacy, and the majority of the officer corps
emanated not from the public schools, certainly not from the universities,
but from local grammar schools. The higher standard of education in
Scotland than in the rest of the kingdom partly accounts for the strikingly
large number of Scots officers.

How an aspiring officer obtained a commission depended on which
branch of the service he entered. Candidates for the artillery and engineers
attended the Royal Military Academy at Woolwich, where they underwent a
professional course that trained them for their subsequent appointments.
Satisfactory performance at Woolwich led to the award of a commission and
thereafter promotion was by seniority. This was a totally fair system, but
because there were no pensions and no compulsory age for retirement it led
to the higher ranks being clogged up by men too old and too infirm to
perform their duties properly, with promotion blockages which went all the
way down. The Chief Engineer in Wellington's army in the Peninsula was
only a major, and the commander of all his artillery a captain.[6]

For the infantry and the cavalry the system was different. There was no
formal training for officers and no equivalent of the Royal Military Academy,
and there would not be until the establishment of the Royal Military College
in 1802. Candidates for commissions in these, the combat arms, had to be
certified as 'gentlemen', whether they were or not, recommended by an
officer of at least the rank of major and acceptable to the Secretary at War (in
the absence of a Commander-in-Chief) as being fit for commissioning. They
also had to be able to find the necessary cash, for most peacetime commissions were purchased. Today it seems extraordinary that a man could obtain
rank and authority over the King's soldiers by merely buying it, but the
system was not as iniquitous as it may seem to twenty-first-century eyes. A
man who had bought his commission in a regiment had a vested interest in
making the regiment work. In an age when the law existed more to enforce
property rights than to promote any concept of egalitarianism or of individual rights, something bought and paid for could not be taken away other
than for reasons of disgrace, and purchase of commissions was a safeguard

against an overmighty monarch attempting to pack the army with his own supporters, as James II had tried to do.

Having purchased his first commission, an officer then rose through the ranks by buying each step in promotion, at which time he would also sell his previous rank. Promotion depended not only on producing the cash but also on there being a vacancy into which the officer could be promoted, which often led to officers serving in a bewildering array of regiments as they progressed upwards. Finally, when he left the service, an officer could 'sell out' and the money obtained served as his pension, for pensions were not provided by the government. While there had been suggestions in the past that purchase should be abolished, it would not be until 1870, and the arrival of Gladstone, that the Treasury felt able to provide the funds necessary to compensate those officers who had paid for their commissions. Much the same applied to the abolition of slavery in the British empire in 1807 (which Wellington supported). Most people accepted that slavery was a bad thing, but, as it was legal, the slave owners would have to be compensated financially before it was made illegal.

Abuses abounded. At the time when Arthur Wesley joined there was neither age limit for a commission, nor any laid down period in one rank before an officer could purchase the next. Rather than laying down a pipe of port, gentlemen bought their godchildren commissions. There were cases of thirteen year olds holding the rank of lieutenant colonel, although they had never seen the inside of a barrack room or the outside of a soldier. The augmentation of the army in 1787 led Sir George Yonge, the Secretary at War and a man corrupt even by the standards of his time, to sell commissions to all who wanted and could pay for them. Despite these evils, many of which would be swept away when the Duke of York assumed the post of Commander-in-Chief in 1795, two years after Arthur Wesley became a lieutenant colonel by purchase, the system was not all bad. It often allowed men of real talent and motivation to rise quickly through the ranks to a position of command when they were mentally and physically capable of exercising it. As a corollary, officers who were utterly unsuited to army life were spared having to stay for the pension – as selling out would raise at least some capital. Officers who were incompetent, or otherwise failed to fit in, could usually be 'persuaded' to sell and go. At the famous camp at Shorncliffe, set up under the aegis of Sir John Moore to train light infantry and riflemen, many overweight and idle officers sold out when they found that the course included running up hills before breakfast.

While positions up to the command of a battalion could be purchased, all promotions above lieutenant colonel were by brevet. This meant that such promotions were granted in batches by authority of the King, although in practice by the Secretary at War, and, theoretically at least, the step from lieutenant colonel to colonel depended upon merit alone (although almost invariably such promotions were by seniority). Above colonel promotion was by brevet according to seniority; it could not be declined and meant that a man would eventually become a general provided he lived long enough. Officers holding ranks above colonel only received pay for their rank if they were actually employed in it, otherwise, if they were employed at all, they drew the pay of their regimental rank. The lack of a vacancy in which a man could be employed gave him the option of selling out his regimental rank and retiring, or of going on half pay while he waited for employment, which might or might not come. Actual employment was by selection and was therefore a means of ensuring that brigades and divisions, when they existed, were not commanded by complete dunderheads. Certainly the officers of the British army, once the long wars with Revolutionary and Napoleonic France began, appear to have been no worse, and in many cases a good deal better, than their contemporaries in the French and Allied armies, all of whom were supposedly promoted on merit and seniority alone.

A criticism of the system was that it discriminated against the poor but able, and to an extent this was so. There were, however, loopholes and methods of entry through the back door. Because a commission was not inheritable property, it died with the holder; and vacancies created through death, whether by enemy action, disease or accident, could be filled without purchase. By the end of the Napoleonic wars the enormous expansion of the army and a sizeable butcher's bill ensured that about half the officers doing duty in infantry battalions had achieved their 1815 rank without purchase. Another method of gaining a commission without purchase, only applicable when the army was expanding, was 'Recruiting for Rank'. A man who could recruit a company's worth of soldiers was given the rank to go with it, usually that of captain, without purchase. This was a source of considerable grievance to existing officers because it allowed men of less experience, and sometimes of less ability, to obtain seniority over those already in the regiment. It had long also been possible for commissions to be awarded to deserving sergeants, usually for gallantry in the field but sometimes for meritorious service in peace. Commissioned sergeants often became adjutants of battalions, whose responsibility was for drill, ceremonial, training and discipline.

In the eighteenth and early nineteenth centuries, before rifled weapons, machine-guns and sophisticated artillery forced dispersion on the battlefield, drill was synonymous with tactics. In the early years of the eighteenth century the pike and matchlock were replaced by a more reliable musket and a ring bayonet. The slow rate of fire, the inherent inaccuracy of the weapon and basic safety all dictated that fire was delivered by volley. An individual firing a musket at another individual was most unlikely to hit the target at much more than a hundred yards range, whereas a line of men standing shoulder to shoulder firing together would at least hit something. Tactics therefore involved getting men to the right place in the right formation to deliver effective fire upon an enemy, whether against attacking or defending infantry, or in defence against cavalry.

The ability to march, wheel and manoeuvre, taking a laid down length of pace at a laid down number of paces per minute while retaining cohesion, especially when under hostile fire, was all-important. Ex-sergeants were much more likely to understand the intricate movements and words of command involved in tactical deployment than were officers who had not carried a musket in the ranks. With a few notable exceptions, ex-rankers did not rise very far. Unless they could obtain further steps in promotion by acts of gallantry or exceptional merit when a free vacancy caused by death occurred, commissioned sergeants were unlikely to be able to raise the money to advance further. Many of them were simply unable to fit into the officers' mess. There were, of course, exceptions. The commanding officer of the Scots Greys (a regiment high up the social pecking order) at Waterloo was the son of a private soldier, and a sergeant of the 24th Foot in the Peninsula would retire as a major general.

Promotion free of purchase as the result of an act of extreme bravery was eagerly sought after on active service. Traditionally the commander of the aptly named 'Forlorn Hope' – the body of men first to assault the breach in a wall during a siege – was usually promoted free of purchase if he survived. The prize often went unclaimed. The sending home of the news of a victory abroad was generally entrusted to a junior officer, and here again the messenger was rewarded by promotion. While a commission obtained without purchase could not normally be sold – it had not been paid for in the first place – an exception existed whereby such a commission held for twenty years could be sold when the holder retired, so that he too had a pension to help him to live on. The various exceptions to the system were all very well in war, when the army was expanding and officers were being killed, but in peace there were few outlets for the deserving but poor. Surprisingly, most of these seem to have accepted their lot, despite being constantly passed over by men with less experience.[7]

Whether Arthur Wesley actually felt himself called to a military career is unknown, but it seems unlikely. He had to find gainful employment, for there were no estates for him to live off. Whatever his private inclinations may have been, his habit of duty, already being formed, would have persuaded him against objecting to anything his mother and elder brother suggested. The Lord Lieutenant of Ireland at the time was the Duke of

Rutland and it was to him that Richard Wellesley, Lord Mornington, wrote to obtain a commission in the army for his younger brother. The letter written by Richard is often quoted as showing that his younger brother was regarded as indolent and unworthy of much consideration, for in it Mornington says: 'He is here at the moment and perfectly idle', before going on to say that it was a matter of indifference what commission he got, provided he got it soon. Mornington's only reservation was that the commission should not be in the artillery, as this 'would not suit his [social] rank or [lack of] intellect'. The word 'idle' was surely being used in its original meaning of unemployed, rather than lazy, and Mornington merely making the point that it was important for the family that the boy should begin to make his way in the world without delay.

On 17 March 1787 the Hon. Arthur Wesley was gazetted as an ensign in the 73rd (Highland) Regiment. The commission cost Lord Mornington £400, which at a time when an ensign's pay was 5s. 3d. per day represented more than four years' salary. In the years prior to Arthur Wesley's joining, when commissions were harder to get, men often paid well over the laid down price for a commission, negotiated through a commissions broker, but the increase in the size of the army in 1787 ensured that the Wellesleys paid the official going rate. It was Pitt who had espoused the raising of regiments from the Scottish Highlands. These were originally clan levies and tended to be raised for a specific campaign and disbanded after it, few remaining on the permanent order of battle. This peripatetic existence was largely due to their propensity to mutiny. Of the eight Highland regiments raised in 1778 for the American War five mutinied. Of the thirty-one Highland regiments raised during the Napoleonic Wars between 1793 and 1803 eight mutinied.[8]

The 73rd had started life in 1758 as the 2nd Battalion of the Black Watch. It had not mutinied (although its parent battalion had done so in 1739) but was disbanded in 1762. Reraised in 1779 it had been retitled the 73rd Highland Regiment of Foot in 1786, the year before Arthur Wesley joined. Whether Wesley actually joined the battalion for duty is unclear. Anecdotal evidence says that he did; according to Croker, one of the new ensign's first actions was to weigh a private soldier and all his kit. In later life Wellington denied this (although he had certainly done it when in command of a battalion, and as Commander-in-Chief had questions as to the weight of equipment carried by soldiers included in officers' promotion examinations) and the tale seems unlikely. Whatever training the new officer underwent was minimal, probably not much more than a few hours in a quiet place being instructed in drill movements by the adjutant, or by a senior sergeant.

Even if Arthur Wesley did serve with the 73rd it was not a long stay, for in October 1787 the Duke of Rutland died and was replaced by the Marquess of

Buckingham as Lord Lieutenant of Ireland. Importuning by the Wellesley clan of the new Viceroy, now ensconced in Dublin Castle, secured Arthur an appointment as an aide de camp, with a welcome addition of ten shillings a day to his salary. Added to his ensign's pay and £125 a year from his family, he now had just over £400 a year to live on, before even thinking about paying his brother back for the money advanced to purchase his first commission. This was in fact not a bad salary, indeed it was a respectable income provided a man lived sensibly and exercised a modicum of prudence.

Great men were accompanied by a plethora of aides de camp, or ADCs. Their job was to make their master's life as pleasant as possible, and to ensure that the general, or governor, could get on with what he was paid to do without having to worry about personal administration. At worst an ADC was a dog walker and social ornament, at best he might be taken under the wing of his employer and have the opportunity to learn the skills of high command. An ideal ADC needed to be unmarried, so as to be able to devote all his attention to his job, socially polished, so as to be able to assist the general in his constant entertaining, and have a good memory and an eye for detail. All these qualities the young Wesley had, although his self-confidence was still embryonic, and he seems to have been perfectly satisfactory in this untaxing appointment. He was not the sole ADC, and inevitably the presence of a number of young, single and underemployed sprigs of the nobility led to a lifestyle that was boisterous and expensive. Although abstemious in later life, Arthur Wesley in Dublin more than held his own in drinking and at the gambling tables. On one occasion he is said to have walked (more probably run) six miles in fifty-five minutes to a finishing point in Leeson Street to win a wager of 150 guineas – an enormous sum, even if a speed of just over six miles an hour posed little difficulty. It is also said, although hard evidence is missing, that he was arraigned before the magistrates and fined for beating up a Frenchman in a Dublin bawdy house.

On Christmas Day 1787 Arthur Wesley purchased, or rather his brother Richard purchased for him, a lieutenancy in the 76th Regiment of Foot. The 76th had been raised in 1756, disbanded in 1763, reraised as a Highland regiment in 1777, disbanded again in 1784 having mutinied, and again reraised without its Scottish title the year Arthur Wesley came nominally onto its books. He did no duty with the 76th, and probably never even visited it. (By a wry turn of fate, in 1881 the 76th amalgamated with the 33rd Foot and acquired the title 'Duke of Wellington's', the 33rd having held that title since 1853.)

In January 1788 the 76th was due to be posted to India. Coincidentally, it was being mooted that all ADCs should be put on half pay, on the grounds that they were not doing duty with their regiments. The proposal failed. If it had been carried, financial pressures would have impelled Wesley to go with his regiment. As it was, his lieutenant's pay secure, he had no wish to leave Dublin Castle and so he exchanged into the 41st Foot. Exchange was a method frequently employed by officers who either sought promotion opportunities or who did not wish to go to a particular station. When a vacancy for promotion arose it was first offered to the senior officer of the regiment of the rank below, who, if he could afford it and wanted the step, would purchase that next rank. If he could not afford it, the offer was then made to the next man down and so on. Officers who were well down the pecking order in their own regiments might look for a regiment where their seniority would put them higher up the list, so as to swap regiments (for a consideration) with a man of the same rank who could not afford to buy a promotion if it came up. The incoming officer could then buy the next step in promotion at an earlier stage than he could have done had he stayed in his original regiment, while the outgoing officer made some money.

Much the same applied to officers who did not wish to go to India, to the West Indies or to any other insalubrious or remote clime. They would exchange with someone who did not mind going, or who was so impecunious that he had to go. How much Arthur Wesley, or his brother, paid for the exchange is not known, but the family was still short of money, despite Mornington's rapid climb up the ladder of political office. It was at this time that Arthur Wesley's grandmother, Lady Dungannon, was arrested and imprisoned for debt, only to be rescued by Mornington and deposited in France, well away from her creditors. The debts were all paid off and Lady Dungannon was able to return to England, just six months before the French Revolution broke out.

Life as an ADC in Dublin Castle, by no means an arduous occupation, was frivolous and expensive. Increasingly, however, Arthur Wesley began to take on responsibilities connected with the management and ultimate liquidation of the family estates in Ireland, in dealing with which he appears to have acted well by the standards of the time. He also took over from his brother William, who had himself succeeded Mornington as the Member of the Irish Parliament for Trim. Trim was almost, but not quite, a pocket borough. Prior to election Arthur Wesley succeeded to membership of the town corporation, where he made a speech opposing the granting of the freedom of Trim to Henry Grattan, the Irish Nationalist leader. He expressed great personal respect for Grattan, while persuading the corporation not to grant the freedom. In the election of March 1790, after expending a great deal of his own money (or more properly Mornington's and borrowed money) on beef and beer for the electorate, the Hon. Arthur Wesley was duly returned as the MP for Trim. During his first few years in the Dublin Parliament he appears to have said little but to have attended regularly. He did speak, however, in seconding the speech from the throne in January 1793, when he deplored the imprisonment of Louis XVI and the invasion of the Netherlands by the French revolutionaries. In a foretaste of his own future attitudes, he also expressed the hope that the government would adopt a liberal attitude towards Roman Catholics. In February of the same year, the month the French National Convention declared war against Britain, he spoke in favour of extending the vote to Catholic landowners: 'I have no objection to giving Roman Catholics the benefits of the constitution', denying protests that they would all vote as their priests ordered and in doing so annihilate the Protestant establishment:

> He has founded his assertion on the supposition that the Roman Catholics will, in voting, be directed by their priests. But have not Roman Catholics, like Protestants, various interests and various passions by which they are swayed? The influence of their landlords, their own interests and a thousand other motives? It appears to me at they will not vote as a body, as has been supposed ...[9]

Life for the young officer did not entirely revolve around attendance upon the Viceroy, management of the family estates and parliamentary duty, for he also found time to pay court. The object of his attentions was the Hon. Catherine Dorothea Sarah Pakenham, known as Kitty, second daughter of Edward Pakenham, 2nd Baron Longford, a captain in the Royal Navy. The Pakenhams, like the Wesleys, were Anglo-Irish Protestants, and Kitty, three years younger than Arthur Wesley, had been brought up in the family home of Pakenham Hall, sixty miles west of Dublin. In the relatively small social circle of the Anglo-Irish, the families knew each other and Arthur and Kitty often met at week-end country house parties and at levées in Dublin Castle. The Pakenhams liked the young Wesley, and had no doubts about his breeding, but they were well aware that he had no money and no apparent prospects. Anything other than platonic friendship, thought the Pakenhams, was out of the question: Wesley did not have the money to provide the standard of living that they expected for their daughters, and the Pakenhams, with eight children, had none to settle upon her. The prospects for matrimonial bliss can only have seemed bleak.

Meanwhile Arthur Wesley was buying his way up the ranks of the army, rapidly but by no means unusually so. In June 1789 he exchanged into the 12th Light Dragoons, returning to the Infantry when he purchased a captaincy in the 58th Foot in 1791, and moving back to the cavalry (18th Light Dragoons) on 31 October 1792. On 30 April 1793 he purchased a majority in the 33rd Foot, from Major Ralph Gore, for £2600. The sale of his captaincy on promotion would have netted him around £1500, but still his indebtedness to Mornington was mounting.

It was on assuming the rank of major that Arthur Wesley first reported to a battalion for serious military duty. He was aged twenty-four, was in debt to his brother, the family land agent, the proprietor of his lodgings – even his bootmaker – and a recent proposal of marriage to Kitty Pakenham had been turned down. He had absorbed social polish, some understanding of the rumbustious world of politics, done his best by his family and failed in his first foray into romance. He had not done a day's soldiering worthy of the name.

2

Early Days

The 33rd Regiment was raised in 1702 as the Earl of Huntingdon's Foot, becoming the 33rd Foot in 1751 and the 33rd (1st York, West Riding) Foot in 1782. It was not a socially smart regiment but it had the great advantage, from Arthur Wesley's point of view, of being stationed in Ireland, from 1794 in Cork. This allowed Major Wesley to continue to hold his appointment as an ADC, and to remain in contact with Kitty Pakenham, even though it had been made clear that a penniless major with no obvious prospects was not an acceptable suitor for a Longford daughter.

Despite its title, the 33rd was by no means entirely composed of men from the West Riding of Yorkshire. Regiments recruited where they could, and Ireland, being an impoverished part of the kingdom, was always a good source of recruits. Catholics had been officially allowed to join the ranks of the army from 1775, although they had been enlisting unofficially for many years before that. It has been estimated that up to 30 per cent of the men in supposedly English regiments were Irish, and hence Catholic (the Ulster Protestants made up a much lower proportion of the Irish population than they do today, and being economically relatively better off did not join the army in any numbers anyway). The 33rd's absentee colonel of the regiment, effectively its proprietor, was the fifty-five-year-old Marquess Cornwallis, elevated to that rank in 1793, the year Arthur Wesley joined for duty. Despite being forced to surrender at Yorktown, when his 8000 strong force was surrounded by 17,000 French and American troops under Washington, Cornwallis was one of the best British generals in the American war. It was a war which Cornwallis had done his best to avoid, having been a fierce critic of the government's tax policies towards the colonists, but once there even Lafayette confessed to having been 'devilish fearful of him'.[1] Returning from America, he was appointed Governor-General and Commander-in-Chief in India, only coming back to England in 1795, to be appointed Master General of the Ordnance with a seat in the cabinet.

There were two majors on the establishment of a battalion in 1793, although one was often away, on leave or in an employment other than with the regiment. The duties of the majors, or more often the major, included acting as deputy to the commanding officer, a lieutenant colonel, and overseeing the internal economy of the regiment. If he was conscientious, the major spent the greater part of his time ensuring that accounts and records were up to date and accurate. There was the clothing account, showing the entitlement to replacement items of uniform, the ration account, the pay records, the reimbursement due to sutlers and contractors for work done or items provided for the regiment, and there was a plethora of returns showing recruiting, training, ammunition expenditure, deserters and punishments awarded, as well as correspondence in and out. While much of the communication between the lieutenant colonel and his superiors was handled by the adjutant, the rest fell to the major.

On joining the 33rd Arthur Wesley found that Cornwallis, despite his military reputation, had allowed the accounts of the regiment to get into a muddle – or rather by his long absences he had allowed the lieutenant colonel to get them into a muddle. The annual monetary grant to the colonel of the regiment came in two parts: 'subsistence' and 'off-reckonings'. Subsistence paid the men while the off-reckonings covered equipment, food and clothing. The colonel of the regiment was in India and the regiment had many unpaid debts. While there does not appear to be any suggestion of corruption, it was not at all clear where the money had gone and what had been paid and what had not. Arthur Wesley, perhaps to his own surprise, found that he had a head for figures and an eye for detail. He set himself to work unravelling the mysteries of the 33rd's accounts, and later said that it was that appointment which taught him the importance of detail in the administration of an army. Certainly he retained a grasp of minutiae and an understanding of figures to the end of his days, often taking an inordinate interest in minor aspects of management, to the frequent irritation of his subordinates. Such attention to detail too far down the chain might be regarded as a negative quality in a commander, implying as it does an inability to delegate. Yet, in a period when the knowledge and capacity of subordinates was at best patchy, there was often no alternative for a more senior officer but to oversee many minor matters himself, and to retain close personal control of the organisation and administration of his command, whether a battalion or an army.

In September 1793, five months after joining the 33rd, Arthur Wesley bought (or rather Lord Mornington bought on his brother's behalf) the lieutenant colonelcy in the same regiment from Lieutenant Colonel John Yorke for £3500. Yorke was an experienced soldier, having been in command of the 33rd since 1781. It would not have been surprising if there was muttering in the ranks and apprehension amongst the officers as to how they might fare under a twenty-four year old with no previous experience of troops. A lieutenant colonel's pay was £1 10s. od. a week in 1793 and the cost of the latest promotion was £900 more than Wesley got by the sale of his majority. His indebtedness was rising, but he was in command of a battalion of the King's soldiers in an army that was now at war.[2]

The French Revolutionary and Napoleonic wars from 1792 until 1815 not only changed the nature of war in the purely military sense, they also changed war conceptually. Previously warring nations had observed 'the courtesies of the age', at least when dealing with Christian powers. Now war would be fought to the limit, with levies drawn from entire populations, with the very existence of the state at risk and with patriotism a major reason for fighting.

In 1791 Prussia and Austria had declared themselves ready to intervene in France to protect the monarchy of Louis XVI, under threat from his own subjects. Russia and Sweden agreed to provide contingents of troops while Spain offered a financial subsidy. The French Assembly hastened to raise armies to protect its eastern frontier and declared war on Austria in April 1792. England remained aloof. In August 1792 the French mob stormed the Tuileries, massacred the King's Swiss Guard and forced the royal family to accept the protection of the Assembly, which first abolished the monarchy and then executed Louis on 21 January 1793. England, alarmed by a French threat to Antwerp the previous year, broke off diplomatic relations. France, already at war with Austria, Prussia and Piedmont, promptly declared war on England, the Netherlands and Spain. The first of seven coalitions to fight the French was formed. By July 1793 France was assailed by enemies without and by royalist risings at home. Its armies, composed of old regulars of the Bourbon army and untrained volunteers, fell back. The Reign of Terror began and the Committee of Public Safety's *levée en masse* in August raised new armies which were flung, largely untrained and poorly equipped, into the field. The British Royal Navy despatched a fleet under Admiral Hood to Toulon, which captured the port and the entire French Mediterranean fleet. In a farcical example of British unpreparedness, Hood found himself with insufficient sailors to remove the prizes to England, being himself besieged by the French before sailing away in December. A young colonel of French artillery, Napoleon Bonaparte, was promoted to general of brigade for his part in the recapture of Toulon.

French governments now rose and fell on their ability to prosecute the war. A mixture of terror, panic, patriotic zeal and the execution of failed generals saved the Revolution. It was beginning to dawn on the other continental powers, and reluctantly on the British, that there could be no accommodation with France. The age of stately manoeuvring, with a few pitched battles fought between armies led by professional soldiers and ending in a treaty and the exchange of a few islands and trade concessions, was at an end. The year 1793 was also the one in which the Hon. Arthur Wesley was gazetted as commanding officer of the 33rd Regiment of Foot and the year in which he burnt his violin.

The English ruling class was aghast at the flood of refugees from the Terror, and its reaction to events on the Continent was to panic at the thought that a similar revolution was a real possibility at home. In hindsight, this seems unlikely. The English may have cut off the head of their King in 1649, but the 'Glorious Revolution' of 1689/90 had established a system of government which, for all its faults, was the most liberal in Europe. Unlikely or not, Habeas Corpus was suspended in May 1793 and any agitation for constitutional reform was suspected as sedition.

Meanwhile Arthur Wesley was reduced to importuning for a job. He cannot have enjoyed the experience of humbling himself for the sake of an appointment with Lord Moira's expedition to Normandy (cancelled) or in the civil sector (no vacancies), nor can he have relished the necessity of applying in sycophantic and self-abasing terms. His later reluctance to seek favours for those who had served him well may have been conditioned by the rebuffs he suffered in 1793 and the early part of 1794.

The purpose of England's involvement in the war against France was not the elimination of the Revolution, nor the restoration of the Bourbons; these two war aims were added later. It was that age-old British concern for the security of Holland and of Belgium, then the Austrian Netherlands, which prompted intervention. The Rhine delta and the Netherland Channel Ports constituted England's main entry to Europe. They could not be allowed to be dominated by a potentially hostile power. The British had never planned for a war in Flanders but, once the immediate threat to Holland had been averted, Britain could only persuade the Austrians to hold onto the Netherlands (as opposed to exchanging them for Bavaria) by the promise of retaining British troops there in support the Austrians, with the additional aim of expanding Holland at the expense of France. Soon after the outbreak of war in 1793 the British Prime Minister, William Pitt the Younger, sent a brigade of three battalions of the Guards to Holland, under Major General Gerard Lake, followed by further reinforcements of infantry and four regiments of cavalry. Included in the force were Hanoverian and Hessian contingents financed by Britain. The whole army was commanded by Frederick, Duke of York, second son of George III.

The sons of George III were not such as to engender pride in the breast of an essentially decent, hard-working and abstemious king. His eldest son, later Prince Regent and George IV, was a political intriguer, lacking financial prudence, who almost certainly contracted an illegal marriage. Although undoubtedly intelligent, witty and a connoisseur of literature and the arts, he was thought of by most of the King's subjects as a dissolute rake. The third son, William (later Duke of Clarence and William IV), had been put into the navy as a boy. While not an incompetent sailor, he had paid little attention to his academic tutors, was loutish in manner and far too fond of the lash. He was an incorrigible womaniser who contracted venereal disease and, on one occasion, had to be rescued from an unsuitable attachment to the daughter of the Spanish admiral on the Cuban station by Captain Horatio Nelson. The fourth son, Edward (later Duke of Kent and father of Queen Victoria), was wildly extravagant and fathered at least one illegitimate daughter in Germany. He behaved like the worst sort of martinet while in command of a battalion and, when Governor of Gibraltar, his insistence on draconian discipline caused a mutiny in the garrison. Prince Ernest (later Duke of Cumberland and King of Hanover), the fifth son, was a cruel reactionary. He was believed to have been a lover of the Princess of Wales, suspected of fathering an illegitimate child on his own sister and accused of murdering his valet. That he was at least brave was shown by his loss of an arm and an eye while serving with the Hanoverian cavalry. He was eventually given general's rank in the British army, although refused a command abroad. The next son, Adolphus (later Duke of Cambridge), seems to have been the opposite of his brothers. Obedient and generally well behaved, he avoided debt and unsuitable liaisons. He too served with the Hanoverian army and was wounded. Many years later, however, Wellington dismissed a proposal to appoint Cambridge Commander-in-Chief on the grounds that he was mad. The seventh son Augustus, later Duke of Sussex, was in sickly health, contracted an illegal marriage, associated himself with the King's political opponents and may also have been mentally deranged.[3]

Frederick, Duke of York, had been born in 1763, so was six years older than Arthur Wesley, and was always the King's favourite son. Appointed a colonel at the age of seventeen and a major general before he was twenty, he was given the command of the 1793 expedition at his father's behest. Initially he had some success. By the end of March 1793 the immediate French threat to Holland had been removed, largely by Austrian action. The British contingent then took part in the successful siege of Valenciennes, which surrendered (to the Austrians) on 28 July. British insistence on obtaining a settlement in accordance with their own agenda forced the retention of a British army in Flanders. As early as April 1793 the British government had come to the conclusion that Dunkirk, occupied by the French, should be the focus for British efforts. If captured it offered a safer and better supply port than Ostende. In British hands, it would prevent the French navy (or rather French privateers) from raiding British shipping in the North Sea. It could be presented to the Austrians as an example of England 'doing her bit', and could be used as a bargaining chip to persuade the Austrians to make conces-

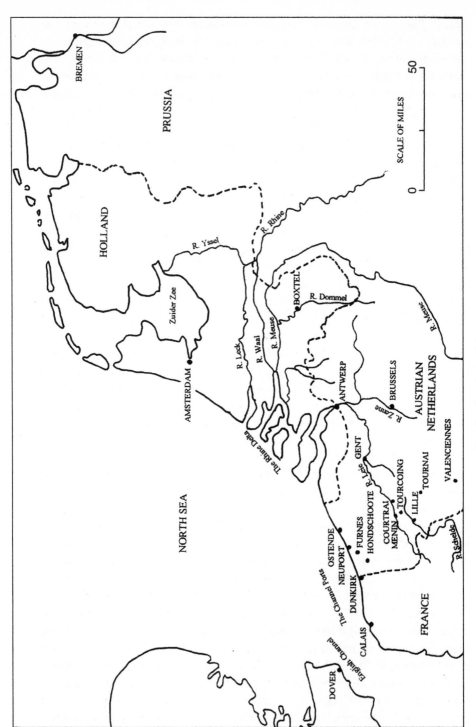

1. The Flanders Expedition, 1794–95.

sions to the Dutch. A subsidiary, and not openly stated, aim of the siege of Dunkirk was to massage British public opinion into an acceptance of further cooperation with the Dutch. While, as we have seen, many in England were opposed to continental adventures, believing that war should be conducted at sea, British war aims made intervention on land a necessity.

England was to find herself at odds with her coalition partners, not for the last time in this series of wars. The other powers had agreed that that the aim of intervention was to recapture French conquests. Britain wanted a comprehensive settlement with guarantees and indemnities to enforce a lasting peace. There were tensions between Austria and Prussia, between Austria and Sardinia, and between England and Spain: all of these were to affect the British conduct of the Flanders campaign.

The Duke of York and his army marched for the Flemish coast from Valenciennes on 15 August 1793, arriving at Nieuport on 21 August, where they failed to make rendezvous with the artillery train and other stores which should have arrived by sea, and reached Dunkirk on 23 August. While an immediate bombardment might have compelled the French garrison to surrender there and then, lack of guns forced York to invest the port while he waited a fortnight for his siege train to arrive. It was now a race: whether York could reduce and capture Dunkirk before the French could find sufficient troops to lift the siege. It was a race that York lost: due to squabbling between the Allied powers, the French were able to cobble together an army of 46,000 men from the Ardennes, from the Rhine and from the Moselle; men who should have been engaging the Prussians and the Austrians, had these two latter powers done what they had contracted to do. The opening of the Dunkirk sluice gates by the French, and the consequent flooding of the marshes surrounding the port, now forced York's force of 14,500 to disperse over a much wider area than had been envisaged. The French army under General Houchard, which moved up from Lille and attacked York's army on 6 September, was composed largely of recruits raised by the *levée en masse* the previous month. Most of them had received only the most basic of training, but weight of numbers and the sheer ferocity of their attacks, fuelled by patriotism and fear of the guillotine, drove the British back to Hondschoote. A further attack on 8 September forced a retreat to Furnes. While the Duke did manage to extricate his army, with losses of about 3000 men, he had to abandon most of his siege train to the enemy. It was the only effective siege train that the British possessed. Houchard, a competent commander, was recalled five days later and guillotined: he had defeated the British at Dunkirk, and then the Prince of Orange at Menin, but had failed to drive the Austrians out of eastern France. French generals, thus encouraged, redoubled their efforts, and a mix of terror and patriotic fervour was begin-

ning to turn an armed rabble into an army. England had by now lost the
initiative in Flanders. Her army could no longer pursue independent objectives and there was no choice in the immediate term but to unite with the
Austrians, while still hoping to prop up the Dutch.

The British government, having failed to secure Dunkirk as a way of paying
for the war so far (or as a bargaining counter to persuade the Austrians to
make some concessions to the Dutch), sought other options. One was an
expedition to the French West Indies, whose capture would not only hurt the
French economy but might also provide the British with a useful trade off in
negotiations with her allies. To provide the troops for this expedition, which
would be led by General Sir Charles Grey, all battalions in Ireland, including
the 33rd, were ordered to give up their flank companies. Every battalion of
British infantry was organised into ten companies, each theoretically of one
hundred men (but more usually about eighty) and commanded by a captain.
Two of the companies were denoted as 'flank': the grenadier company, which
occupied the right of the battalion line; and the light company, which acted as
the battalion skirmishers before taking their place on the left of the line. The
grenadiers, originally men who carried and threw primitive grenades, but
who were now armed as standard infantrymen, were usually the tallest men
in the battalion and its best physical specimens. Men of the light company,
because of their skirmishing role which required them to act individually or
in pairs, were generally the more intelligent of the soldiers. Both companies
were the cream of their battalion, and a force composed entirely of flank
companies would be high grade indeed.

Lieutenant Colonel Wesley, desperately seeking employment which
offered more prospects than garrison duties in Ireland, applied to go with the
force: 'they may as well have me as anyone', he said. His application was
rejected, but it is well for British military history that it was. The force set sail
in November 1793 and initially all went well. In an excellent example of naval
and military cooperation (the naval commander was Sir John Jervis, later Earl
St Vincent), the expedition captured Martinique, St Lucia and Guadeloupe,
cutting off a large proportion of the French sugar trade. Then, as so often in
the West Indies, disease began to take its toll. Cholera, dysentery, yellow fever
and malaria caused far more deaths than the French. According to the
Military Secretary's digest of service of the 33rd Foot, its flank companies
were 'totally destroyed'. Much the same happened to all the battalions which
took part. Wesley, whose health as a young man was delicate, would have had
little chance of returning, had he accompanied them. The damage done to the
33rd, and to the other battalions whose best men had been taken away, took
far longer to repair than the time taken to simply replace them with recruits.

Meanwhile the 1794 campaign in Flanders was not going well for the Allies nor for the Duke of York, whose army was now tied to the Austrians. The battles of Courtrai (11 May) and Tourcoing (18 May) were French victories, while Tournai (23 May) was an expensive draw. When the French continued to press, it was apparent that reinforcement had become imperative. At last Arthur Wesley's opportunity came. Lord Moira was now to lead an expedition to reinforce the Duke of York. The force would consist of twelve battalions from the Isle of Wight and three, the 8th, 33rd and 44th Foot, from Ireland. Arthur Wesley embarked with his battalion at Cork, and by the end of June the whole force had arrived at Ostende.

Just before the force embarked, the government authorised a second lieutenant colonel for each battalion. This was an expedient, occasionally resorted to in time of war, designed to compensate for the commanding officer of the battalion being often employed to command a brigade or other grouping, when the second lieutenant colonel would take over command of the battalion. Modern units are already allocated to their brigades, divisions and corps in time of peace, and such higher formations have their integral staffs and commanders ready to deploy for war. In the 1790s there was no peacetime organisation higher than a battalion or regiment, and brigades were ad hoc bodies formed from whichever units were available. The command and staff arrangements had to be extemporised and, in what was hoped would be a short war, there was a reluctance to sanction overgenerous promotion. Commanding officers of battalions were an obvious source of temporary brigadiers.

The 33rd were lucky in the appointment of their second lieutenant colonel, or rather in the man who was able to obtain the new vacancy. John Sherbrooke, five years older than his commanding officer, had been commissioned into the 4th Foot in 1780. He had been serving in the 33rd since 1783, when he had purchased a captain's vacancy in the regiment. He had become a major in the same regiment, again by purchase, on the day on which Arthur Wesley assumed command. With long service in the 33rd, and far more experience than his young commanding officer, Sherbrooke did the regiment, and Wesley, well. He acted as an effective and loyal deputy and provided a knowledge of the men and of regimental procedures that was invaluable. Wesley thought Sherbrooke 'A very good officer, but the most passionate man I think I ever knew'. Despite a rough manner and a propensity for using his fists, Sherbrooke never forfeited his superior's confidence, serving with him in India and the Peninsula.

On arrival at Ostende, Lord Moira now organised his force into brigades, the three battalions from Ireland being in the 2nd Brigade, with Lieutenant Colonel Wesley appointed to command it, leaving Sherbrooke to command the 33rd. If the appointment of a very young and inexperienced officer to command a brigade on active service seems unwise, there was no alternative: despite his youth, Wesley was the senior of the three commanding officers and the appointment was his by right.

The approach of a French army under General Pichegru, including the young Colonel Murat, gave the British little choice but to evacuate Ostende. Lord Moira left Wesley's brigade behind to protect the evacuation of inessential men and stores, while the main body marched off to join the Duke of York. Arthur Wesley was not troubled by Pichegru, and his men covered the final evacuation of Ostend before themselves re-embarking and sailing to Antwerp, from where they joined the Duke of York's army just before Moira's leading troops got there overland. Arthur Wesley's first independent command had shown him as moderately capable, with an understanding of the usefulness of seapower.

Things continued to get worse for the British. The Austrians were showing less interest in the Flanders adventure and began to reduce their troops in the theatre. There were suspicions that even the Dutch might treat with the French, and the Duke of York had perforce to retreat north, into Holland. The army had been reorganised and Wesley found himself sometimes in command of his own regiment, sometimes commanding a brigade.

On 15 September the French attacked and took the town of Boxtel, capturing its garrison of 1500 Hessians in British pay. This was serious: if the French could hold Boxtel they could cut off the British withdrawal. The Duke of York ordered a counter-attack to be mounted the next day, with two brigades supported by cavalry, the whole to be under the command of the sixty-one-year-old Lieutenant General Sir Ralph Abercromby. The two brigades selected were the Guards and the 3rd Brigade, this latter now consisting of four battalions, including the 33rd, and commanded by Arthur Wesley. That such an important operation should include the Guards is not surprising but, even given that there was a shortage of senior officers, the employment of the 3rd Brigade, commanded by a lieutenant colonel with so little experience, indicates that even then Wesley was seen as sound.

Abercromby advanced against the town but then, meeting a far stiffer resistance than he had anticipated, decided to pull his men back. British armies have always had a problem with withdrawals, and this was no exception. The infantry became disordered and got mixed up with the cavalry, junior commanders lost control and, when two French regiments came on in pursuit, an orderly withdrawal was in danger of becoming a rout. The day was saved by the 33rd, who formed line, waited until the French were within fifty yards and then fired two disciplined volleys. The carnage was considerable; the French had had enough and left the field. Contrary to most accounts, the 33rd was actually commanded by Sherbrooke, not by Wesley, but it was

Wesley's brigade and he got the credit, although he praised the 33rd for their efforts and thanked them handsomely.

The retreat went on and winter began to set in. The drainage ditches and canals, which would have hindered the pursuers, froze and the newly consti-tuted wagon train – known irreverently to the soldiers as the 'Newgate Blues' – was unable to cope. Medical facilities were primitive and men starved, became diseased or froze to death. Contrary to previous practice, the French showed no signs of going into winter quarters. The British army began to disintegrate, while even their better-organised Prussian allies had problems, but still the retreat went on: a scramble to a river line; a pause to reorganise and fend off the pursuing French; then a rush to the next river. It was the coldest winter in living memory and most of the troops lacked greatcoats. In December 1794 the Duke of York, having become the subject of a rhyme sung even today in every British nursery, was recalled. That he had a lot more that 10,000 men and that he marched up very few hills and down even fewer was irrelevant: the campaign was clearly not a success and public and parliamen-tary opinion demanded a scapegoat.

Arthur Wesley spent most of that terrible winter with the rearguard, either commanding his own battalion or a brigade. He was frequently in action as the French tried to mop up the British between the rivers Waal and Leck, until eventually the British government realised the futility of persisting with the campaign and ordered the evacuation of the army by sea from Bremen. The 33rd embarked in April 1795. While the battalion had lost only six men killed by the enemy, 200 had died of disease and 'other causes', and 162 men had been left behind in hospitals. Wesley returned to England early - for further employment had to be sought – and the twenty-four-year-old lieu-tenant colonel was not reticent in commenting on matters relating to the defence of the realm.

On 13 March 1795 a motion came before the Irish House of Commons censuring the government for supposedly allowing the total of regular troops in Ireland to fall below the agreed figure of 12,000. Pointing out that the exigencies of war had forced the government to send troops abroad, Wesley reminded the House that enlistment of new recruits and the availability of the Militia more than made up for the troops removed:

Were the new levies just recruited to be sent abroad, or the disciplined soldiers? The question answers itself, and justifies sending the old regiments out of the kingdom and retaining the new corps. An Honourable Baronet [Sir L. Parsons] has called the new levies 'ragamuffins'. I congratulate the Hon. Baronet on his military sagacity, for who would send ragamuffins upon foreign service? But I assure the Hon. Baronet that, however he may treat the new levies with contempt, they were not objects of contempt to the enemies of their country.[4]

Wellington was later quoted as saying that the Flanders campaign had taught him how not to do it 'which is always something'. We must beware of such comments, however, for they were made much later, to Arbuthnot or to Croker or to Stanhope, when the great man was possessed of hindsight and had time to review his life and his actions. We do not know what Arthur Wesley thought at the time, but he must have pondered and he must have learned – for there was much to learn. History has blamed the Duke of York for the abject failure of the 1794/95 campaign in Flanders, and as the Commander-in-Chief he must be held at least partly culpable. Whether anyone else could have done any better is a moot point. After years of neglect and reluctance to spend money on the army, it is hardly surprising that when an underfunded and underequipped body was launched onto the Continent of Europe things did not go well. There was political interference from Prime Minister and Foreign Secretary, dithering by the recently appointed Secretary at War, Henry Dundas, and bad blood between the Master General of the Ordnance, the Duke of Richmond, and the Duke of York.[5] There were failures of intelligence, there was a lack of grip at headquarters and there was an absence of professionalism amongst many of the generals and staff officers, some of whom preferred to dine well with dubious female company rather than go forward to the troops and see for themselves what was happening. It could hardly be otherwise. The sale of commissions to virtually anyone who wanted one, and a complete lack of training in the basic aspects of command and management of men, had given the army a body of junior officers – and some senior ones – who were simply not up to the job. Major General Craig, chief of staff to the Duke of York and a competent officer, wrote from Holland in November 1794: 'Out of fifteen regiments of cavalry and twenty-six of infantry, which we have here, twenty-one are literally commanded by boys or idiots – I had the curiosity to count them over'. It was not the officers' fault: the reforms so far instigated had not yet worked through the system and no one had bothered to tell the young gentlemen how to lead their men. Such animal transport as was available in Flanders spent far too much time moving officers' personal baggage and not enough in shifting stores and wounded. Inherent incompetence and inexperience, coupled with an almost complete breakdown of the supply and logistical arrangements, made disaster inevitable. The age-old military adage that men are only as good as their officers was certainly not lost on the young Wesley: later, in the Peninsula, not only would regimental officers be expected to know their business, they would be lucky to have one baggage mule between four of them.

While the much-depleted 33rd Foot now went into camp at Warley in order to recruit and refit, Arthur Wesley returned to representing Trim in the Irish Parliament and to his duties as an ADC in Dublin Castle. Once more he began to importune for jobs, and it is evident that at this stage he was by no means committed to the army as a lifetime career. He applied, somewhat optimistically, for the post of Secretary at War in Ireland and for 'something in the Treasury or Revenue boards'. His pleas fell on deaf ears, for the Viceroy was no longer the Wellesleys' friend Lord Westmoreland but Lord Camden, who had his own patrons to placate and his own protégés to advance. The one post he was offered, which he turned down flat for obvious reasons, was that of Surveyor General of the Ordnance, which far from being vacant was occupied by Kitty Pakenham's uncle. We may reasonably assume that the post was solicited by Mornington, rather than by Wesley himself, and without the latter's knowledge.

Meanwhile, in October 1795, the government concluded that a further expedition to the West Indies was now imperative. Sir Ralph Abercromby, Wesley's superior during the Boxtel affair, was nominated to command and the force was to have twenty-five infantry battalions, including the 33rd. After delays due to problems in getting the necessary equipment together and unfavourable weather, the force eventually set sail on 16 November from Portsmouth, only to run into a hurricane almost immediately. The storm sank a number of the ships and forced the remainder to seek shelter in a variety of coastal harbours. Here there is some confusion as to Wesley's whereabouts. The 33rd may have accompanied the expedition when it was ready to sail again, in December, or, along with a number of other regiments, it may have been incapable of being re-embarked for active service due to disease, desertion or the loss of vital equipment. These battalions were left behind, and the 33rd may have been sent to Lymington. Whatever the exact sequence of events, neither the 33rd nor Arthur Wesley went to the West Indies.[6]

Whether Wesley was at sea or not, he was certainly ill that winter, as he had been on his return from Flanders. The illness was described at the time as being some kind of fever, and what we now call malaria was abroad in the Flanders of 1795. In view of his excellent health in later years and his longevity, it may be that the various bouts of ill health in Wesley's early years had a psychological origin. He was undoubtedly frustrated by his failure to obtain what he would have seen as worthwhile employment, he was increasingly in debt and he was suffering from what would now be recognised as stress. Life must have seemed bleak. Later, when he had responsibility, a place in the councils of the great and increasing status, he seems rarely to have been ill. He was described at this time as being of just over average height (variously reported as five feet eight, nine or ten inches) with a spare, erect figure; light blue or hazel eyes; light brown hair and aquiline features. His prominent nose is not mentioned in contemporary accounts until much later.

In early 1796 any idea of sending the 33rd to the Caribbean was abandoned, and instead the battalion was ordered to India. While the troops embarked in April 1796 Wesley was still recovering his health and did not accompany them, catching them up at Cape Town having followed in a fast frigate of the Royal Navy. Wesley left Portsmouth to rejoin the 33rd Foot in the last week of June 1796, but before he left was promoted to the rank of colonel. Colonel was an army, rather than a regimental, rank and promotion to it was generally by brevet, that is a number of officers all being elevated together, without purchase. This promotion was too late to appear in the Army List of 1796, the year in which it occurred, but the List of 1797 shows that forty-three lieutenant colonels were appointed as colonels with a common seniority date of 3 May 1796, retaining amongst themselves the seniority that they had as lieutenant colonels. Of the forty-three so promoted one was in the artillery (the father of Congreve of rocket fame), seven were in the cavalry (including two officers of the Life Guards), thirteen, including Wesley, were in various regiments of foot, twenty were in the Foot Guards and one was on half pay. This latter promotion was unusual but there were officers who had gone on half pay for one reason or another but who were still considered employable and worth promoting. The large proportion of officers of the Guards is misleading. Guards officers, as befitted their exalted status as the King's personal troops, held two ranks: regimental rank and army rank. Army rank for these officers was two ranks above regimental rank; thus a captain commanding a company in a Guards battalion was a lieutenant colonel in the army. While doing duty with his regiment he was a captain and drew a captain's pay, but should he be for any reason employed outside the regiment – for example as an ADC – he held his army rank and drew the pay of it. The thirteen Guards officers promoted on the May 1796 list were actually captains being promoted to major in their Guards regiments. A further twenty lieutenant colonels, all senior to those promoted to colonel, were not promoted, but all were marines, or on half pay (and presumably considered unemployable), or invalids or otherwise ineligible in one way or another. Of the new colonels Wesley was the junior but one.[7]

Given the overall size of the army at this stage in the French wars there could not be vacancies in the new rank for all those promoted. The promotions cost the state nothing, however, for colonels without a vacancy as such simply continued to do duty in their regiments drawing the pay of their regimental rank – that of lieutenant colonel. As for the man so promoted but without a colonel's post to fill, he obtained some status, was eligible in his turn for the next colonel's appointment that came along, and was on the first rung of a ladder that would, subject to survival and good behaviour, eventually take him to the rank of general, even if he might never actually be employed as such.

It was a long voyage to India. Having learned at Eton never to get involved in something about which he knew nothing, Wesley took his library with him. A few of his books were relics of his fledgeling political aspirations in Ireland, such as Clarendon's *Irish Affairs*, and some dated from his abortive participation in the West Indies expedition, but of an astonishing total of 240 books a very large number were about India, its history, languages, people and economy. Classical works with a military bias were included, as were more modern treatises on tactics and strategy. Chapman's *Venereal Disease*, a copy of the Bengal Army List and a number of Persian grammars and dictionaries are all listed as accompanying their owner on the voyage.[8] All this indicates that Wesley was resigned to a long stay in India, and that he was beginning to take soldiering seriously.

It has been suggested that Arthur Wesley underwent a sudden conversion to a military career, but the truth is almost certainly more prosaic. He wanted – he needed – gainful employment. He had failed to find political preferment and there was nothing left but to make his name as a soldier. He had made a reasonable start in the Flanders war and had tried to get to the West Indies, or had at least not objected to going. To shine in the army he needed not only active service, with the chance of responsibility and promotion, but service in a theatre which offered opportunities for financial reward. A campaign in the West Indies, had he survived it (and many did not, carried off not by the enemy but by disease), would not have offered the sometimes spectacular sums of prize money available to the successful commander in India. Wesley was always a pragmatist. His best chance of success in life lay in the army, so that is what he would do and he would do it to the best of his ability. India was the place to go.

Although at this stage a colonel in the army, Arthur Wesley remained in command of the 33rd and drew the pay of a lieutenant colonel. At Cape Town, taken by the British from the Dutch the previous year to forestall a French seizure, he was reunited with the 33rd and also found time to make the acquaintance of two young English ladies, sisters fresh out of school and on their way to India, presumably two of the early members of the 'Fishing Fleet'. Wesley described one, Miss Henrietta Smith, as having 'a pretty little figure and lovely neck'. Necks were not an object of titillation in the eighteenth century: the term was a euphemism for bosom.

The voyage continued in the East Indiaman *Princess Charlotte* and Wesley and his regiment reached Calcutta on 17 February 1797. It had been a long and tedious voyage. Even allowing for the stopover at Cape Town, the regiment had been on the move for ten months and Wesley for eight. During the journey there was little for the officers to do besides reading and talking, and ensuring that the men kept themselves and their cramped quarters clean.

European interest in the potential of trade with India had been sparked by Marco Polo's travels there in the thirteenth century, and had increased after the Portuguese Vasco da Gama visited Calicut, on the extreme south-western coast of India, in 1498. In the early 1500s Portugal sent an expedition fitted out not only for trade but for conquest, under an admiral who had been granted the title of Viceroy of India. That venture failed, the local rajah having been assisted by the Venetians, ever ready to destroy a trading competitor, but for most of the remainder of the sixteenth century Portugal, with mastery of the Far Eastern seas, was the major European power on the subcontinent. Portugal lost her independence to Spain in 1580, and her pre-eminence in India began to decline. Increasingly other powers were anxious to establish their influence in this huge and seemingly endlessly rich market. The Dutch began to appear in the Indian Ocean, and Elizabethan England, having removed the threat of Spanish sea power by the defeat of the Armada in 1588, was not far behind.

In 1600 Queen Elizabeth I granted a charter giving a monopoly of British trade with India to 'The Governor and Company of Merchants of London Trading to the East Indies'. The constitution of the Company remained largely unchanged for two hundred years: initially gentlemen were prohibited from joining (trade not being an acceptable occupation for them); British ships trading in Indian waters and not belonging to members of the Company were to be seized and their cargo confiscated; and the Company was expressly prohibited from giving offence to any other Christian (that is European) power already trading in the area and which objected to the presence of British ships. Almost inevitably this latter prohibition was widely flouted from the outset. At first individual voyages – which could take three years from start to finish – were financed by individual members of the Company who shared in the profits. Some captains found it faster and more profitable simply to seize the cargoes of other European ships, and in the early days of the Company piracy made a not inconsiderable addition to the profits of honest trading.

As the Moghul empire in India declined, throughout the late seventeenth and early eighteenth centuries, European trading companies became more and more involved in Indian affairs. Trading stations were established and forts built to protect them. In order to secure trade advantages the companies made alliances and signed treaties with local Indian rulers and, to protect their trading concessions, were inevitably drawn into conflict to prop up their native clients. Conflict meant the need to raise troops, initially native guards, then native and European regiments, and then, in the case of the British, regular units of the British army paid for by the Company. By the mid eighteenth century Dutch influence had been eradicated and Portugal confined to a few small territories including Goa. Only the British and the French were now serious contenders for influence in India, but the French, despite their occupation of Pondicherry, had less money and the English had mastery of the seas. India did not lend itself to colonisation and France was more interested in its possessions in North America. By 1763 East India Company armies had defeated the French and their Indian allies and held a tenuous supremacy over Indian affairs, a situation recognised by the Treaty of Paris in that year.

By the time that Colonel Wesley and the 33rd arrived in Calcutta the East India Company had become yet another Indian power, one of a number that arose after the collapse of Moghul rule. The Company now had far less to do with trading than with the administration of government. In the British Parliament the Regulating Act of 1773 had recognised the right of the Company to administer territories, but had made it clear that this right stemmed from Parliament. The Company effectively ruled parts of India on behalf of the British government, which now created the post of Governor-General, who would be assisted by a council and would serve a five-year tour. Salaries (generous for the time) of Company officials were fixed, officials were formally forbidden to take bribes, and were no longer to be permitted to trade on their own accounts. The Company could sign treaties and wage wars; it had a diplomatic service; it raised taxes; it negotiated with Indian states not directly controlled by it; and it had three armies, one for each of the British controlled presidencies of Bengal, Madras and Bombay.

The armies of the East India Company consisted of three types of unit. British regular units (of which the 33rd Foot was one), sent to India for a period of anything between seven and ten years, whose costs were paid by the Company out of Indian revenues; European regiments raised and paid for by the Company and owing loyalty to it alone, consisting for the most part, but not exclusively, of officers and men of British origin; and native regiments consisting of locally recruited soldiers, or sepoys (from the Persian *sipahi* or soldier), with their own native officers and NCOs promoted from the ranks but with British officers filling the senior command appointments. These officers were career soldiers, but at the time when Wesley arrived in India there was some legal doubt as to their exact status, for they held their commissions not from the King, like officers in the British army, but from the Company. The Company was allowed to grant commissions by its charter, but the regulation was imprecisely worded and referred to 'military officers' or 'persons serving as officers'. This did not matter within the Company's armies, but it did make a difference when officers of the Company were serving alongside King's officers, as officers of the regular British army in India were known. Even though the Company had no formal training establishment for the officers of its armies, until starting to send potential artillery and engineer officers to the Royal Military Academy Woolwich in 1798, and the Company's establishment of a military seminary at Addiscombe in 1809 for the cavalry and infantry, Company officers considered themselves to be professionally superior to their British counterparts. Officers of the Company commanded much larger bodies of (albeit native) troops and were constantly on active service. They nevertheless felt at a disadvantage: there was no system of purchase in the armies of the Company and so promotion was much slower than it was in the regiments of the King. A holder of the King's commission was also senior to an officer with a commission in the Company's armies, regardless of the actual difference in rank. This system would change while Arthur Wesley was in India, but it was a cause of friction until it did.[9]

India in early 1797 was, for the moment, relatively peaceful. In 1789 Lord Cornwallis, the Governor-General, had invaded Mysore and in March 1792 Tippoo Sultan, the 'Tiger of Mysore', made peace by ceding half of his dominions to the British. For the moment Tippoo was neutralised. (Tippoo is probably best remembered now for his working model, complete with sound effects, of a tiger devouring a British soldier, which may be seen in the Victoria and Albert Museum in London). Calcutta was the seat of government for the Bengal presidency and for the whole of British India. It was also the centre of such British society as existed in India. As the 33rd and their twenty-seven-year-old commanding officer were not for the moment required to concern themselves overmuch with matters military, the officers of the regiment rapidly made a name for themselves as socially smart. Heavy drinking was rife, as was gambling, although Wesley set his mind against the latter, paying off at least one officer's dues (thus increasing his own indebtedness) and making him promise never to gamble again. Wellington in later life was abstemious, at a time when a bottle of hock, followed by a bottle of claret and finished off by half a bottle of port and several brandies, was regarded as a reasonable intake for a gentleman at dinner. He realised early on that the Indian climate combined with a high intake of alcohol was not conducive to long life. Many of officers of the army and officials of the Company in India who are shown as having expired from 'apoplexy' were almost certainly laid low by a propensity to dine well if not wisely.

While in Calcutta at this time Arthur Wesley again met Major General James Craig, one time chief of staff in the Flanders campaign and now serving in India, and Major General John St Leger, a crony of the Prince of Wales and the founder of the race which bears his name. Wesley got on well with Craig, as might be expected, but not with St Leger, with whom he had an altercation as to the feasibility of forming a horse artillery arm for the Company's armies. St Leger wanted it to be horse-drawn: the problem being that no suitable horses were available. Wesley agreed that mobile artillery to support the cavalry would be a useful asset but, as a practical man, suggested that the guns should be drawn by bullocks, of which there were plenty.

News from Europe about the war travelled slowly to India. In April 1797 sailors of the Royal Navy at Spithead mutinied, followed by those at The Nore. The causes were low pay, bad food and poor conditions. Although the mutineers were at pains to state that if the French fleet put to sea then they would not be found wanting, the government's fears of an export of French revolutionary ideas intensified. The mutinies were put down, but considerable concessions were made and the sailor's lot improved.[10] Then in August of the same year Spain, which had opted out of the anti-French coalition, changed sides and declared war on Britain. While there was little the British could do in the European theatre, Spain had colonies in the Far East and these might be usefully sequestered by an expedition from India. Sir John Shore, Cornwallis's successor as Governor-General, ordered Lord Hobart, Governor of the Madras presidency, to despatch a force to capture Manila. As Bengal had more troops available than Madras, the bulk of the force was to come from the Bengal army. Wesley had hopes of commanding it, although it is difficult to see why, as he had only just arrived and there were many available officers senior to him. He did not command, but the force sailed in August 1797 and Wesley and the 33rd were part of it. Even a relatively short voyage was hazardous in those times, for if the weather did not threaten the ships then cramped conditions, bad food and disease certainly did, and Wesley had a dispute with the Royal Navy as to who had responsibility for the health of the embarked troops. The navy said it was theirs, while the commander of the 33rd insisted it was his and that it would be his regimental surgeons who would administer to the men. Wesley personally promulgated a regimental order which is a model of what would now be known as regulations for health and safety at work. Strict injunctions as to hygiene and cleanliness, feeding, laundry of clothing and physical exercise were laid down, and subordinate officers were made personally responsible for their enforcement. A not ungenerous allowance of half a pint of spirits per man, watered down to seven parts spirit and three parts water, was authorised. The 33rd being without a regimental chaplain, shortly before sailing Wesley acquired the Reverend Stephen Blunt, a minister recommended by William Hickey. Hickey was a retired official of the Company, a resident of Calcutta, a *bon viveur*, diarist, socialite and sometime drinking companion of the officers of the 33rd. Three days out of harbour Blunt got roaring drunk and emerged from his cabin to caper stark naked amongst the somewhat bemused, and no doubt amused, soldiers and sailors. Despite Colonel Wesley's assurances that the incident would quickly be forgotten, sobriety brought alcoholic melancholia, and the wretched Blunt expired 'from contrite repentance' a few days later. It was not the last problem that Arthur Wesley was to have with chaplains during his long career in command of troops. As it happened, the force never reached Manila, for on arrival at Penang they were recalled. Now that Prussia, Austria and Spain had all left the coalition, there were spare French armies available for operations out of Europe, French influence in Mysore was growing and all available troops were required for the defence of India itself. Wesley and the 33rd returned to India via Bombay and were back in Calcutta by November 1797.

Now Arthur Wesley's fortune began to turn, for Richard Wellesley, Earl of Mornington and recently advanced to Baron Wellesley in the English peerage, was appointed as Governor-General of India. He was originally to have taken over from Lord Hobart as Governor of Madras, with Sir John Shore (who had resigned as Governor-General, apparently fearful of his settlement with Tippoo coming unstuck) being superseded by Lord Cornwallis, who had held the post once before. Events in Ireland, however, where there had been yet another rising, required Cornwallis to remain at home to command the army, so Mornington leapfrogged Madras and went straight to Governor-General.

The career of Wellington has rather eclipsed that of Mornington in modern history books, but if his brother had never been then Richard Wellesley would have come down to us as a great man. Far more of an intellectual than his younger brother, he was a brilliant classical scholar, although lack of money had forced him to leave Oxford without taking a degree. He had enormous capacity for hard work; he had impressed Pitt and Grenville who had advanced him; he had been an effective Junior Lord of the Treasury; and, in an age where what we would now regard as corrupt behaviour was generally seen as a perfectly normal way of conducting business, he seems genuinely to have regarded himself as having a higher mission. He was also subject to violent mood swings, having a tendency to sulk when matters did not go entirely to his liking, and had a very high (but to be fair, usually justified) opinion of his own talents. He was ambitious and wished to advance the interests of himself and his family, but his recorded statements and letters show a desire, unusual for the time, to rule for the good of the ruled and for the greater advantage of the British world position – which he would have seen as being synonymous. With him to India he took his youngest brother, Henry, as his secretary. (A fourth brother, Gerald, between Arthur and Henry, made a career in the church).

Mornington too paused at Cape Town on his way to India and there he met William Kirkpatrick who was on his way home to England, having spent twenty years in the service of the Company, latterly as the British Resident at the court of the Nizam of Hyderabad. Kirkpatrick spoke a variety of Indian languages, knew as much as any Englishman about the politics and plottings of the native rulers and spent long hours discussing them with Mornington. Kirkpatrick was so taken with Mornington – he saw him as a man whose hour had come and who could bring the whole of India under British sway – that he abandoned his thoughts of retirement to England. When Mornington left Cape Town to continue his voyage, Kirkpatrick followed him on the next available ship to Calcutta. The regard was mutual, for Mornington created the post of Political Secretary to the Governor-General especially for Kirkpatrick.

Richard Wellesley, Earl of Mornington; landed in Calcutta on 17 May 1798 and in the same month Arthur Wesley changed his name to Wellesley. Mornington threw himself into the task of getting to know his council and understanding Indian affairs, briefed verbally and by letter by his brother Arthur. In September, when the 33rd were ordered to proceed by sea to Fort George in Madras, Arthur Wellesley accompanied them. Although the voyage was short it was eventful. The ship almost foundered on a reef and the whole of the 33rd went down with 'flux', probably dysentery. Fifteen men died, for which Arthur Wellesley blamed the captain's slackness in failing to ensure a supply of clean drinking water. It was not simply military capriciousness that had called for the move of the 33rd, but stark necessity. Tippoo Sultan had recovered his courage and, egged on by the French, was once more emerging as a threat to British interests. The Fourth Mysore War was about to begin.

3

Learning the Trade

The arrival of the Wellesley brothers in India came at a cross-roads in the history of that land; indeed had it not been for their actions in the political and military spheres the British Raj might never have been. In the 1790s there was much debate in England as to Britain's – and the East India Company's – exact role in India. To the Company, now a quasi-official arm of the British government as well as a trading organisation, India showed as a debit balance on its books. Whilst individuals had made and were making fortunes in the subcontinent, the costs of administering British India far exceeded the revenues raised. The Company's profits came not from India but from China. There were those in the Company's councils who thought that the British should revert to their original role as traders pure and simple, and give up any attempt to administer territories. There were others who felt that what had been gained must be held, but no further territorial acquisitions should be made. Richard Wellesley, in contrast, was an exponent of a forward policy: he believed, and in this he was actively encouraged by Kirkpatrick, that British influence should be confirmed and expanded, and that it should be Britain that would rule India. At home the government was ambivalent, reflecting the differences of opinion within the Company. If Mornington was to succeed in his mission of establishing Britain as the paramount power in India, he would have to proceed carefully; and he could not afford mistakes. In all this he was helped by the war situation: the French were threatening Egypt and there were rumours that the French Governor of Mauritius was offering troops and money in support of Tippoo Sultan. In hindsight it is difficult to see how the French in Mauritius could have done very much, but the threat of it was all grist to the Governor-General's mill.

In all of India's long and rich history it had rarely been united, and such unity as had occasionally existed had been imposed from without, generally by a conqueror who had entered from the north. Most of these invaders had been Moslems and had exercised indirect control, allowing existing local rulers who had not opposed them, or who had come to terms with them, to continue to govern, or misgovern, in their own areas while acting as tax collectors for the central power. The latest arrivals had been the Moghuls (the word is a derivation of Mongol), who had come into northern India from

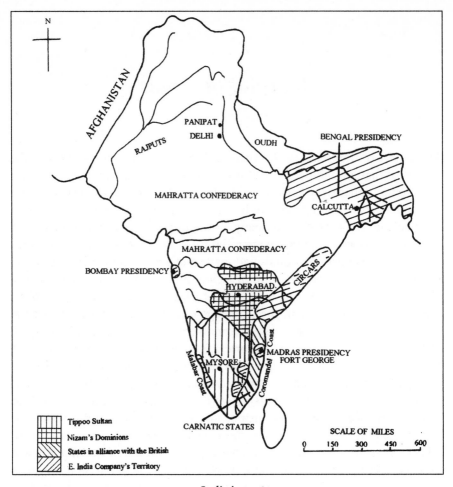

2. India in 1798.

Afghanistan, originally as traders and then as conquerors. Moghul rule had, however, been on the decline for a hundred years, and now few paid more than lip service to the Emperor in Delhi. The British held territories centred on Bengal, Madras and Bombay, nominally from the Emperor, but it had been many a year since the Emperor had been asked about, or been informed of, anything the British were up to.

Bengal was the largest, and wealthiest, of the three presidencies. Administered from Calcutta, in the productive Ganges delta, it had only been ruled directly by the Company for the past forty years, but because of the richness of its land it provided the bulk of the Company's Indian revenues. Bordering on Bengal was the state of Oudh, which would eventually fall to the British but which in 1798 was bound to the Company by treaty. The Madras presidency, administered from Fort George, was not much more than an enclave on the Coromandel coast, although it now also included a portion of what had been Mysore, and was linked by a series of diplomatic agreements to the client states of the Carnatic. Bombay too hugged the coast, on the west this time, and included the environs of the city itself and the immediate hinterland. Each territory had a Governor, with the Governor of Bengal also being the Governor-General of the whole of British India. The Company had an army in each of its three demesnes. In 1796 Bengal, the largest, had three battalions of European infantry, three regiments of European artillery, ten regiments of native cavalry and twenty-four battalions of native infantry. Madras had two battalions of European infantry, two regiments of European artillery and fifteen companies of native artillery, four regiments of native cavalry and twenty-two battalions of native infantry. Bombay had eight battalions of native infantry, relying on local allies for the provision of cavalry and on the other presidency armies for artillery.

There were, apart from the British, four major powers in India or on its borders. Mysore stretched from the west coast, roughly opposite Madras, about 300 miles inland where it bordered on the Company's dominions. It was ruled over by Tippoo Sultan, the so-called Tiger of Mysore and son of the great Hyder Ali. Tippoo was much given to consulting soothsayers and to putting himself into mystical (and possibly drug-induced) trances. He was inclined to the casual and capricious execution of prisoners and had no love for the British, having been forced into ceding half his dominions to the Madras presidency in 1792 when a Company army led by Lord Cornwallis had stormed Bangalore and encircled Seringapatam, Tippoo's capital.

To the north of the Madras territories of the Company lay Hyderabad, a huge area four hundred miles square, whose Moslem ruler, the Nizam, ruled over a largely Hindu population. He was inclined to favour the British, or at least make use of British support to advance his own interests. Such support as he might lend the British was, however, constrained by the fact that his army was trained and led by Frenchmen, whom the Nizam suspected might also pose a threat to him.

North of Hyderabad and stretching in a crescent to its west, but to the east of the Bombay presidency, lay the Mahratta Confederacy, a loose assembly of semi-independent states ruled over by a plethora of chiefs who all owed a nominal allegiance to the Peshwa of Poona, the Mahratta state nearest to Bombay. The Confederacy covered a vast area, stretching 900 miles from south to north, where it reached almost to Delhi, and 1000 miles from east to west. Of all Britain's potential enemies in India it was the Mahrattas who posed the greatest threat; but to deal with them it would first be necessary to bring Tippoo Sultan and Mysore to heel. Of less immediate concern, but a potential threat nonetheless, were the Afghan tribes, who might once again descend through the passes of the north and menace Delhi. This was to be a major consideration affecting the government of India for the next hundred and fifty years.

All these states had armies which varied in effectiveness, depending upon how much their patrons were prepared to spend on them; and, of equal importance, how much could be spent to procure the services of European mercenaries to lead and train them. Had these 'country powers', as they were known, been able to unite, the precarious British toehold in India could not have lasted six months, but they were riven by dissent, both internally and in their relations with each other. It was this factor which the Wellesley brothers used to eliminate their enemies one by one, establishing the foundations of British India in so doing.

In his wish to begin his great mission by the reduction of Mysore, Mornington was assisted by rumours circulating in the Calcutta newspapers. Tippoo had asked the Turks for assistance to remove the British; he had appealed to Paris; he was recruiting more European mercenaries; and he was practising appalling barbarities on prisoners in his gaols. This last, at least, was true, and Mornington, with all the enthusiasm of the politician who has never actually participated in organised killing, urged an attack on Mysore at the earliest possible moment.

Any assault on Tippoo would fall mainly to the Madras army, but here there were problems. The Commander-in-Chief in Madras, and currently acting Governor pending the arrival of Lord Hobart's replacement, was Major General Sir George Harris. Harris, then fifty-two, had attended the Royal Military Academy at Woolwich and had been commissioned into the artillery at the age of fourteen in 1760. Transferring to the infantry, he had served in the American war (where he was wounded at Bunker Hill) and in St Lucia before going to India, where he made his name in the Third Mysore War. A cunning old warrior, well aware of his own limitations, he knew that there was no money in the Madras treasury for military adventures. His reply to Mornington's initial urgings was to prevaricate, but the Secretary to the government of Madras, Josiah Webbe, replied in blunter terms, with a bald statement that there was no money and no credit to finance a war, and implying that if the Governor-General persisted he might be impeached. This infuriated Mornington, who was only persuaded to hold off immediate military action by Arthur Wellesley, who explained to his brother that it would take time and money to build up a force capable of decisive action against Tippoo.

Even when Mornington, in a storm of vituperation, had made it clear to Madras that he would brook no shirking and that an expeditionary force was to be prepared for action against Mysore, there was still Hyderabad to consider. The Nizam, essentially a weak man, distrusted Tippoo and feared the Hindu Mahrattas. He was already loosely connected to the Company by treaty, but his own army included sixteen regular battalions of infantry commanded by French officers. These officers were adventurers pure and simple, although they appear to have had republican sympathies and some had clothed their men in 'cap of liberty' buttons and equipped their battalions with the tricolour. The concepts of liberty, fraternity and equality had no place in the Nizam's government, nor indeed in that of any eastern potentate, and the Nizam had a suspicion that the time was not far off when these French officers might use his own army against him. British methods might not be entirely to the Nizam's liking either, but at least the British had been and were now a power in India, which the French were not. Added to this was the evidence of the Nizam's own eyes, which told him that the two British-officered native battalions of the Company present in Hyderabad appeared better trained and more effective, besides having European-manned integral artillery, than his own, French-officered, units.

From the British point of view the Nizam had now to be brought into the anti-Mysore front. Feelers were put out. The Company would protect Hyderabad against the depredations of the Mahrattas and of Tippoo, provided that the Nizam agreed to replace his French military advisers by British. In September 1798, in a brilliantly engineered and almost bloodless coup, led by the commanders of the two Company battalions in Hyderabad, the Nizam's French officers – around a hundred altogether – were rounded up and put under arrest. The Nizam's army was now under British control and the French officers were sent home in an East India Company ship.

In Madras the build up of troops proceeded, but very slowly. The new Governor, Lord Clive, son of 'Clive of India', initially joined the peace party. It was at this point that Mornington sent Arthur Wellesley and the 33rd to Fort George, the citadel and capital of Madras. The arrival of a King's regiment would add some muscle to the Madras army, and the presence of the Governor-General's brother would, Mornington hoped, impart some sense of urgency to Clive and General Harris.

In fact, Arthur Wellesley got on well with both. He eventually persuaded Clive that the best interests of Madras and of the Company lay in taking control of Mysore. Harris, impressed by the supplies of money, men and equipment now arriving from Bengal, credited Wellesley with having achieved this, and appointed him as officer-in-charge of mobilisation, which was taking place at Arcot and Vellore, within British territory and still a hundred miles or so from the border of Mysore. There had already been an officer appointed to this post, Colonel Aston of the King's 12th Foot.

Promoted to colonel in the same batch as was Wellesley, Aston was two places higher on the seniority list. Both colonels had come out to India at about the same time and they were friends. Aston, a normally competent and intelligent officer, had foolishly fought not one but two duels with one of his own officers. This had not only attracted the displeasure of General Harris, it had also led to his being incapacitated by having a bullet wound in the side (from which he eventually died). He could no longer command the concentration area, so Wellesley was appointed in his stead. Cynics might say that Harris had got the inconvenient brother (and spy) of the Governor-General well away from Fort George, while ensuring that if things went wrong the blame would fall on the Wellesleys, and not on him.

Mornington now sent an emissary to ask Tippoo for an explanation of his seemingly unfriendly policies. Tippoo answered that he was about to go hunting and had no time to reply to the Governor-General's request. While this was hardly a reason for war, it was at least an excuse. Mornington ordered General Harris to prepare to advance into Mysore with a view to capturing Tippoo's capital, the fortified city of Seringapatam.

Arthur Wellesley had been in Madras since early September 1798. While he saw the personal advantage to be gained by war, he was sufficient of an embryo strategist to have doubts as to its wisdom and to dissuade his brother from precipitous action. At one stage he even suggested that all that was required was for Tippoo to expel the French from his court and his lands and accept a British Resident instead. Mornington's grand scheme demanded conquest, however, and so Arthur Wellesley continued to steer Clive towards that end, while working assiduously to gather the stocks of rice, carts, bullocks, forage and all the impedimenta that the army would need once it crossed the frontier. Of particular importance was the provision of a siege train: those heavy guns with their crews, transport and ammunition which would be needed to reduce the fortress of Seringapatam. Wellesley was unimpressed by the two Company officers sent to assist him; he thought they were incompetent and expressed surprise that they were unable to speak the local language. The implication is that he, despite his short time in India, had managed to master at least a smattering of the languages and dialects of Madras. He would have needed some Urdu (a hybrid language loosely based on Arabic) to deal with the senior officers of the Nizam's army, and Hindi for general use. Wellesley's letters during this period are peppered with dialect words, and we may assume that his already noted fluency in French now extended to Indian languages. The problems of administering an army in the field in Europe have already been referred to, and in India too there were difficulties brought about by a reluctance to spend money in peacetime on something which would only be needed in war. The Company did have a rudimentary commissariat, but much of the transportation and provision of rations and forage was contracted out to civilian suppliers. Inevitably this led to corruption and Wellesley angrily reported that suppliers who had supposedly won their contracts in open and fair tendering were in fact controlled and financed by officials of the Company. Even at this early stage in his career he showed an antipathy for any form of personal enrichment at the expense of what he called 'the public interest'.

There were a number of factors which dictated when an advance into Mysore could be made. The Madras army needed to be prepared for the campaign. Due partly to the difficulty in concentrating an army and all the stores and supporting elements that an advance would need, and partly due to the inherent bureaucracy of the Madras government, which decided everything by committee, this would take time. Should Tippoo attack Madras before the Company's expeditionary force was ready, then the 33rd would have to bear the brunt. There was also the possible threat posed by the Afghans, who might invade northern India and then attack Bengal while the bulk of both presidencies' resources were tied up by Tippoo. There were also the Mahrattas to consider. While they were probably too busy quarrelling amongst themselves to attack the British, there was always the possibility of one or more of the semi-independent chiefs seizing an opportunity. Finally there was the weather. Any large-scale military operations must be complete before the arrival of the monsoon, which generally broke around the end of May, rendering movement difficult if not impossible.

All these points were addressed: the army was steadily amassing the men and equipment it would need and inquiries among the Mahratta chieftains indicated that they were far more concerned about a threat from Afghanistan than by any wish to support Tippoo against the Company. Memories of the battle of Panipat in 1760, when an army of Afghans and Rohillas had defeated the Mahrattas, killing, so it was said, 200,000 of them, were still fresh. The Mahrattas were unlikely to make common cause with Tippoo or to move against the British – at least yet.

At this point Mornington himself arrived in Madras, and at one stage even considered accompanying the army when it marched off into Mysore. Arthur Wellesley, rightly, saw that such close political supervision would make the task of the Commander-in-Chief, Harris, almost impossible. On 29 January 1799 he wrote to his brother (as 'My dear Mornington'), to tell him so:

> it appears to me that your presence in camp, instead of giving confidence to the general, would deprive him of the command of the army ... Everything which the general might think necessary will be thwarted and canvassed, not by you probably but by those whom you will naturally wish to consult ... Your presence will

diminish his powers, at the same time that, as it is impossible you can know anything of military matters, your powers will not answer the purpose, which [whereas] even those which he [Harris] has at present may.[1]

It was remarkably perspicacious advice from a young colonel not yet thirty. Mornington wisely heeded it, and in a reply dated 2 February 1799 said that he entirely agreed and claimed that accompanying the army had not been his idea, but that of his advisers.

On 29 January 1799, with the army almost ready to take the field, General Harris and his staff arrived from Fort George. Instead of being in sole charge of mobilisation, Arthur Wellesley now found himself well down the chain of command. He cannot seriously have expected to be put in charge of the oper-ation – armies did not work that way and seniority ruled – but he was certainly disappointed. Harris, nobody's fool and no doubt anxious not to have an officer so closely connected to the Governor-General as a direct subordinate, appointed Wellesley as adviser to the Hyderabad contingent, provided by the Nizam to cooperate with the Company's army in the conquest of Mysore.

Wellesley's position now called for the exercise of tact and diplomacy of a high order. Although technically only the adviser to the contingent, which was nominally commanded by the Nizam's chief minister, Mir Allum, there was no doubt in British minds that Wellesley would be responsible for all that the contingent did, and that he would have to exercise command without appearing to usurp the authority of Mir Allum. Happily, his relations with Mir Allum, and with Indians generally, were excellent; indeed the Mir had asked Harris for Wellesley by name. The Hyderabad contingent consisted of, in Arthur Wellesley's own words, 'six excellent battalions of the Company's own sepoys, four rapscallion battalions of the Nizam's, which, however, behaved well, and really about 10,000 (which they called 25,000) cavalry of all nations, some good and some bad'.[2] While the 33rd were not originally intended to be part of the Hyderabad contingent, they were added to it at Wellesley's suggestion. He himself could not of course command the 33rd directly, and Lieutenant Colonel John Sherbrooke was also unavailable, as he was now required to command a brigade, so the 33rd passed into the tempo-rary hands of its senior major, Major John Shee, not an officer whom Wellesley held in high regard.

The plan was for the Madras army under Harris, who would combine command of that army with the overall appointment of commander-in-chief, to advance westwards from Vellore, linking up with the Nizam's contingent at Amboor, still inside British territory, whence it would move to the Mysore border, on the way picking up the Baramahal force (a mixed all arms grouping of Company and Hyderabad troops numbering about 5000 all ranks and commanded by Lieutenant Colonel Read, an officer of the Company). Simultaneously 6500 men of the Bombay army under Lieutenant General James Stuart would advance from the west, while the Coimbatore army of 4500 men under Lieutenant Colonel Brown, also of the Company, would move up from the south. The three prongs of the attack would converge at Seringapatam. As the senior British officer of one of the columns, Wellesley would be expected to entertain and feed his staff: he wrote to his brother Henry Wellesley, Mornington's secretary, asking to have tureens and serving dishes for twelve sent to him, the custom being for the host to provide the food and the serving dishes, while those dining would supply their own plates and cutlery.

Harris's Madras army totalled around 20,000 effectives. The two brigades of cavalry, under Major General Floyd, had two King's regiments, the 19th and 25th Dragoons, and four sepoy regiments. The infantry, in six brigades, included four King's battalions, eleven sepoy battalions and one Swiss battalion, this latter having been inherited by the Company from the Dutch when the British acquired Ceylon in 1796. Altogether, including the Nizam's contingent, Harris deployed around 55,000 troops in the war and was well provided with artillery. The field artillery consisted of fifty-six guns, ranging from eighteen pounders to 5.5 inch howitzers, while the siege train, gathered together by Arthur Wellesley with considerable difficulty, had two twenty-four pounders, thirty eighteen pounders, eight twelve pounders and three eight inch howitzers.

On 3 February 1799 Richard Wellesley, Earl of Mornington and Governor-General of British India, ordered the armies to begin their advance on Mysore. War had not yet been declared, so Harris was ordered to stop at the border. Harris moved off from Vellore on 11 February and reached Amboor on the 18th, where he joined up with the Hyderabad contingent. Moving in two parallel columns about three miles apart, the two armies continued their movement to the Mysore border, which they reached on 3 March 1799. It was now clear that war was inevitable, for Tippoo failed to come to terms with the Governor-General's demands and, adopting a not very efficient scorched earth policy, concentrated his army, of about 30,000 men, in Seringapatam. The two huge columns crossed the border and began advancing through enemy territory.

Covering an area of about eighteen square miles, with the troops on the flanks and the baggage and stores in the centre, the two columns moved at a stately rate of between five and ten miles a day. While this may seem a crawl, it was reasonable progress over bad or non-existent roads with the need to forage on the way. While the troops themselves moved in disciplined formations and were equipped with tents, the armies, like all armies of the time in the east, rapidly took on the appearance of a travelling circus. Harris disposed of 20,000 troops in his Madras army, but they needed 9000 'official' civilian followers to support them. In addition the families of many of the sepoys followed the column and all manner of tradesmen came along too, setting up booths from which they dispensed their wares whenever the army stopped. There were money changers, shoemakers, food stalls, wine and liquor shops, goldsmiths and jewellers, fortune tellers and apothecaries, jugglers, dancing bears and their attendants. There were grass cutters and grooms for the horses, and sweepers and latrine orderlies for the men. European merchants established mobile grocery shops to cater for the British element and there was, of course, a group of what were euphemistically termed 'dancing girls'. All the tentage and stores for the troops, to say nothing of the belongings of the great travelling bazaar which accompanied them, had to be carried, and while most of the military transport was by bullock cart (around 100,000 bullocks) there were donkeys, ponies, oxen, camels and a few elephants in attendance. The supporting train for the Hyderabad contingent was even larger. Altogether there were probably 100,000 non-combatants trailing along after the 50,000 or so soldiers.

It was during this advance that Arthur Wellesley noted men of the 33rd deploying in what he considered to be a sloppy fashion, some without their weapons. He sent the men back to the battalion telling them they were not to behave in such a fashion again. Major Shee, temporarily in command of the 33rd, and like Wellesley Anglo-Irish, but perhaps more Irish than English, took this as a personal insult and sent a most intemperate letter to Wellesley, protesting against what Shee saw as interference in what was now his battalion. Wellesley replied:

This is not the first time that I have had occasion to observe that, under the forms of private correspondence, you have written to me letters upon public duty, couched in terms to which I have not been accustomed ... I cannot but reflect that no sensible man ever writes a letter in a passion: that he inquires and considers, and, in the end, finds that he had no reason to be displeased. However, it is necessary that I should inform you that the next letter of that kind that I receive I shall send to the Commander-in-Chief, and leave it to him to make such answer as he may think fit. It will be much better, and it will make both your situation and mine more comfortable to us both, if you will understand one thing, that I have no intention whatever of doing anything which can have any effect unpleasant to your feelings, and that the best method of coming to such an understanding as we ought to live upon is, to inquire before you act in consequence of anything that passes. Of this you may be certain, that however my attention may be engaged by other objects, whenever I find it necessary I shall interfere in everything which concerns the 33rd. I have written more than I intended, and in hopes that I shall hear no more of it.[3]

Arthur Wellesley understood people. He could so easily have taken the matter of Shee's impertinence higher but chose to be conciliatory, while still showing that the iron fist could be employed if necessary. Shee appears to have got the message.

As they moved into and through Mysore, Harris's armies entered the area which Tippoo had attempted to lay waste. As the British carried enough rations to last the troops three months, this had little effect on the men; but the bullocks which were essential to the force had to feed on locally obtained forage. If Tippoo could starve the bullocks he could bring Harris to a halt. Progress slowed and from 10 March Tippoo's cavalry began to harry the force. While the lightly armed Mysore cavalry could not stand against the better disciplined and equipped Company troops, they were a nuisance. Constant small-scale raids against the flanks of the columns, with the risk to the baggage and the siege train in the middle, necessitated constant vigilance and frequent deployments to drive them off. Wellesley was well aware of the threat and moved the Hyderabad contingent accordingly, with flank guards composed of companies of his own 33rd Foot interspersed with detachments of the Company's Madras infantry, and a cavalry screen supported by guns to the fore. At one stage on 10 March a host of about 2000 hostile cavalry attacked Wellesley's column from the rear. Galloping to the threatened area, he organised his troops, beat off the Mysore horsemen and personally led a counter attack of Company and Hyderabad cavalry. The attackers withdrew. Already we see Wellesley's almost uncanny ability always to be at the point of maximum risk and to take such measures as were required. While his force suffered some casualties - twenty killed and about twice as many wounded - the disciplined volleys of the 33rd and the Madras Native Infantry wreaked far more damage among the enemy. The Mysore troops were not to attack in such force or with such determination again.

On the same day, away to the west, a large Mysore detachment attacked the Bombay army but, despite operating on their own interior lines and having a numerical superiority of over five to one, the men of Mysore achieved nothing despite fierce fighting which went on all day. The Company was victorious and their attackers withdrew back into Seringapatam to rejoin the rest of Tippoo's forces.

Harris's columns moved on, roughly to the north in the direction of Bangalore, but a combination of Tippoo's scorched earth policy and disagreements with the civilian contractors and the bullock drivers caused delays. Wellesley had persuaded Harris that the system of peacetime accounting for transport and bullocks was inefficient in the field, so the whole system had been simplified and stores not considered necessary had been dumped. Many of the contractors did not like the new system and pilferage of equipment and absenteeism began. If he stuck to his intended route, Harris could not reach Seringapatam with enough time in hand to capture it before the monsoon set in. Harris now changed his line of march and headed south west. Within a few miles he was out of the area devastated by Tippoo, forage for the bullocks was plentiful and guards placed on the baggage reduced the haemorrhage of stores and ammunition. Tippoo's cavalry, caught out by this sudden change of route, took some days to start attacking the columns again and there was a welcome respite from their pinprick raids.

By 21 March Harris had swung onto the main Bangalore to Seringapatam road, bordered on both sides by thick jungle. After four days of slow movement through this difficult country, where visibility off the road was reduced to a few yards, the force emerged into a flat, clear plain short of the town of Mullavelley. Here, on 27 March, some of Tippoo's troops made a stand and Arthur Wellesley was once more to the forefront. Both the Madras army and the Hyderabad contingent were involved, with John Sherbrooke commanding the Madras pickets and Stapleton Cotton the cavalry.[4] Wellesley personally took command of the 33rd, ordering them to fire when the Mysore infantry were no more than sixty yards away. The British were the victors, but in Wellesley's view Tippoo had wasted an opportunity by not attacking the columns when they were moving through the jungle. He nevertheless thought that the Mysore infantry and cavalry had fought well at Mullavelley and were only defeated by a failure to coordinate the movement of their infantry, cavalry and guns, and by a mass panic which set in once they were charged by the 33rd.

The Madras and Hyderabad armies were now only thirty miles from Seringapatam, but the entire direct route had been laid waste by Tippoo, who had reverted to his scorched earth methods. Harris once more changed direction, turning south to cross the Cauvery river, where he found bullocks and forage aplenty, and then turning west once more to approach Seringapatam from the south. On 4 April the British were within five miles of Seringapatam and their objective could be clearly seen. Tippoo had now given up any hope of being able to stop the British, or even delay them, short of his capital. He was now firmly ensconced in Seringapatam with all his chiefs and his army. His only hope was to resist the coming onslaught until the monsoon turned the Cauvery into an impassable torrent.

The Cauvery river, which rose in the Western Ghats and flowed to the Bay of Bengal on the east coast, was a major obstacle. At Seringapatam it flowed roughly east to west and was between 500 and 600 yards wide, before dividing into the north Cauvery and the south Cauvery to form an island on which the fortress of Seringapatam stood. The island was about five miles from east to west and just over a mile from north to south at its widest point. The fortress loomed over the western end of the island and was about a mile long on its north side and three quarters of a mile long north to south. The fortifications were impressive, the walls being mainly of granite with some brick. Trenches formed an outer protective line and the one ford over the south Cauvery was well protected by guns and dug in infantry. Along the south wall were around a hundred guns. Beyond the south Cauvery, and between fifty and five hundred yards from it, was a rivulet, not a major obstacle to infantry or cavalry, but a line that could be easily defended. Further out from the rivulet was an artificial watercourse, which was steep and faced with stone. It zigzagged roughly parallel to the south Cauvery and about a mile from it.

On 5 April the two armies, those of Madras and Hyderabad, camped in the area from where they would assault Seringapatam, south west of the fortress island and four miles from it. They had covered 150 miles in thirty-one days (not all of them marching days) and had suffered remarkably few casualties. Most of the stores and equipment had arrived intact, the commissariat had thirty-three days rations for 30,000 men and the Hyderabad contingent alone had arrived with 3000 artillery rounds. The Madras army was to the north, astride the water course, while the Hyderabad contingent camped 500 yards south of them, the soldiers in orderly lines of white tents, the followers in all manner of huts, palm leaf shelters and makeshift bivouacs. Wellesley now had the complete confidence of Mir Allum and was firmly, in fact if not in name, in command of the Hyderabad contingent. This was to cause some

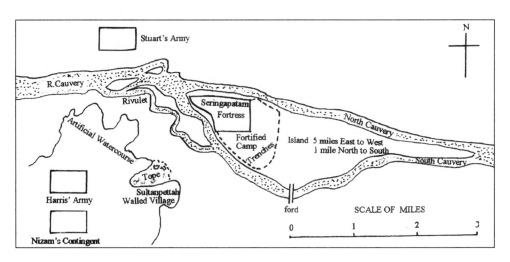

3. Seringapatam.

jealousy amongst both King's and Company officers who were senior to him and who would have preferred Wellesley's position to that of command of a brigade in the Madras army.

Before the siege proper could begin, the area between the allied camps and the south Cauvery had to be cleared. There were two areas of particular importance, which if not taken by Harris would make an escalade of Seringapatam impossible. To the east of Wellesley's camp was a wood in one bend of the watercourse and a walled village in the next bend to the south. The wood, more properly a patch of thick jungle a quarter of a mile across and half a mile deep and known as the 'Tope' (Hindustani for wood, or clump of trees), was behind the watercourse, while the village, Sultanpettah, was in front of it. The watercourse here was between forty and fifty feet across and about six feet deep. It was banked on each side and from the British side it was impossible to see what lay beyond.

At about four o'clock in the afternoon of 5 April, while Wellesley was setting out his pickets and flank guards to protect his camp, a message arrived from General Harris ordering him to attack and capture the watercourse, Tope and village. A second attack, commanded by Colonel Shaw, would take place simultaneously across the watercourse, parallel to and about half a mile north of Wellesley's line of advance. Wellesley found the order unclear. He rode off to seek clarification from Harris and, failing to find him, left a note saying that he did not know what Harris meant, adding: 'When you have got the watercourse you have got the Tope'. Wellesley was wrong.

There was no time for any reconnaissance, so galloping back to the Hyderabad camp Wellesley began to gather together a force to capture the designated area. Taking his own 33rd and two battalions of Madras Native Infantry with some guns, Wellesley moved off at around seven o'clock, by which time it was fully dark. He himself led with the grenadier and light companies of the 33rd, followed by Major Shee and the rest of the 33rd in column, supported by the two Madras battalions.

A night attack, even today, is always difficult, particularly over unfamiliar country. Visibility is reduced, landmarks cannot be seen and navigation can easily go wrong. Men must keep in close personal touch and use simple formations. Progress is slow, control can easily be lost with the risk of men attacking the wrong objective, mistaking each other for the enemy or of attacking at different times, thus losing the impetus and momentum of the attack. In an age when there were no pocket compasses, and in a land where maps were but sketches, the problems were magnified.

The attack was a disaster. Accounts are vague and contradictory but what appears to have happened is that Wellesley arrived short of the watercourse and left his guns there, with a Madras battalion to protect them and act as a reserve. The 33rd then attacked the defended but dry watercourse, helped by the light of rockets being fired at the British camp from Seringapatam, and drove the enemy back down the bank and into the Tope. Pursuing into the thick woods the men became disorientated and scattered. Wellesley had dismounted short of the watercourse and accompanied the flank companies into the Tope, but he too became lost and separated from his men. Scrambling about in the clumps of bamboo and falling into the drainage ditches that criss-crossed the Tope, the attackers came under fire from both flanks and there were a number of instances of hand to hand fighting, bayonet against tulwar. Some of the men of the 33rd fell into the watercourse; control had been lost and no one had much idea where they were or in which direction they were supposed to be going. Wellesley eventually met one of his own officers and together they recrossed the watercourse and tried, and failed, to find the reserve. Wellesley did however find his horse, and remounting he cantered along the watercourse trying to discover what was happening and attempting, largely unsuccessfully, to restore order. In the meantime, the battalion companies of the 33rd, under Major Shee, having crossed the watercourse and got lost, re-emerged and eventually joined Colonel Shaw's force further north, where they were able to be of at least some assistance.[5]

Wellesley galloped back to the Madras camp where he found General Harris and told him that the attack on the Tope had failed. He was described as being much agitated. Having delivered his report, he flung himself full length on a mess table and went to sleep, totally exhausted and still suffering from the mild dysentery which he had contracted some days before.

Although in hindsight the attack on the Tope and surrounding area was only a minor skirmish – British casualties were in the region of twenty-five – Arthur Wellesley had nevertheless presided over a failure: he had lost control of the action and of himself and he had panicked and deserted his men. There is little sign here of the calm, controlled and personally courageous commander of the future. Looked at two centuries later it is an extraordinary story: behaviour which would not have been tolerated in a subaltern much less a colonel. It is difficult to excuse, but a measure of the man is that he did not try to excuse himself. He admitted he had got it badly wrong and made no attempt to lay the blame other than squarely upon himself. He could have claimed that he was badly briefed (true); he could have accused Shee of not following up closely enough and then of going almost a mile off course in completely the wrong direction (again true); he could have blamed the two Madras battalions of not using their initiative and of failing to press on when things began to go wrong (not true, but a common excuse for King's officers). As it was, he availed himself of none of these pleas in mitigation but pondered on what had gone wrong and learned from the affair.

Arthur Wellesley had his enemies – as the brother of the Governor-General and favoured by Harris over officers much senior to him it could hardly have been otherwise. Had he not been the brother of the Governor-General, Seringapatam might have spelled the end of his career. Instead, he survived; but he never forgot the lessons he had learned there and they were to stand him in good stead for the rest of his life. He realised that the overall commander of an operation should not be so far forward as to get personally involved in the fighting, to the detriment of his ability to control the actions of the whole force. He learned never to launch a night attack against a position that had not been properly reconnoitred in daylight – apart from assaults on the breaches of fortified towns that he was besieging, he would never initiate a night attack again – and he learned the importance of self-control. Harris did not hold Wellesley's failure against him, although some of the senior officers did. Wellesley was not only well connected in Indian terms but Harris had already come to a favourable impression of his abilities. Next morning Wellesley renewed the attack on the watercourse and the Tope and this time took it easily – the enemy having in fact withdrawn.

The work of reducing Tippoo's outposts went on and by 17 April all had been taken by assault or abandoned. The Bombay army had arrived and Tippoo and his army were now walled up inside Seringapatam. The siege proper could begin. Guns were hauled into position, trenches dug to allow the assaulting troops to approach the walls, and scaling ladders were made from locally obtained bamboo. By 3 May, the heavy siege guns having smashed a breach in the north-west wall of the fortress, the engineers declared it 'practicable': that is, capable of being ascended by a man walking upright without having to use his hands.

Harris decided to assault the fortress through the breach at one o'clock in the afternoon of the following day, 4 May 1799. It would be the hottest hour of the day and not when an assault would be expected: the defenders might literally be caught napping. While a longer battering by the guns, which still had ample supplies of ammunition, might have made the attack easier, the monsoon was approaching and Harris wished to be safe inside Seringapatam before it broke. While Wellesley seems to have hoped, somewhat unrealistically, for command of the attack, Harris nominated Major General David Baird, up to now commanding a brigade of the Madras army. Baird was a Scot and had been commissioned into the British army in 1772, at the age of fifteen. He had gone out to India in 1779 and had been wounded and captured by Hyder Ali, Tippoo's father, during the Second Mysore War in 1780. He had spent four uncomfortable years in chains as a prisoner in Seringapatam before being released at the end of hostilities in 1784. He then served in the Cape and returned to India at about the same time as Mornington took up the Governor-Generalship. Baird was a big, strong man, brave to a fault and a fighting leader of men. Unfortunately he was somewhat lacking in intelligence and he had an exaggerated view of his own importance, constantly seeing slights where none were intended. He was no friend of Arthur Wellesley and had objected when Wellesley was placed with the Hyderabad contingent. Harris had been able to explain this seeming supersession of Baird by referring to an obscure Company rule which said that no officer on detachment could hold a rank higher than that of colonel – Baird was a major general – but it was the right choice nevertheless. Arthur Wellesley often fulminated against Indians, particularly Indian contractors – but then he fulminated against all contractors, Indian, Portuguese, Spanish or English – but he liked Indians, respected their customs and culture, got on well with them and made considerable efforts to learn some of their languages. Baird, perhaps understandably given his enforced sojourn in Tippoo's jail, neither liked nor understood Indians. He would have been completely the wrong choice for the Hyderabad contingent, but was exactly the right choice for the assault on Seringapatam.

Wellesley played no part in the assault, which took place as planned on 4 May. He was in command of the reserve, which was not needed. Two columns, one led by John Sherbrooke, crossed the almost dry bed of the south Cauvery and stormed the fortress town. By four o'clock in the afternoon the union flag flew over the royal palace, Tippoo was dead along with 10,000 of his men and the British had Seringapatam.[6] British and allied casualties amounted to less than 900, of whom 200 were killed.[7]

Order had now to be restored in Seringapatam, the leaderless Mysorean soldiers rounded up and disarmed, and the British and allied troops, engaged in their usual occupation of plundering a captured town, brought under control.[8] A governor of the town had also to be appointed. Baird, having led the successful assault, had every reason to believe the command would be given to him, but Harris had other ideas. The army had a system of duty officers at every level, and there was a duty brigade commander roster, which included Arthur Wellesley. Baird had been the duty officer on the day of the assault, but Wellesley's name was due to come up on the following day. Colonel Wellesley was appointed as Governor of Seringapatam, to the considerable discomfort of Baird who received the news from Wellesley himself at breakfast, thus adding yet more fuel to his resentment.

The Governor-General was elated. The first step in his grand design to establish the British as the paramount power in India had been a triumphant success. Company rule in Mysore must now be consolidated, for it was from here that further expansion could take place. Mornington established a commission to run Mysore. It was headed by General Harris with Arthur

Wellesley as the next senior military officer. It also included Henry Wellesley and Lieutenant Colonel Barry Close, a Company officer and the man who probably knew more about India and the Indians than any other European alive, and John Malcolm, who had commanded one of the Company battalions in Hyderabad and had played a major part in the coup which removed the Nizam's French officers. By July 1799 General Harris had returned to Madras and Wellesley was effectively the commander of the army in Mysore. Just why he was entrusted with such an important task, with wide-ranging discretion and responsibility, when there were so many officers with far more experience than he had, is no real mystery. Mornington as Governor-General had never been a soldier and had little time for the protocols of military rank and seniority: Arthur Wellesley was his brother and he trusted him totally. General Harris, despite the failure at the Tope before Seringapatam, had observed Wellesley closely both while he assembled the expedition for Mysore and organised its administration, and also as adviser and de facto commander of the Hyderabad contingent. He too had full confidence in Wellesley, confidence that was not misplaced. The colonel had shown as the temporary, later permanent, commandant of Seringapatam that he had the administrative ability, the tact, diplomacy and the understanding of the natives to organise and manage a sizeable city where previously disorganisation had been the norm. Despite the great powers delegated to him, he was careful not to upset his distant superiors – even Baird became almost reconciled to him – and he quickly won the respect of the local notables. Arthur Wellesley was never a good second-in-command, but when given responsibility he rose to it. He acquired a reputation as a fair but firm administrator, who respected local customs while bringing law and order never previously known to the territory under his command.

Wellesley was adamant that the good name of the British and their reputation for fair play must not be besmirched. On Christmas Eve 1799 we find him turning his mind to the problems of the inhabitants of the late Sultan's harem. A number of the women in the harem had been married to Indian Christians before being forcibly added to Tippoo's and his nobles' collections. Now a French priest wanted them returned to their original husbands. Wellesley set out a reasoned opinion: while the normal reaction of any Englishman would be to have these women released, the British had guaranteed the sanctity of the families of the nobles, and to release all the women now would be going back on their word. As some of the erstwhile husbands wanted to remarry, the best that could be done, in Wellesley's opinion, was to make a list of the women and inform the priest which of them were dead, allowing the husbands to be remarried under Christian rites.[9] Somewhat to their surprise, the inhabitants of Mysore found that they rather liked the rule of the

Company, headed by Colonel Wellesley. While brooking no deviation from its rules, it was at least consistent, allowing the population the peace and order to farm and follow their trades, without the constant disruption of petty wars and endemic banditry.

Being at the top of the slippery pole in Mysore was no sinecure. One of the problems brought about by the British take-over of the territory, and one which would be repeated elsewhere as British India expanded, was the host of unemployed soldiers formerly in the service of Tippoo who had now taken to the hills and jungles, where they existed as brigands, ambushing, raiding and thieving. They had to be hunted down and dealt with, either by execution or imprisonment, or by persuading them to turn to more peaceful occupations. Neither the British nor the East India Company armies had much experience of what would become known as guerrilla warfare, against an enemy which did not wear uniform and did not stand and fight, and in a country where movement was difficult and everything the troops needed had to be carried with them. Some of these freebooters, those in gangs small in number and with little support in the countryside, were easily dealt with. Others were not, and restoration of law and order in Mysore soon turned into a full-scale counter-insurgency war. There were no textbooks to guide Wellesley, and tactics for an army hitherto accustomed to operations in close column and line, using volley fire against an identifiable enemy assembled in mass array, had to be improvised.

The methods that Wellesley used could have served as a model for the Briggs Plan, devised to defeat the Communist insurrection in Malaya a century and a half later. Those opposing the British expansion were largely mounted and lived off the country. Lacking uniforms and conventional tactics and discipline as they did, they were nevertheless described as the best light cavalry in the world. They did not stand to fight but would ambush roads, raid supply columns and mount lightning attacks on formed bodies of troops before scattering and withdrawing back to the jungle or to remote fortresses, leaving their pursuers far behind. To defeat them the British had to have intelligence of their movements, and deny them food and support from the local population so as to try to force them to concentrate where they could be defeated by superior firepower. At the same time the British forces had to be able to communicate with each other, to be able to move quickly to threatened areas, and to be supplied while on the march.

To try to guard every vital point and every road would have been impossible, and would only have dispersed the troops available into penny packets, too small to be effective. Wellesley's aim was to position his forces where they could react in strength once he knew where the enemy was located. In an age when military intelligence was neglected and often despised as not being the

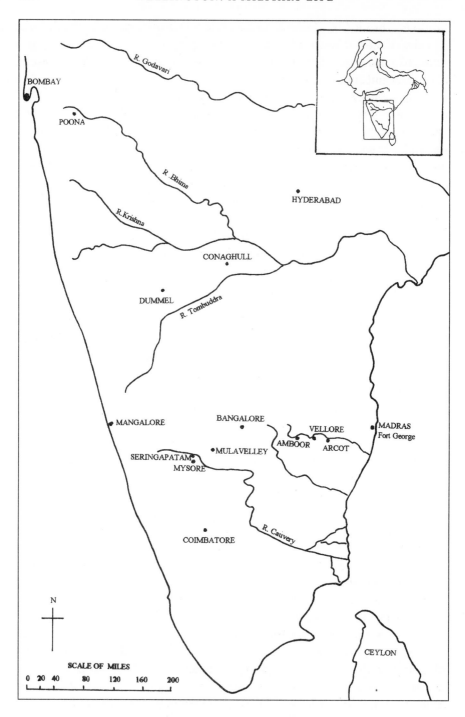

4. India: Area of Operations, September 1798 to February 1801.

concern of a gentleman, Wellesley set up a combined communications and intelligence service using existing channels. There were two means of communicating over long distances in India: one was by using the hereditary caste of letter writers and messengers, who carried letters and small packets over long distances. High caste Hindus (mainly Brahmins but many educated in the Persian idiom), they were usually mounted on racing camels, which could travel at up to fifteen miles per hour, or on ponies. These men were organised not only as messengers for the Company army but also as intelligence agents. Well paid and well looked after, they were remarkably efficient. Even when Wellesley's forces were split into four groups operating at distances of several hundred miles from each other and from headquarters in Seringapatam, each component always knew what the others were up to and Wellesley was able to coordinate their movements and receive reports from them. The other method of communication was by using the *dhak,* literally a post or small cottage erected at intervals along main routes, manned by runners and kept in order by the local authorities.

The existing roads were the fastest means of movement for Wellesley's forces, but they were also dangerous and liable to ambush, particularly when trees and jungle grew along the edges. To prevent the insurgents using the cover of the jungle to ambush the columns, all roads were cleared of vegetation for up to a hundred yards on each side, and columns of troops moving along the roads were accompanied by one or two guns, usually the light galloper guns originally intended to support the cavalry. Firing canister these guns could fire into jungle and scrub and cause horrific casualties amongst men hiding in it. The canister round in use in the 1790s was a tube of tin packed with one-ounce lead musket balls. When fired from a normal artillery piece the tube split, sending a swathe of balls in an expanding cone from the muzzle of the gun. Although with a relatively short range, it was particularly effective against massed cavalry and infantry in the open. Canister is sometimes – and wrongly – referred to as 'grape shot'. The latter was a naval weapon firing nine golf ball sized projectiles designed to foul rigging and break spars. It was rarely used on land.[10]

To prevent the bandits obtaining food Wellesley ordered the burning of crops in areas sympathetic to his enemies, and ensured that grain merchants and professional carriers did not supply them from the coast. He instructed his subordinates to let it be known to the merchant community that supplying the enemy would be considered a serious offence: 'I am in the habit of hanging those whom I find living under the protection of the Company and dealing treacherously towards [the Company's] interests. I spare neither rank nor riches!'[11] Wellesley was much given, then and later, to threatening the ultimate sanction, although he rarely put it into effect.

It was generally accepted that armies in India did not move during the monsoon: the weather and the rains hugely increased the difficulties in supply and transport. Like Slim a hundred and fifty years later, Wellesley decided to ignore this: by strict orders regarding hygiene and close attention to the commissariat, he succeeded. Supply columns of bullocks moved (relatively) swiftly along the now cleared roads, escorted by troops and supported by guns. Wellesley said that if he had bullocks he had rice, and if he had rice he had men. He ensured that he had plenty of bullocks.

The most dangerous opponent of the Company in Mysore was now a chieftain of Pathan origin known to the British as Dhoondhia Waugh. He came from humble origins (but so had Hyder Ali) and styled himself 'King of the Two Worlds'. Dhoondhia Waugh operated in the scrubby, almost desert, country where Mysore, Hyderabad and the Mahratta countries met. By the early summer of 1800 had up to 50,000 men, mostly mounted, under his command. In June 1800 Wellesley was ready to move against Dhoondhia. Dividing his forces into four he began to reduce Dhoondhia's outposts and small forts, while flushing him ever northwards and away from his sources of reinforcement and supply. In this the British found the Mahrattas cooperative – Dhoondhia was as much a threat to them as he was to the Company.

In June Wellesley took the field himself, with two King's battalions (but not his own 33rd), five battalions of Madras sepoys, and two King's and three Company regiments of cavalry. On 26 July Dhoondhia's main fortified base, at Dummul, was offered terms of surrender. When these were refused, the forty foot high granite walls were stormed. Within an hour the fort was in Wellesley's hands and the thousand men of the garrison dead or prisoners. Dhoondhia himself was not among them, but he had now no base from which to operate. It could only be a matter of time before the Company caught up with him: it was just a question of mopping up. Dhoondhia's army split into two in order to forage. On 30 July a portion of Wellesley's force, having been warned by the Brahmin intelligence service, marched twenty-six miles in nine hours, caught one half of Dhoondhia's army in camp and destroyed it. Wellesley's four miniature armies were closing in, although Dhoondhia managed to evade them for over a month. On 10 September fate caught up with him. On that day, near the town of Conaghull, Dhoondhia was retreating from the force commanded by Colonel Stevenson (incidentally senior to Wellesley) when he ran into Wellesley himself. Dhoondhia had 5000 men with him, Wellesley but two regiments of British dragoons and two regiments of Madras cavalry, perhaps 1600 men in all; but without hesitation Wellesley formed his entire body into a single line and, putting himself at the head on his charger Diomed and with sword drawn, charged Dhoondhia. Wellesley had no reserve and it was not a manoeuvre that he would have attempted against the French, but he knew his enemy. Dhoondhia was killed trying to rally his troops, his men were scattered or put to the sword. It was the end of any serious opposition to the British in Mysore and brought a further huge tranche of territory under direct Company rule.

In just two and a half months Arthur Wellesley had reorganised the supply system of his army, created roads that it could move along, and manoeuvred a doughty enemy who was operating in his own country into battles which could only have one result. As was now his nature, Wellesley thought about the lessons learned in the pacification of Mysore. He used those lessons later on, in the mountains and undeveloped areas of the Iberian Peninsula where he appreciated the value and vital importance of the Spanish guerrillas whom he used there to good effect.

On the financial side things were looking up. In accordance with the rules and customs of the time, a successful capture of an enemy city and the seques-tration of its treasury led to a disbursement of part of the booty to those who had taken part. The total prize money for the taking of Seringapatam, which came to nearly one million pounds, was distributed according to rank. General Harris got £150,000, a British private soldier £7 and a sepoy £5. Wellesley's share came to £4000, which allowed him to make a considerable reduction in his indebtedness.

Mornington had now returned to Calcutta, where the complete success of his plans for Hyderabad and Mysore reinforced his belief in an expansionist policy. While the members of the British Cabinet were not as enthusiastic as the Governor-General – they only conferred an Irish marquessate instead of the English one upon which Mornington had set his hopes – the time was now ripe to consider the next step. In the meantime he could now do some-thing for his brother, whose abilities as a soldier were now confirmed in Marquess Wellesley's mind, if not in the minds of all those officers with more seniority.

The Governor-General decided to mount an expedition against the French: whether to Mauritius or to the French-controlled Dutch colony of Batavia was not yet decided. At the end of 1800 Arthur Wellesley was ordered to hand over his post in Mysore and to proceed to Ceylon, where he would take sole command of a force of 5000 British and Company troops supported by ships of the Royal Navy. Now was his great opportunity. Such an expedi-tion would surely result in rich pickings, perhaps enough to cover his remaining debts and leave some to spare, while success in a sole command would confirm his rising reputation as a soldier. He quickly put together a headquarters staff from volunteers among the garrison of Mysore and left for Ceylon in December 1800. As it was intended that he should eventually return to his Mysore command, his political duties were delegated to Lieutenant

Colonel Barry Close. Close, as a Company officer, could not hold the military command, however, so this was assumed by Colonel Stevenson, a King's officer.

The purpose of the expedition had not been properly thought out, and orders soon arrived direct from London, received in both Calcutta and Ceylon, for the expedition to forget about Mauritius and Batavia and to proceed instead to Egypt, via the Red Sea, as part of a pincer movement against the French army in Egypt. The original purpose of the expedition would not have been easily achieved in any case: the admiral commanding the ships considered that the Royal Navy was not subject to orders from India, and would accept orders only from the King. The new orders, sent overland, were dated October 1800 but arrived in Calcutta in February 1801. Wellesley, seemingly upon his own authority, decided to embark his force and head for Bombay, as the first step on the journey to Egypt. In India news of the new destination for the Ceylon force was seized upon by the irascible General Baird. He argued that, as the force was now to be engaged in much more than just a simple raid on a not particularly well-defended island, command should be in the hands of a general rather than in those of a mere colonel. The Commander-in-Chief in Bengal, the senior British military officer in India, agreed and the Governor-General decided to appoint Baird as commander of the expeditionary force with Wellesley as his deputy. It was a perfectly reasonable decision. Given that the Governor-General was being presented with military advice by his constitutionally appointed senior military adviser, he had little option but to concur. Wellesley, who heard the news while on the high seas, did not see the appointment in that light. He saw his great opportunity being snatched from his grasp, flew into a tantrum and, on arrival in Bombay, took to his bed with a recurrence of that, possibly psychosomatic, illness which had regularly afflicted him in his early days when he did not get his own way. Whatever it was that laid him low was exacerbated by his contracting 'Malabar Itch', one of the many skin complaints inherent in service in a tropical climate.

Meanwhile Baird had arrived in Ceylon, found his army gone, and had to turn about and follow to Bombay. Baird and the troops then duly sailed for Egypt. Wellesley was intended to follow, missed the ship which was to take him (which sank with all hands), then, after a series of angry remonstrations with his brother, demanded of Lord Clive, Governor of Madras, that he should be allowed to return to his regiment, the 33rd. Wisely Clive refused, and in April 1801 Wellesley returned to his old command in Mysore.

4

Sepoy General

Richard, Marquess Wellesley, recovering his spirits after the disappointment of finding that the British government had not viewed the successes in Mysore in quite the same rosy hue as he had, now began to consider his next move, designed to bring the Mahrattas under control.[1] In this he was helped by Pitt and the British government, who directed the Governor-General to expel the remaining French from India. As most of the remaining French were in the employ of the Mahrattas, this instruction was seen by the marquess as giving him a free hand to take such action in the Mahratta domains as he saw fit.

On 29 April 1802 Colonel the Honourable Arthur Wellesley was gazetted a major general in the British army, although the news did not reach him until September.[2] As has been explained, general officers only received the pay of that rank if they were actually employed as such. As far back as November 1800 the Duke of York, now Commander-in-Chief of the British army, had promised that once Wellesley became a major general he would be given a permanent appointment as such. That appointment was in fact not made, but General Sir James Stuart, Commander-in-Chief Madras in place of Harris (who, like his predecessor, knew Wellesley well), created a vacancy for him on the Madras establishment. Arthur Wellesley now was not only a general: he would be paid as one.

As a general officer Wellesley had to relinquish his command of the 33rd Foot, although in practice he had rarely exercised it directly. His last months as commanding officer were not entirely happy, largely due to the propensity of the 33rd, now on garrison duty in Seringapatam, to wile away the idle hours by drinking and brawling. These habits appear also to have extended to the officers, for there was more trouble with the alcoholic and obstreperous Major Shee. Shee was eventually manoeuvred by Wellesley into tendering his resignation, which he then withdrew, but was sent home on sick leave and eventually allowed to sell out.

Arthur Wellesley had commanded the 33rd for nearly ten years. Although he had been employed on other duties for most of that time, he had always maintained a close interest in the regiment and in its welfare and discipline. He had also involved himself in the selection of officers for the regiment.

When it was proposed that two half-caste officers be appointed, he demurred: however competent they might be, the 33rd was not a sepoy regiment.[3] It was generally held, not least by General Harris, that the 33rd was the best King's battalion in India at the time. The selection of Wellesley's successor as commanding officer of the 33rd Foot was in the hands of the colonel of the regiment, Lord Cornwallis, who, with Wellesley's agreement, wanted to appoint John Sherbrooke. Unfortunately Sherbrooke's health, like that of so many of his contemporaries, had broken down in the Indian climate and he had returned to England in 1800. Instead, Major Arthur Gore, brother of Ralph Gore from whom Wellesley had bought his majority, and until now an officer of the 78th Highlanders, was appointed. He was already in India and had served under Sherbrooke in the storming of Seringapatam. Gore was not Wellesley's first choice but was given his full support.

While Wellesley was still putting his energies into the good governance of Mysore, not all his time was devoted to weighty matters of economics and administration. In June 1802 he took care to meet a request from Major Kirkpatrick, the British Resident in Hyderabad, who had asked that the bark from a certain tree be found and sent to him, as the Nizam considered it to be a remedy for 'palsy' (possibly malaria). Assuring Kirkpatrick that the tree would be searched for, Wellesley wryly added that he feared the only benefit the Nizam would obtain from it would be the hope of a cure.[4] That Wellesley had absorbed the diplomatic niceties of India is shown in his letters to the Nizam, where he addresses him as 'the Presence, the treasury of bounty, of the unsullied Nabob of extended titles, whose turrets are the heavens and whose origins are celestial, be his dignified shade extended'.[5] Whatever Wellesley may have thought of his local allies in the privacy of his own quarters, he knew how to treat them formally.

The Governor-General and his brother, now reconciled after their differences over the command of the Egypt expedition, continued to ponder the Mahratta question. The Mahratta confederacy was in practice a loose grouping of five great Mahratta families, those of Dowlat Rao Sindhia, Jaswant Rao Holkar, the Gaikwar of Baroda and the Rajah of Berar, with the head of the fifth, Baje Rao the Peshwa of Poona, being the nominal overlord.[6] What the Governor-General had failed to realise was that these great chiefs bore a closer resemblance to medieval robber barons or Chinese warlords than they did to conventional heads of states. As the Peshwa was in fact the weakest of the five, both militarily and in treasure, much of the infighting that had so far diverted the Mahrattas' attentions from the British was motivated by a struggle to control the Peshwa. The current holder of that office was a young man of twenty-five, plausible, outwardly pleasant but described as a born intriguer whose motto was said to be 'deceive everybody and trust nobody'. In October 1802 the Sindhia family controlled the Peshwa, but it was then defeated by the Holkar army near Poona. In revenge the Peshwa had Holkar's brother executed by being stamped on by an elephant, while he watched in glee. Opposed now by both Sindhia and Holkar, the Peshwa fled to Bassein, near Bombay, and appealed to the British for help. Marquess Wellesley saw his chance: if the Peshwa could be brought under British control, the other Mahratta leaders would follow their paramount chief. Although he did not know it at the time, the Governor-General was wrong; he had failed to appreciate that loyalty to the Peshwa was only superficial. Any agreement struck with him would not be willingly accepted by the other Mahrattas but would have to be imposed upon them by force of arms.

The treaty of Bassein was signed in December 1802. The British would restore the Peshwa to his throne and guarantee his continuing rule. In return, all French soldiers and traders would be expelled from the Mahratta country (not just from that portion ruled by the Peshwa); the Company would have the right to station troops in the Peshwa's dominion (whose running costs he would pay); and the Governor-General would control the Peshwa's relations with other states. It was what had become to be termed a 'subsidiary alliance', similar to that which the Company already had with Hyderabad and Oudh. It was totally unacceptable to the other Mahratta families, who, not unreasonably, saw it as unwarranted interference in their affairs.[7]

The immediate problem was how to put the Peshwa back on his throne in Poona. He was to be escorted deep into Mahratta territory, 500 miles from Mysore, and his rights restored. All this was to be done without, as yet, provoking war with the Mahrattas. It was an almost impossible task, and, although he did not yet know it, it was to be given to Wellesley. How he prepared for this task, and how he restored the Peshwa and fought the inevitable war which the restoration precipitated, was to revolutionise British campaigning in the east, and was to give Wellesley experience upon which he would draw in his subsequent career.

Various elements of the Madras, Bombay and Bengal armies began to prepare for the coming expedition. Wellesley built upon his experience gained in the organisation of the army for the Mysore campaign. He realised that the major difficulty facing an army with a European component in an underdeveloped country was that it moved far too slowly to bring an enemy living off the country to battle. It was partly the necessity to carry rations and stores for the European troops that slowed progress – rations for native troops could be obtained along the way – and partly the problems in moving over country covered in jungle or arid scrub and crossed by rivers which were impassable in the monsoon. Along with these difficulties were the injurious effects of the Indian climate and the easy availability of strong drink, both

imported and local. Wellesley had himself been no stranger to alcoholic rois-
tering, but he now became more temperate in his habits, encouraging moder-
ation in his officers and enforcing it on his men. He did not attempt to
impose complete abstinence on a soldiery, whose only escape from the
rigours of campaigning was in drink, but he ensured that the daily ration of
arrack, a locally distilled spirit, was provided by reputable contractors and
had not been adulterated with ingredients which could cause blindness or
even kill.[8] He insisted on barracks, when available, being airy, spacious and
kept clean, and in an age where medical science had not yet appreciated the
link between bad water and cholera and other diseases of the East, Wellesley
seems to have realised that a supply of clean drinking water promotes health.

There would inevitably be a vast amount of baggage accompanying the
army, but this could be reduced and made more efficient. Wellesley had
already begun to breed a heavier type of bullock from Tippoo's stud farms of
fine white animals. Twelve of these could pull a six pounder field gun faster
than the infantry could march. While he intended to obtain, and pay for, as
much animal fodder as he could while on the march, there would still be a
need for resupply of rations for the soldiers and forage for the cavalry horses,
which would be done by protected convoys from Madras. Each supply
column would consist of six to eight thousand bullocks, each carrying 120 lbs
of pre-loaded stores, which, while not as fast as the bullock-drawn guns,
could still cover eight miles a day. Gangs of labourers were hired to clear the
jungle on either side of the roads, and the convoys were escorted with
infantry supported by small detachments of cavalry and guns. As they were
far too formidable to be targets for Mahratta raiders, they would always get
through. In support of these military convoys Wellesley used his well-tried
system of local carriers. He also revived his intelligence and communication
network.

Wellesley had already noted, as far back as his days in the Flanders
campaign, the propensity for officers to encumber the army with far too
much personal baggage. Henceforth officers' baggage wagons would be
banned, with the exception of one cart for the headquarters paperwork, and
officers' personal kit would be carried only on pack animals, which could
move off the road. Even with economies and innovations, which included
improvements in the fashioning of cart wheels, there would still be a very
large number of non-combatant followers (each cavalry horse had a groom
and a grass cutter, who walked). These men and women were strictly
enjoined to stay in their allotted place in the order of march and forbidden to
straggle. While these measures appear to us today as mere common sense,
they were highly innovative at the time. While Harris's army in the invasion
of Mysore had moved at a stately five miles or so a day, Wellesley could move

at twenty miles a day, which he would have to do in a war with the lightly equipped and mostly mounted Mahrattas. All this cost money. Despite the profits from the Mysore operation, there was little money to be had in the Company's treasury and London was complaining about the expense of further military expansion. Mornington solved the problem by appropriating bullion from the Company's China Fleet and making it available to the army. This was to infuriate the directors of the Company, but they were far away in London and it would be months before they knew.

Three armies were available for the restoration of the Peshwa, although only one – Wellesley's – was actually used. Wellesley himself had 15,000 men, King's and Company cavalry and infantry, and a good quantity of guns, mainly six pounders, although he decided against large field pieces (as opposed to siege artillery, which he did take), on the grounds that one howitzer or twelve pounder gun would require as many bullocks as an entire six-gun battery of six pounders.[9] With Wellesley was Colonel Stevenson, with 9000 men plus a somewhat mixed bag of 15,000 men, mostly cavalry, from Hyderabad.

In late 1802 General Baird returned from Egypt, where he had done well. He was senior to Wellesley, although they both now held the same rank, and he was on the permanent Madras establishment whereas Wellesley's position was only temporary. Baird insisted upon being sent to where the armies were concentrating and duly took overall command. Uncharacteristically, Wellesley seems to have accepted Baird's arrival without protest.

The decision as to which army, or armies, to use to restore the Peshwa was that of the Commander-in-Chief in Madras, Stuart, and he chose Wellesley. Since his return from Ceylon in April 1801 Wellesley had been commanding in Mysore for more than eighteen months. There he had shown himself to be a master of logistics. He had also established good relations with the minor chiefs through whose territories he must pass. Wellesley would command the entire expedition and Stevenson and the Hyderabad contingent would support him. Stevenson and the Hyderabad troops would move separately. Stevenson would be logistically independent and the Hyderabad force would be supplied from home under their own arrangements.

Considering himself ill-used by his own Commander-in-Chief, by the Governor-General and by the Company generally, Baird refused a pension offered for his services in the storming of Seringapatam, and set off for England in a huff. His ship was captured by a French privateer and he was imprisoned, although later exchanged. Despite his view that Wellesley had been unfairly favoured over him, Baird's career was not yet at an end, as he reappeared as second-in-command to Moore in the Peninsula. Many years later he was reconciled to the then Duke of Wellington. Wellesley, writing to his friend Croker nearly thirty years later, summed it up:

Baird was a gallant, hard-headed lion-hearted officer, but he had no talent, no tact; had strong prejudices against the natives; and he was peculiarly disqualified from his manners, habits etc, and it was supposed his temper, for the management of them.[10]

The march to restore the Peshwa began on 9 March 1803. Wellesley, with John Malcolm (now a major) as his political adviser, had, after some reorganisation to increase the striking power of Stevenson's force, one King's regiment of cavalry (the 19th Dragoons) and three regiments of Company native cavalry, one King's infantry battalion and six battalions of Madras native infantry. His field artillery consisted of sixteen six pounders, and the horse artillery had twelve six pounders of which four would be in direct support of the infantry. The siege train had six twelve pounders. In addition there was a Mysore contingent of 2500 Silladar light cavalrymen, to act as scouts and reconnaissance troops.[11] Wellesley's only regret was that he could not have the 33rd Foot as part of his force, but they were with General Stuart, back in Mysore as a reserve and as a warning to Mahratta chieftains not to interfere.

By fast marches, avoiding Mahratta forts and paying for everything that his troops required along the way, Wellesley managed to avoid trouble. He issued strict orders against looting, threatening dire consequences to any who disobeyed. His Mysore army paid far more attention to this than would his Peninsular army later – but then the Mysore army was paid up to date and plentifully supplied with all their wants. The inhabitants of the lands through which Wellesley's army passed were amazed: no army in history, friendly or hostile, had ever passed them without plundering. A final cavalry dash of sixty miles saw the British in Poona on 20 April, with the army of Sindhia taken so by surprise that his men evacuated the city. The Peshwa was formally restored to his throne on 13 May.

The question now was the reaction of the other Mahratta rulers. The Peshwa hoped to embroil the British in fighting all his enemies for him, while Richard, Marquess Wellesley, in Calcutta, hoped for a period of diplomatic negotiation and the conclusion of treaties, or subsidiary alliances, with the other Mahratta states. The Governor-General realised that, as it took over a month for a message from Calcutta to reach Poona and for an answer to come back, his brother must be given some leeway. The Governor-General instructed that Arthur Wellesley was to have sole discretion and that he should rely entirely upon his own initiative in dealing with the other Mahrattas. Richard rightly realised that only the man on the spot, in touch with the daily shifts and nuances of Mahratta politics, could act promptly in pursuance of British, Company and the Marquess's own policies. Trusting the man on the spot totally, on 26 June 1803 he delegated all powers of decision-making to

Wellesley. In addition, the Governor-General gave the same discretion to General Lake, commanding a Bengal army away to the north in Hindustan. He had already refused to return Pondicherry to the French, as stipulated in the Peace of Amiens. This was the right decision, as the peace was short lived. Wellesley now had the power to make war or peace.

Barry Close, now British Resident at the court of Sindhia, suggested the possibility of a subsidiary alliance to Sindhia. The proposal was rejected, and Sindhia threatened to combine all the Mahratta chiefs in a war against the British. When he was asked to declare his objections to the Bassein treaty, Sindhia gave no answer, but instead began to manoeuvre his cavalry for what looked like a raid into Hyderabad. When Sindhia would neither withdraw his cavalry nor agree to talk, Wellesley, on his own authority, declared war on 6 August 1803.

The Mahratta field army of Sindhia was largely cavalry and could live off the country. Wellesley's problem was to bring them to battle where his superior firepower and discipline could tell. Between the British and Sindhia lay the Godavari river, and it was now the monsoon. In order to ensure that Sindhia could not use the Godavari as an obstacle to hinder movement, Wellesley established a series of crossing points, with bridges of boats strongly guarded along its length. Then he could cross the river, with only 7500 regular troops, 2000 of them British or Company Europeans and 6000 light cavalry from Mysore and the Peshwa. In his pursuit of Sindhia Wellesley crossed and recrossed the Godavari many times. Ahmednuggar was taken by a mixture of storm and bluff between 8 and 12 August and Baroach on the 29th. Even Wellesley's new model army could not move as fast as Sindhia's horses, however, so his plan was to use both his own and Stevenson's force to manoeuvre the main Mahratta army into a position where it could not avoid having to stand and fight.

Sindhia could still not make a clean break, and so he at last abandoned his plans for a raid into Hyderabad and called south his trump card: his elite infantry. Altogether Sindhia was able to summon seventeen of these battalions. They were elite because no expense had been spared in their training, equipment and uniforms. They were as well armed as were the British and Company troops and they were commanded by European officers. These officers were somewhat of a rag-bag. There were Dutchmen, Germans, Englishmen, half-castes and the inevitable French. Most were mercenaries pure and simple, but they were by no means incompetent and were well supported by their own artillery. The largest brigade, or compoo, with eight battalions and five guns, was that commanded by Colonel Pohlmann, an ex-sergeant in the Hanoverian army and thus technically taking up arms against his King. George III was, of course, King of Hanover, even if that country had been occupied by the French. The Governor-General had offered pensions and a guarantee of no loss of income to subjects of the crown who forsook the Mahratta armies, and proceedings for treason to those who did not. Despite this, there were still British subjects in Sindhia's armies. A further brigade, of five battalions and twenty-five guns, belonged to the Begum Rheinhart, the Indian widow of a former German soldier, although field command was actually exercised on her behalf by the French Colonel Saleur. The third brigade had four battalions and fifteen or so guns and was commanded by Baptiste Filoze, of mixed Italian and Indian parentage. All brigades had some integral cavalry and pioneers, and the whole force totalled around 20,000 regular troops.

Wellesley and Stevenson advanced separately on either side of a range of hills towards Borkardan, where they believed the main enemy army to be, and which they intended to attack on 24 September. On 23 September 1803 Wellesley's force moved out at first light. As was now the standard deployment, the irregular cavalry scouted ahead, Wellesley followed at the head of the regular King's and Company cavalry and the infantry brought up the rear, the by now reduced number of followers in the centre. By eleven o'clock in the morning they had marched fourteen miles and had halted at the village of Naulniah, about ten miles south of Borkardan, where they intended to spend the night preparatory to joining Stevenson the following day and attacking the main Mahratta force. At this point a cavalry patrol of the 19th Dragoons discovered, from questioning local merchants, that Sindhia's main army, complete with elite infantry, was much closer than had been thought. It was in fact camped in a fork of the rivers Juah and Kaitna by the town of Assaye and well east of Borkardan. Wellesley himself galloped off with only a few men as escort to where he could see the enemy camp. The Mahrattas were spread out over about six miles between Borkardan and Assaye, and their total was estimated as something between forty and fifty thousand, the regular battalions being augmented by Sindhia's own infantry and a swarm of cavalry. They seemed to be in the process of breaking camp, having probably become aware of the British approach. Here was a chance to smash Sindhia once and for all.

Some of Wellesley's staff warned him that the Mahrattas' regular infantry would fight well, pointing out that the British were grossly outnumbered. Wellesley, however, considered that the presence of the elite infantry was an opportunity, because its presence meant that the Mahrattas could no longer strike and disappear, but were reduced to the speed of a conventional army. The huge disparity in numbers was not as bad as it seemed, for only the elite infantry could be expected to stand and fight: the remainder could be brushed aside by the disciplined formations of the Company. A more

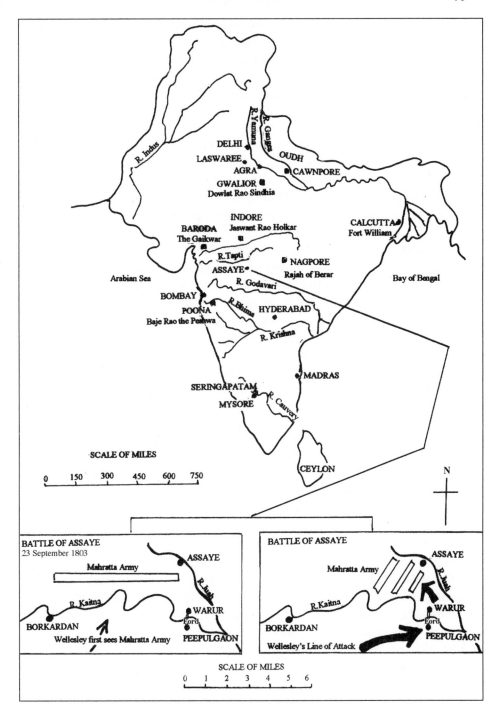

5. India in 1803 and the Battle of Assaye.

prudent commander might have waited for Stevenson to arrive – he was expected the following day – but even a delay of twenty-four hours might have allowed Sindhia to slip away, forcing the pursuit to continue. Wellesley decided to attack at once. He has been criticised for this decision, accused of wishing to keep all the glory for himself rather than share it with Stevenson, but this is surely naive. Wellesley was anxious to acquire glory – it was the only way to progress – but he was already far too professional a soldier to allow personal aggrandisement to take priority over military necessity. The longer the war went on, the greater was the risk that the British would be forced onto the defensive, as Sindhia attracted more of the Mahratta chieftains to his cause; and the more likely it would be that the British government would seek a compromise, to halt the outflow of money needed to finance the war. Now was the opportunity to finish Sindhia at a stroke. Wellesley galloped straight back to his main body and left a battalion to guard his camp for use as a rallying point should he have to retreat. He sent his cavalry forward to cover the Kaitna river in case the Mahrattas tried to cross and attack him. He then ordered the rest of the army to march forward. Between the British and the Mahrattas was the Kaitna, with the elite infantry drawn up to cover it. To get to grips with the enemy Wellesley would have to get his men across the river, but the only ford seemed to be right in front of the enemy line of battle. To try and cross there would be suicide: his men would have to concentrate into one narrow column and would be slaughtered by the Mahratta guns. Further to the east, downstream, were two villages on opposite sides of the Kaitna: Warur and Peepulgaon. Whether it was Wellesley himself who worked out that two villages on opposite sides must have a means of communication between them, either a bridge or a ford, as most accounts relate and as he himself claimed, or whether he discovered it from locals does not matter. He personally reconnoitred the river bank, found a ford and waved the infantry over.

As the Mahratta elite infantry, hinging on Assaye, changed their front, a difficult movement but well executed, and now turned to face the British line of advance rather than the Kaitna and the western ford, Wellesley ordered an attack. It was a bloody battle: the British regular cavalry were badly mauled in getting too close to Assaye, which was strongly held, and at one stage got out of control after a charge to clear the line of the Juah; the infantry had to form squares to repel Mahratta cavalry charges which were pressed home gallantly. Wellesley himself lost two horses, including his favourite Diomed stabbed by a Mahratta spear. (Diomed recovered, was later rescued from a horse market and returned to his master.) The British and Madras infantry were too good, however, and in the late afternoon the Mahratta infantry broke and ran, abandoning most of their guns – over a hundred – and much of their equipment.[12]

It was a convincing victory, but not without cost. Of the six thousand King's and Company Europeans engaged 1600 were dead or wounded. The 74th Highlanders alone had 60 per cent casualties and the Madras infantry too suffered severely. Altogether, in a battle lasting a few hours, Wellesley's casualties were about 27 per cent. With the exception of Waterloo (28 per cent), this was the highest casualty rate in any battle commanded by Wellington throughout his career. Wellesley is sometimes criticised as only being able to fight a defensive battle, and it is true that, for very good reasons which will be examined later, many of his Peninsular battles were defensive, but Assaye surely gives the lie to any suggestion that he was always cautious or lacked the speed of reaction to fight an encounter battle. Immediately upon realising that the Mahratta army were as close as they were, he had galloped straight to where he could see for himself, then in minutes had decided that the best option was to attack at once, had made his plan, issued his orders and had got the army under way. If he had not reacted as he had and instead had waited for Stevenson, for which no one would have blamed him, he would have lost the window of opportunity and the pursuit might have gone on for months. The result was worth the butcher's bill. In his old age Wellington would be asked what was the best he ever did in the way of fighting. 'Assaye', he would reply, and even years later the thought of that battle would give him pause.

The army was exhausted. They had been marching since dawn, had crossed a river and fought a battle. No pursuit was possible and the men slept where they were, Wellesley on a pile of straw in a farmer's hut. The war was not yet over but, like in Mysore, it was mostly a question of mopping up, although there was another three months of fighting to come. On the 24th Stevenson's army was directed to follow up the Mahrattas while Wellesley's men saw to their wounded: many had been left on the field and were not recovered until well into that day. There were insufficient surgeons to deal with the unexpectedly high number of casualties, and it was three days before Wellesley could organise makeshift field hospitals, collect the wounded, bury or burn the dead and prepare his army for further action. The British and Company dead were buried in neat rows of graves while the Mahratta bodies were counted and tipped into one mass grave dug by the Madras infantry and followers. Those Mahratta guns which could fire British calibre ammunition were added to the artillery. Those which could not were sent back to Poona, where their brass would fetch a good price.

Stevenson's pursuit began. All along the trail of the beaten army were the signs of panic and disorder. Abandoned carts, guns, equipment and wounded Mahrattas littered the route, and the villagers complained of wanton destruction of their property and looting of their belongings. Wellesley's immediate problems were the replacement of his casualties and what to do with his wounded. He summoned a Madras battalion from Poona, where it would no longer be needed, and began to look for a site to establish a hospital. He could not leave his wounded in Assaye, as he could not spare men to guard them. The town was not strong enough to withstand an attack should some of Sindhia's men double back, or should another Mahratta chieftain join the war. Initially Wellesley wanted to locate the hospital in Dowlutabad, a strongly fortified town belonging to the Nizam of Hyderabad and about fifty miles from Assaye, but the fort commander distrusted the British, did not wish them to examine his fortifications at close range and refused to let Wellesley's men anywhere near the place. To attack and take Dowlutabad would have been counter-productive and so Wellesley fixed upon Ajanta, also belonging to the Nizam. While not as strong as Dowlutabad, it was suffi- ciently well fortified to be able to resist any attack by the Mahrattas until help could arrive.

Once the wounded were all transferred into Ajanta, by the first week in October, Wellesley was able to move north, moving separately from, but supported by, Stevenson. By 24 October Stevenson had taken Berhampore by storm and persuaded Assergurh to surrender. The laws and usages of war at the time, in so far as the laws of war were applicable to India, allowed a city or fortress to be invited to surrender once the besiegers had made a breach in the walls. Should surrender not be forthcoming and the attackers had to storm the walls, with inevitable heavy loss, the city could be given up to plunder and sack. As the Company was running short of ready money to meet Wellesley's insistence on paying for all forage and to pay the carriers, followers and intel- ligence operatives a decent wage, Stevenson gave the inhabitants of Berhampore a choice: pay up or be plundered. Wisely they agreed to impose a levy on all occupants. The inhabitants were spared three days of uncontrolled licence by the soldiers, while the Company treasury gained hard cash.

Sindhia's army had been soundly beaten at Assaye and most of his elite infantry disbanded. Many, although not all, of the European officers trans- ferred their allegiance to other masters (Pohlmann eventually taking service with the Company), but an army of sorts was still in being and now allied itself with the Rajah of Berar. These two armies, of Sindhia and Berar, had to be kept on the move, harried and driven, and denied a fortified base. Stevenson's army was given the task of capturing and reducing Mahratta fortresses, while Wellesley's troops were the mobile strike force. The Mahrattas would move against Poona; Wellesley would move to head them off. The Mahrattas would threaten Hyderabad; Wellesley would intercept them. Often he would cover twenty miles a day, infantry, cavalry, siege train and all, constantly replenished by relays of Indian carriers which he had

1. Arthur Wellesley, first Duke of Wellington (1769–1852),
by Thomas Heaphy, 1813.
(*National Portrait Gallery*)

3. Vignette of Arthur Wesley as a boy, by an unknown artist.

2. Merrion Street, Dublin, the house where Wellington was born.
(*Gale Scanlon*)

4. Wellington as a young officer, by an unknown artist, 1804.
(*National Portrait Gallery*)

5. Kitty Pakenham, Wellington's wife, by Sir Thomas Lawrence, 1814.

6. Richard Colley Wellesley, Marquess Wellesley (1760-1842), by J. Pain Davis, 1815. As Governor General of British India from 1798 to 1805, he laid the foundations of the British Raj.
(*National Portrait Gallery*)

7. A stylised depiction of the storm of Seringapatam, 17 May 1799. (*National Army Museum*)

8 The battle of Assaye, 23 September 1803, the victory of which Wellington was most proud.

9. The north gate of Gawilghur. (*National Army Museum*)

10. The storm of Gawilghur, 15 December 1803, which brought the war with the Mahrattas to an end.

11 Robert Stewart, Viscount Castlereagh (1769-1822), by Sir Thomas Lawrence, *c.* 1800-4.
(*National Portrait Gallery*)

12. William Pitt the Younger (1759-1806), after John Hoppner, 1805.
(*National Portrait Gallery*)

13. Sir John Moore (1761-1809), whose death at Coruña opened the way for Wellington's command in the Peninsula, by Sir Thomas Lawrence.
(*National Portrait Gallery*)

organised. Meanwhile, in the north, General Lake, like Wellesley operating with unfettered discretion, had moved out of Cawnpore, marched up the River Ganges and had taken Agra and Delhi, Moghul cities occupied by the Mahrattas. On 31 October he had soundly beaten an army led by Sindhia in person at Laswaree. The noose was tightening.

Sindhia was now having second thoughts and opened negotiations with the British. On 22 November a cessation of hostilities, effectively an armistice, was agreed to give Sindhia time to consider the Governor-General's terms. One of the conditions of the armistice was that the Mahratta armies were to withdraw to an area where they could not threaten any British protected state. Until they did this both Wellesleys were determined to continue the war. Eventually, after much marching and counter marching, on 29 November 1803 the Mahratta armies of Sindhia and the Rajah of Berar were reported to have halted at Argaum. On receipt of the news Arthur Wellesley and Stevenson were twenty miles apart. Both armies moved at first light, covering twenty miles each until they had met and were within sight of the Mahrattas. Once again Wellesley had to make a decision: whether to attack now with his tired army, or wait until the men had rested – in which case the Mahrattas might slip away. Again he demonstrated the flexibility and willingness to attack that some later critics have denied him, ordering an immediate assault. Moving his horse artillery guns to a flank where they could give fire support, he directed his infantry along a line of approach through fields of millet, which grew taller than a man and gave his men some cover from view. He then launched his cavalry against the Mahratta left wing. Sindhia's army left the field, but Berar's stood its ground. The British infantry came under heavy fire from the Mahratta guns and two Madras battalions broke. Wellesley rallied them personally and sent them into a village where they were under cover from fire and could regroup. The Mahratta right disintegrated: their light cavalry was no match for the disciplined charges in tight formation of King's and Madras troopers with tempered steel sabres. In the centre Wellesley's infantry, supported by bullock-drawn guns moving with them, approached to within a few hundred yards of the Mahratta line. The bullocks wheeled about, a devastating bombardment of solid round shot and canister decimated the enemy front rank, and volley fire and a charge with the bayonet by the infantry did the rest. The Mahratta army dissolved into panic flight, pursued by the British cavalry for two days. While British and Company casualties were a handful, those of the Mahrattas numbered thousands. By personal reconnaissance, swift and positive action and skilful handling of combined infantry, cavalry and artillery groupings, Wellesley had now decisively beaten the last Mahratta field army of any consequence.[13]

Wellesley's and Stevenson's armies marched again, taking their few wounded with them this time, and on 3 December Wellesley made camp fifteen miles south of Gawilghur. Gawilghur was the hot weather capital of the Rajah of Berar and was said to contain most of his treasury. It was double walled, well provided with guns and had a commanding field of fire over the surrounding countryside. Inside were around 6000 troops, led by a Sikh mercenary, and the fort was well provisioned with food, water and ammunition. From the south, as Wellesley initially inspected it, the fortress looked a difficult objective, but intelligence from the Brahmin messengers and from the Nizam of Hyderabad's agents suggested that an attack from the north was feasible. Here the walls were not so high and there was a covered approach up to about 200 yards from the walls. To get to the north side of Gawilghur meant a difficult flanking march through hilly jungle, but, by using double teams of bullocks and elephants, with Madras pioneers to widen the existing path, the artillery was moved to within 300 yards of the northern wall. On the morning of 12 December two eighteen pounder and three twelve pounder siege guns began to batter the walls. The old masonry began to crumble and soon stones were tumbling down with every shot. A further breach was attempted in the south, but difficulty in moving the guns over rocky terrain and up small cliffs made progress much slower. Despite the size of the defending garrison, morale in the Mahratta armies was low, many of the soldiers inside the fort having already been beaten by the British. There had been little attempt to prevent Wellesley's army from moving round from the south, and little action to prevent the breaches being enlarged. By the evening of 14 December Wellesley's few engineers pronounced the breaches practicable. Wellesley decided upon an assault the following morning, a cannon loaded with canister being fired at each breach every twenty minutes throughout the night to prevent the garrison making repairs.

The assault was set for ten o'clock on the morning of 15 December 1803. It would be a two-pronged attack, Stevenson's army going for the northern breach while Wellesley would demonstrate against the south, although with little hope of being able to get in. The defenders would, however, be forced to split to defend both walls and one at least of the storming columns was likely to succeed. Stevenson was by this time ill – he had directed his share of the operations at Argaum from a sick bed on top of an elephant – and two lieutenant colonels of the Company were in charge in the north. A lesser man than Wellesley might have led the northern assault – it was the one which had most chance of success – but he had looked at all the breaches carefully, had given detailed orders to Stevenson's officers and chose to accompany the less glamorous but tactically (because of the lack of cover) more difficult southern attack.

The assault went in. The northern attacking force stormed through the

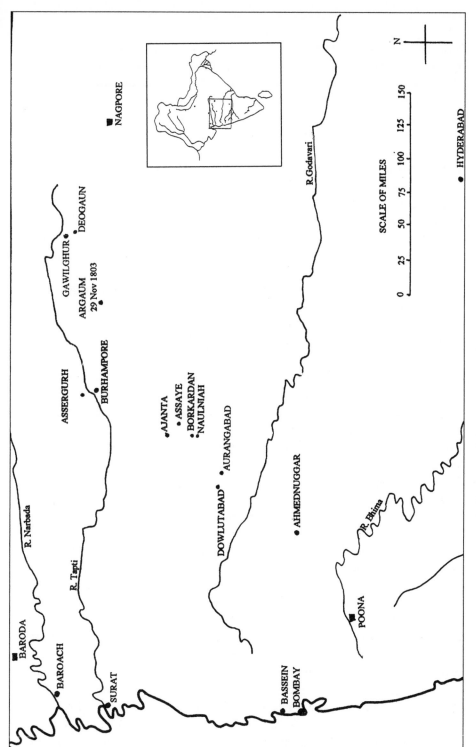

6. India: Area of Operations, May 1803 to December 1803.

breach and fought their way over the second wall and into the inner fort, opening the gate to the column from the south. Although some of the Mahrattas fought bravely, particularly when cornered in the inner fort, they were beaten before they started: they no longer believed in victory. The British and their native soldiers were not invincible, but the Mahrattas thought they were. British casualties were remarkably light: 130 or so. Nobody knows how many defenders died: the Sikh commander was certainly killed and Wellesley thought that most of the garrison had perished. The treasury was never found.[14] The capture of Gawilghur ended the Mahratta War. The very next day the Rajah of Berar's representatives arrived to sue for peace. Sindhia too had had enough. The treaty of Deogaun, negotiated by Wellesley himself with Berar on 17 December and with Sindhia on 30 December, ceded vast territories to the British, gave concessions to the Nizam and bound the Mahratta states in subsidiary alliances.

Arthur Wellesley, as the man on the spot, was intimately involved in the terms of the treaty. Once again a difference in viewpoint is evident between the soldier in the field and his brother, the diplomat, in Fort William. The Governor-General still thought that the Indian rulers could be negotiated with in the same way as European powers. Arthur Wellesley recognised the reality, which was that the Mahrattas were still only a step away from being a collection of bandits, individuals bound together by a very loose common-ality of interest, without fixed boundaries and without a foreign policy as such. To impose subsidiary alliances upon them, and to disband their armies, would alienate the chiefs and throw up hordes of unemployed soldiers who knew only one trade. Arthur Wellesley would have drawn the borders of the Company, albeit with some enlargement of British territory, and then by a policy of divide and rule would have ensured a balance of power and kept the Mahrattas under control, while leaving them alone within their own lands. It was an outlook which he would later apply in Europe. Marquess Wellesley would have none of this, argued with his brother, and in the end had his way. When John Malcolm pointed out in a note to Calcutta that everything that had been agreed by Wellesley had been 'in the public interest', the Governor-General replied tersely that it was Malcolm's job to obey orders. He, the Governor-General, would look after the public interest.

Arthur Wellesley was perhaps being somewhat naive, and was in danger of being outmanoeuvred by Watel Pant, Sindhia's chief minister. Pant was a wily negotiator. In later years Wellesley would say that Talleyrand, the consummate French politician who had served the Bourbons, the Revolution, Bonaparte and the Bourbons again while still keeping his head, was like Watel Pant 'but not so clever'. Pant managed to exclude Sindhia's major fortress of Gwalior from the treaty. The Governor-General insisted that Gwalior be ceded to the British and would not sign the treaty until it was. As far as he was concerned, the Mahrattas had either to be brought to heel or destroyed. Wellesley was much more concerned with the British reputation for keeping their word, pointing out that while the war might be over and quickly forgotten, the treaties would last for a hundred years. As it transpired, the Governor-General was probably right. While his treaties caused unrest in the Mahratta domains, and while military action to keep the peace continued long after Wellesley's departure, the subjugation of Mysore and the treaties imposed after the Mahratta war finally established Britain as a major power in India. British power was not yet secure, and would not be until after the Indian Mutiny of 1857 (more properly a mutiny by part of the Bengal army), but Richard Wellesley the politician and diplomat and Arthur Wellesley the soldier had between them increased the size of British India fourfold in a mere six years. The beginnings of one of history's greatest, mutually benefi-cial, imperial achievements had been written, and in due time the Mahrattas would become faithful friends and loyal allies of the British. The Mahrattas remained loyal during the Great Mutiny of 1857, and they fought on the Western Front and in the Middle East during the First World War and in Burma, North Africa and Italy in the Second.

Wellesley's job in the Mahratta domains was not quite over. Now in command of all the forces in the Deccan, he still took the field when neces-sary. In February 1804 he made a near incredible forced march of sixty-six miles in thirty hours to defeat and disperse a predatory band of freelance Mahrattas at Munkaiseer.[15] Despite this and other annoyances, the campaign was effectively at an end and Wellesley could reap the benefits. Financially these were considerable – and most welcome. He received his share of the prize money paid to the army for their conquests. He was voted the sum of £1000 by the citizens of Calcutta, as well as being presented with numerous ceremonial swords, plate and laudatory addresses. He could now, at last, repay his debts.

When Jaswant Rao Holkar began to take a belated interest in the war, the Governor-General summoned his brother to Calcutta for discussions. General Lake had the situation well in hand and there was no job for Wellesley, who had now achieved all that he could achieve in India. It was time to look for further opportunities. As he himself said, he had served in India longer than any man ought. He had made his name as a competent and fair administrator, and as a fighting soldier with flair and tactical acumen. This was recognised by the government at home by the award of a knight-hood of the Bath on 1 September 1804.

Major General Sir Arthur Wellesley was now thirty-five, and had been in India for seven and a half years. Despite his lapses into 'fever' when things did not go his way, his health had held out remarkably well, no doubt due in part to his observation of proper hygiene and sensible drinking, and his continued physical exertions (in the Gawilghur campaign he rode at least thirty-five miles every day, on bad roads, between his own and Stevenson's armies). He had arrived in India with very little military experience. Despite being on the books of various regiments as a captain, he had never commanded a company. He had spent a brief period as a major with the 33rd Foot, but commanded nothing, being immersed in administration. On purchasing the lieutenant colonelcy of the 33rd he had hardly exercised that command at all, being otherwise employed in Flanders. While it is true that he had commanded a Flanders brigade – and very well too, in the opinion of senior officers present – the tasks given to that brigade allowed for little exercise of initiative by its commander. Wellesley always had men like John Sherbrooke, who had come up the hard way, to back him up. On arrival in India he owed everything to the influence of his brother, who gave him his chance over the heads of many others with more seniority and far more experience. Had it not been for his brother he would have remained in command of the 33rd, and had it not been for his brother he would never have come to the attention of General Harris. No doubt Harris's motives for backing Arthur Wellesley lay partly in a wish to curry favour with the Governor-General, but Harris also recognised latent talent when he saw it. Without Richard Wellesley, however, that talent might never have been noticed.

The Tope before Seringapatam was a disaster which would have wrecked the prospects of many another officer, but Arthur Wellesley learned from it and never made the same mistakes again. Perhaps the main lesson that became engraved on his mind was the need to control himself, and here we observe the seeds of what was later seen as a somewhat cold, unapproachable and unemotional personality. Wellesley was far from cold, nor was he devoid of emotion. He was musical, artistic and often sentimental, but he realised in time that to control others you have to control yourself. For the rest of his life, save for rare occasions, he would conceal his innermost feelings from the world.

Wellesley's preparations for the Mysore campaign, and his extrapolation of the lessons from that to the Mahratta war, were masterly. His creation of an intelligence service using indigenous operatives, and his logistic arrangements which ensured that his men were always fed and, as important, paid in hard cash, contributed in very large measure to victory. While some of his King's regiments and many of his Madras sepoys were excellent material, well trained, fully equipped and competently led, it was Wellesley's arrangements and Wellesley's almost uncanny knack of reading his opponents minds that got the army to where they could do the business. Soldiering is not now, and never has been, a cerebral profession, but command in battle requires a cool head, a calm assessment of the situation and the ability to use one's (usually limited) assets to best effect. It also requires a controlled ruthlessness and a willingness to take chances on occasion. Wellesley showed that he had all these qualities: and, in his coordinated handling of cavalry, infantry and guns, allied with an instinctive knowledge of when to attack and when to manoeuvre, we see the first signs of the greatness that was to come. While men like Malcolm, Close and Kirkpatrick were much more knowledgeable than Wellesley in matters Indian, and the friendship that was forged between them undoubtedly contributed to the successful outcome overall, it was Wellesley and Wellesley alone who, without teaching, training or instructional manuals to help him, devised the tactics and organisation which won the war.

In the modern age we have become accustomed to, and take for granted, the total incorruptibility of British civil servants and administrators. At a time when that was by no means so, and when many – civilians and soldiers alike – made huge fortunes by what we would now consider dishonest means, and were thought none the less of for it, Wellesley's unfashionable insistence on scrupulous honesty and paying for all that his army took was to have far-reaching effects on the future of British India. Of course Wellesley made money out of his service in India, but all that he took was in strict accordance with the law. By the standards of the time it was honestly earned. Later, British administrators in what came to be the Indian Empire earned a reputation for incorruptibility. Perhaps that is the most fitting legacy of the Wellesleys in India.

After a hectic round of farewell parties, loyal addresses, the publication in General Orders of the thanks of King and Parliament, and exchanges of correspondence with individuals, regiments (including the 33rd) and the native nobility, Sir Arthur Wellesley took ship for England in March 1805.[16] The journey lasted six months and he was seasick for much of it. His ship stopped off at the island of St Helena, where his greatest opponent, Napoleon Bonaparte, was to die in exile sixteen years later.

As a young and inexperienced officer sailing to India eight years before, Colonel Arthur Wesley had been accompanied by a library which included many worthy tomes, classical and philosophical. One wonders how many he ever read. He must have absorbed something, however, for he did occasionally quote from them, carefully avoiding Latin. On the homeward journey, his reputation made – in the eyes of the Indian establishment at any rate – he could relax. Now his reading material consisted mainly of novels, some utter trash, many of them cheap love stories, then as now considered by many to be fare for shopgirls rather than for major generals and knights of the Bath.

There were, however, more serious matters to consider, and Wellesley found time to compose a detailed paper on a government-proposed scheme to send sepoy battalions of the East India Company's armies to the West Indies, and Negro soldiers of the West Indian corps to India. This was an extraordinary idea. While it is true that troops so transported would not be susceptible to local influences, many Hindus would have objected to such a long sea voyage (it carried ritual pollution) and the standards of the West Indian soldiers of the time would have made them of little use against Mahrattas. Sir Arthur suspected that the scheme was really aimed at running down the strength of British troops in India, which he advised strongly against. While many of the customs and much of the behaviour of British soldiers caused offence to Indians, British troops, once long enough in theatre to become acclimatised, were held in high regard because of their fighting qualities. It would, thought Sir Arthur, be a mistake to think that they could ever be replaced.[17]

Sir Arthur Wellesley arrived in England in September 1805. Pitt asked to see him, as did Castlereagh, now Secretary for War and the Colonies.[18] Much had happened while Wellesley had been away – it had been well over nine years since he had last set foot in England – and in both political and military fields there was much to ponder on.

In 1795 the French National Convention had been dissolved and replaced by a five man Directory after a monarchist rising in Paris had been put down by the young General Bonaparte. The following year, 1796, saw the nature of the war changing. Having started as an attempt to export French revolutionary ideas and to defend French national boundaries, the war turned into one of territorial expansion – France could no longer maintain the huge citizen armies which she had raised by levy, and needed to seize resources beyond her own frontiers. Under Carnot, French armies began to expand into Germany and Italy. Spain joined the war against England, its rival for overseas trade and sea power. After a lightning campaign in Italy Bonaparte, on his own initiative and without instructions from the Directory, negotiated the treaty of Campo Formio which ceded Belgium to France and expelled the Austrians from Italy. The following year an army to invade England was assembled at Dunkirk. Bonaparte knew well that such an enterprise could not work – the Royal Navy would prevent it – but it was useful in the message that it sent to England's allies, for it was English money that kept the coalition in being. The same year the French occupied Rome, a Swiss republic was established as a French client state, and a French landing in Ireland and a rebellion in support of it were defeated. The French began to wrest Egypt, cross-roads of the world, from the Turks. This enterprise was eventually foiled by a

British expedition in 1801, after General Bonaparte had abandoned the *Armée d'Orient* in 1799, an act of betrayal for which he was never held accountable. A second coalition was formed and in 1799 the British once more ventured onto the Continent, when a force of 27,000 men under the Duke of York landed in Holland, now the French-dominated Batavian Republic. Due to poor co-ordination with the Russians in the north and – by now depressingly familiar – logistical breakdown, the force achieved little on land. Before withdrawing, however, it did at least capture the Dutch fleet, thus rendering it useless to France. In November Bonaparte, by a *coup d'état*, established himself as First Consul, effectively dictator of France. By the battle of Marengo and using tactics which would become familiar in the years to come, Bonaparte snatched victory from defeat and the result persuaded the Russians to leave the war. He offered peace to his remaining enemies, but the war went on. By the end of the year 1799 the French had been driven out of Italy by the Austrians, but they had held everywhere else. In 1801 the French recaptured Italy, while they lost Egypt to a combined British and Turkish force, which included Baird's contingent from India.

A brief respite – the Peace of Amiens – from March 1802 until May 1803 achieved little other than allowing British merchants to fulfil a contract to supply the French army with greatcoats, which must have been of good quality, for the French army were still wearing them when they invaded Russia ten years later. The mills of Lancashire might have been better employed providing their own army with greatcoats.

The war resumed with a British blockade of French ports, and a second army to invade England was assembled, at Boulogne this time. It seems unlikely that Bonaparte ever intended to attempt the crossing, but a fleet was assembled in the Rhine ports and landing craft were constructed and concentrated, only to be destroyed by Sir Sidney Smith's fireships in October. The British were not a land power, but their ships continued to block French expansion beyond the coasts of Europe. In Parliament Earl St Vincent pointed out that while he did not say that the French could not come, he did say that they could not come by sea. The year ended with the coronation of Napoleon Bonaparte, now Emperor of the French at the age of thirty-five.

The year of Sir Arthur Wellesley's return to England from India, 1805, saw the formation of the Third Coalition with Austria, Russia and Sweden joining England in the prosecution of the war. With the concentration of the *Grande Armée* on the Channel coast, the only other French army of significance was 50,000 men under Masséna in northern Italy. The Allies saw an opportunity to smash Masséna and then to strike west, deep into France. Napoleon's intelligence was now well developed. He well knew what the Allies would try to do and in August abandoned plans for an invasion of England (if they ever seriously existed) and began to withdraw his army from Boulogne. They slipped away quickly at night. By the time the Allies realised that Napoleon was on the move it was too late. In a brilliant turning manoeuvre, in October he forced the Austrian General Mack von Leiberich to surrender at Ulm. Then, in December, came Bonaparte's crowning glory – the battle of Austerlitz. The Austrians were knocked out of the war and the shattered Russian armies reeled back towards home. On land Napoleon now controlled most of western and southern Germany.

Things, however, had not gone so badly for Britain. The threat of invasion disappeared when, on 21 October 1805, Admiral Viscount Nelson utterly routed the combined French and Spanish fleets at Trafalgar. It was this victory, perhaps more than any other event, which, by giving Britain world domination of the seas, allowed the British to continue to wage war and to use the tiny British army as an intervention force virtually anywhere along the coasts of Europe. If Waterloo would eventually seal British victory and French defeat, it was Trafalgar that made Waterloo possible.

The organisation of the army had changed much since Colonel Wesley had embarked for India. The Duke of York, as we have seen, was no great field commander – although the blame for the reverses of his two Flanders campaigns cannot be laid entirely upon his shoulders. On his return to England he was promoted field marshal on the staff and appointed Commander-in-Chief of the British army. The promotion and appointment were made at the behest of the King, for York was still his favourite son. It did not meet with the unqualified approval of ministers or generals, but it was nevertheless an excellent appointment. Frederick, Duke of York, was a born administrator. He well knew what was wrong with the army – wrongs which had contributed to his own failures as a commander in the field – and he was determined to do something about them. He was fortunate in that he was supported by William Pitt the Younger, who realised that this would be a long war and that, if it was to be won, the British army must be reformed. York set to work with a will, but there was a limit as to how much he could do. As Commander-in-Chief he could affect officer selection and promotion, infantry and cavalry training and deployment, but he could do nothing about the supply services, which remained the preserve of the Master General of the Ordnance. Even in war there was a reluctance to spend, and such reforms as York was able to implement depended on the money being made available by the Treasury and the Secretary at War.

York knew from his experiences in Flanders that one of the brakes on British military achievement was the lack of professionalism amongst the officers. A commission was still regarded by many as a social cachet, rather than an opportunity to lead the King's soldiers competently in battle. York considered the abolition of purchase, but found that the continental systems which he examined were not necessarily better. In any case, if purchase was to be abolished, where was the money to refund officers to come from? Purchase would remain, but now officers would have to spend a laid down minimum period in each rank and be certified as efficient before being allowed to purchase the next step. There would be no more teenage colonels. The right to confer commissions, promotions and appointments was removed from the Secretary at War, a civilian appointee, and given instead to the Military Secretary, a serving officer who reported directly to the Commander-in-Chief. Education was not neglected and in 1802, as a result of pressure from the duke, a military college, the forebear of the Royal Military Academy Sandhurst, was opened at High Wycombe, for the purpose of educating and training potential officers. Tactical training of the troops was not neglected and Dundas's tactical instructions were widely promulgated and enforced. Light infantry, virtually neglected by the British army since the American war, was revived and a new branch of the infantry – the rifle regiment – instituted. All these reforms were to have much influence on the army which Sir Arthur Wellesley would eventually command in Portugal and Spain.[19]

5

Vimeiro to Coruña

Both Pitt and Castlereagh were interested in Sir Arthur Wellesley's views on various proposals for expeditions to the Continent, and Pitt was particularly impressed by the major general's ability to explain his opinions clearly and concisely, whether verbally or in writing. They were also interested in his views on India, particularly when criticism of Marquess Wellesley's methods and policies grew. Despite these favourable opinions, the best that could be offered him in the military sphere was command of a brigade, which he accepted in November 1805. In December Sir Arthur Wellesley and his brigade were ordered to Hanover. After a particularly unpleasant week at sea, tossed about, constantly wet and frequently seasick, the brigade arrived at Bremen, sat there for six weeks, did nothing, and returned in February 1806. Wellesley was now appointed to command a brigade at Hastings, supposedly guarding the coast, including, as he pointed out, the area where William the Conqueror had landed. A French invasion, if it ever came, would be most unlikely to land at Hastings and the command there was boring and frustrating, although Wellesley did manage to keep the troops busy with training and weapon drill.

In April 1806 Wellesley married Kitty Pakenham in Dublin. Having made his name and a reasonable fortune, he was now regarded as a suitable husband for a Longford daughter. His reasons for marrying Kitty seem to have stemmed from an exaggerated sense of duty. Before going to India he had intimated that, despite the rebuff from her family, he would still feel the same about her on his return, provided that she too retained her affection for him. He never wrote to her from India, as far as we know, although he did keep track of her through Olivia Sparrow, a mutual friend. On Wellesley's return Kitty was still unmarried (although she had nearly married Lowry Cole, who was to serve under Wellesley in the Peninsula); indeed she was now of an age when prospects were receding fast, and she had lost the prettiness and bloom for which she had been noted as a young girl. It was not a happy marriage, for although Kitty was devoted to her husband and remained utterly loyal to him until her death, she could not give him the intellectual stimulus that he needed, nor the domestic happiness that he craved. She did provide him with two sons and, although he had many close female friends there is no reliable evidence that he was ever unfaithful to her.[1]

A few days after his wedding, Wellesley resumed his political affairs. It would be unthinkable today that an officer of the army, much less a major general, should be a Member of Parliament – indeed it is forbidden by law - but such was not the case in the early nineteenth century. On 12 April 1806 Wellesley was returned to the House of Commons as Member for the town and port of Rye, conveniently close to his military command, joining his brother William Wellesley-Pole, who was already a Member. [2]

Wellesley had no great wish to become involved in politics, and had made his decision to follow a career in the army. He was nevertheless sorely needed in Westminster, for his brother Richard was now in trouble. As Governor-General of British India Marquess Wellesley had turned the East India Company from a trading organisation into a power in its own right. It was his strategy that had brought Hyderabad and Oudh into the British fold, had conquered Mysore and had humbled the Mahrattas. Despite his very considerable achievements, which had earned him a marquessate and the thanks of Parliament, the members of the Court of Directors of the Company had not forgiven him for using bullion from Canton to finance his wars, and many of them were in any case fundamentally opposed to his forward policy. 1805 was the year of Austerlitz, and Britain's seeming lack of progress in the war brought the government under increasing pressure to halt the flow of money needed to consolidate the British hold on India. Marquess Wellesley was recalled and arrived back in England only shortly after his brother.

The new Governor-General and Commander-in-Chief in India was Marquess Cornwallis. He had already been head of government and army in India, and then Master General of the Ordnance until 1801, while combining that post with Lord Lieutenant and Commander-in-Chief in Ireland from 1798, when he defeated the French General Humbert and the Irish rebels. In 1801 he had been one of the negotiators of the Peace of Amiens, gaining the respect of Napoleon Bonaparte in so doing. He was now sixty-seven years old and had no wish to return to India - but, like Sir Arthur Wellesley, he was a man who put duty first. He went, only to die at Gahzipur, in the province of Benares, in October 1805. Wellesley was appointed colonel of the regiment of the 33rd Foot in place of Cornwallis, an appointment that he retained until 1813. The colonelcy of a regiment was supposed to confer financial benefit on the holder – even an honest holder – but in this case it actually cost him money. This was partly because the battalion's establishment was reduced (thus providing fewer 'blank files' for the colonel), and partly because the 33rd remained in India until 1812, and the colonel had to pay the cost of transporting uniforms and other items by sea to India and then overland to Hyderabad, or wherever the regiment was.[3] Later Wellesley was offered the colonelcy of a regiment with two battalions, financially a much better deal, but he refused it saying that he had no wish to sever his association with the 33rd. It was only in January 1813, when the Prince Regent ordered Wellesley (by then General the Marquess Wellington) to assume the colonelcy of the Royal Horse Guards, household troops, that he reluctantly parted company from the 33rd.

On 22 April 1806 Marquess Wellesley's stewardship of India was raised in Parliament. A Mr Paull, a sometime merchant in the Indian trade and a member of the Court of Directors of the Company, presented to Parliament an 'Article of Charge of High Crimes and Misdemeanours against the Said Marquis [sic] Wellesley' in that:

> in all the recited proceedings and deeds the said Marquis Wellesley had been utterly unmindful of the solemn engagements entered into, had set at naught the authority and orders of his employers the East India Company, had daringly contemned the Parliament, the King and the Laws, and has therein been guilty of high offences, crimes and misdemeanours.[4]

The newly elected Wellesley, in his first speech in the Westminster Parliament, was there to defend him:

> This house will doubtless recollect how often that Noble Marquis has been thanked by this House itself, and by the Honourable Court of Directors, for those very measures, many of which are now brought forward as matters of serious charge against him ... the services upon which I was myself employed in India enable me to speak to some of the facts connected with this Charge. I have had considerable experience and personal knowledge of his lordship's system of government, and I can take it upon myself to state positively that there is not the slightest foundation for the present charge. Some of the facts have been greatly misrepresented, some are utterly without foundation ...[5]

The debate dragged on, and Wellesley was in the thick of it. Never one to shirk responsibility, on 28 April he told the House:

> to many of the facts and proceedings charged against my noble relative, as most culpable, most reprehensible and deserving of the most severe punishment, I was myself accessory. My short reply to that observation, sir, is this: that whatever I did in India was done in obedience to orders, which I had from proper authority; and for the manner of that obedience, and for its immediate results, I am ready, at any time, to answer either to this House, or to any other tribunal in the realm.[6]

On 3 June, in addition to charges of financial impropriety, disobedience and 'private depravity' against the marquess, murder was alleged. His brother was quick to rebut it:

Instead of complying with the law they [the Mahrattas] combined to resist it. They assembled together their armed forces ... they retired to their forts; they set the laws at defiance; they refused to pay any tribute; and it was found necessary by the Governor-General, in support of the laws, to reduce those men by force. So formidable were they that it required the whole of the Bengal army, with the Commander-in-Chief at their head, to effect this service. They were attacks in their forts, and, in the course of their obstinate resistance, some persons fell; some blood was spilt; and this is what the honourable gentleman imputes to the Noble Marquis as murder. It was an act of public power, done in support of the laws of the country, like what would have been done against any class of British subjects in similar resistance to the laws passed by Parliament. The House will now judge how far it is just to describe such a measure by the epithet of 'murder'.[7]

The motion of censure was defeated in both Houses of Parliament, Paull's suicide during the hearings no doubt having helped. Most of the charges were groundless; those which were not related to matters where Marquess Wellesley's high-handedness actually resulted in great benefit for both country and Company. Marquess Wellesley's political career continued and he would in time fill the offices of ambassador to Spain, Foreign Secretary and Lord Lieutenant of Ireland.

Meanwhile Sir Arthur Wellesley was still seeking employment. The trouble was that, at the moment, there was very little on offer. He turned down the proposed command of an expedition to Mexico, via Singapore, a somewhat far-fetched whimsy that never actually happened. British strategy, such as it was, was in disarray. The navy ruled the seas, but the tiny army had been bustled unceremoniously out of Europe whenever it had tried to intervene. The capture of the French islands in the West Indies (notably Guadeloupe and St Lucia) had brought some rewards, until most of them were recaptured, but the high death toll from disease made any extension of campaigning there hardly worth the effort.[8] After 1805 the British were scratching around trying to find some way of extending their maritime strategy and making themselves felt in the prosecution of the war. Wellesley himself thought – or said he did, much later, to Croker - that his lack of employment in anything that he considered to be worthwhile was due to prejudice against those whose military experience was in India – the 'sepoy generals'. He also thought that his origins in the Anglo-Irish nobility militated against him. As some of the most senior generals in the army had served in India – Cornwallis, Cavendish-Bentinck, Craddock and Clarke to name a few – this may have been exaggerated in his mind, but it is true that there was a consistent thread of suspicion of 'Indian' officers that was to continue until the British Indian army passed into history. If his origins were Irish and aristocratic, he did his best to ignore the former and his status as an aristocrat was a lowly one. It is far more likely that any prejudice which existed was due to his family's political connections. Wellesley realised this to be a factor, for he said later that a politician could not be a soldier. Perhaps he should have said that a soldier could not be a politician. Wellesley was also very junior. While some of his seniors could be passed over on grounds of age, not all could be disregarded, even if the government and the Commander-in-Chief had been convinced that Sir Arthur was the coming man, which at this stage they were not.

On 23 June 1806 William Pitt, worn out by illness, disappointment at the French victories of 1805 and overindulgence in strong drink, died, aged only forty-seven. Prime Minister from December 1783 at the age of twenty-five, he had held office until his death, except for the period 1801 to 1804, when he had resigned when unable to persuade George III that the Act of Union with Ireland carried with it an obligation to remove restrictions on Roman Catholics. Pitt was essentially a reformer. He had refined the fiscal system, carried through the Act of Union and wished to reform the constitution. A brilliant orator and a man of high intellect, it was his misfortune that the war with France prevented him from carrying out many of his plans, and made him the chief opponent of social change. He was never able to create a credible British strategy on land and the expense of maintaining the various coalitions, formed at his instigation, caused real hardship at home. Pitt was succeeded by the so-called Ministry of All the Talents under Grenville, which lasted only a year. In March 1807, when the Whigs left office, Sir Arthur Wellesley was offered the important post of Chief Secretary for Ireland, under the Duke of Richmond as Lord Lieutenant. Wellesley accepted, having first obtained assurances from the Commander-in-Chief, the Duke of York, that such employment would be no bar to his selection for a military appointment and could be discarded should a command come up. There had been no Irish Parliament since the Act of Union of 1801 and Irish voters now returned Members to the Parliament in Westminster. The Chief Secretary was effectively the Prime Minister, without the necessity to explain everything to an electorate, and the head of the administration under the King's representative the Lord Lieutenant. As the law then stood, anyone appointed to government office had to resign his parliamentary seat and fight a by-election. Wellesley gave up his seat and was returned for both Newport, Isle of Wight, and Tralee in Ireland. It was then not uncommon to stand for more than one constituency, although the successful candidate could represent only one. Wellesley chose to represent Newport, possibly because his constituents would be less likely to badger him than Irish ones might have done.

As Chief Secretary Wellesley concerned himself with all manner of issues, from the creation of a police force for Dublin and coastal defences against invasion, to the appointment of bishops. He ordered the Yeomanry not to celebrate the anniversary of the 1798 victory of Vinegar Hill over the Irish rebels, on the grounds that it would be unnecessarily provocative, and he devoted much time to the thorny question of education for Roman Catholics (he thought that they should have opportunities equal to those of the Protestants). He had considerable patronage at his disposal but he exercised it sparingly: a dunderhead would not be given a post however eminent the petitioner, a practice that he was to continue throughout his life.

Sir Arthur Wellesley had not forgotten India, and he corresponded with John Malcolm, who sought his advice on the state of the country and of the Company's armies. In 1806 there had been a serious mutiny by sepoys of the Madras army stationed at Vellore. Peace in Mysore and Hyderabad had led to the cutting of field allowances. An order that sepoys could no longer wear caste marks and ear rings and must wear leather caps caused great offence to Hindus. Discontent was stirred by the dead Tippoo's relatives, living in Vellore as pensioners of the Company. Sir Arthur told Malcolm that he would be happy to return to India to sort matters out, but doubted that he would be allowed to go. He nevertheless gave cautious and sound advice as to how matters might be handled and conditions improved.[9]

On 25 June 1807 Alexander, Tsar of All the Russias, and Napoleon Bonaparte, Emperor of the French, met on a raft in the middle of the River Nieman. Alexander disliked the English but was fascinated by Napoleon. The result of their meeting was the Treaty of Tilsit, by which Russia left the Fourth Coalition in favour of an agreement with France to carve up eastern Europe. Prussia, defeated by Napoleon, lost all of her territories west of the River Elbe. East Frisia went to Holland, while the grand duchy of Berg acquired some of Westphalia, the rest being formed into the new kingdom of Westphalia to be ruled over by Napoleon's brother, Jerome. Virtually all of Prussia's Polish lands went, to be included in the Grand Duchy of Warsaw under the suzerainty of the King of Saxony, but with a constitution which pleased most Poles, despite the stationing of a French army there to ensure good behaviour. Both the Grand Duchy and Westphalia would be part of the French dominated Confederation of the Rhine. Prussia, thoroughly humiliated, was to be reduced to just four provinces occupied by French troops until a huge war indemnity was paid.

Territory and alliance were not the only subjects of discussion between Alexander and Napoleon, however, for it was agreed that, in return for French support for Russia against the Turks, the Tsar would try to persuade England to settle her differences with France and, failing that, would attempt to persuade the Baltic states and Portugal to join Napoleon's Continental System, under which all member countries agreed to refuse any trade with Britain.

British intelligence very quickly discovered the terms of the Treaty of Tilsit. A main point of concern was the position of Denmark. Having recovered from Nelson's depredations of 1801, the Danes possessed a large and reasonably efficient fleet. While neutrals, their Crown Prince was pro-French. If French influence in the Baltic was to grow, there was a very real risk that France might obtain possession of the Danish fleet and thus once more threaten British naval supremacy, won at such cost at Trafalgar. The British invited the Danes to hand over their fleet for safekeeping, an offer indignantly refused even when Britain offered to hire it for the duration of the war. Peaceful persuasion having failed, plans to take the fleet by force began to be formulated. Security was virtually non-existent, and everyone, save possibly the Danes, seems to have known what was in the offing. Sir Arthur Wellesley in Dublin got wind of what was afoot, thought it unlikely to succeed but wrote to Castlereagh (Secretary of State for War) to ask if a place could be found for him.

> It will be understood and said that I had avoided or had not sought for an opportunity of serving abroad in order to hold a large civil office. As I am determined not to give up the military profession and as I know that I can be of no service in it unless I have the confidence and esteem of the officers and soldiers of the army, I must shape my course in such a manner as to avoid this imputation ...[10]

A place could be found, and Wellesley wrote to the Lord Lieutenant of Ireland, the Duke of Richmond, to explain:

> whatever may be the chance of success of the expedition it would not answer for me to allow it to go on without expressing a desire to be employed upon it. I accepted my office in Ireland solely on the condition that it should not preclude me from such service when an opportunity should offer ...[11]

The collection of troops for the Danish expedition was not as difficult as it might otherwise have been, for there was already a force assembled for yet another proposed expedition to South America. Plans were hastily altered, and its destination changed to Elsinore. Admiral Gambier would command the naval contribution, while Lieutenant General Lord Cathcart commanded the troops. Cathcart, fifty-two years old in 1807, had commanded in Scotland prior to being appointed to the Danish operation, and Wellesley had served with him in the Flanders expedition of 1794/95. One of his sons, a captain in the Royal Navy, died of yellow fever in Jamaica in 1805; two others would serve under Wellington at Waterloo.

In July 1807 Wellesley sailed from Sheerness in the troop transporter HMS *Prometheus,* as a divisional commander in Lord Cathcart's force of 15,000 troops. A fellow divisional commander was his old enemy David Baird. A

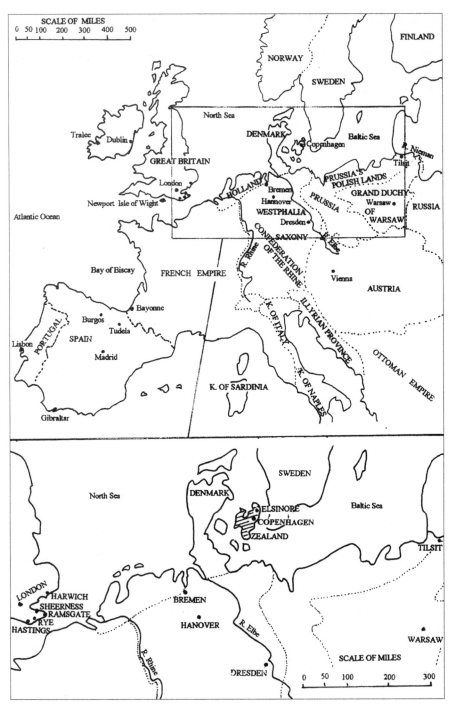

7. Europe in 1807.

division was very much an ad hoc formation in 1807, indeed British expeditionary forces were rarely large enough to require formations above brigade level, and Cathcart's 'divisions' were really only augmented brigades. Wellesley was fortunate in that his division consisted of two crack battalions of light infantry, the 43rd and the 52nd Foot, and a battalion of the recently formed 95th Rifles along with the 92nd Highlanders, all at a good state of training and up to strength. In support he had a troop (modern battery) of Royal Horse Artillery, some foot artillery and a Hanoverian cavalry detachment.[12] From 7 August, when the fleet gathered off Elsinore, the Danes now knew what was up. Small British cavalry patrols, landed with representatives of the commissariat, found the locals unhelpful, the Danish militia fully aware of British intentions and tradesmen unwilling to sell fresh food.

Cathcart arrived on 14 August and on 16 August began disembarkation. Wellesley's men were first ashore, their task being to seize and hold a beachhead to allow the remainder of the force to land. This was achieved without difficulty and by 21 August the suburbs of Copenhagen had been cleared and siege lines established. Copenhagen was well fortified, and the British lacked a siege train. Assaulting the city was not, therefore, an option. It was decided instead to bombard the inhabitants into submission, using field artillery, naval guns firing from the ships off shore and Congreve rockets, which were intended to set alight the wooden buildings inside the city walls. Wellesley's division was not involved in the siege itself, except briefly and temporarily when his men filled a gap intended for the King's German Legion, who were late. His main role was far more difficult: protecting the lines of communication from the fleet to the troops ashore, and preventing the Danes from raising the siege. The Danish army was small, but a sizeable militia had been embodied and was fired by indignation at being attacked despite their neutrality. Their strategy was to hit and run, mounting swift raids in rear of the British lines and interfering with supply columns on land and convoys at sea. Here was a task exactly suited to Wellesley's experiences in Mysore and against the Mahrattas, and to the training and tactics of his light infantry and rifles. In a series of sweeps and swift encircling movements, he cleared the whole of Zealand of Danish troops and militia by 3 September, at a cost to his own division of six killed and 115 wounded. On 8 September the Danes surrendered, to avoid further destruction to their capital, and negotiations began.[13] The agreement handed the Danish fleet of eighteen ships of the line to the Royal Navy, who towed the ships back to English ports, and allowed British occupation of Copenhagen until the sequestered fleet was safe and all damage to British property made good. Wellesley was one of the chief negotiators and the British signatories were himself, George Murray of the Adjutant General's department on Cathcart's staff (he would serve under

Wellesley in the Peninsula) and Captain Home Popham of the Royal Navy.[14]

The Copenhagen affair caused outrage in Europe, even amongst those powers friendly to the British, and provoked parliamentary opposition at home. Even the army, including Wellesley, was sympathetic towards the Danes. It has to be admitted that the action was totally illegal, infringed all the usages of war and was seen to be - and was - arrogant and high-handed. That said, it achieved its object of denying a very useful fleet to the French and of augmenting the Royal Navy by the same. The end may not always justify the means in everyday life, but in war it often does. In hindsight the British action was militarily justified. The last British troops left Denmark in October, but Wellesley departed after the capitulation had been signed and, *faute de mieux*, returned to wrestling with the problems of Ireland. He did not languish in Dublin for long.

The Peninsular War, the major British contribution to the struggle against Napoleon on land, need never have happened. It began because of French overconfidence, a failure by Napoleon to assess the mood of the common people of Spain, and a subsequent reluctance on his part to extricate himself once it became apparent that Spain would continue to tie up French troops which could have been used to far greater profit elsewhere. If it was never the major theatre of the war, from the Allies point of view it was an extremely effective side-show. It also established Wellesley as England's greatest general. It was to be some time, however, before he would find himself in supreme military command of British and Allied troops in Iberia.

In 1807 Spain was a half-hearted ally of France. There were those in Spain who considered the Spanish constitution and administration in need of reform – as indeed it was – and that this could only come about by the import of French revolutionary ideals. Others were suspicious of the French but more so of Britain, a traditional trading rival, while there were those who considered that a French alliance might give Spain control over Portugal with its ports on the Atlantic coastline and its colonies in South America. Since being frustrated in Denmark, Napoleon had been plotting to bring Spain firmly under French control. French troops were in Madrid, supposedly to cooperate with the Spanish armies but in reality in preparation for a coup.

In November 1807 a Franco-Spanish army invaded Portugal, hoping to seize the Portuguese fleet in Lisbon. The British appealed to the Regent, Prince John, to stand by his country's oldest ally. When John dithered and then looked as if he would throw in his lot with the French, the British navy removed both John (to the Portuguese colony of Brazil) and the fleet (to British ports). Initially the Portuguese welcomed the French – they bitterly resented what they saw as the desertion of the Regent – but when French oppression became severe, risings occurred all over the country and the district of Oporto set up a Junta under the bishop. Although most of the Portuguese regular troops had been sent to northern Europe by order of Napoleon, the militias were able to force the French to abandon most of the hinterland and concentrate in the Lisbon area and in the major fortresses. Soon the Portuguese appealed for British help.

In March 1808 the French effectively kidnapped the Spanish royal family, whisked them across the border to Bayonne and announced that the King, Ferdinand VII, had been deposed and replaced by his father, Charles IV, who had previously abdicated.[15] Charles was then persuaded to abdicate once more and Napoleon declared his brother Joseph Bonaparte to be King of Spain. Although the French expected some resistance, its extent came as a surprise. In Madrid civilians rioted and attacked French soldiers. Order was firmly restored by French troops under Murat, but the example set by Madrid began to spread, with spontaneous risings all over the country. French actions had pushed Spanish pride and xenophobia too far, but the French still thought that the disorder was only temporary and caused largely by the machinations of British agents. These latter did, of course, seize on any opportunity to discommode the French, but there were very few of them and their activities were very far from being enough to rouse almost the entire Spanish population against the French.

Spanish leadership came not from the nobility in the capital but mainly from local leaders. Districts set up their own Juntas with command exercised by village headmen, mayors, landowners and churchmen, the latter wanting nothing to do with French anticlericalism. Here was the beginning of a problem which was to tax the British throughout the war: most decisions were taken locally and no one seemed to speak for the whole country; or if anyone claimed so to speak, they were unable to enforce their wishes nationally. It was not all that different from the situation in Mysore and in the Mahratta country, where local chiefs decided what happened in their locality without paying much attention to the centre.

The Spanish, in turn, now appealed to Britain for help. The Duke of Portland, who had succeeded Grenville as Prime Minister with George Canning as Foreign Secretary, was ecstatic. Here at last was a European nation prepared to stand up to Napoleon, and where one nation led others might follow. Somewhat bedazzled by the exaggerated claims of death and destruction being dealt out to the French, which were seized upon by the British newspapers and engendered widespread public enthusiasm, the British government decided to support the Spanish and the Portuguese. On the principle of 'my enemy's enemy is my friend' the Spanish Juntas, by the end of the year, received over one million pounds in specie and 200,000 muskets.

On 25 April 1808 Sir Arthur Wellesley was promoted to the rank of lieu-tenant general. There were thirty-two major generals promoted in the same brevet, with Wellesley twenty-ninth on the list. Whatever may have been his suspicions as to prejudice against him, it was clear that the Commander-in-Chief wanted him for an important command. Of those senior to him and promoted on the same brevet, many were never actually employed. Of them, Sir John Stuart was already Lieutenant Governor of Grenada; Sir William Congreve Bt, father of the inventor of the military rocket, was comptroller of the Royal Laboratories; and only Henry, Lord Paget (later Earl of Uxbridge), was to play a significant part in the rest of the war. It would have caused an outcry to have promoted Wellesley over the heads of so many generals senior to him: the solution was to promote them all but employ only a few.

To the British government it now seemed that it might be possible to do more than just supply money and weapons to the Spanish. The obvious first target was the French occupying force in Portugal under General Jean-Androche Junot. Junot had commanded the invasion of Portugal, sent there from Paris to get him away from simmering scandal, both financial and sexual (including a liaison with Napoleon's sister Caroline). He was now the Governor-General but, it was reported, supported by only five thousand French troops. Confined to Lisbon and a few outlying areas, and cut off from the French armies in Spain by the insurrection there, he might profitably be eliminated. The British government decided that this could be achieved by a swift operation and that the ideal officer to command it would be Sir Arthur Wellesley, who would take seven thousand men from the Irish garrison. As it would be a rapid affair, and over quickly, he need not relinquish his post as Chief Secretary for Ireland.

It soon became apparent that intelligence reports from the Peninsula were grossly inaccurate. The Spanish and Portuguese had exaggerated their successes and understated the number of French troops. Far from having only 5000 troops, Junot, it now appeared, had nearer 15,000. The operation would still proceed, but it would require a much larger British contingent and could not now be under Wellesley's sole command. Instead, the necessary troops would be found from an expedition just returned from Sweden, combined with those under Wellesley and augmented by five thousand men from Gibraltar under the recently knighted Major General Sir Brent Spencer. Spencer would land at the head of Cadiz Bay, itself under the control of the Royal Navy since it had been seized in June, when the French ships moored there were appropriated by the British.

The British had recently sent ten thousand troops on a largely nugatory foray to Sweden when the Crown Prince, neutral but anti-French, had asked for help to defend his country against any French agression. Once there the Crown Prince tried to have the force placed under his own command to be used in furthering purely Swedish interests. The troops were recalled. This expedition was commanded by Sir John Moore, a lieutenant general since 1805. Moore had many qualities in common with Sir Arthur Wellesley, but in some aspects they were quite different personalities. Moore, eight years older than Wellesley, was commissioned in 1776 at the age of fifteen. He had fought in the American war, in Corsica, in the West Indies and in Holland. Like Wellesley, he was a thorough professional and believed in hard and realistic training. While the redevelopment of light infantry tactics and the institution of rifle troops in the British army was probably as much the inspiration of the Commander-in-Chief, the Duke of York, as it was of Moore, his enthusiastic support for the famous training camp at Shorncliffe did much to inspire that arm of the service.[16] One of Moore's most noteworthy qualities was his understanding of the private soldier. While he often placed far more trust in what he saw as their essential decency and good nature than was justified by the evidence, there is no doubt that his genuine concern for the soldiers' well-being made him revered by the men placed under him. He abhorred flogging and hanging, and believed that self-discipline, individual initiative and pride in race and regiment would make the British soldier the envy of the world. He may not have been right, at least in the early nineteenth century, but his concern and his honestly-held beliefs were universally respected. Wellesley took a much more sceptical view of the other ranks of the army. He did believe in hanging and flogging (or at least said he did). While equally concerned for his men's welfare, it was less a personal concern for the man and more a realisation that a soldier who is uncared for will not fight, and that disease and hunger reduce the human assets available to a commander. The difference, perhaps, is that Moore understood soldiers intimately, whereas Wellesley did not. Moore had taken fourteen years to achieve the rank of lieu-tenant colonel, during most of which time he had actually commanded a company of infantrymen. Wellesley rose to that rank in only six years and had never previously commanded anything.

Against this, Moore was constitutionally incapable of getting on with his military superiors, with politicians or with the navy, with all of whom he frequently quarrelled. Intelligent and forward-looking soldier though he was, and a master tactician, he had great difficulty in working in concert with others. Wellesley was related to politicians and had political experience, understood how government worked, had shown in India that he had the tact and discretion to work within a coalition, and took care not to upset the navy, or at least its commanders.

Command arrangements for the expedition were muddled. The obvious commander was Sir John Moore, but instead the overall Commander-in-Chief appointed was Lieutenant General Sir Hew Dalrymple, aged fifty-eight, who had until recently been a perfectly competent Governor of Gibraltar (before which he had held a similar post in Guernsey), but who had not seen active service for fourteen years. The appointment was probably due to seniority - the Duke of York, for all his genuine reforming zeal, still had to pay due deference to length of service – and it was not politically contentious. Moore was the favourite of the Whig opposition and had argued with Castlereagh, while Wellesley was the holder of a political office and in any case thought to be too junior. The post of second-in-command to Dalrymple went to Lieutenant General Sir Harry Burrard, fifty-three years old and lately a fellow divisional commander of Wellesley's under Cathcart in Denmark, an appointment which he had combined with that of second-in-command of the expedition. Of the various generals involved in the Iberian intervention, Moore was the third senior and Wellesley the eighth. Moore, despite his doubts as to the feasibility of the expedition, was unhappy not to be in sole command himself, writing in his journal:

> I understood from Gordon [secretary to the Duke of York] that there had been much intriguing about the command. Ministers had done everything in their power to give it to Sir Arthur Wellesley; but he was so young a lieutenant general that the Duke had objected to it, and afraid of disgusting the army and the nation by such an appointment they had given it up. Disappointed in their favourite object, they were determined it should not be given to me, and to prevent the possibility of its falling to me, Sir Harry Burrard was named as second.[17]

On 14 June 1808 Sir Arthur Wellesley was appointed to command the troops sailing from Cork, totalling 10,728 all ranks, and on 12 July he sailed in HMS *Crocodile*. Altogether the Cork force consisted of eleven battalions of infantry, a regiment of cavalry and supporting engineers and artillery. As the infantry had been mainly engaged in recruiting and training, all battalions were up to strength; the smallest, the 45th Foot, having 594 all ranks and the largest, the 5th Foot, 1107. Less satisfactory was the state of the one cavalry regiment, the 20th Light Dragoons, which had 381 all ranks but only 215 horses. There were only six officers, one sergeant and eleven other ranks of the Royal Engineers and a mere fifty Royal Artillery drivers, including a subaltern and a drummer.[18] Wellesley's orders were simple: he was to secure Lisbon as a base for the Royal Navy and then assist the Portuguese in expelling the French. At this stage Wellesley still thought that his troops would be the only ones involved and that he would command them, but this changed quickly. Suspicion of information emanating from the Spanish and Portuguese was such that Wellesley was instructed to call in at Coruña on his way, in order to assess for himself the true situation. In late July Wellesley was reinforced by a further four battalions of infantry sailing from Ramsgate, and two battalions of infantry, two companies of the 95th Rifles and two batteries of foot artillery from Harwich.

Reaching Coruña on 20 July Wellesley took soundings from the Galician Junta. Their reports were optimistic, assuring him of the support of 2000 troops under their command, with a further 5000 at Coimbra. They estimated the French forces as being no more than 14,000 and said nothing about the Junta's defeats – of which there had been several. Not entirely convinced, Wellesley sailed on and rendezvoused with Vice Admiral Sir Charles Cotton off Fort Figueira. Cotton, commanding the Royal Navy's Tagus Squadron, had been supporting the Spanish and Portuguese along the coastline. Like everybody else who hoped for French defeat, he had initially believed the Junta's claims, passing them on to London. Now, however, he had managed to find out the true situation and was able to report that Junot had actually got 20,000 French troops, all close to Lisbon and well aware that a British landing was imminent. Cotton's advice was to land the men at Mondego Bay, about 120 miles north of Lisbon. While this would mean a landing across open beaches with heavy surf, the Royal Navy could cover the landings, local roads were bad, the French could not approach without difficulty, and Fort Figueira was in the hands of the Navy. The troops began to disembark, being ferried through the surf in small boats crewed by sailors. Horses were winched over the side in slings and swam to shore, and artillery and heavy equipment was moved by pontoon and raft. The landings took four days.

Three days after Wellesley had set sail from Cork, Sir John Moore arrived at Dover in HMS *Victory*, having escaped from virtual house arrest ordered by the King of Sweden. King Gustavus IV of Sweden may well have been mad, but he was an ally who had a personal hatred for the French. While the British government could not fault Moore in his decision to withdraw from Sweden, ministers were less than happy by the way in which he did it. Moore was surprised to find no one at Dover to meet him. Hurrying to London he saw Castlereagh, who told him that he was to proceed to Spain or Portugal. The command arrangements were explained to him. Moore was unhappy at not being placed in overall command and set off for Portsmouth after parting acrimoniously with Castlereagh. The Secretary for War and the Colonies was not one to ignore insubordination from soldiers, and a letter to Moore, received just before he sailed from Portsmouth, made it clear that were it not now too late to alter arrangements for the expedition, Moore would not have a command at all. Moore sailed from Portsmouth on 31 July 1808.

At Mondego Bay, with all his troops now landed by 3 August, Wellesley found a depressing situation, all too reminiscent of Flanders twelve years previously. There were insufficient rations and those that had arrived were of poor quality. There was a shortage of cash to buy food locally and many of the commissariat officials – tools of the Treasury rather than of the army - were incompetent or uninterested. There was a severe shortage of artillery horses and drivers, and a message from Sir Brent Spencer, now hurrying to join Wellesley, said that Spencer had been forced to abandon his artillery through lack of horses to pull the guns. Wellesley sent a flurry of dispatches back to Castlereagh. Things would improve, but not yet.

Some good news did arrive. While most Spanish armies were of dubious military merit in the war, one, commanded by General Francisco Xavier Castanos, had met a French army under General Dupont at Bailen on 21 July. While it is difficult to avoid the judgement that both Castanos and Dupont were incompetent, Castanos was slightly less so. Dupont was soundly beaten and forced to surrender his army.

Waiting for Sir Brent Spencer to arrive, Wellesley issued a stream of orders to subordinate commanders, situation reports to the British government, to the navy and to other generals. Having now been informed that Dalrymple had been given the overall command with Burrard as second-in-command, he took care to keep them informed by letter, transmitted by fast frigate. Wellesley was always a prodigious worker. In a not untypical day, 8 August 1808, two days before he intended to march from Mondego, he penned no fewer than ten letters and memoranda, altogether amounting to the remarkable total of almost 5000 words. Of these, two went to Castlereagh, three to Dalrymple, one to Burrard, one to Lieutenant Colonel Robe, commanding the artillery, one to Captain Malcolm RN, captain of HMS *Donegal,* one to Brigadier General Fane who would command the advance brigade, due to leave a day before the main body, and one to Colonel Trant, commanding the Portuguese contingent.[19] While some of the shorter letters may have been prepared by Wellesley's staff for his signature, and some may have been dictated by him to clerks, all are written in his unmistakable style, so would certainly have been vetted, and if necessary altered by him, before despatch. When one remembers that all correspondence of this nature was written by quill pen, the magnitude of the work is apparent.

On 10 August Wellesley, now united with Spencer's force, marched off in the direction of Lisbon, staying close to the coast and naval support. The troops were in good heart and Wellesley was optimistic. Before leaving Ireland he had said that, while he acknowledged that so far French armies had defeated all that had been sent against them, he suspected that those who had been vanquished were half beaten before they started: he at least was not afraid of the French.

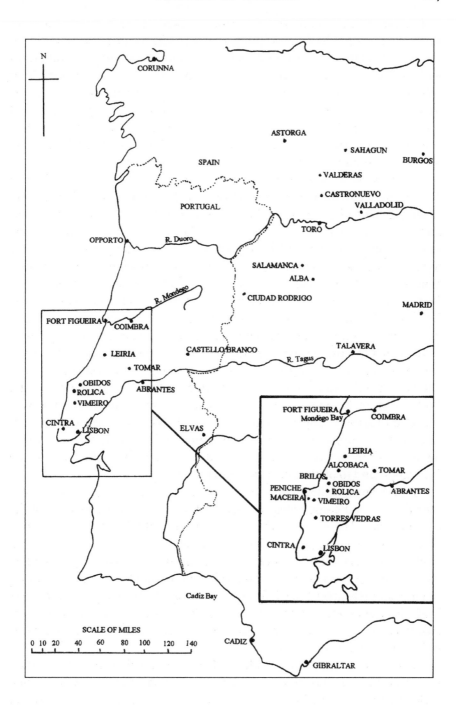

8. Portugal and Spain: Area of Operations 1808.

The extravagant promises of Portuguese and Spanish troops failed to materialise – they had no commissariat and the British had insufficient rations to feed them – but a contingent of around 1500 Portuguese did march with Wellesley, under command of a British officer, Nicholas Trant. Trant was Anglo-Irish and the same age as Wellesley. Commissioned into the infantry in 1794 after serving as a Volunteer in Flanders in 1793/94, he had transferred to the Royal Staff Corps in 1803.[20] He never held rank higher than colonel in the British army, but was a brigadier general in the Portuguese service in 1808 and was eventually promoted to major general.

Gradually, as Wellesley's men moved nearer to Lisbon, the true facts as to the French deployment emerged. While he had not yet organised the system of intelligence gathering that he would use to such good effect later in the war, and had insufficient cavalry to range far ahead of the main body, officers mounted on good, fit horses forging ahead of the marching troops were able to see for themselves where the French were, and could obtain information from friendly Portuguese. It now appeared that there were around 12,000 French troops in and around Lisbon, with a mobile force of 6000 men under Delaborde blocking the Lisbon road at Obidos, and a further 9000 men under Loison somewhere between Obrantes and Tomar. Additionally there were French troops, of unknown number, in the area of Leiria. This was not necessarily bad news. Delaborde and Loison might unite, but even so they would still only number 15,000, compared to the combined British and Portuguese total of 17,000, with the extra 5000 from Ramsgate and Harwich expected to arrive at any moment. Even if the French moved troops up from Lisbon, these could only be a small proportion of their occupying army, as to denude Lisbon of French troops would be to hand the city back to the Portuguese and to invite a British landing.

On 14 August Wellesley reached Alcobaca, having covered sixty miles in four days - good going given the state of the roads and the vagaries of the commissariat. The next day the first skirmish of the Peninsular War took place when three companies of the 95th Rifles, scouting ahead of the main body, drove a French piquet out of a windmill at Brilos. The French scuttled back three miles to Obidos, and the riflemen followed them up, when they ran into a much larger French force. Impetuosity on the part of their officers might have got them into trouble, but Sir Brent Spencer with a battalion was able to extricate them with little difficulty. Total British casualties were one officer and about twenty men.

On 16 August the French abandoned Obidos and withdrew back into their first main blocking position, at Rolica. The British camped in Obidos that night and reports came in which indicated that only Delaborde's army was at Rolica, but that Loison was only half a day's march away. Wellesley's men were under arms and formed up an hour before daybreak on 17 August. The approach from Obidos to Rolica was into a broad valley, leading into a horse-shoe of hills. The British moved off in the direction of Rolica in three columns. Wellesley's column, in the centre, with just over half of the British infantry, the 20th Light Dragoons less one troop, some local Portuguese cavalry and twelve guns, about 9000 men in all, moved straight along the valley. To the east and west Wellesley sent two arms of a pincer movement. The eastern column, under Major General Ferguson, had the rest of the British infantry, a troop of the 20th Light Dragoons (about forty horsemen) and six guns, or about 4500 men all told. Colonel Trant led the western column composed of his own Portuguese. The plan was for Wellesley in the centre to fix the French army while the two flanking columns would converge behind them, cutting them off and allowing Wellesley's infantry to destroy them. Ferguson's force was the stronger of the two pincer arms, as he had also to watch out for any attempt by Loison to come to the aid of his fellow general.

As the centre column got to within about two miles of Rolica, Wellesley could see the French under Delaborde formed up in line. There was no sign of Loisin. The French position was near the head of the valley and well in front of the line of hills. It was protected by lines of *tirailleurs*, or skirmishers, deployed in front of the main line, and there seemed to be rather a lot of cavalry. Up to now the British infantry had been marching in column of route; now they deployed into battalion columns. A little closer, and Wellesley ordered his guns to deploy and to open fire. It was too great a range for the guns to have any effect; but if the attention of the French could be held for just a little longer the arms of the pincers would begin to converge and the French would be unable to move.

To Wellesley's right, as Ferguson's light companies engaged the French *tirailleurs*, the trap was about to close. Delaborde, however, was a wily old soldier. He had enlisted in the ranks of the Bourbon army in 1783 and had advanced rapidly after the Revolution, becoming a *général de division* in 1793. He had served in the Pyrenees and fought in Germany and commanded a division under Junot in the invasion of Portugal. Now, watching events from the top of a windmill to the French rear, he realised exactly what his opponent was trying to do. He ordered a withdrawal and, screened by his cavalry which was too numerous for the British to counter, he skilfully moved his men back two miles, up onto the line of hills overlooking the British advance. The hill on which Delaborde now took his post was one of a series of lozenge-shaped features. His line was almost a mile long and each flank was protected by a deep gully. The slope facing the British was steep, and cut by numerous dry rivulets and re-entrants. In front of the position, and providing a natural

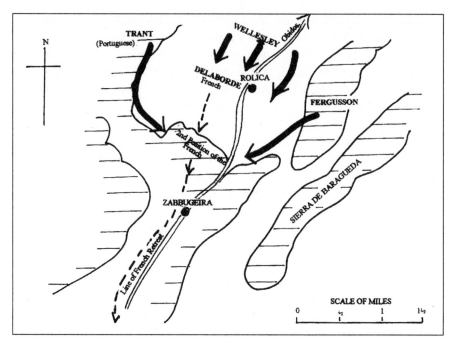

9. The Battle of Rolica, 17 August 1808.

breastwork, was a dry rocky ditch. The French artillery had a clear view of the British approach and could fire down on the advancing infantry, whereas the British guns could not elevate their muzzles sufficiently to make much reply.

The two arms of the British pincers continued to manoeuvre, and local battles between the opposing skirmishers grew more intense. Figures in black and green dashed across the valley, for men of the 95th Rifles were used as runners to keep Wellesley informed of what the other two columns were up to. It was clear that there was no alternative, short of retreat, to launching a general attack, and 500 yards from the bottom of the French slope Wellesley ordered his battalions to form line. The drums beat, the sergeants screamed and the columns moved up and around, at seventy paces per minute, until the battalions were in line advancing on the French. Both sides' skirmishers were now engaged, and the broken ground made the preservation of the British line increasingly difficult. At this point something happened which was to become all too familiar in the early stages of the war. The 1st Battalion of the 29th Foot, commanded by Lieutenant Colonel Lake, should have been advancing in line with its light company out ahead in the skirmish line. For some reason known only to Lake, he led half his battalion straight up a re-entrant that ran towards the French position and then turned east. Lake and the men of the 29th eventually emerged about 200 yards in rear of the French position. They found themselves in a cramped depression with fire directed at them from all sides. Lake tried to form his men into a firing line, but it was too late. The French left centre fell upon him and Lake and many of his men were killed, with four officers and thirty men taken prisoner. A few managed to scramble back down the gully to safety. Perhaps Lake was using his initiative, or perhaps he simply became confused and disorientated, but it was to confirm Wellesley in his view that no local commander should ever do anything which had not been ordered.

The main British line was now ascending the slope. Maintenance of a neatly dressed line was made impossible by the ground and the battle degenerated into an untidy series of company-sized actions, with the British steadily inching themselves up the hill. The British superiority in numbers could not, at this point, be used but at last groups of redcoats began to emerge onto the top of the western half of the ridge. Companies reformed into battalions and battalions into brigades. To the east the fighting was harder – the French were waiting for Loison – but when Delaborde realised that the British would soon be in control of the high ground he began a withdrawal of his four battalions. The retreat was carried out in an orderly manner with two battalions covering the withdrawal of the other two, being covered back in turn. The British were held off by the French cavalry, very much in its commander's grip, and keeping the British at arms length by a series of short, controlled charges, never pressed home and so incurring few casualties. Just south of the village of Zabbugeira was a defile that ran right across the area. Here there was some confusion as the French crossed the defile, and Delaborde was forced to abandon three of his guns, but, once across and onto the flat and open ground beyond, the British were unable to pursue: the French had far too many cavalry and the British far too few. Local Portuguese reconnaissance reported that Loison was only five miles away, so the British bivouacked on the field for the night, with their guns and most of the infantry facing south and east.

By the later standards of the war Rolica was only a minor skirmish, but its importance was out of all proportion to its strategic significance or to the casualties incurred (roughly 700 French and less than 500 British). The British army had become accustomed to being beaten by the French; almost every time they had attempted to intervene on land in Europe they had been driven unceremoniously out again. Now, for the first time for many a year, a British force had attacked a French army in a defensive position and had driven it from the field. True the British greatly outnumbered the French, but even so they were taking on vastly more experienced soldiers with a long tradition of winning against everything thrown at them. British morale soared.

During the night of 17 August the men slept in their stand-to positions, and at Wellesley's headquarters messengers came and went: dragoons, mounted officers, Portuguese auxiliaries and civilians. There appeared to be no move of French troops out of Lisbon; Delaborde and Loison had come together but were still moving away to the south east. The expected British reinforcements had arrived offshore and the navy intended to land them at Maceira, about fifteen miles south west of Rolica. By eleven o'clock on the morning of 18 August Wellesley and his army were on the march towards Maceira, arriving there just before last light.

The landings began at first light on 19 August. The beach where the Maceira river flowed into the sea was easily protected from the land side, and the navy could prevent any interference from the sea, but there was a very heavy surf. Many of the small boats used to transfer the soldiers from the troop transports to the beach were swamped, drowning a number of men, but by 20 August both reinforcing brigades were ashore and Wellesley now commanded, for the time being at least, in the region of 16,000 men. He was anxious to continue his advance on Lisbon, for the longer he delayed the more time the French would have to prepare for his approach.

On the evening of 20 August Lieutenant General Sir Harry Burrard, overall second-in-command of the British forces in Spain and Portugal, arrived in a fast sloop off Maceira. Wellesley was rowed out to Burrard's ship for a conference, which lasted several hours. Burrard thought that Wellesley was underestimating the number of French troops in the area, and their state of readiness, and considered that any further advance in the direction of Lisbon would be too dangerous. He ordered Wellesley to remain where he was, to await the arrival of Sir John Moore and his force, expected to land at Mondego Bay shortly.

If Sir John had not yet landed (Moore arrived off Mondego Bay on 19 August, but hove to offshore waiting for an order to land), this might mean a delay of at least a week. Wellesley felt that Moore would be better employed striking inland and cutting off the French line of retreat, but he had no option but to obey. By last light he was back on shore and disposing of his troops in a defensive posture.

Burrard was and is much ridiculed for his caution (he was known to all as 'Betty' Burrard), but his decision was not unreasonable. Wellesley and his rudimentary intelligence staff had underestimated the number of French troops, the British were very short of cavalry and there was no sign of Spanish assistance. The addition of Moore's force of 12,000 men would give the British a clear superiority in numbers over all French forces in Portugal, and, assuming that the French could not be reinforced, would make victory for the British almost certain. The British had had enough defeats. Burrard would not risk the gains from Rolica by being overconfident. Having made his views plain, he transferred his office to a frigate and remained there writing letters.

From Maceira Bay the river ran east behind a ridge, before cutting through the ridge to the south. Just north of the ridge was Vimeiro Hill, and it was on the ridge and the hill that Wellesley's, or more properly now Burrard's, men were placed. They bivouacked just behind their stand-to positions, and throughout the night intelligence and reconnaissance reports came in. A patrol of the 20th Light Dragoons reported that a French force was moving up towards Vimeiro and would be there by the morning. Although Wellesley did not know it, Junot had decided to concentrate Delaborde's and Loison's force at Torres Vedras. With the hostile population of Lisbon behind him, and the likelihood of British reinforcement, Junot did not want an enemy army to approach any nearer. True, the English had won the battle of Rolica, but their lack of coordination and their generalship had not impressed the experienced French commanders. Now this troublesome British intrusion could be brushed aside.

Just before first light on 21 August Wellesley ordered his men to stand to, with no noise, no drums and no bugles. They were drawn up along the ridge and on Vimeiro Hill itself, with fourteen artillery pieces spread amongst the infantry. At about eight o'clock, well after dawn, the French could be heard, and then seen, approaching. There was little attempt to manoeuvre, just an attack in column straight up the centre, and a sweep to the east, trying to turn the British flank. The British infantry, in lines two deep, waited until the French came up the hill and then repulsed them by volley fire and canister from the artillery. All the French attempts to strengthen the flanking movement could be clearly seen from the ridge where the British stood, and Wellesley was able to reinforce the threatened parts of his line by moving men along the reverse slope, out of French fire and view. There was little tactical initiative required by the British: they simply stood and fired their volleys at French columns trying to advance up the slope; and when the columns tried a different approach British troops were there to meet them. Unlike in Flanders, senior officers were well to the fore. By about half past ten it was all over; the French gave up and began to withdraw, leaving around 2000 casualties. With only about 600 British killed and wounded, now, as Wellesley saw it, was the time to follow up and destroy Junot utterly. The British force was numerically roughly equal to that of the French, and three brigades had not been engaged and could be pushed on to Torres Vedras, thus blocking Junot's retreat towards Lisbon. The remainder of the army could harass the French and drive them into the hinterland, where lack of supplies and the Portuguese guerrillas might force a surrender; otherwise they could be defeated in detail.

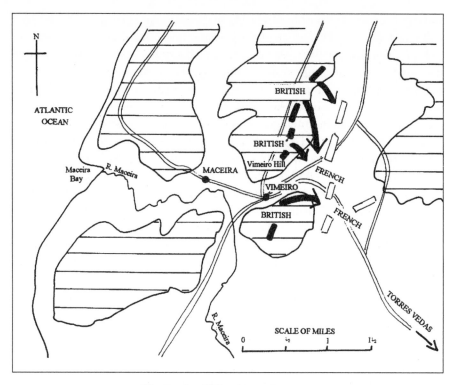

10. The Battle of Vimeiro, 21 August 1808.

Unfortunately, as Wellesley saw it, Sir Harry Burrard now came ashore and would countenance no further move. The British had driven off the French and that, as Burrard saw it, was quite enough for one day. Lieutenant General Sir Hew Dalrymple (known to the army as 'Dowager' Dalrymple) arrived that same night and confirmed his second-in-command's orders. The British would stay where they were and wait for reinforcement.

Matters now came to a head, for on 22 August a group of French cavalry carrying a flag of truce appeared at the British outposts. General Kellermann had been deputed to ask the British for an armistice, which was agreed that day. Over the next week negotiations between Kellermann, Dalrymple, Burrard and Wellesley continued. It may be that Junot's original plan was simply to stall for time, in the hope that he might gain assistance from a Russian fleet, allied to France since the Treaty of Tilsit and now off the mouth of the River Tagus. When it became apparent that the Russians would not cooperate, the negotiations began in earnest. The French, seeing their position in Portugal as hopeless and without any chance of help from Spain, agreed to surrender all Portuguese fortresses still in their hands and to evacuate Portugal.

On the face of it, this is exactly what the British government had wanted: the French driven from Portugal. What angered Wellesley, and ultimately the British government and public, was the manner of their going. By the terms of what came to be known as the Convention of Cintra (the British moved their headquarters to Cintra, the summer capital of the kings of Portugal, on 31 August), the French army, complete 'with all military baggage and equipment' was to be returned to France in British ships. As the French interpreted military baggage to mean huge quantities of looted treasure and artefacts, and included officers' mistresses collected on campaign, the Portuguese were far from satisfied. There was also no clause to prevent the use of those same troops against the Portuguese or British in the future. Wellesley was fully involved in the negotiation, and when the agreement was signed at the end of August his name was on the paper, but he was unhappy with it and took the precaution of writing to Castlereagh to tell him that he disagreed with the terms. His unhappiness can only have been increased by the arrival of his superiors, for now, instead of being commander of an army, he had perforce to revert to being a divisional commander under Dalrymple and Burrard.

While all this was going on Sir John Moore had reached Vigo, sailed on to Oporto, and had reached Mondego Bay on 19 August. On 22 August he began to land his men, when a message from Burrard, sent by fast sloop, told him to cancel the landing: the battle of Vimeiro had been won and he was now to sail direct to Maceira Bay. Moore arrived off Maceira on 24 August, when he sent a congratulatory note to Wellesley. On 25 August Moore reached the British headquarters where, according to his journal:

> I was sorry to find everything in the greatest confusion, and a very general discontent. Sir Hew [Dalrymple] had been announced to the army but had not yet taken the direction of it. Much was still done by Sir Arthur Wellesley, and what was not done by him was not done at all.[21]

Moore agreed with Wellesley that the terms of the Convention were dishonourable, and that the French should have been followed up and smashed after Vimeiro. Given that the French had been allowed to get away, however, Moore considered that the terms of the Convention were probably as good as the British could now obtain. Moore kept aloof from the negotiations, but his admiration for Wellesley grew:

> The Army List is a bad guide in the choice of a military commander. Sir Arthur Wellesley seems to have conducted his operations with ability, and they have been crowned with success. It is a pity, when so much has been thrown into his hands that he has not been allowed to complete it ... I have told both Sir Hew and Sir

Arthur that I wished not to interfere; that if hostilities commenced Sir Arthur had already done so much that I thought it but fair he should have the command ... I considered this his expedition.[22]

If Wellesley had a low opinion of Dalrymple and Burrard, he was more than happy to serve under Moore. On 17 September he wrote to tell him: 'The Commander-in-Chief must be changed, and the country and the army naturally look to you as their commander.' Alluding to the difficulties over the Swedish affair, he offered to mediate with the politicians on Moore's behalf. Moore was initially suspicious: he hardly knew Wellesley, had only met him once or twice, and wondered what his motives might be. The two generals met and Moore, having made it plain that he would have no part in any intrigue, agreed to his fellow general's suggestions. Wellesley saw no point in remaining in Portugal when no operations were in progress and none likely, particularly now that he had been superseded in command. He left for England on 21 September and, having arrived on 4 October, began to make his position on the Convention clear. Because of the storm in Parliament and the press, the British government convened a court of inquiry into the negotiations, and, on the day that Wellesley arrived in England, Dalrymple, recalled, left Portugal with Burrard following later. All three generals were required to give evidence before the court. There was no need for Wellesley to importune on behalf of Moore. Despite the government's suspicions, with the departure of Dalrymple and Burrard there was no alternative but to appoint Sir John Moore Commander-in-Chief in Spain and Portugal, which was duly done on 6 October 1808. On 22 October, in England, Sir Arthur Wellesley began his evidence to the court of inquiry into the Cintra affair.

In Portugal Moore was hurriedly preparing his army for action. His instructions were vague - he described them as the sort of nonsense spouted by holders of office pretending to be military men – and required him to strike into the north of Spain with a view to cooperating with the Spanish armies to expel the French from Spain. Moore was unhappy with this and considered any stab into Spain as being very risky indeed; the farther he moved from his ports, the more difficult it would be to supply his men; and the greater the likelihood of his being cut off by the French and destroyed. Due to the state of the roads, such as existed, it would be quite impossible for the army to march along one route, so Moore instructed Sir David Baird, now on his way from Falmouth with reinforcements, to land at Coruña and march from there, while Brigadier General Hope would move from Elvas via Madrid, all three columns aiming to meet at either Burgos or Valladolid.

As with Wellesley's army, there were problems with the commissariat: there were no stockpiles of stores, the military chest was bare, maps were rudimentary and there was a shortage of carts to carry the heavy equipment and artillery ammunition. The weather had turned very cold and daily sickness rates went up as morale went down. The promised Portuguese and Spanish help either did not appear at all, or they would only cooperate if their administration and rationing was catered for by the British – an impossibility given that Moore had barely enough food for his own men.

Moore himself marched from Lisbon on 27 October 1808. On 3 November he crossed to the south bank of the River Tagus at Villa Velha, then pushed on into Spain. Moving via Castello Branco and Ciudad Rodrigo, he reached Salamanca on 13 November. Here he heard to his dismay that the French had taken Burgos - a town which Moore had hoped to occupy himself - and were now in Valladolid, only seventy miles or three to four days march away. Despite mounted messengers urging Baird and Hope to hurry, they were unlikely to arrive before the end of the month. At this point it seemed to Moore that retreat back to the coast was the only sensible option. To stay in Salamanca or to advance further would invite the French to destroy him in detail. Even if all three elements of his army joined they could still be cut off, and there were alarming reports of French reinforcements. Although Moore did not know it, Napoleon himself was on his way, his only visit to the Peninsula, in order to supervise the expulsion of this impertinent English interference.

All Moore's military training, experience and instincts told him to retreat now, while he still could, but there were political restraints to be taken into account. London wanted to be seen to be supporting the Spanish, and the British envoy in Madrid, John Hookham Frere, was determined that Moore and his men should stay. Whether Frere knew the danger the British army was in but considered even its destruction worth the political gain, or whether he was genuinely ignorant as to the inability of the Spanish military to provide meaningful support, can be debated. Whatever his motives, Frere pressed Moore to abandon any idea of a withdrawal and constantly promised military and material help from the Spanish. Reluctantly Moore agreed not to retreat, but he did instruct Baird to come no nearer to Salamanca but to halt on the Coruña road. News came in that every Spanish army save one had now been defeated and scattered. The one remaining army was poorly equipped, and somewhere between Salamanca and Madrid, under Castanos. It was never the purpose of the British army to defend Spain alone, yet it now seemed as if that was exactly what they were being expected to do. Frere still insisted that Moore stay, although by now French troops were probing Baird's defences at Astorga. Given that Moore was forbidden to retreat, there were only two options open to him. He could stay where he was and risk almost certain defeat; or he could cancel his previous orders to Baird, unite the army and go on the offensive. A further advance seemed as dangerous as a retreat, but at least it would meet Frere's demands, and by extension the politicians'.

On 27 November, just as Moore's messenger to Baird cancelling the previous orders to come no closer was setting off, the worst possible news arrived at Moore's headquarters in Salamanca. Castanos's army, the sole remaining Spanish one, had been roundly defeated at Tudela on 22 November. There was now nothing to stop the French falling on Salamanca. On 28 November Moore took the decision to retreat, whatever the politicians might say. Militarily he was right: even if Baird and Hope could join him before the French arrived the British would simply be surrounded and starved into surrender, while the French could supply themselves from Burgos. Orders went off to Baird and Hope telling them to fall back on Coruña ready for evacuation by sea. The withdrawal would not begin just yet, however, for frenzied remonstrations began to pour in to Moore's headquarters. Frere, the Spanish Junta and individual Spanish officers all appealed to the general not to desert Spain in its hour of greatest need. Even the British Minister in Madrid, Charles Stuart, suggested that the French successes had perhaps been exaggerated, the Spanish losses had not been so serious after all and more Spanish armies were being formed. Late on 2 December Moore was informed, by a letter from Frere in Talavera, that Spanish resistance around the capital was stiffening. Their success or otherwise would depend on what Moore might do. Once again messengers galloped off into the night with orders cancelling the retreat. Despite Moore's better judgement, the army would unite and would strike into Spain.

On 4 December Hope at last arrived at Alba, within easy reach of Moore, and with him were the bulk of that cavalry and the artillery, perforce sent with Hope as the road along which Moore's men had marched was considered unsuitable for either. Also on that day, although Moore did not know it, the French occupied Madrid.

Moore waited for ten days, hoping against hope that some sort of help might be forthcoming from the Spaniards. When it was not, Moore moved. He reached Toro on 15 December, Castronuevo on the 17th and Valderas on the 19th. On 21 December the army moved north east, towards Sahagun, and the British cavalry, moving ahead under Lieutenant General Lord Paget, occupied the town. It was to be a brief occupation, however, for Moore now heard that the French were moving north at last. The British were far from their naval support, had outrun their supply lines and were in grave danger of being cut off and destroyed. On Christmas Eve 1808 the retreat began. The weather was now bitterly cold, and snow and driving rain beat into the faces of the soldiers as the turned round to move in the direction of Coruña. On

Christmas Day, Portuguese scouts reported that Napoleon himself was only fifty miles away, with the main body of the French army. On Boxing Day, French advance patrols began to harry the retreating army, only just held off by the cavalry, the horse artillery, the light infantry and rifles who formed the rearguard. Discipline began to break down and half-starved men, who could not be supplied by the commissariat, looted such food as they could find along the retreat. Inevitably, when the men could not find food, they did find plentiful supplies of wine. Drunkenness, always the curse of the British army, became rife. Even the humanitarian Moore found himself forced to order the execution of more than one miscreant. Cavalry horses were shot because there was insufficient fodder for them all; drunken soldiers fell out of the line of march and either froze to death or were captured by the French; women unable to keep up were raped by French dragoons. It was a terrible retreat – one of the most harrowing in British military history – and it went on until 11 January 1809, when the remnants of Moore's once proud army straggled back into Coruña, to the waiting ships of the Royal Navy. In French eyes it was a resounding victory. Bonaparte returned to Paris on 2 January, leaving Marshal Soult to administer the *coup de grâce*.

The embarkation began, with Coruña now under siege by the French, but with British ammunition stocks now resupplied by the navy. Most of the troops got away, with only a few of the sick still there when the French marched in on 18 January. One who remained, and who would never return to England, was Sir John Moore. Fatally wounded by a cannon shot, he died on 11 January and was buried on the ramparts at night, wrapped in his general's cloak. Soult mounted a guard of honour on the grave and fired an artillery salute in his memory. Had Moore survived he would almost certainly have commanded the army in the Peninsula; but, given the importance of the navy and of working with allies, the result might have been quite different. Perhaps it was as well that Moore was left alone in his glory.

While Moore was doing his best to maintain British military prestige in the Peninsula, the court of inquiry into the Convention of Cintra completed its deliberations. All three generals were cleared of any impropriety, but only Wellesley left the court with his character unblemished. The court, while not expressly condemning Dalrymple and Burrard, made plain its disapproval. Neither was ever employed in a military capacity again.[23]

6

Talavera

On 22 January 1809, six days after Sir John Moore's death and burial at Coruña, and with the remnants of his army beginning to come ashore at Portsmouth, Sir Arthur Wellesley received the thanks of the House of Lords for his victory at Vimeiro. He replied by letter in a modest fashion, pointing out that to be given command of His Majesty's troops was in itself honour enough. On 27 January, when the House of Commons followed by voting their thanks, he replied briefly, thanking the House for the trust they had reposed in him. Shortly after Wellesley had resumed his seat, Colonel Gwylym Lloyd Wardle, radical MP for Okehampton, proposed that the House should examine the conduct of the Duke of York. The motion was precipitated by rumours and accusations that had been circulating for some time. It was alleged that certain commissions granted and appointments made by the Duke, as Commander-in-Chief of the British army, had been obtained by bribery, and that the Duke had enriched himself from public funds. The matter revolved around the Duke's mistress, Mary Anne Clarke, who was said to have acted as the go-between, taking money from those who sought the Duke's favours. Mrs Clarke, the wife of a bankrupt stonemason, was thirty-three in 1809. By all accounts pretty and vivacious, she had become the Duke's mistress in 1802, when he settled £1000 a year on her. Her favours do not appear to have confined to York, and there seems little doubt that she did take bribes against promises to influence her lover. When the Duke found out what was going on he ceased the association, cutting Mary Anne off with £400 a year. Heavily in debt, she attempted to resolve her financial difficulties by extorting money from the Duke. When he refused to be blackmailed, she persuaded her friend Wardle to raise the matter in the House.

Replying to the motion, the Secretary at War, Greville Leveson-Gower, promised that the House would have a full opportunity to examine the imputations against the Commander-in-Chief, and remarked that 'my gallant friend near me' could probably tell the House what state the army was in. The 'gallant friend' was Sir Arthur Wellesley, who, having ridiculed the suggestion that the Commander-in-Chief had embezzled funds from the public purse, told the House that, judging by the troops which he had taken over in Portugal in 1808, the army had never been in a better state. This happy circumstance, he insisted, was entirely due to the exertions of the Commander-in-Chief. There had, of course, been a great deal wrong with the army taken over by Wellesley in Portugal, but the deficiencies – lack of horses and an inefficient commissariat – had not been within the powers of the Commander-in-Chief to rectify, but lay with the Secretary at War and the Treasury. An inquiry was set up, by a Committee of the Whole House, and in February and March Wellesley gave evidence before it. The affair rumbled on.

Political memory is fickle. The House had congratulated Wellesley on the results of Vimeiro on 27 January, but on 2 February Samuel Whitbread MP, of the brewing family and an Opposition politician throughout the wars, demanded whether it was true that Sir Arthur Wellesley had, while fighting on the Continent, continued to draw his salary as Chief Secretary for Ireland. Wellesley replied that it was indeed true. He had made it clear to the Duke of Rutland, Lord Lieutenant of Ireland, that should another person be appointed to the Secretary's post in his stead then that would be perfectly in order, but the Duke 'out of personal kindness to myself' had chosen not to do so, and he had continued to receive part of his Secretary's salary. He made the final point that, while he was in command of the troops in Portugal, he had not received the full allowances for that appointment, 'one liable to very heavily increased expenses, which I did not feel in a position to be able to afford'. The matter was dropped. During what would turn out to be but a short sojourn in England, Wellesley also spoke in Parliament about the Irish Militia, the conduct of various officers of the army, telegraphs in Ireland, Cintra (again) and the Marquess of Wellesley's conduct as Governor-General of India (again). On 29 March 1809, in his last speech before resigning his seat, he introduced a Bill to extend inland navigation in Ireland.[1]

The British government had to decide what its next steps in the prosecution of the war should be. Moore, before his death, had said that Portugal was indefensible; and that if the French succeeded in Spain then they could not be resisted in Portugal. Wellesley thought otherwise. In a succinct memorandum, dated 7 March 1809, he suggested that Portugal could be defended, regardless of what might happen in Spain; and that, if that were done, then the situation in Spain too might be altered to the British advantage. He urged that the reconstitution of the Portuguese forces should be a priority. If the Portuguese regular and militia units were supported by British money (which Wellesley estimated as one million pounds for 1809), weapons and clothing, and trained and commanded by British officers, then a relatively small British force could, in conjunction with the Portuguese, not only defend that land but cause the French to commit a large number of men to the Iberian Peninsula. Wellesley thought that the British force should be in the region of 30,000 men. Although he did not expressly say so, Wellesley was advocating what came to be called the 'Spanish Ulcer', whereby the French could be bled of resources at relatively small cost to the Allies, or at least to the non-Iberian Allies. In his memorandum Wellesley stressed the necessity of the British army in Portugal having a sufficiency of cavalry and artillery - for the Portuguese had none, or very little - and that the commissariat must be British. Wellesley emphasised the importance of security. While British journalists were sometimes prosecuted for spreading what the government considered to be revolutionary propaganda, this was an age when the freedom of the Press was jealously guarded in England. As soon as the French read in the English newspapers that British staff officers had embarked for Portugal, then their troops in Spain would move in opposition. It was important, he concluded, that all men and stores must be in place before the public at home discovered what was happening.[2]

The British government did not, at this stage, accept that the Peninsula should be the primary focus of the British war effort. There also existed the possibility of operations on another front, in conjunction with Austria, which was anxious to take up arms again as soon as possible. The validity of Wellesley's proposal was recognised, however, and it was agreed that operations in Portugal should continue. Command of the Portuguese army by a British officer had already been conceded by the Portuguese, and they had actually asked for Wellesley. Impressed by Wellesley's memorandum on the defence of Portugal, Castlereagh and the Commander-in-Chief of the army had other plans for him, and on 2 March 1809 William Beresford was promoted to lieutenant general in the British army and appointed as Commander-in-Chief of the Portuguese army, with the Portuguese rank of marshal. Beresford was the illegitimate son of the Marquess of Waterford. Born in 1768 he had been commissioned in 1785, served with the 69th Foot at the siege of Toulon and had commanded the 88th Foot (the Connaught Rangers) as a lieutenant colonel in India, where Wellesley had first made his acquaintance. After India, Beresford accompanied Baird's force to Egypt, then served at the Cape, again under Baird. As a colonel he commanded the disastrous expedition to Buenos Aires in 1806/07, where his 1500 man force was hopelessly outnumbered and he was captured, but later escaped. In late 1807 he had been lent to the Portuguese as Governor and Commander-in-Chief of Madeira, before serving under Moore in Spain. Beresford's British promotion, which elevated him over many major generals who had been his senior, caused resentment, but he was a first-class administrator who spoke Portuguese. He at once began an energetic reform and rebuilding of the Portuguese army, using a nucleus of British officers who were persuaded to transfer by a free step in rank. With a few exceptions, Beresford got the sort of officer he needed, including a number of British sergeants commissioned as

11. Portugal and Spain: Area of Operations, 1809.

ensigns. In due course Portuguese battalions, integrated into British brigades, were to be a vital component of Wellesley's army.

The French soon recovered from their reverses at Rolica and Vimeiro. Capitalising on the expulsion of Moore from Spain, Marshal Nicolas Soult invaded the northern provinces of Portugal. Like many of the French revolutionary and Napoleonic generals, Soult had originally enlisted in the ranks of the French army. He was commissioned in 1792, after seven years' service, and moved rapidly upwards, being created a marshal in 1804. He was an experienced and highly thought of officer, having fought with distinction at Fleurus, in Germany, Switzerland, Genoa and Naples, and at Austerlitz, Jena and Eylau. By the end of March 1809 Soult's men had captured the whole of northern Portugal as far south as Oporto. There was panic in Lisbon. In London successively more frenzied appeals for help arrived from the Portuguese regency.

The British troops remaining in Portugal after Moore's withdrawal were under the command of Lieutenant General Sir John Craddock. Craddock, aged forty-seven in 1809, had served in the West Indies and as a brigade commander in Egypt, before being sent to India in 1803 as Commander-in-Chief Madras. While there, his insensitivity to Indian customs and culture was largely responsible for the mutiny of the East India Company's troops at Vellore in 1806, and he was recalled. After the removal from Portugal of Generals Dalrymple, Burrard and Wellesley following the Cintra affair, and with Moore away to the north in Spain, Craddock was appointed to command what was left of the army in Portugal. He was not an incompetent commander, but he lacked vision and was not considered by either the politicians (particularly Castlereagh) or the Commander-in-Chief of the British army as being suitable to command Britain's main overseas army. Craddock was now informed that he was to hand over the army to Sir Arthur Wellesley and transfer to Gibraltar. With Moore dead, Dalrymple and Burrard discredited, Craddock unsuitable and most others either already in posts elsewhere or unemployable for one reason or another, the way was now open to appoint Wellesley, his reputation untarnished by the Cintra inquiry, to the command in Portugal. He at once resigned both his seat in Parliament and his post as Chief Secretary for Ireland, and left England. More than five years would elapse before his return.

Lieutenant General Sir Arthur Wellesley KB, newly appointed commander of the forces in Portugal, left England on *HMS Surveillante* on 15 April 1809, after being delayed for a week in Portsmouth by bad weather. His career almost came to an abrupt end there, for the *Surveillante*, recently captured from the French and pressed into the service of the Royal Navy, very nearly sank off the Isle of Wight on her first night out of Portsmouth.[3] Colin Campbell, Wellesley's ADC, went down to the general's cabin to tell him that the ship's captain was considering ordering the 'abandon ship'. Finding Wellesley sleeping, Campbell shook him awake: 'we are likely to go to the bottom, put your boots on sir, and come on deck'. 'Boots be damned, I can swim better without them', was the reply, 'besides, there is a deal too much commotion on deck already'. The weather abated, and the ship did not sink.

Also travelling to Portugal, some on the same ship as Wellesley, others on ships which departed shortly after he did, were reinforcements for the army in Portugal. Two regiments of heavy dragoons, a regiment of hussars (light cavalry), the 24th Foot from Jersey and a brigade of light infantry would bring the total entrusted to his command to around 20,000 men. Horses were being shipped out as well, some for the artillery and two hundred for the commissariat. As there were no men of the commissariat available to care for their horses on the voyage, Wellesley had instructed the commanding officer of the 22nd Light Dragoons to furnish a hundred soldiers to act as grooms. On 22 April he landed in Lisbon and immediately threw himself into gathering together his new command. The next day he wrote to Beresford, commanding the Portuguese, and to Craddock, who had moved north to Leiria with the army, asking them to come and see him. He wished to discuss arrangements for the handing over of the army with Craddock, and consider future plans with Beresford. Craddock was known to be most unhappy at being superseded. In his letter, couched in courteous and placatory terms, Wellesley asked that the Adjutant General, the Quartermaster General, the officers commanding the Royal Engineers and the Royal Artillery, and the Commissary General should also come south. These were the principal staff officers of the army and Wellesley would need to impress his ideas and plans upon them without delay.[4]

In India Wellesley had been innovative, both in matters of organisation and of tactics. He had been able to create his own organisation and develop his own tactics because there had been little there to begin with. In the Peninsula Wellesley was rarely innovative. He took what was there and improved upon it, and made what was already in place more efficient, but the existing structure of the British army was not to be trifled with. As Wellesley often said, you must do the best you can with what you have. As has already been seen, there were no permanent staff officers nor dedicated headquarters in peacetime, these being found when necessary for an operation of war. British armies were deployed, administered and managed by the commander and his staff. In British armies there was neither chief of staff, nor any staff branch directly responsible for operations.

As in all European armies, the British infantry and the cavalry, supported by the artillery and the engineers, did the fighting. It was not enough just to have fighting troops, however, for they had to be directed, supplied, fed, paid, housed, moved, treated when sick or wounded and buried when dead. Without these functions an army could not operate; however brave and well trained its fighting soldiers might be, it would soon disintegrate without an organisation to keep it in the field.

At the top, and directing the whole army was the Commander-in-Chief, Wellesley, although he was more usually known as the 'Commander of the Forces'. He had a personal staff, which included a military secretary, who was responsible for promotions and appointments and confidential correspondence, and a number of ADCs. We have already seen that in peacetime an ADC might be little more than a well-bred ornament, but on campaign the role was very different. In addition to looking after the commander's personal administration in camp and in the field, these young officers – and

Wellesley had up to a dozen – were also the eyes, ears and messengers of their master. They often galloped long distances under fire to take an order to a subordinate commander, or to assess a situation on the commander's behalf. Lastly, the commander's personal staff contained a headquarters commandant, who was responsible for the siting and administration of the headquarters, and who worked for the Adjutant General in his spare time.

Immediately under the Commander of the Forces, and reporting directly to him, were the two main staff branches, those of the Quartermaster General and the Adjutant General. The Quartermaster General was originally responsible for movement, as well as supply. As movement was largely dictated by the particular operation in hand, so it was the Quartermaster General who became responsible for operations. The Quartermaster General looked after embarkation and disembarkation (particularly important when Britain relied on its navy to insert and supply troops on the coast of Spain and Portugal), military equipment, the provision of barracks in towns and cities, billeting when on the move, and the allocation of camp sites when billets could not be found. The more the army grew, the more work fell to the Quartermaster General. To assist the Quartermaster General there were Deputy Quartermaster Generals (DQMGs), Assistant Quartermaster Generals (AQMGs) and Deputy Assistant Quartermaster Generals (DAQMGs), some of whom were seconded to divisions. At a time when the ranks of staff appointments was not yet fixed, DQMGs were usually lieutenant colonels, AQMGs majors and DAQMGs captains, but they were often a rank lower. One of the AQMGs was responsible for the baggage of the army, assisted by a baggage master, usually an ensign or lieutenant found from one of the units in the army. As the care and movement of the army's baggage required some skill, and knowledge of the proclivities of soldiers and civilians to steal from it, the baggage master was often an officer commissioned from the ranks.

The Adjutant General was responsible for duties (the provision of sentries, advance guards, duty officers, fatigue parties and escorts); returns, of which there was a myriad, including ration states, sick and wounded, deaths, desertions, discharges and leave; general correspondence and discipline. To assist him he had Deputy Adjutant Generals (DAGs), Assistant Adjutant Generals (AAGs) and Deputy Assistant Adjutant Generals (DAAGs), some of whom would be attached to the various divisions. Later a civilian Judge Advocate General was added, his responsibility being to oversee courts martial and inquiries.

Attached to the headquarters and normally moving with it were the Staff Surgeon, who exercised a supervisory function over the army's medical officers, or surgeons, and was the commander's adviser on medical matters; a chaplain; an assistant commissary general, who not only saw that the headquarters was fed but was the commander's link to the commissariat service; an assistant provost marshal; and an assistant baggage master. Present too were the Officer Commanding the Royal Artillery and the Commanding Royal Engineer. The Officer Commanding the Corps of Guides had charge of a group of officers mounted on good horses who operated partly as route finders and partly as intelligence gatherers. This officer was also responsible for the army's post office and for communications within the army. The Officer Commanding the Staff Corps of Cavalry was in charge of the police and also responsible for what was described as 'other duties of a confidential nature' – which meant spying and the carrying out operations not allocated to a specific unit. The Provost Marshal, with his non-commissioned Assistant Provost Marshals (APMs), dealt with prisoners of war, deserters from the enemy and the army's own prisoners. While offences committed by officers and men subject to military law were normally brought to trial before a court martial, the Provost Marshal and his men were authorised to impose a summary sentence of death where they had actually witnessed the offence. On several occasions Wellesley found it necessary to remind officers of the army that this power lay with the provost staff alone, and other officers were forbidden to order the provosts to carry out such a sentence. APMs were supposed to be selected from amongst the more responsible NCOs of the army. Occasional errors were made, however, and in one general order Wellesley ordered the dismissal and return to his regiment of a sergeant APM after the commandant of Lisbon reported him as being often in a state of intoxication and incapable of doing his duty.

In addition to the military staff, enumerated above, there were a number of civil departments attached to the headquarters. The Inspector of Hospitals had his staff of deputy inspectors, physicians, staff surgeons, apothecaries, dispensers and hospital assistants. The Inspector, who was responsible for the medical aspects of hospitals, worked closely with the Purveyor to the Forces, who concerned himself with the hospital buildings, medical stores, the arms, accoutrements and clothing of men in hospitals, and the burial expenses of men who died in hospitals. The Paymaster General with his assistants and clerks ensured that the army was paid, albeit usually in arrears, while the Storekeeper General took charge of field equipment, tentage and heavy baggage. The post office reported to the Officer Commanding the Corps of Guides, and the mobile printing press produced all manner of orders, notices, proclamations and forms. Over all, military and civil, loomed the Comptroller of Army Accounts, with his inspectors and examiners, who spot-checked all accounts, from company to army, and carried out regular audits. The one account safe from the attentions of the Comptroller was that of the commissariat, which had its own audit team.

The commissariat was perhaps the most important, and certainly the most visible, of the civil departments attached to the army. The Commissary General, with his deputies, assistants, deputy assistants and commissariat clerks, presided over two branches: stores and accounts. Stores branch procured and provided the army's rations and much of its transport, while accounts ensured that everything supplied was authorised, signed for and, if necessary, paid for. Commissariat officers were civilians but held equivalent officer rank to their civil grade in order to imbue them with the authority they needed to carry out their functions. In 1809 the Commissary General was John Murray.

Also accompanying the army was the battering train, under the senior artillery officer. The battering train contained all the guns, ammunition and stores need to reduce a fortified town. Wellesley initially had none. Even when a battering train was added to the army it was never large enough, and there were always problems with its transport and movement. The pontoon train (again almost non-existent in April 1809) came under the Commanding Royal Engineer, and consisted of the equipment needed to bridge a water obstacle. The engineer park contained the equipment and stores needed for a siege – including shovels, gabions, fascines and scaling ladders - and also came under the chief engineer. The wagon train (somewhat improved since 1795 in Flanders but still known as the 'Newgate Blues') belonged to the Quartermaster General, as did the ordnance stores train (ammunition and explosives), while the commissariat had its own commissariat wagon train. One shadowy group, which reported directly to the Commander of the Forces, was a group of 'officers in observation', charged with collecting topographical information and intelligence about the enemy. These officers ranged much further than the corps of guides and often went well behind enemy lines. They were mounted on the best horses in the army and always wore uniform, to ensure that if captured they would not be shot as spies. They usually had to buy their horses themselves and, when a standard officer's charger cost around £18, some of the observing officers paid as much as £50. When the army occupied a town, or used it as a base for supplies or communications, a town major was appointed, with a town adjutant and an APM.[5]

As for the fighting troops, in the British line infantry the smallest recognised unit was a company. It could be split down into two half companies, or platoons, and was commanded by a captain assisted by two subalterns (ensigns or lieutenants). It consisted of eighty non-commissioned officers (NCOs) and men. Eight 'battalion companies' and two 'flank companies' (the grenadier and light companies) made up a battalion, theoretically commanded by a lieutenant colonel but, as we have seen, often by a major or even a captain. The established strength of a line infantry battalion, the ten companies plus officers and a small headquarters, varied from 850 to 1000 men (Guards battalions often being even larger). All the men in a battalion wore the same badge and the same colour of facing on their tunics, the identifying symbols of the regiment to which the battalion belonged. This caused confusion, for the British often used the terms battalion and regiment synonymously. Some British regiments had only one battalion, others two, some three or even four. The regiment in the British infantry was not a tactical formation: a regiment might have one of its battalions in India and another in Gibraltar (although more often one would be abroad, and the other at home recruiting and supplying drafts to its sister battalion on foreign service). The term regiment in all French and most continental armies *was* a tactical formation, of anything from three to six battalions all operating together.

The cavalry equivalent of a battalion was a regiment, numbering around 500 all ranks at full strength, and divided into troops (later squadrons). The role of the cavalry was changing, although not all cavalrymen realised it. Originally used for shock action, with heavily armoured troopers charging knee to knee, the cavalry in this war was be employed in reconnaissance, outpost duty, in pursuit, as a covering force and with rearguards, only occasionally being used to charge opposing cavalry or to finish off disorganised infantry.

Between two and five infantry battalions were grouped into a brigade, the number of battalions being dependent on the role of the brigade. A colonel, a brigadier general or a major general commanded a brigade. He had one ADC and one staff officer: the brigade major (actually a captain) and a deputy assistant commissary general.[6]

Up to now the British army had rarely been large enough to require any grouping larger than a brigade. On the few occasions when British expeditionary forces had been formed into divisions, these had been purely tactical formations and not administratively self-contained. Wellesley now formed his army into divisions, but constructed them so that they could operate independently, with their own artillery and administrative staff. In 1809 Wellesley disposed of four divisions; by 1814 there would be nine divisions, eight cavalry brigades, a number of independent infantry brigades, besides Portuguese formations and, occasionally, Spanish ones. Originally put together in an ad hoc fashion, the establishment of a division soon settled down. It was normally commanded by a lieutenant general or major general who was entitled to two ADCs. The divisional staff consisted of an assistant adjutant general and a deputy assistant adjutant general seconded from the army's AG staff; an assistant quartermaster general and a deputy assistant quartermaster general from the QMG; one or two officers of the Royal

Engineers (although initially these were in very short supply, and the army never did have sufficient); a staff surgeon; a chaplain; an assistant provost marshal; a baggage master; a detachment from the staff corps of guides; and a storekeeper of ordnance, who was responsible for the reserve ammunition and who came under the direction of the senior artillery officer of the division. To see to the division's supplies was an assistant commissary general with deputy assistants and clerks. The cavalry was excluded from the divisional organisation, being held separately, but sometimes with brigades or regiments detached to divisions for a specific task.

The army that Wellesley took over from Craddock in 1809 was relatively small, and not all the branches and departments were complete, but this was the basic organisation that would hold throughout the war, even though the number of staff officers and the size of the various departments increased as the army grew. Wellesley was fortunate in the Quartermaster General he inherited. Major General George Murray (no relation to the Commissary General) was three years younger than Wellesley and was a professional staff officer to his fingertips. He had been commissioned in 1789 and, after regimental service with the 3rd Foot Guards, entered the Quartermaster General's department in 1796. With one brief absence in 1811, he would serve Wellesley until 1814. The Adjutant General was Major General Charles Stewart, half brother of Castlereagh. Unlike Murray, who had no pretensions to being a field commander, Stewart saw his staff employment as merely a stepping-stone to command of armies. He was competent enough, but his search for involvement in operations, and a tendency to try to concentrate more and more power in his own hands and in that of his staff, meant that Wellesley could never trust him to the same extent as Murray. At this period the main headquarters staff officers were appointed by the Horse Guards, while all assistants and divisional staff officers had to be found from units in the army, which meant that regiments with a reputation for attracting intelligent and well-educated officers, like the 95th Rifles and the Guards, often found themselves short of officers with the troops, despite a regulation that not more than two captains and two subalterns from any one battalion were to be employed on the staff. Although there was by now an embryo staff college in England, it was not popular, largely because officers had to pay fees to attend and the lectures were mostly in French. Of the eighty-one officers who served in the Quartermaster General's department during the Peninsular War, a mere thirty-five had attended the college, while the Adjutant General's department had only one graduate. A commander, whether Wellesley himself or a divisional or brigade commander, had little say in the appointment of staff officers. He either took whomever the Horse Guards sent out from England, or such material as was offered up by regiments in the field. The exception was the appointment of ADCs, who were very much the commander's choice. The Commander of the Forces was entitled to three ADCs but he needed, and employed, more. Similarly, divisional and brigade commanders required more than the two and one ADCs allowed for in regulations. These extra officers had to be paid for and rationed by the commander, for which he received an allowance. In Wellesley's case the allowance was 9s. 6d. per day, insufficient to cover one extra ADC, much less the eight or nine that Wellesley actually had. Command of an army was not for the impecunious.

At this stage the French had over 325,000 men in the Peninsula, including 40,000 cavalry. Of these no fewer than 58,000 were in hospital, 25,000 were in garrisons, manning forts, guarding stores depots or on escort duties, while 50,000 protected the lines of communication back to France. This left 192,000 men available for operations, but in truth the French were severely overstretched. They had insufficient men to pacify Spain and to complete the occupation of Portugal. The French were consistently dispersing Spanish armies, but these dissolved into the countryside only to reform again. The French could control the towns and cities but increasing guerrilla activity meant that the countryside remained hostile. A combination of jealousy between the marshals and a French commissariat that was rudimentary prevented the French from concentrating their various armies except for short periods.

Wellesley was concerned with three French armies. Occupying northern Portugal, as far south as Oporto, was Marshal Soult with three weak infantry divisions and a cavalry division, or about 20,000 men in all. To the east, along the Tagus valley in Spain, was Marshal Victor with his corps of another 20,000 men, while further away, off to the north west of Spain, was Marshal Ney with a further corps. Victor (the name by which he was known - his full name was Claude Victor Perrin) had served in the ranks of the Bourbon army for ten years. When the Revolution came he joined a local volunteer corps and rose swiftly. He served at Toulon, where he came to Napoleon's attention. He fought at Marengo and Friedland, becoming a marshal in 1807. In Spain he had beaten Blake's Spanish army at Espinosa in November 1808. In Wellesley's view the immediate threat to the security of the British army was Soult, who was nearest and was actually in Portugal. The risk of Victor attacking the British flank, rear or supply lines by an advance across the (flooded) Tagus could be guarded against by sequestering all the boats along the river and having the Portuguese watch the river line to give early warning of any approach. If Soult could be dealt with quickly, then the British could go on the defensive in northern Portugal, turn eastwards and, in conjunction with the Spanish, confront Victor. It was unlikely that Ney could do very much in the immediate future, as he was too far away.

Wellesley's reorganisation of the army into a divisional structure was carried out without delay and, in a departure from established tactical wisdom, he attached a company of rifles to each division. Rifle regiments are often confused with light infantry, and both had a skirmishing role. Light infantry, an extension of light companies but formed into battalions, took their place in the line when their skirmishing role was over. Like all other soldiers of the line infantry, they were armed with the smooth bore musket and wore red tunics. Men in rifle regiments, on the other hand, were armed with the Baker rifle, which was accurate up to 300 yards (more in skilled hands), and dressed in dark green and black. Originally titled the Experimental Corps of Riflemen, the British now had two regiments of rifles, the 60th Rifles and the 95th Rifles, with five battalions between them. Riflemen were trained to work in pairs, ahead of the army and on the flanks, as skirmishers, snipers, scouts and ambush parties. They were highly trained and amongst the best troops of the army, although the slow rate of fire of the Baker rifle made it impractical to put them in the line. Rifle companies attached to divisions came either from one of the British rifle regiments or from the King's German Legion (KGL). This latter organisation, a miniature army in its own right, was formed from the remnants of the Hanoverian army after Napoleon had overrun their homeland. Their depot was on the Isle of Wight and they comprised line infantry, rifles, cavalry and artillery. While their quality deteriorated as the war went on, as reinforcements from any part of Germany had to substitute for Hanoverians, they were high grade troops and their standards of discipline were far higher than that of British units.

For the action against Soult, Wellesley had three British divisions, the British cavalry and a joint British and Portuguese force. His three divisional commanders were Major Generals John Sherbrooke, Edward Paget and Rowland Hill. Sherbrooke, commanding the 1st Division, was well known to Wellesley from his days with the 33rd Foot and India, and had become a major general in 1805. He had then served in Sicily and arrived in the Peninsula in June 1809. Edward Paget, commanding the 2nd Division, was a brother of Henry Paget, who had commanded Moore's cavalry with great distinction in the Coruña campaign. He had served in the Netherlands and in Egypt and led the reserve division under Moore. Originally nominated as second-in-command to Wellesley, this appointment was assumed by Sherbrooke (Paget's senior) on his arrival. Rowland Hill, commanding the 3rd Division, was one of sixteen children of a Shropshire gentleman and a nephew of the founder of the London Missionary Society. Commissioned at the age of eighteen in 1790, he had served at Toulon and commanded the 90th Foot in Egypt, a brigade at Vimeiro and a brigade at Coruña. He had great concern for and kindliness towards the common soldiers, to whom he was known as 'Daddy' Hill. Commanding the cavalry was Major General Stapleton Cotton, MP for Newark and, like Hill, the son of a Shropshire landowner. He too was well known to Wellesley from the Mysore War in India.

Sherbrooke's 1st Division had three brigades, the others two. With the exception of the Guards brigade (1st Division) and the KGL brigade (2nd Division), each brigade had a battalion of Portuguese. At this stage the Portuguese were very much learning their business, although Beresford's reforms were beginning to take effect, and many of the original elderly Portuguese officers had been replaced by younger men or by Portuguese-speaking British officers. Both the 1st and 2nd Divisions had two companies of British rifles each; the 2nd Division relying on KGL riflemen. The Anglo-Portuguese division, under Beresford, had two brigades, one composed of two British and one Portuguese battalions and five companies of rifles, and one of five battalions of Portuguese infantry. Cotton's cavalry numbered around 1500 men, from four British and one KGL regiments. The British artillery, of four batteries each of six guns, was held under Wellesley's personal command. Beresford's division had its own artillery (twelve guns) and cavalry (two squadrons or about 160 men) from the British 14th Light Dragoons.

Wellesley's plan was to mount a direct assault on Oporto from the south, under his own command. He sent Beresford's force off to the east, to get behind the French and cut them off should they be forced out of Oporto, and to prevent them linking up with Marshal Victor. In case of any interference by Victor, who might get across the Tagus and attack Lisbon, Wellesley created a fourth division to act as a covering force for the Portuguese capital. This division had two brigades, one British of four battalions and one Portuguese of ten battalions; two regiments of British and five squadrons of Portuguese cavalry; and three batteries of foot artillery and one of horse artillery (six pounders). The division was commanded by Major General John MacKenzie, from the Black Isle in Ross and fifty-six in 1809. He had originally joined the Marines, transferring to the 78th Foot in 1794. Beresford left Coimbra on 6 May 1810, while Wellesley himself departed on the 8th.

Wellesley marched north, covering eighty miles in four and a half days, meeting some French opposition on the way. This was only a covering force of cavalry with some infantry support and horse artillery, not the main French army. Wellesley attempted to cut them off, sending Hill's division along the coast in a fleet of small boats, but the French would not stand, and at two o'clock in the morning of 12 May they withdrew over a bridge of boats, across the Douro and into Oporto. The Douro runs east to west and reaches the sea at Oporto. As the British navy controlled the sea, Marshal Soult considered that a British attack on Oporto, if it came, would be by seaborne landing. He felt secure behind the Duoro, which was a formidable obstacle, being deep, fast flowing and 300 yards wide. The bridges had been destroyed and the French army had commandeered all boats in the area. Soult saw little threat from that direction and left only General Foy, with around 10,000 men, in and around Oporto, with the main army farther north watching the sea. Farther still to the north was a force of about 6000 men under General Loison, too far away to be able to affect what might happen at Oporto. Morale in the French army was not high, largely due to rumours of an incipient mutiny, which Wellesley knew about, which was said to be because of Soult's alleged ambitions to declare himself King of Northern Lusitania.[7]

Wellesley established his headquarters in a convent to the south of the river. From there he could see the town, its surrounds and the roads leading to it. French observation of the south bank was desultory, no more than a few piquets and roving patrols. On the far bank Wellesley noted a seminary, surrounded by a high wall which ran all the way down to the riverbank. The seminary was in a bend of the river, and seemed to be empty of French troops. Even if there were some French soldiers inside the seminary they could not see the stretch of river flanked by the wall. As no commander will march on a major water obstacle without means to cross it – and Wellesley's pontoon train was in embryo at this stage, and in any case many miles behind on the road – we may assume that he had a good idea that some means of crossing would be found. His observing officers had been scouting ahead of the main body, and one in particular had found the means to get at the French. This officer was Lieutenant Colonel John Waters, probably the most capable espionage agent in the Peninsula. Aged thirty-five and a native of Glamorgan, he was an accomplished linguist, speaking not only Spanish but the patois of many regions of Spain, which, along with his swarthy appearance, enabled him to pass himself off as a Spaniard. He also spoke fluent French, with a German accent, and often operated behind the lines, wearing uniform under a civilian cloak and hat, mixing with French troops, who took him for a native of Alsace. Waters had discovered a skiff moored on the south bank and had persuaded the inhabitants of Oporto to bring four barges, each of which could carry about thirty-five men, over to the south bank. Additionally, he reported that there was a ferry at Barca de Avintas, three miles upstream, which was not guarded by the French.

The British artillery was hauled up to the convent, from where it could fire at the town and on the roads leading to it. Wellesley ordered one brigade to move up the river and cross by the ferry as soon as possible. This was the KGL brigade in Paget's 2nd Division and was commanded by Major General John Murray (no relation to the quartermaster general or to the commissary general). The remainder would cross by barge. At ten o'clock in the morning of 12 May 1809 the first British troops, a lieutenant and twenty-five men of the 3rd Foot, crossed the river, ran into the seminary, found it empty of French soldiers and began to prepare it for defence. More men piled into the barges and began to cross. This was a highly risky operation. With a turnaround time of twenty minutes it would take an hour to get one battalion across, and it would take at least a battalion to hold the bridgehead long enough to be reinforced. If the French saw what was happening and reacted quickly enough, then the initial landings could be defeated. Wellesley's luck held, and more and more men piled into the seminary. At last, at about eleven o'clock, General Foy discovered what was happening and launched the first ill-prepared and hasty counter-attack. The seminary, surrounded by a stout wall nine feet high and with a strong parapet round its roof, was ideal for defence. The French attack, made with skirmishers and three line battalions, was beaten off. By now both Hill and Paget were across, and the British strength was building up, slowly but steadily. The French sent more battalions from the town to contain the crossing, but British artillery in the convent was able to cause considerable destruction as the French columns approached. As French battalions left the town the inhabitants swarmed down to the river, released the sequestered boats and brought them across to the British bank. By two o'clock in the afternoon the French realised that their position was untenable and began a disorderly withdrawal to the north, chased by Hill's division. Meanwhile John Murray, one of Wellesley least impressive brigade commanders, had got his brigade across by the ferry but had failed to position it where the French retreat could be cut off. Soult got away, but Wellesley, at a cost of around 150 killed and wounded, had driven the French out of a secure position, inflicting 500 casualties and capturing 1500 sick and wounded and fifty-eight guns, and had taken the second city of Portugal.

Wellesley was unable to begin the pursuit of Soult until the 15th. The British army was exhausted; and, while there was infantry, and some cavalry, on the northern bank of the Duoro, the guns, wagons, heavy baggage and stores all had to be ferried across. Beresford, however, supported by Murray's brigade, and helped by the Portuguese General Silveiro and the northern militia, was able to harry the retreating French. Cut off by Beresford and Murray on 14 May, Soult was forced to destroy his transport, blow up his guns and stores, and head off into the mountains by mule tracks, reaching Guimaraes on 15 May, where he was joined by Loison, whose men had been soundly trounced by the Portuguese militia on 10 May. There too was General Lorges, who had gathered together the various garrisons of northern Portugal, which had also destroyed much of their baggage and stores before evacuating their posts.

The pursuit went on, but the rain, which had been falling since the 13th, made the tracks along which Wellesley's army had to move almost impassable to wheeled transport. The infantry and the cavalry could move but they could not be adequately rationed. By 16 May Wellesley had heard from Beresford that he had blocked all routes to the east: Soult could not link up with Victor. In the early hours of 18 May Soult's army crossed the frontier into Spain. By now the British army had marched about 150 miles in ten days and could do little but snap at the heels of the French. Men began to fall out through exhaustion and hunger; to pursue any further would be to extend the thin line of communication and supply to breaking point. In any case, on the same day, 18 May, Wellesley heard from Major General MacKenzie that Marshal Victor had moved at last. He was reported to have come north across the Tagus and to be now at Castello Branco. It was time for Wellesley to turn south and east. Soult's army had been driven from Portugal, it had lost all its baggage and heavy equipment and had no artillery. Altogether Soult had lost around 4000 men, killed or captured by the British, or murdered by the Portuguese peasants when they left the line of march. Many of the survivors were without boots or weapons. It would be months before they could be effective again. Moore was avenged.[8]

Leaving the Portuguese militia, under Silveiro, to guard the northern borders of Portugal, Wellesley moved south. He soon found that Victor had not, after all, entered Portugal. There had been a reconnaissance in force across the border but the French had withdrawn. Wellesley had time to reconstitute his army, and it was time that was sorely needed. There was a shortage of clothing – especially boots – and insufficient hard cash to purchase supplies. The British government had hoped that the Portuguese authorities would accept bills of exchange drawn on London, but the Portuguese peasants were suspicious of bits of paper, and even the authorities would only accept them at a heavily discounted rate. Britain was Portugal's ally, and Portugal would cooperate totally in matters military, but if Napoleon defeated England then the bills would be worthless. Not for the last time Wellesley wrote to Castlereagh about the lack of professionalism among his officers, and the lack of discipline amongst the men. He was particularly concerned about a new procedure for courts martial, which placed more emphasis on evidence to prove the guilt of the accused, rather than the previous system, which largely relied on the opinion of the officer or officers sitting in judgement. 'They [the soldiers] are never out of the sight of their officers that outrages are not committed', Wellesley wrote. He was particularly concerned as to the effects of the behaviour of the troops towards the local inhabitants: 'there is not an outrage of any description which has not been committed on a people who have uniformly received us as friends, by soldiers who never yet, for one moment, suffered the slightest want, or the smallest privation'. That the soldiers were in fact underfed, and suffered because of cheap boots which wore out in a few weeks of marching, was irrelevant to Wellesley. As in India, he insisted that everything taken from the civilian population was to be lawfully requisitioned and paid for. To do otherwise would only turn the population against an army which some Portuguese (and more Spanish) thought was composed of heretics.

British army discipline was strict, and even the Prussians remarked upon its severity. The British flogged, imprisoned and executed far more than did their allies or their enemies, but still discipline broke down when the men were not directly under the supervision of their officers. The continental armies were conscripted from the broad mass of the population, which meant that there was a higher standard of education and morality in the ranks than was the case in the British army. The British army was composed entirely of volunteers, which led to a better standard of training, better marksmanship and an ability to carry out complex tactical manoeuvres, but inevitably reflected the society from which it was drawn. Taking the King's shilling was, for many, the last resort of the hopeless and underprivileged. Although the quality of recruit improved as the war went on, the majority of those who enlisted (and up to 1812 enlistment was for life) came from insanitary urban slums or from the impoverished countryside; many were on the run from the law and most had come from a life where simply to survive was a struggle. Life in the army was not easy either, although the soldiers did get fed, usually, and paid, eventually. The outrages referred to by Wellesley were a mix of thoughtlessness and deliberate crime. Men would cut down cork trees to construct makeshift shelters from the wet, or steal beehives, or despoil orchards, or catch and eat chickens and piglets, all of which destroyed the peasants' livelihoods. More serious was deliberate crime, often fuelled by drink. Stealing of plate from churches, robbing shopkeepers and thieving from billets were all prevalent offences. Military equipment was not immune, and the selling of cartridges, plundering of stores depots and the selling of army mules were regular occurrences. Commissariat convoys were more often at risk from British soldiers than they were from the French, and even in secure areas they had to be guarded by armed sentries to prevent their comrades from pilfering from them. If an officer or a sergeant did not command the guard, even it could not be trusted to deliver the convoy intact. Rarer were the crimes of assault, murder and rape, although these too did happen, and not only after the storming of a fortified town, when licence was generally tolerated in the immediate aftermath. In a life of strict discipline and drudgery, the only easily available outlet for the soldiery was in drink, and they would go to extraordinary lengths to get it, although in a country where almost every civilian made or stored wine this was not difficult. Wellesley wanted the law to be strengthened, to make it easier to punish offenders, and to have less reliance on legal niceties which could delay the carrying out of a sentence for weeks. Wellesley also made the point to Castlereagh that the old-established custom, whereby provosts could carry out a summary sentence of death if they had witnessed the offence, was itself of doubtful legality under the new regulations. Wellesley's other problem was his officers. If they sinned – and many did – it was, he felt, pointless bringing them to court martial because they were being judged by men who themselves were equally guilty. Things would improve, but Wellesley was always concerned about the discipline of his army, which throughout the war had a distressing tendency to break down during retreats, bad weather, periods of idleness, when opportunities for plunder were presented or when supplies were short.[9]

Wellesley also wrote to Huskisson, the Secretary to the Treasury, complaining that, of the £400,000 promised for operational expenses (mainly food, forage and local transport), only £100,000 had arrived. By 30 May he was demanding the outstanding £300,000 immediately. The problem was that, as Victor and the French had withdrawn, they had destroyed crops and farm implements in an area already known for its poor soil. Lack of hard cash and an inexperienced commissariat exacerbated the difficulties, which were inevitably blamed on the commissariat officers. August Schaumann, commissary to the 14th and 20th Light Dragoons at Braga, could produce only goat's meat and rye bread for the men and rye grass for the horses. The wrath of the exasperated brigade commander, Major General Payne, descended upon him. Schaumann explained that he had only just been appointed to the cavalry, that a Spaniard had stolen his mule, and that only rye grass grew in the area. It was not his fault. 'Very well', said Payne, 'then I forgive you, but in that case allow me to shit and spit on your commissary general, who is squatting comfortably in Oporto while he leaves us here to starve.'[10]

During this period the four infantry divisions were able to settle down in their new organisation, and more reinforcements arrived from England. Wellesley was in communication with the Spanish Supreme Junta and planned to cooperate with General Cuesta, the Captain General of Estramadura, against Victor. The latter, in accordance with orders from King Joseph Bonaparte in Madrid, had now withdrawn to Talavera in the Tagus valley, but had seized Alcantara, where the Tagus could be crossed. He might yet launch an attack towards Lisbon. Officers from Wellesley's staff were inside Spain, negotiating with General Cuesta, who promised much, including rations and transport for the British army once it crossed into

Spain, but discussions were long drawn out. Aged sixty-nine in 1809, Cuesta had consistently been beaten by the French since 1793. Grossly overweight and unfit, he travelled everywhere in a heavy coach, and on the rare occasions when he mounted a horse had to be held in the saddle by orderlies. He had the overweening pride of the Castillian nobleman that he was. Although he usually managed to conceal his resentment of a British army engaged in liberating his homeland – a feeling which many Spanish generals shared - his attitude, combined with his incompetence as a field commander, made him a difficult ally. The British never really understood Spanish mistrust, and could not comprehend why Spain refused to accept the status of Portugal, with the British directing the war effort. Cuesta knew well that John Hookham Frere, now British representative to the Spanish Supreme Junta, and the man who had refused to let Moore retreat in good time, was asking for Cuesta to be dismissed and for Wellesley to be appointed supreme commander of the Spanish forces. All this added to Wellesley's difficulties in a coalition war.

Unlike the Spanish, the Portuguese had no difficulty in surrendering supreme military command to the British. In order to make it clear that Beresford and the Portuguese army was under Wellesley's command, the Portuguese regency created Wellesley a marshal general of Portugal, one rank above that held by Beresford.[11]

On 11 June Wellesley received permission from the British Cabinet to take his army into Spain. By early June the army was marching to Abrantes, fifty miles on the Portuguese side of the frontier. The men had not been paid for two months, food was still short and indiscipline increased. A group of looters from the 42nd Foot (the Black Watch) were given 500 lashes each, and a murderer of a civilian was hanged. A company commander of the 43rd Foot was arrested and court martialled for negligence, after he and his officers had abandoned their men, who then dissolved into an unruly rabble.

The army reached Abrantes on 27 June and on the same day cash at last arrived, having taken ten days to travel the hundred miles from Lisbon. Wellesley often said that only a battle could restore the British army to its allegiance, and he intended that a battle should take place. His intention was for Spanish forces to prevent any reinforcements reaching Victor, while he and Cuesta would attack at Talavera. By 10 July a series of forced marches, covering 150 miles in thirteen days, had brought the army to Plascenia, where Wellesley and Cuesta met. Wellesley was late, and an inspection of the Spanish army was carried out by torchlight. Wellesley was not impressed by what he saw. As Cuesta refused to speak French and Wellesley knew no Spanish, joint planning took place through the medium of a Spanish colonel (later major general), O'Donohue.[12] On the assumption that Victor could not be reinforced, the Anglo-Spanish armies, numbering 53,000 in total,

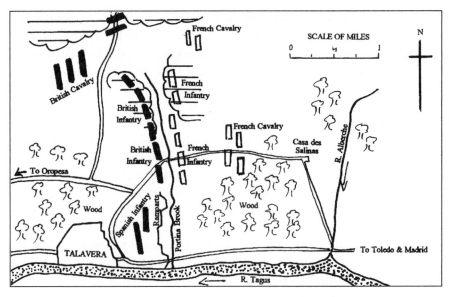

12. The Battle of Talavera, 27 and 28 July 1809.

should be more than a match for Victor's 20,000. Unfortunately, the Spanish had been unable to prevent Victor being joined by 22,000 men under General Horace-François-Bastien Sebastiani. Aged thirty-seven and a Corsican, like his master Bonaparte, Sebastiani had originally been intended for the priesthood but instead had accepted a commission in the French army in 1789. He had served in Italy, at Marengo and Austerlitz, and was sent to Spain in 1808. He was regarded as brave but careless and indolent.

The British and Spanish armies concentrated at Oropesa, and on 21 July began to advance eastwards, on either side of the Tagus. French intelligence, unable to move in bodies less than a squadron of cavalry strong for fear of being ambushed by guerrillas, failed to detect the Allied approach. By 23 July Wellesley was within striking distance of the French and wanted to launch an immediate surprise attack. The opportunity was lost when, after Cuesta refused to take part, the French located the Allied armies and Victor withdrew down the Madrid road. Cuesta, recovering his courage, insisted, against Wellesley's advice, on pursuing the French. Wellesley and the British army occupied Talavera but, when Victor was reinforced by a further 12,000 men rushed up from Madrid, Cuesta's army received a bloody nose and scuttled back to Talavera and the protection of the British. The British were furious, particularly when they had to detach troops to cover the Spanish retreat on 27 July, suffering casualties in the process. Most British officers blamed Cuesta personally. Even Wellesley began to form a contemptuous view of the

Spanish army that would never be completely eradicated, although he was enough of a diplomat never to allow the Spaniards to see his true feelings.

The tables were now turned: far from pursuing an inferior French army, the British and Spanish were now outnumbered by Victor. There was no alternative but for the Allies to take up a defensive position at Talavera and wait for the French. Wellesley spread his troops along two miles of rising ground running south to north, with his right flank on the River Tagus. He placed the Spanish army in and around the town, where they were partially protected by the old town walls and by hurriedly constructed ramparts. The British and KGL infantry occupied the rest of the line and the cavalry was placed on the northern, left, flank to prevent the French attacking the Allied flank or rear and to give warning should any of the other French armies approach. The main line followed a small brook, the Portina, which, while no great obstacle, did give cover for skirmishers and marksmen. Wellesley himself was nearly captured by French light infantry on the morning of 27 July when reconnoitring along the Tagus, but his horse soon outpaced the heavily burdened French.

On the same evening, as Wellesley and his staff were marshalling the Spanish battalions into their positions in front of Talavera, some French dragoons appeared to the front of the Allies, about a mile away across the plain. The Spanish panicked. Somebody gave the order to fire and from the entire Spanish army there erupted a volley of musketry, none of which had any effect whatsoever upon the distant French. Frightened by the noise of their own firing, four Spanish battalions dropped their weapons and fled to the rear. Included in the flight was Cuesta's coach, although Cuesta himself was not in it. The terrified soldiers ran back about four miles, plundering the British baggage train on the way, before order was restored. In Wellesley's own words:

> This practice of running away, and throwing off arms, accoutrements and clothing, is fatal to everything, excepting a reassembly of the men in a state of nature, who as regularly perform the same manoeuvre the next time an occasion offers. Nearly 2000 ran off on the evening of the 27th, from the battle of Talavera (not 100 yards from the place where I was standing), who were neither attacked nor threatened with an attack, and who were frightened only by the noise of their own fire: they left their arms and accoutrements on the ground, their officers went with them; and they, and the fugitive cavalry, plundered the baggage of the British army which was sent to the rear. Many others went whom I did not see. Nothing can be worse than the officers of the Spanish army; and it is extraordinary that when a nation has devoted itself to war, as this nation has, by the measures it has adopted in the last two years, so little progress has been made in any one branch of the military profession by any individual, and that the business of an army should be so little understood.[13]

King Joseph Bonaparte and his military adviser, Marshal Jourdan, were now present with the advancing French army. Jean-Baptiste Jourdan owed his military career to the Revolution, and had been both politician and soldier. Although he had fallen out with Napoleon over the coup of 1799 – Jourdan favoured a republic over a consulate or an empire – he had been rehabilitated and had followed Joseph from Naples to Spain. Jourdan's position was difficult. The other marshals in Spain were nominally subject to his instructions, but they were forever quarrelling amongst themselves and would appeal directly to Napoleon over Jourdan's head. While the King was supposedly in command of the French army at Talavera, with Jourdan to advise him, the strategy was largely dictated by the more forceful Victor. Having chased the Spanish all the way back to the British defence line on 27 July, Joseph and Jourdan took a cautious view. The French did indeed, just, outnumber the Allies, but they had nowhere near the three to one superiority generally considered necessary for a successful attack on a defended position. Other French armies – those of Soult (now reconstituted after its defeat at Oporto), Ney and Mortier – were hurrying south. Once they arrived – and their vanguards might begin to appear on 28 July – the French would have overwhelming superiority in infantry, cavalry and guns, and could cut the British off from their bases in Portugal and rout them utterly. Victor, dissenting, urged an immediate attack. He had considerable experience of beating Spanish armies, and believed that Cuesta's force could be discounted. What little he had seen of the British so far had not impressed him. An attack now would be a walkover. Victor, no doubt partially motivated by a wish to keep the anticipated victory for himself rather than share it with the other marshals, had his way.

The battle of Talavera began with a French night attack, which very nearly succeeded owing to British staff officers having placed the troops in the wrong position. The assault was beaten off by a counter-attack organised by Hill, and resumed the next morning with a French artillery bombardment. By seven o'clock in the morning of 28 July the skirmishers of both sides had begun their private war. Then the French launched an infantry attack in column against the British centre, which was beaten off by superior musketry. There was now a brief and unofficial armistice, during which both sides brought in their wounded and drank from the brook. Again the French attacked, with 30,000 men this time, and again they were driven back. A bayonet charge in pursuit by the Guards and the KGL had to be recalled when it hit the French reserve columns, but the men rallied just in time to stop the French exploiting the gap left in the British line. Again the disciplined volleys of musket fire from the British line tore into the French columns, and the French reeled back, pursued this time by Cotton's cavalry. A French attempt to turn the northern flank using nine battalions of infantry was foiled by British and KGL cavalry supported by horse artillery. The cavalry charged into an unseen valley, almost a ravine, and took around two hundred casualties, but the survivors pressed on and engaged the French cavalry. The French infantry formed squares, the KGL cavalry could not penetrate them, but they made excellent targets for the horse artillery. By late afternoon French enthusiasm had petered out. They had made no impression on the British position and withdrew during the night.[14]

Strategically the Battle of Talavera brought few advantages to the British, except, of course, that the army was still in being. It was one of Wellesley's fiercest battles, and his casualty return showed 857 killed (including forty officers and twenty-eight sergeants), 3553 wounded (including 195 officers and 165 sergeants) and nine officers, fifteen sergeants and 159 rank and file missing.[15] This was almost a quarter of his strength. The casualty figures were made worse by a grass fire in no man's land, in front of the British centre, and probably started by burning musket wads, from which many wounded could not be extricated. The French lost about seven thousand, or a sixth of their strength; Wellesley's returns also showed the capture of fifteen guns and two howitzers. He had given the British a victory, even if his half-starved soldiers, still on half rations as they had been for the past month, hardly appreciated it. On 26 August Lieutenant General the Honourable Sir Arthur Wellesley KB was created Baron Douro of Wellesley and Viscount Wellington of Talavera in the English peerage. It would be over a year before the British army would fight another major battle in the Peninsula.

7

The Defence of Portugal

Major battles are much more than the simple sum of individual efforts. The difference between an army and a murderous mob is concentration of effort brought about by discipline, training and tactics. If strategy can be defined as the art of winning wars, then tactics are the art of winning battles. As Talavera was, in many ways, a microcosm of Wellington's way of making war, it is apposite to examine the tactics of the period.

All belligerents of the early nineteenth century adopted similar tactics, which were dictated by the weapons available and the ground upon which those weapons were employed. In essence, war could be divided into four phases: attack, defence, withdrawal and siegecraft. The attacker's aim was to assemble his army in a location from where he could launch an assault on his opponent, who might be well aware of the threat and be in a defensive position. While on the move the attacking army had to be protected from being attacked itself. Moving long distances in battle formation was slow, so armies generally moved in what was known as column of route until they were within striking distance of the enemy. For the infantry this was a simple 'crocodile', of three or four ranks of men, each following the man in front. Company commanders and above rode horses, while their juniors marched on foot. The baggage would either bring up the rear or, in relatively safe areas, leave well before the main body so as to be available when the army halted for the night. The marching column, which could stretch for miles, would be protected by the cavalry and by the infantry's own skirmishers – light infantry and rifles.

The battle would generally begin with an artillery bombardment, whereby the attackers hoped to break up the enemy defence line and cause casualties. The defenders would use their artillery to disrupt the attacking formations. The next stage would be the clash of the skirmishers. As we have seen, the British army had recently introduced light infantry and riflemen, who would go ahead of the main attack to drive back the enemy's own skirmishers and to cause casualties to the main defence line. The skirmishers fought in open order, spread out and using cover. Wellington used a much higher proportion of his army as skirmishers than did the French, whose infantry often thought they had reached the main British line when they had in fact only come up against skirmishers. The French equivalent of the British light infantry battalion was the *tirailleur* battalion, while their line battalions' own integral skirmishers were the *voltigeurs*. The French army had no rifles: Bonaparte had ordered this weapon withdrawn in 1802 because of its slow rate of fire. This meant that British riflemen could begin to cause casualties to the attacking French at a range at which the French could not reply. While riflemen could not cause the mass destruction of close range volley fire, they could pick off officers and colour bearers and, as the French infantry could make no reply, this had a considerable effect on morale.

Once within artillery range of the defenders, the main body of the attacking army would move from column of route into column. At battalion level, each company pivoted on its leading man and wheeled right or left until each company was in line, with the companies one behind the other. Once within musket range, or preferably just before, the battalion would perform another drill movement to bring it into line, with each company level and the whole battalion in an extended line. The purpose of this latter formation was to allow maximum use of firepower against the defenders. At a range of around one hundred yards the attackers would halt, fire one or two volleys and then fix bayonets and charge the enemy. In fact bayonet charges were very rarely pressed home: either the defenders would drive the attackers off by their own volleys of musketry, or they would retire, leaving the ground to the attackers. Attack was not solely the preserve of the infantry. All armies advocated the use of cavalry and artillery to support the attacking infantry, the artillery to move up behind the attacking battalions and the cavalry to attempt to turn the flanks.

So much for the theory of the attack. The problem was that the performance of complicated evolutions while under fire needed steady troops with a great deal of training. The French knew perfectly well that an attack should be delivered in line, so that all the defenders were engaged and so that the maximum weight of fire could be delivered. In reality, partly due to lack of training in their conscript armies, but more often due to an inability to co-ordinate their efforts, the French nearly always attacked in column. This was of course good for morale – men were packed more densely than they would be in line – and if the column did close with the defenders then shock action would punch a hole in the defence, allowing the whole line to be rolled up. Against France's European enemies this tactic generally worked: the sight of a French column rolling on, seemingly unstoppable, with the drummers beating the *pas de charge* and the men cheering '*Vive l'Empereur!*', must have been terrifying to inexperienced troops, who often fired one ragged volley and then disintegrated.

An army in defence would try to protect its flanks, either by anchoring them to geographical features impassable to the enemy, or by posting its cavalry there. The infantry would line the front, in three or four ranks, and would hope to blast the attackers away with musket fire. Wellington's army in the Peninsula was almost always outnumbered by the French, and so most of his battles were perforce defensive ones. Wellington's defensive tactics were not new but an adaptation of those in Dundas's *Regulations*. Dundas laid down that infantry in defence should form in four ranks, the first three ranks available to fire while the fourth provided battle casualty replacements. Wellington almost always formed his men in two ranks. This not only allowed him to cover a wider frontage – important when his army was almost always numerically smaller – but it meant that every man could make his fire felt. Despite the financial stringency imposed upon it, the British army was the only one that regularly fired live ammunition in peacetime training. The British soldier spent mind-numbing hours of every week practising loading and firing his musket, an operation which required no fewer than twenty separate actions just to load and fire one round. The weapon itself had been standardised in 1716 (and would remain in service until 1845). Known as the 'Brown Bess' (from an earlier matchlock issued under Elizabeth I), the standard infantry musket was a smooth bore, muzzle-loading flintlock. The barrel was thirty-nine inches long and had a diameter of .76 inch. The musket weighed eleven pounds and fired a one ounce lead ball. The diameter of the ball was .71 inch, which made for ease of loading but also inherent inaccuracy. As the French musket was similar, but of slightly smaller bore, the British could fire captured French ammunition, but not vice-versa. The only way to ensure effective musket fire was to pack men shoulder to shoulder and have them fire in unison at close range. Musket cartridges came made up and wrapped in paper. To load, the soldier canted his musket forward, gripping it by the point of balance in his left hand. He then opened the pan and pulled the cock back to half-cock. Taking a cartridge from his pouch he bit off the bullet end, retaining the ball in his mouth, and sprinkled a little powder in the pan of his musket, closing the frizzen to prevent the powder from falling out. Bringing the butt of his musket to the ground the soldier then poured the remaining powder down the barrel, spat in the ball and followed this with the cartridge paper, which formed a wad and prevented the ball from rolling out. He then withdrew the ramrod from its keepers under the barrel and rammed the load well down the barrel. Once he had replaced the ramrod the musket was loaded. To fire, the man brought his musket to the front of his body in the 'present' position, pulled the cock back to full cock, aimed (there were no sights, so he looked along the barrel) and pressed the trigger. The trigger action allowed the cock to spring forward, when a flint held by a screw struck the frizzen, simultaneously opening the pan and causing a spark. The spark ignited the powder in the pan, and this mini-explosion flashed through a small hole from the pan to the main charge in the barrel, firing the round. The musket had a fierce recoil and the ammunition used black powder; after firing a few rounds men had bruised shoulders, a raging thirst from biting into the powder, and could see very little. Each man also had a bayonet, seventeen inches of good quality steel in the case of the British; very inferior steel in the case of the French (whose bayonets often bent).

The rate of fire was two, or at the most three, rounds a minute. To make sure that fire was continually directed at the enemy, volleys were staged, either by having one rank firing while the other reloaded, or firing by companies or half companies, in which case the volleys rippled up and down the line. Within a battalion a common method of staging volleys was to begin with the flank companies, that is those on the extreme left and right, followed by those next to them, and so on until the two centre companies had fired, after which the whole process began again. At a rate of fire of two rounds a minute, and with men packed shoulder to shoulder in two ranks, firing straight to their front, an attacker would face at least four rounds a minute for every yard of front. An attacking column, however, covered a smaller frontage than defenders in line, so the latter would concentrate all their fire at the column, with those men not directly opposite the enemy firing inwards. This would double the number of rounds per yard of front. Heavily laden infantrymen took about thirty seconds to charge a hundred yards, with four volleys directed at each attacker. Small wonder that charges were rarely pressed home against defending infantry who stood their ground and continued to fire what Wellington referred to as clockwork volleys. British infantry did stand their ground, and the superior firepower of the line almost always beat the column, where only those men in the front two or three ranks could fire their weapons. [1]

As the musket was too long to be loaded in the lying position, defending infantry had perforce to stand up, thus presenting a target themselves. Wellington made great use of reverse slopes, that is he began a defensive battle with his infantry behind the feature which he was defending, with only his skirmishers and artillery forward. Often he would have the infantry lie down, giving them some protection against artillery rounds which came over the hill. At the critical moment, as his skirmishers began to withdraw, Wellington would have his infantry stand up and move forward over the slope, from where they could begin their drilled volleys. The attackers could never be sure exactly where the British infantry was, while Wellington could move men along to threatened areas using the cover of the reverse slope. This required careful coordination and a cool head, both of which Wellington had in abundance.

In the attack officers led from the front, while in defence they controlled the fire from behind or between companies and battalions, their orders being relayed by drumbeat (light infantry and rifles passed orders by bugle and whistle). Sergeants usually brought up the rear, using their halberds (a form of poleaxe) held horizontally to keep men in line and to level musket barrels.

Unsupported infantry were at risk from cavalry, who would try to turn their flanks or attack from the rear. The standard drill for infantry caught in the open by cavalry was to form battalion squares, a complicated drill movement, which took a well-trained battalion twenty seconds. The square was actually a rectangle, thirty-five yards by twenty-five yards, with three companies on each of two faces, and two on the others.[2] Men were packed into four ranks on each side of the square, with the front rank kneeling with bayonets fixed. As no horse will charge something that he cannot jump over or gallop through, infantry in square were perfectly safe provided they did not panic and break the square. If the square was broken and cavalry could get inside, then the end was usually swift and certain. In square, the men in the front rank rarely fired at all, except in emergency, while those behind them fired by ranks. The men of the fourth rank, while they could fire, were more often used to replace men killed or wounded. The accepted ploy when attacking infantry with cavalry was to use the cavalry to force the infantry into square, then use artillery to blast holes in the squares through which the cavalry could pass. This required a degree of coordination which the French hardly ever managed and which the British rarely attempted.[3]

In the immediate aftermath of Talavera Wellington's inclination was to march on Madrid, the capital of French-occupied Spain. This plan came to nothing when General Cuesta, smarting with jealousy and having suffered a stroke, withdrew his contingent and abandoned Wellington's wounded, which he had undertaken to protect, to the French. It was also confirmed that Ney's French army was marching south. Left on his own, Wellington was in real danger of having his tenuous supply lines to Portugal cut by the French. The Spanish were unwilling or unable to provide the needed supplies and eventually, on 13 August, with only one day's rations left, Wellington had no alternative but to withdraw his hungry soldiers to the Guadiana valley, where they were spread out over forty miles to watch the frontier. He established his own headquarters in the fortified Spanish town of Badajoz. For the time being he was safe, but the area was infested with mosquitoes and men began to go down with 'fever' (actually malaria) and there were serious outbreaks of dysentery. For all this, they could at least be fed and supplied, and could begin to recover from the rigours of the campaign so far. At this point Richard, Marquess Wellesley, was appointed British Minister to the Spanish Supreme

Junta, whose seat of government was Seville. Once again the Wellesley brothers could work together to further British interests, although the marquess found it more difficult than his younger brother to be civil to the Spaniards, once telling a member of the Junta that he would not trust the protection of his favourite dog to the Spanish army.

Despite Wellington's elevation to the peerage, vociferously opposed by the Whigs, the British government had not yet decided to place all its military resources at his disposal. [4] There was still a yearning to do something nearer home, in conjunction with the Austrians. On 11 August 1809 40,000 British troops, escorted by thirty-five ships of the line and twenty-three frigates, landed on the island of Walcheren, part of Zeeland in Holland and at the mouth of the strategically important River Scheldt. The land forces commander was the Master General of the Ordnance, Lieutenant General John Pitt, 2nd Earl of Chatham, and elder son of Pitt the Elder. Aged fifty-three in 1809, Chatham had followed a political as well as a military career. In the administration of his brother, Pitt the Younger, he had been First Lord of the Admiralty from 1788 to 1794, Lord Privy Seal from 1794 to 1796 and then Lord President of the Council until 1801. He was Master General of the Ordnance from 1801 to 1806, and again from 1807, and had been (briefly) considered for command of the Peninsular expedition. Chatham had been a useful cabinet member, and a more competent Master General of the Ordnance than many of his predecessors, but while he had commanded a brigade in the expedition to North Holland in 1799 he was not a field soldier, being excessively idle and lacking breadth of view. At first things went well, however, and Flushing, on the western Scheldt, was captured on 13 August. Chatham should now have marched on Antwerp, which would probably have fallen to him, but instead he allowed himself to be distracted by the inevitable supply problems and remained on Walcheren. The Austrians, having been soundly beaten by Napoleon at Wagram on 5 and 6 July, were in no position to help, and Napoleon sent Marshal Bernadotte to command the defences of Antwerp. [5] Bernadotte, who had been sent off the field in disgrace at Wagram for his mishandling of the 9th Saxon Corps, cobbled together sufficient troops, mainly local volunteers, to defend Antwerp and to seal off Walcheren from the mainland. [6] There was now nothing that Chatham could do but re-embark his troops, which he did on 20 September. He had lost 106 men killed in action, and four thousand dead of disease (mostly from malaria).

The British government could not escape censure for the failure of Walcheren. The Prime Minister, the Duke of Portland, had a stroke and resigned in October 1809, dying shortly afterwards. Canning, the Foreign Secretary, resigned, fought a duel with Castlereagh, and, having been shot in the thigh, was absent from politics for some months. Castlereagh then resigned as Secretary for War and the Colonies. All this was not necessarily to Wellington's disadvantage, although he regretted the passing of Castlereagh (who would return as Foreign Secretary in 1812). The new Prime Minister, Spencer Percival, recalled Marquess Wellesley from Seville and appointed him Foreign Secretary, while Lord Liverpool (a staunch Wellington supporter) became Secretary for War and the Colonies. One of Marquess Wellesley's first acts as Foreign Secretary was to appoint his brother Henry as British Minister to the Spanish Supreme Junta. It was beginning to dawn on the British government that the only British army in being on the European mainland, and likely to achieve anything, was that commanded by Wellington.

The Walcheren fiasco reignited the furore over the Duke of York's alleged corruption in the selling of commissions. The parliamentary committee which was supposed to be looking into the affair had been quiescent of late but now hearings began again in earnest. It could not be shown that York had ever profited from his mistress's activities (and he had probably not), but the matter was a major embarrassment and the Duke was forced to resign his office. (It was a temporary absence, for he was able to resume his post in 1811, to the great benefit of the army and the nation.) In York's place as Commander-in-Chief the King, on the advice of ministers, recalled from retirement General Sir David Dundas, author of *Regulations* and known to all as 'Old Pivot' from the style of manoeuvres which he advocated. Dundas (no relation to Henry Dundas, Secretary at War) was seventy-four when he became Commander-in-Chief. He achieved little in that office, being noted mainly for a conviction that age equalled suitability for promotion, but he did little harm either and he supported Wellington to the best of his (somewhat enfeebled) ability.

After Talavera Wellington knew that Portugal was safe for a while. His immediate task was to keep it safe. Only then could he consider what to do to help the Spanish. Despite his increasing irritation with the Spanish, their broken promises and their badly led armies, which he expressed in letters to Castlereagh, to British ministers with the Spanish and, couched in more restrained language, to the Spanish Supreme Junta itself, Wellington knew very well that he could not win the war without them. Britain and Spain had few interests in common, other than a desire to defeat the French, and when Spain had been allied to the French Britain had attempted to wrest its South American colonies from it. Even now, the British were sympathetic to independence movements in those colonies, pressing for trade advantages from Spain in return for help against the French. Despite lack of military capability, the Spanish did tie down large numbers of French soldiers and their cooperation was essential if a British army was to have any hope of remaining in the Peninsula. Spain had to be kept in the war, but relations were not advanced by the insistence of the Spanish on embarking on an ill-advised autumn offensive. This was roundly defeated everywhere, notably at the battle of Ocana, on 19 November 1809, when Cuesta's replacement, General Ariezago, with 53,000 men, lost 5000 killed and wounded and 20,000 prisoners to a French army half his size commanded by Jourdan and Soult, whose casualties were only 1700.

Wellington was still concerned about the discipline of his army, and now he was having problems with the women as well. The army discouraged marriage, but a number of soldiers' wives were officially on the strength (that is they had married legally, with their commanding officer's permission and within the permitted quota) and were allowed to be taken on service. The number allowed in the Peninsular army was six wives per company, chosen by lot. These women were entitled to half the soldier's official ration, with a quarter ration issued for each child. Apart from the issue of rations, no arrangements whatsoever were made for the wives, and it was not until much later in the century that married quarters would be provided. The wives were an encumbrance to the army but they did perform useful services, assisting the surgeons and earning pin money by cooking, doing laundry and carrying out repairs to clothing. They were supposed to move in the rear of the army, with the baggage train, but were often worse plunderers than their husbands, roving far and wide in the search of extra food and comforts. Often the commissariat officers arrived at a village to purchase victuals for the troops, only to find that all available foodstuffs had already been bought up by the women. On 23 August 1809 Wellington issued a general order requiring women leaving camp to have a passport signed by the commanding officer of their regiment, and forbidding them to buy bread within six miles of the location of any division of the army. Wellington was later accused of permitting the flogging of women caught looting by the provosts – thirty-six lashes on the bare bottom was quoted – and it probably happened.[7] On 7 September Wellington was complaining about a resurgence of the stealing of beehives, and the next day he wrote to John Charles Villiers, British ambassador to Portugal, to clarify the position of Catholic soldiers wishing to attend Mass. Wellington explained that the law as it stood prohibited the attendance at Mass of soldiers of the British army, except in Ireland. As far as he, Wellington, was concerned, soldiers could attend Mass in Portugal, and no one would ask any questions, provided that the men actually participated in the service and were not there simply to 'gawk'. He pointed out that while there were whole regiments of Catholics in his army, who were not in any way prevented from attending Mass, he knew of no cases where they actually did so, unless it was to wheedle drink out of the Portuguese by making the sign of the cross. Wellington's only caveat was that he would not tolerate attempts by local priests to persuade and induce soldiers to practise their religion – attendance was to be left to the individual's own conscience.[8]

Officers were not immune from censure, and on 12 October Wellington wrote to Brigadier General Slade, commanding a cavalry brigade, expressing his displeasure at the result of a court martial over which Slade had presided. Lieutenant William Pearse, of the 45th Regiment, had been accused of taking part in an affray in a brothel. The court found that Pearse had actually assisted in quelling the affray and ordered an honourable acquittal. Wellington did not dispute the facts of the case, but pointed out that, as Pearse should never have been in a brothel in the first place, the word 'honourable' must be deleted from the findings of the court. (Pearse was to be killed at the storming of Ciudad Rodrigo in January 1812.)[9]

Wellington realised that the French were bound to invade Portugal. Of the 325,000 French troops in Spain a large number were already engaged in attempting to subdue the interior and in besieging Cadiz, but around 85,000 might be available for operations in Portugal. Wellington, with his 40,000 Anglo-Portuguese, could not possibly confront this number in open conflict. All he could do was to plan for a campaign of delay and attrition for the coming year, 1810, while avoiding a pitched battle. Whenever the French came, Lisbon had to be defended. It was the Portuguese capital, and the main British base, where the Royal Navy could land supplies and reinforcements. Without Lisbon neither the British army, nor an independent Portugal, could survive.

As early as October 1809 Wellington, with his Chief Engineer, Major (acting Lieutenant Colonel) Richard Fletcher, was riding round the hills north of Lisbon examining how a French advance might be countered. Fletcher, who served as chief engineer until his death at the storming of San Sebastian in August 1813, was aged forty-one in 1809 and was one of the small band of the all-officer Corps of Royal Engineers.[10] The roles of the corps included route reconnaissance, road making, the bridging of obstacles, siegework, the preparation of defence works, surveying and map-making, the establishment of water points and the building of barracks. Without engineers an army could neither move nor properly defend itself.

It was a common complaint of commanders in all armies that there were never enough engineers. At the outbreak of war in 1793 there were only seventy-three Royal Engineers in the whole British army, spread around the world from Canada to India; even at the height of the war there were never more than 300. Of even this small number not all were effective, for the system of promotion by seniority alone meant that many of the senior officers of the corps were incapable of taking the field. Engineer officers were highly qualified and their training, and the equipment they needed to put it into practice, was expensive. Moore had only thirteen engineer officers for his Coruña expedition, and Wellington had only the same number when he took command in Portugal in April 1809. The Royal Engineers came under the Master General of the Ordnance and had no non-commissioned ranks. Instead they were supported by the Royal Military Artificers, consisting of carpenters, bricklayers and other tradesmen. They were organised as companies, commanded by a sub lieutenant (always a commissioned sergeant) and a staff sergeant from the Royal Artillery, from which small detachments were sent on campaigns as required. In November 1809 Wellington had only two artificer sergeants and twenty-three other ranks, of whom four were sick and two were absent without leave. At Wellington's urging they were reinforced by twenty-five other ranks, who while qualified in their trade had no experience of the construction of trench works or gun emplacements. In order to have some engineering support subject to the Horse Guards rather than the Master General of the Ordnance, the Royal Staff Corps had been raised in 1798, largely due to the insistence of the Duke of York. Originally intended as skilled overseers of labour, their duties gradually expanded and by 1809 overlapped those of the Royal Engineers and the Artificers. The corps was organised with officers and other ranks, and by 1809 was formed as a battalion, which had to support the army all over the world, leaving very few for the Peninsula. The situation would improve, but while the Royal Engineers and the Royal Staff Corps, assisted by the Artificers, could plan, design and supervise, the hard labour involved in engineering tasks fell to the unskilled infantry or locally recruited labour. Fletcher himself was very experienced. He had served in the West Indies expedition of 1794 as a lieutenant, was lent to the Turks from 1799 to 1800, when he designed and built the fortifications of El Arish and Jaffa. He was one of Wellington's engineers in the Copenhagen operation of 1807 and was Moore's Commanding Engineer during the Coruña campaign.

Having carefully examined the area north of Lisbon, Wellington made his plan for the defence of the capital, although he also planned for an evacuation of the whole British army, should his plans fail. He saw that Lisbon could only be approached from the north or the east, the western (seaward) approach being protected by the Royal Navy. To the south and east lay the River Tagus, which in winter posed a major obstacle to any French attempt to cross, but which they might attempt to ford in summer. The most likely approach was from the north. Wellington's plan was to guard against any attempted crossing of the Tagus, while fortifying the northern approach. On 20 October Wellington wrote a memorandum to Fletcher explaining his plan for the

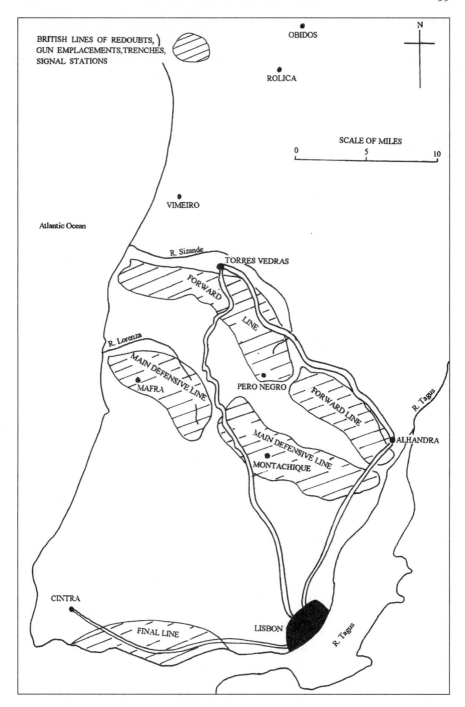

13. The Lines of Torres Vedras, 1810.

defence of Lisbon. He instructed Fletcher to examine the possibility of damming the rivers running into the Tagus in order to create further obstacles, and to submit his estimates for the time, equipment and manpower needed to destroy roads which the French might use, build roads for British use, and to construct a series of various redoubts, gun emplacements, trench lines and signal stations, which would form the defence works themselves. The result was one of the greatest feats of military engineering ever undertaken in such a short time. What became to be known as the Lines of Torres Vedras were actually three lines. There would be a forward, or outpost, line running from the River Sizande on the Atlantic coast through Torres Vedras to the River Tagus near Alhandra. This line would have thirty-two redoubts and 158 artillery pieces. Between six and nine miles behind and to the south of the outpost line would be the main defensive line. Sited so as to block any approach through the hills to the north of Lisbon, this ran through Mafra, Montachique and Alhandra with sixty-five redoubts and 206 guns. The final line, constructed to protect an embarkation of the British army should all else fail, was sited eleven miles to the west of Lisbon, round the port of Sao Juliao. It would have eleven redoubts and eighty-three guns and would be guarded by two battalions of Royal Marines.

The lines were not continuous works but a series of mutually supporting fortresses and entrenchments. Each redoubt was self-contained; and even if one should fall the French would still come under fire from at least two others. The defence works were sited in depth, so that a penetration of one part of one of the lines merely forced an attacker onto another protected position further back. North of the Lines Wellington intended a scorched earth policy: the inhabitants, with all the supplies, food, machinery and personal property that they could carry, would withdraw inside the defended area. What could not be removed would be destroyed, and unharvested crops burnt. For swift communication along and behind the Lines a series of signal stations, using shutters which could be opened and closed (later to be replaced by semaphore arms) would be constructed.[11]

The memorandum to Fletcher was long and detailed.[12] On the same day, 20 October 1809, Wellington, prodigious worker that he was, wrote six further letters, some of them of several pages long. Three of these concerned prisoners of war. To the French General Kellermann he wrote, in French, assuring him that any British officer prisoner of the French who misused his parole to escape back to the British lines would immediately be returned to French custody. In the same letter he regretted that Kellermann's ADC, Lieutenant de Turenne, could not be exchanged for the British Lieutenant Cameron, owing to the fact that de Turenne was actually held by the Spanish, who refused to give him up. Instead Lieutenant Véron de Farincourt, held by the British, would be returned. To de Farincourt Wellington wrote that, while he would now be exchanged, there was no chance of his surviving the journey through Portugal and Spain unmolested, so he would be provided with an escort by Marshal Beresford. Wellington's final letter regarding prisoners was to write a *carte d'exchange* confirming that Farincourt was to be exchanged for Cameron.[13] To Castlereagh, still just in office, Wellington wrote three letters: the first explaining the position of British officers in the Portuguese army, and referring to a recent case where two had absented themselves from duty without leave. Pointing out that these officers could not be punished under British military law, Wellington asked that the sort of officer who was likely to misbehave should not be sent to the Portuguese. The second letter concerned the problems faced by British officers with the Portuguese who were due for promotion in their own army, but could not be given it because they were no longer on the British strength. Wellington's recommendation was that the return of these officers to the British service – when they could be promoted – would have a deleterious affect on the Portuguese army and that an exception should be made, whereby they could be promoted but remain where they were. The final letter dealt with the requirements for stores and equipment for the Portuguese army.[14]

Work started immediately on the Lines of Torres Vedras and their associated outworks. It was supervised by Fletcher and seventeen officers of the Royal Engineers. The work was mainly carried out by 300,000 members of the Ordenança, the Portuguese home guard, at 4d. per day, and 10,000 locally employed labourers at 1s. per day. Control and discipline was exercised by 150 British NCOs carefully selected for their ability to remain sober and close mouthed. The whole project cost £100,000 and was cheap at the price. Security was paramount. Wellington hoped that the French, if they came, would come by the northern approach. If they did, then every hill, ridge, village, defile, ravine and river would be opposed to them. They would be dragged ever deeper into the peninsula bounded by the Tagus to the east and the sea to the west, as the Allies conducted a fighting withdrawal. The French would take more and more casualties as they advanced and, if they could not force the Lines, would be faced with starvation in an area cleared of everything of use to them. All this depended upon the French not finding out what Wellington's plans were. The French had nothing to equate to Wellington's officers in observation, and any French spy or roving patrol would be ambushed and killed by the Spanish or Portuguese guerrillas. There was little risk of the French discovering what was afoot, but equally important in Wellington's mind was the need to conceal the plan from his own army. Military censorship of mail was unknown and freedom of the Press a jealously guarded right at home. In the event, he did succeed in keeping the secret of the works, which went on for the whole of the winter and spring of 1809 and 1810. Even when the army eventually withdrew into the protection of the Lines most officers and men thought they were about to embark for England. Effective security carried with it mixed blessings, however, for the impression within the army, and in Parliament at home, was that the army was doing nothing. A vote of thanks to Wellington for the battle of Talavera, moved in the House of Commons on 1 February 1810, was only carried against the vociferous protests of the Opposition, as was a vote on 16 February to award Wellington and his two immediate male heirs a pension of £2000 per annum. Wellington became increasingly irritated by what he termed 'croakers' in the army, officers who wrote to friends in Parliament and the press criticising the command of the forces. His anger was only marginally abated by the Supreme Junta appointing him a captain general of the Spanish army, although he refused to accept the pay, saying that it would be a burden on a poor country at war.

The army was now redeployed to conform with Wellington's plans for defence. Major General Hill, with his 2nd Division, was posted along the Tagus, while Wellington retained the bulk of the army under his own command at Mondego. To the north he detached the Light Division (until recently a brigade) to watch the line of the River Agueda. The Light Division was commanded by Major General Robert Crauford, aged forty-six in 1810. Crauford was probably the most competent of Wellington's major generals, but he was not an easy subordinate. From a family of old Scottish gentry, he had been commissioned in 1779. The rules as to time in each rank had not yet been introduced, and within a year, aged only nineteen, Crauford was a captain commanding a company in the 75th (Prince of Wales's) Foot. There he stuck, however, and took a further nineteen years to become a lieutenant colonel. Despite his lack of advancement, he was intensely interested in his profession. He served in the Third Mysore War, during which secondment in Holland, and on attachment to the Austrian army, he met Frederick the Great of Prussia. In 1801, still a lieutenant colonel, he went on half pay and entered Parliament as member for East Retford, a pocket borough in the gift of his brother, where he was a consistent critic of Pitt the Younger. After the death of Pitt, the Whig 'Ministry of All the Talents' was better disposed to him and, after Beresford's capture in South America, Crauford was appointed to command a brigade in General Whitelock's ill-fated venture to the same continent in 1806. Although he had to surrender in Buenos Aires in 1807, he was one of the few officers to return with his reputation unsullied. Crauford was short and dark, bitter and with a violent temper – which may have contributed to his early lack of advancement. He was a fierce disciplinarian, and probably flogged, shot and hanged more British soldiers than any other general of the Peninsular army – yet he took an inordinate interest in his men's welfare. The Light Division, although smaller than other divisions, was an elite formation, and on 28 July 1809 had completed a near incredible forced march of forty-two miles in twenty-six hours from Lisbon to Talavera, arriving just too late for the battle. One of its two brigades contained the 1st battalion 43rd (Monmouthshire Light Infantry) Regiment, half of the 1st 95th Rifles, and a battalion of *cacadores* (Portuguese light infantry). The second brigade consisted of the 1st Battalion 52nd (Oxfordshire Light Infantry) Regiment, the other half of the 1st 95th Rifles, and a battalion of *cacadores*. Despite Crauford's formidable reputation as a martinet, his men had great regard for him, or at least the well-behaved ones had. They knew that Crauford would ensure, to the utmost of his considerable ability, that his men would be trained and prepared for whatever operations they might have to undertake. They also realised that as an elite division they would have to take on some of the more dangerous tasks of the army.

Meanwhile Napoleon was anxious to complete his conquest of western Europe, currently being held up by the infuriating, but seemingly insignificant, British presence in Portugal. In April 1810 he appointed Marshal André Masséna to command the Army of Portugal. Masséna was another example of Napoleon's oft-quoted maxim to the effect that every soldier had a marshal's baton in his knapsack. The son of a wine merchant, he originally joined the ranks of the Bourbon army. Taking his discharge as a sergeant major, he had set himself up as a fruit seller and occasional smuggler, until in 1792 he was elected as the lieutenant colonel of a Revolutionary volunteer unit. By the end of the following year he was a major general. After service in Italy and Switzerland and command of the Army of Italy, he became a marshal in 1804. He commanded a corps in Poland, lost an eye in 1808 in a shooting accident, and again commanded a corps at Aspern-Essling in 1809. He had a reputation as an incorrigible collector of loot, and that in an army of looters. His current mistress, Henriette Leberten, accompanied him to Spain, irritating the headquarters staff by always appearing dressed in the uniform of an officer of light cavalry. Uneducated, but an instinctive and inspirational leader, Masséna was aged fifty-two when he came to Spain. Although probably past his best, Wellington considered him, next to Napoleon himself, to be the best of the French generals.

By June 1810 Masséna had arrived in Spain with reinforcements and now had around 100,000 men available for the invasion of Portugal. His first move was to instruct Marshal Ney to capture the Spanish fortress of Ciudad Rodrigo, which he had been blockading since February. Ciudad Rodrigo guarded the north-eastern corridor between Spain and Portugal. Its capture would be essential to an advance on Lisbon by the northern route – exactly where Wellington hoped the French would come. By 16 June Ney, with 26,000 men, had invested Ciudad Rodrigo and the siege began. Michel Ney, born in 1769, the same year as both Wellington and Napoleon, was another ex-ranker, having been commissioned in 1792. He was devoted to Napoleon and became a marshal in 1804. He had been a corps commander in the *Grande Armée* and fought at Jena, Eylau and Friedland. Personally brave to a fault, he lacked the strategic vision to hold marshal's rank, and his relations with Masséna were strained.

The Spanish garrison of Ciudad Rodrigo, under General Herrasti, fought well, leading Wellington to modify his low opinion of Spanish fighting qualities slightly. He now considered that Spanish troops placed behind fortifications or earthworks, where they could not run away, could fight well. Wellington made no move to relieve the siege of Ciudad Rodrigo, and he came in for criticism from the Spanish and from his own army for his seeming lack of activity, but it was the right decision. To venture out of his secure and reasonably well supplied positions around Lisbon would only run the risk of his army being cut off from its bases and eventually destroyed by the far greater numbers that Masséna could deploy. Wellington's army was the only army that Britain had: it must be carefully husbanded.

The garrison of Ciudad Rodrigo held out for forty-two days, but by 8 July the French had breached the walls. The next day, to spare the population the horror of a storm and its aftermath, General Herrasti surrendered. In a flagrant violation of the laws of war, the French plundered the town anyway. With Ciudad Rodrigo now in French hands, Wellington ordered the Light Division to pull back from the Agueda. The division had been on the north-east frontier for more than three months, collecting intelligence and keeping French probes from finding out what lay beyond. Ney pushed on, hoping to catch the Light Division with its back to the River Coa, fifteen miles west of the Agueda. In a series of brilliantly conducted small actions, the Light Division crossed the Coa safely; but Crauford infuriated Wellington by disobeying orders and indulging in unnecessary skirmishes, which very nearly allowed the French to catch the division on the wrong side of the river. The French would indeed have caught the division but for the fighting qualities of the British and Portuguese light troops, aided by French mistakes. 'I am glad to see you safe', said Wellington to Crauford after the withdrawal. 'I was in no danger, I assure you', replied Crauford. 'But I was, from your conduct', was the irascible retort from the Commander of the Forces. Shortly afterwards, on 31 July 1810, Wellington ordered a general withdrawal of the non-essential elements of the army into the protection of the Lines of Torres Vedras. The Lines themselves were held mainly by Portuguese militia, with those elements of the British and Portuguese army not occupying outlying defended localities concentrated in rear, ready to move to any threatened point. Civilians too moved inside the Lines, with their goats, sheep, carts of olives, donkeys laden with cork and wine, oxen hauling loads of hay and straw and anything that was portable and which might be used by the French.

The next objective for the French army was the Portuguese fortress of Almeida, twenty miles from Ciudad Rodrigo and just inside the Portuguese frontier. The French were slow to move against Almeida, partly because they wanted to replenish their siege train after Ciudad Rodrigo and partly because of bad roads and the ever-present Spanish guerrillas. At last, on 26 August, the French batteries were in position and opened fire. Wellington had hoped that Almeida might be held until the arrival of the autumn rains, which would slow up French movement. The fortress was well provisioned and had large stocks of artillery ammunition and plenty of guns to fire it. It was commanded by Lieutenant Colonel Cox, a British officer in the Portuguese service with the rank of brigadier. Cox was a competent officer and it was his great misfortune that a French shell, which exploded in the town on 28 August causing little damage in itself, ignited a train of powder which had spilled from damaged powder casks carried from the main powder magazine to the gun positions on the walls. The magazine, under the cathedral, blew up, killing around 500 Portuguese soldiers instantly.[15] The cathedral ceased to exist and surrounding houses were flattened. While the walls were relatively undamaged, there was now no powder with which to continue to defend the town. Cox tried to delay by stringing out negotiations for the surrender of the fortress, but his Portuguese officers insisted on immediate capitulation, and on the evening of the same day French troops occupied Almeida.

Masséna established his headquarters and stores depot in Ciudad Rodrigo and garrisoned Almeida. He was now joined by a further corps of 17,000 men under General Reynier from Talavera. There were 60,000 French troops available for the invasion of Portugal; all that lay between them and complete mastery of continental Europe was the small Anglo-Portuguese army, with half of its Portuguese component made up of untrained volunteers. There was no need, thought Masséna, to manoeuvre or to attempt a southern thrust: he would press on to Lisbon. All this was good news for Wellington. Despite the disparity in numbers, it was clear that the threat lay from the north only, and that the French were not contemplating a pincer movement from the south east. Wellington summoned Hill's division from the Tagus, and Beresford's Portuguese army from Abrantes. They would take up a blocking position at Busaco.

The French continued their cautious and slow advance in the direction of Coimbra. It was cautious because the Spanish guerrillas were swarming in the hills along the route, ambushing French patrols from behind rocks with sporting guns, rolling rocks down on them and mounting hit and run raids at night. Wisely, they never attempted to meet the French in open battle, but any French soldier foolish enough to leave the line of march to forage, or sometimes only to urinate, had his throat cut. The bodies, often mutilated, dumped along the route did nothing to boost French morale. Masséna ordered that civilians found with weapons were to be shot. This was perfectly legal, and sanctioned by the laws of war, but it did nothing to endear the French to the local population. The advance was slow because the roads were appalling and because of the need to forage along the way. The French army had a commissariat, but the policy was for the soldiers to be fed by the occupied country. This entailed either heavy taxes from the population, or the seizure of food and forage. It was a counter-productive system because it restricted the speed of the army to that of the foraging parties, and it fuelled Spanish resentment against the invader. British soldiers looted and plundered too, but the locals knew that this was not officially sanctioned and that perpetrators were punished if they were caught, and compensation paid if thefts were reported.

Captured French soldiers were a valuable intelligence source. As those taken by the guerrillas were nearly always killed, often after torture, Wellington had to institute a monetary reward paid for French prisoners delivered alive and unharmed. Further intelligence came from Captain Somers Cocks, one of the observing officers, who with an escort of British and KGL cavalrymen roamed around behind and on the flanks of the French, passing information as to their progress. Wellington wanted to keep Masséna on the road to Coimbra, for if the French swung north west to Oporto then they would avoid Busaco, and the battle Wellington was planning, altogether. Colonel Trant, with a force of Portuguese militia, unwisely tried to hold up the French advance, and was roundly defeated, but on 24 September the Light Division and an independent Portuguese brigade commanded by a British officer, Major General Denis Pack, had more success at Mortagua. This was an enticement battle, intended to lure the French in pursuit and keep them on the road to Coimbra, and it was entirely successful. The French followed up the withdrawing Light Division and Pack's Portuguese as far as the village of Moura, four miles from Busaco Ridge. Wellington then ordered Crauford and Pack to break clean and move back to Busaco.

Busaco Ridge ran north to south and was eighty miles from Almeida and twelve miles from Coimbra. Provided that the French could be kept on the Coimbra road – as so far they had been – then they could not ignore Wellington's army on Busaco Ridge. If they tried to pass north of it then they would run the risk of having their lines of communication and supply cut off,

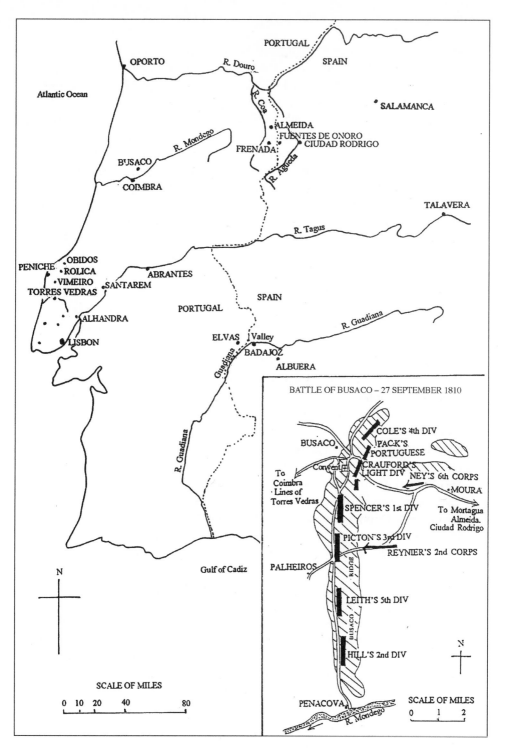

14. Portugal and Spain: Area of Operations, 1810.

and would be caught between the defenders of Lisbon and Wellington. Wellington wanted a battle for Busaco Ridge: it was an ideal defensive position and, now that he had lured the French to it, he hoped to be able to slow them down, inflict casualties on them and then withdraw his own army into the Lines of Torres Vedras, eighty miles to his rear. The ridge was almost ten miles long and from 2000 to 1000 feet above the ground over which the French would have to cross. On the British right, southern, flank the ridge dropped sharply 1800 feet to the River Mondego. The northern end of the ridge was steep and an approach could not be made without being seen by the defenders. Wellington deployed his army in what would later be considered his classic posture for defence. The Light Division and Pack's Portuguese brigade were about two thirds the way down the forward slope, where they would drive back the French skirmishers and take a toll of any French columns climbing the hill. Behind them, on the reverse slope of the ridge itself, were the infantry, now increased to five divisions. There had been some changes in the command structure of the army. The health of John Sherbrooke, now knighted and a lieutenant general, had broken down again and he had returned to England in June 1810. His replacement in command of the 1st Division was Major General Brent Spencer, who had been with Wellington at Rolica and Vimeiro. Spencer was somewhat out of his depth as a divisional commander. Wellington found him 'puzzle headed' and unable to remember Spanish and Portuguese place-names, constantly referring to the Thames when he meant the Tagus. The 4th Division was now commanded by Major General Galbraith Lowry Cole, who had taken over command from Major General Alexander Campbell in October 1809. Cole, another Anglo-Irishman and one-time suitor for the hand of Kitty Pakenham, was thirty-eight in 1810 and the second son of the 1st Earl of Enniskillen. Commissioned in 1787 at the age of fifteen, he was promoted to major general in 1808. Cole probably reached his ceiling as a divisional commander. He had a very quick temper but was popular with his men, to whose welfare he always paid close attention, and with officers, to whom he was known for giving the best dinners in the Peninsula. Wellington cared little for what he ate, living largely on a diet of mutton, bread and cold chicken legs, and there was little competition to be invited to eat at his table. Cole, on the other hand, never lacked dining companions. The commander of the recently constituted 5th Division was Major General James Leith. Forty-seven years old in 1810, Leith was commissioned in 1780, served at Toulon and, a major general since April 1808, had commanded a brigade at Coruña under Moore.

Placed from north to south along Busaco Ridge were Cole's 4th Division; most of Spencer's 1st Division; the 3rd Division, commanded by Picton;

Leith's 5th Division; and finally, on the extreme right, the 2nd Division commanded by Rowland Hill. Forward of the left centre of the main line, and on the forward slope, were Crauford's Light Division and Pack's Portuguese. Altogether Wellington disposed of around 50,000 men and sixty guns, these latter being spread along the infantry line. Beresford and his Portuguese army, and most of the cavalry, was sent off to the north, to guard against any flanking movements, or the – increasingly remote – possibility that Masséna would not take the bait offered at Busaco after all.

Masséna's army was divided into corps. The Napoleonic corps was really a self-contained miniature army, with its own artillery and cavalry, and which could operate independently of the main army. Under Masséna, Reynier's 2nd Corps had 18,000 men; Ney's 6th Corps 24,000 and Junot's 8th Corps 17,000. Between them the three corps disposed of seventy-six artillery pieces. Under Masséna's personal command was the general reserve, a mixed force of infantry and cavalry with thirty-eight guns and totalling around 7000 men in all. Wellington with his 50,000 men thus faced Masséna with 66,000.

The main road from Moura, where the Light Division had broken clear of the pursuing French, ran up the ridge and crossed through the British left centre, passing Busaco convent, where Wellington established his headquarters. The engineers had constructed a rough lateral road, really an improvement and joining together of existing tracks, along the reverse slope of the ridge in order that troops could be moved rapidly to reinforce threatened areas. On 25 September 1810 Wellington's Anglo-Portuguese army began to get into position, the men slept at their posts and no fires were lit. Wellington himself alternated between riding up and down the line ensuring that all divisions were where he wanted them, and watching the French from an observation post short of Moura.

Masséna wasted the 26th of September. His approach was leisurely and he failed to reconnoitre the British positions properly. As most of the troops were on the reverse slope and could not be seen, the French thought that they had only a weak rearguard to contend with. They had a low opinion of the Portuguese, whom they thought would not fight.

The morning of 27 September 1810 dawned in a thick mist. At a quarter to six in the morning the first French attack was launched by eleven battalions of Reynier's corps attacking the Allied centre defended by Picton's division. The British could hear the French columns approach but could see little, hearing the rattle of musketry and rifle fire as their own skirmishers began the attrition battle before falling back. Reynier's men approached the ridge, but British guns sited on the flanks and firing canister began to tear great holes in the advancing ranks. The French pressed on through the mist, reached the top of the ridge and then, fifty yards away, saw an immobile red wall. British muskets came up to the present, and the aim, and the rolling volleys began. The columns began to disintegrate and the French fell back. By half past six Reynier had thrown two further assaults, of seven and then four battalions, at the ridge and they too had been driven back, with men from Hill's and Leith's divisions hurrying along the lateral road to reinforce Picton. In this sector alone, twenty-two French battalions had been defeated by twelve British and Portuguese. At a quarter past eight in the morning Ney sent two divisions, of twenty-three battalions in all, straight up the Coimbra road. His men could hear the firing on the crest to their left and assumed that the left-hand assault had been successful. The French columns first met the Light Division, commanded by Crauford, conspicuous in the centre on his horse. The light infantrymen and the rifles opened fire downhill, and then withdrew behind the crest, where they took post with three Portuguese brigades. One of Ney's divisions, commanded by Marchand, ran into Pack's Portuguese and got no further. The remainder of Ney's attacking columns reached the top of the ridge, but they too then faced the synchronised volleys of the British and Portuguese infantry and fell back, encouraged by the British artillery firing shrapnel.[16] Fighting went on until four o'clock in the afternoon, when Masséna at last abandoned the battle. Altogether he had mounted five separate attacks on Busaco Ridge, with a total of forty-five battalions, and had made no progress whosoever. Although Junot's corps and the general reserve were not employed at all, the French casualties totalled 4500, compared to 1200 for the Allies, about half of them Portuguese. Wellington resisted the temptation to mount a counter-attack: his aim had been to delay the French and to cause casualties on ground of his own choosing. He had succeeded in soundly trouncing Masséna, but to come down off his ridge was a risk he was not prepared to take.[17]

The battle did not delay Masséna for long: next day he found a way round the ridge; but it was too late, for Wellington had withdrawn. The battle was especially good for Portuguese morale: Beresford's reforms were taking effect and the Portuguese battalions had fought well, and would continue to do so. The French ceased to despise the British army and would move with even more caution from now on.

Wellington's army now moved back into the Lines of Torres Vedras, followed up by the French. The cavalry and the horse artillery prevented Masséna from catching up and on 10 October the Allied rearguard moved into the Lines. On 11 October the French arrived at the outer defence works. Masséna was horrified. The French had no idea that any work of such complexity had been undertaken, and now they saw that every hill, defile, road and river was entrenched and fortified, with guns sited on every approach and with a Portuguese garrison in every redoubt. They could only

stand and stare. Soon they began to starve as well, for they could not penetrate the Lines and Wellington's scorched earth policy had left little for the
French to feed on. The policy of laying waste the area where the French would
be had not been as successful as Wellington had hoped: inevitably some of the
peasants had hidden stocks of food, and inevitably the French found them,
but it was never enough to feed the men and the horses. Masséna stayed in
front of the Lines for a month, hoping to lure Wellington out and into a
battle, but the Allies, comfortable behind their defences and well provisioned
by the navy through Lisbon, were not to be shifted. The main Anglo-
Portuguese army was deployed around Mafra, ready to move to any point
where the French might make some progress against the garrisons of the
defence works. The signal stations could pass a message from one end of the
Lines to the other in seven minutes, and a written message from Wellington's
headquarters in Pero Negro could reach anywhere in the Lines in under an
hour. Wellington worried that the Tagus was his most vulnerable flank, but
flotillas of Royal Navy gunboats patrolled the estuary of the river and this too
was secure. At last, on 15 November, with the weather turning cold and
rations exhausted, Masséna recognised the inevitable. He wrote to Napoleon
explaining that the Lines were impenetrable and his army was starving. On
the same wintry night his army stole away, leaving dummies packed with
straw in their outpost positions, and withdrew thirty miles to Santarem,
where some rations and forage could be obtained. The French army stayed in
the area of Santarem for the winter, watched by Wellington's cavalry and
intelligence officers. By the beginning of March 1811, despite receiving some
reinforcement, Masséna's force had shrunk from 60,000 men to 47,000,
largely due to disease, starvation and the fate meted out by the guerrillas to
French foraging parties.

On 5 March 1811 Masséna's last hope of succour – an advance by Soult up
the Tagus – was dashed when it became apparent that the siege of Badajoz
would take up all Soult's energies and assets, and Masséna finally abandoned
the invasion of Portugal. Apart from a brief raid in April 1812, the French were
never to return to Portugal and Wellington had achieved the first part of his
mission. In the whole of Portugal only the fortress of Almeida remained in
French hands.

8

The Keys to the Kingdom

The success of Wellington's defence of the Lines of Torres Vedras and the French withdrawal from Portugal had a significant effect on opinion at home and in the army. Throughout 1810 the British government was still not fully convinced that its army in the Peninsula was making any significant contribution to the eventual defeat of Napoleon. There was still a view that the Peninsula was a side-show, and that such efforts that Britain could make should be in northern Europe, as part of another coalition. Many armchair generals were critical of the army's defensive posture and, even when the French failed to bring Wellington out from the Lines and into battle, could only grumble that Wellington was always lucky. The realisation, in December 1810, that King George III was unlikely to recover from his illness worried Wellington and his supporters, as it was thought that the Prince Regent favoured the Opposition, and might replace the existing cabinet of Spencer Percival with one that would make peace. Wellington said that even if the present government was replaced he was prepared to stay on in command – provided that there was still an army to command – as his appointment (and, he felt, that of his brother Henry in Cadiz) was professional rather than political. In the event the Prince of Wales did not turn to the Opposition, but even so there were concerns as to the cost of the war, which had risen to £6,500,000 for 1810. Wellington thought that the war in the Peninsula was highly cost-effective, in that it not only tied down large numbers of French troops, which would otherwise be used elsewhere, but it encouraged the Spaniards in their resistance and gave hope to other nations in Europe who might be encouraged to rise against French occupation. He insisted that the sums for the costs of the war were wrong: the troops and their rations, stores and equipment would have to be paid for wherever they were. The real cost, Wellington calculated, was £1,500,000. This was a feat of creative accounting – if the regiments had not been in Portugal they would have probably been disbanded – but he had a point. In his later years Wellington claimed that he alone had persuaded the British government to continue the war in the Peninsula. This is not entirely accurate: it was Lord Liverpool, Marquess Wellesley and Castlereagh (once he returned to office in 1812) who ensured that the war went on, but Wellington's opinions, closely reasoned by letter, had considerable influence on the decision-making process.

The members of the Portuguese Regency, previously wholly supportive of Wellington, were concerned too. They felt, with reason, that the scorched earth policy north of Lisbon was impoverishing an already poor country. Wellington's import of seed and agricultural implements, which were issued to the peasants in the area from where the French had withdrawn, helped somewhat, but the increasing inability of the Portuguese to supply even their own army, let alone provide transport and supplies for the British, was a matter of concern. Wellington suspected that the lack of logistical support was due to incompetence at best and corruption at worst. Eventually, in August 1811, he unsheathed the weapon of the annual British subsidy to the Portuguese Regency. The agreed annual subsidy was £2,000,000: from now on it would no longer be paid direct to the Portuguese Regency but into a military chest controlled by the British. Increasingly Wellington accepted that *faute de mieux* the British commissariat would supply the Portuguese army.

Wellington was also concerned about the numbers of men available to him, and often said later that if he had had 10,000 more soldiers he would have fought a very different campaign. The volunteer British army was recruiting around 15,000 men a year, but this was for the whole of the army worldwide, and was insufficient to make a real numerical difference when losses and discharges were replaced. Between April 1809, when Wellington took command of the army in Portugal, and December 1811, when he was watching the Portuguese frontier after Masséna's withdrawal, Wellington had been sent 22,000 men as reinforcements, but his losses during this period were over 16,000. Not all the losses were from enemy action. When Wellington withdrew into the Lines of Torres Vedras he had around 33,000 British troops, of whom 9000 were in hospital or convalescing. Rest and good rations during the winter of 1810/11 improved matters somewhat, but sickness was always to dog his army, particularly when rations were short and the weather was wet or cold.

The French withdrawal from Portugal changed attitudes overnight. The Portuguese were mollified (reserving the right to become unmollified should the French return). The government in London basked in Wellington's achievement, admitted that his strategy had been the right one, and confirmed that the Peninsula would remain as the seat of British land operations against Napoleon. As Masséna withdrew, Wellington harried him unmercifully, keeping him on the move and allowing him no opportunity to rest and refit. Despite having to destroy much of his wheeled transport and shoot or hamstring lame animals, Masséna conducted a masterly withdrawal, and Wellington, anxious not to over-extend his own army, was never able to corner him where the French army could be destroyed. Wellington was not helped by having his experienced and able divisional commanders, Hill, Crauford and Leith, as well as Cotton, commanding the cavalry, all away on leave in England. On 26 April 1811 both houses of the British Parliament passed a vote of thanks to Lieutenant General Viscount Wellington for the liberation of Portugal.

In order to ensure that the French would not attempt another invasion of Portugal, Wellington now wanted to secure the frontiers. There were three major fortresses which protected the main routes into Portugal. To the north east was Almeida, in Portugal, which was complemented on the Spanish side by Ciudad Rodrigo. Farther south and guarding the approaches from the east was the Spanish fortified town of Badajoz. Ciudad Rodrigo and Badajoz had long been known as the keys to the kingdom of Portugal because they guarded the two main routes into that country from Spain. Almeida and Ciudad Rodrigo had been in French hands since Masséna's invasion of Portugal in 1810, and Badajoz had finally been taken by Soult in January 1811. If these fortifications could be recaptured and strongly garrisoned, then Portugal would be safe. Wellington decided that his campaign of 1811 would be concentrated on the three strongpoints. It was a brave decision, as Wellington still had no siege train, which was being assembled in England and then transported piecemeal to Lisbon. Such items as had arrived were on board transport ships off Lisbon. The siege train would not be complete until the middle of the year and would then have to be transported to the army. As Wellington could not yet blast holes in walls, he opted to cordon off the three fortresses, blocking all routes out and in, hoping that he could starve the French garrisons into surrender. This was risky, as there were still two French armies within reach: that of Marshal Victor in Old Castile, and Soult's in Andalusia, while Masséna retained his headquarters in Ciudad Rodrigo. All three could call for reinforcement from French armies elsewhere in Spain, and a further risk was that two or more might combine. Wellington was not overconcerned with the risk of a combination against him. Apart from the marshals' constant internecine squabbling, the French system of rationing their troops – effectively living off the country – meant that any given area could only supply a limited number of troops for a limited time, after which the army must move on in search of further supplies. French armies could and did concentrate, but they could only do so for short periods, and it was this factor that contributed in large measure to Wellington's ability to operate successfully with much smaller forces throughout the war.

Wellington set up his own headquarters at Frenada, where he could menace Almeida and Ciudad Rodrigo, and on 8 March 1811 he sent Beresford, now also commanding Hill's division, off to blockade Badajoz. There

Beresford borrowed some ancient guns from the Portuguese arsenal in Elvas and attempted, unsuccessfully, to breach the walls. A week later Wellington reinforced him with Cole's 4th Division.

While the inclusion of Ciudad Rodrigo in Wellington's blockade programme was perhaps overambitious, plans had been drawn up for the Spanish guerrillas to give adequate warning of the approach of any French reinforcements to the Light Division, who would then move to intercept. As Crauford was at home on leave, the division was under the temporary command of Major General Sir William Erskine. Originally commissioned into the Light Dragoons at the age of seventeen in 1786, Erskine had shown reckless bravery in the Flanders expedition of 1793/94, although it was noted that he was incapable of conducting any business after dinner, owing to his being drunk. Erskine then pursued a political career, being MP for Fife from 1796 to 1805, the year in which he became a major general. Sir David Dundas, the Commander-in-Chief of the British army during the period when the Duke of York was in disgrace, thought highly of Erskine, and sent him to the Peninsula as a brigade commander. Wellington queried the posting on the grounds that Erskine was generally thought to be highly unstable. Colonel Torrens, military secretary to Dundas, replied that, while Erskine probably was a little mad, he was very clever during his lucid moments, although he had looked a little wild when he embarked. At this stage of the war Wellington had very little say in the appointment of senior officers, and he had perforce to accept Erskine. While occasional outbreaks of lunacy in a general might be of no great import, it is useful if a general is able to see the ground over which he deploys his troops, and Erskine's eyesight was so bad that he was very nearly blind. When the guerrillas told Erskine that a French supply column was moving towards Ciudad Rodrigo, Erskine's total incompetence meant that it was not intercepted, and it managed to enter the town, bringing provisions and ammunition. The French garrison was now capable of staying put for a long time and could not be starved out. Wellington abandoned his attempt to blockade Ciudad Rodrigo and concentrated on Almeida.

On 16 April Wellington, accompanied only by his personal staff, rode the hundred miles south to Badajoz in two days. Once there he rode all round the city, conferred with Beresford and then left again for Frenada on 25 April. On his way north Wellington learned from despatches sent by General Spencer that Ciudad Rodrigo was being reinforced by French troops. Masséna was said to be gathering every man he could in order to lift the blockade of Almeida.

Meanwhile there was success for the Allies further south. Cadiz, now the seat of the Spanish Regency Council (the successor to the Supreme Junta), had been under French siege since February 1810. It was, however, eminently defensible, being on a peninsula and easily supplied by the Royal Navy. The garrison had rarely been more than 15,000 Spanish troops and five Anglo-Portuguese battalions, but it tied down 60,000 French troops. The British commander in Cadiz was Lieutenant General Thomas Graham, who had possibly the most unusual background of any of Wellington's generals. As a young man Graham had shown no interest in a military career. He was a Scottish landowner, a Whig MP, a breeder of horses and a fine cricketer. When his wife (who had been painted by Gainsborough) died in the south of France in 1792, Graham was accompanying the body home when he was stopped by French Revolutionary Guards, who insisted on opening the coffin and searching the body for contraband. This conduct so incensed Graham that he became a lifelong hater of all things French. At the age of forty-five, and with no military experience whatsoever, he determined to be a soldier and served at Toulon as an unpaid volunteer on the staff. The following year, 1794, he raised the 90th (Perthshire Volunteers) Regiment of Foot at his own expense, which brought him the honorary rank of lieutenant colonel. He was a British liaison officer with the Austrians in Sicily, fought at Mantua, Minorca, Sicily and Malta, and then went to Egypt, arriving too late to take part in the campaign. Still unpaid and officially unrecognised, he went to Sweden and then to Spain with Sir John Moore, a personal friend, as an extra ADC and was present at Moore's death. At last, and possibly as a tribute to his friendship with Moore, he was formally placed on the Army List as a major general, served at Walcheren as a lieutenant general and was then sent to command the British troops at Cadiz.

When the French besiegers of Cadiz were ordered in January 1811 to send a third of their strength to support the final assault on Badajoz, Wellington saw an opportunity. Graham was ordered to embark an Anglo-Spanish force, sail fifty miles south to Tarifa, and take the remaining French from the rear. The attack was to take place on 3 March and was to be coordinated with an overland sortie from Cadiz. Within Cadiz there was heated argument as to who should command. Wellington had been very clear that Graham was to be in charge of the joint force, but, as there were considerably more Spanish than British troops involved, the Regency Council, fuelled by Spanish pride, insisted that the overall commander should be Spanish. To preserve relations in the coalition Graham reluctantly agreed to serve under General Manuel La Pêna, incompetent even by Spanish standards and treated with scorn by his own officers, who referred to him as *la Donna Manuela* – 'Madame Manuela'. Graham's force of 5500 British, Portuguese and KGL troops sailed from Cadiz on 21 February. When the weather prevented them from landing at Tarifa, they sailed on to Algeçiras, landed, marched to Tarifa and linked up with La Pêna and his 8000 Spaniards. The combined force now began to advance towards the French rear. Progress was slow, due to bad weather and because La Pêna insisted on marching at night and kept getting lost. As the troops approached Chiclana, where the French were, it was apparent that the attack from the French rear could not take place on the planned date. The message to the Spanish General Zayas, who would command the sally from Cadiz, telling him to delay, failed to get through. On 3 March Zayas launched his planned attack, crossed the Almanza inlet and advanced south east along the coast. He made no progress against the French and was pushed back, but did manage to hold a bridge-head about a mile from the inlet, around Bermeja.

By now the French were well aware of what was up, and determined to ambush La Pêna and Graham as they approached Cadiz. Marshal Victor ordered one French division to block La Pêna's route to the bridgehead while he placed two divisions in the Chiclana forest, ready to fall on the flank of the Allies as they moved along the coast towards Cadiz. When La Pêna eventually arrived at Chiclana on 4 March, he decided to abandon the original plan of attacking the French and determined instead to join up with Zayas's men and withdraw into Cadiz. He initially took up a position on Barrosa Ridge, which dominated the coastal route to Cadiz. On the morning of 5 March La Pêna ordered Graham to hold Barrosa Ridge while he advanced towards Bermeja to link up with Zayas. Neither general knew that there were two French divisions concealed in the forests to their north. After an initial rebuff, La Pêna succeeded in driving off the French blocking the approach to the bridgehead and, shortly after noon, ordered Graham to abandon Barrosa Ridge and follow him along the coast road. Graham protested. To move off Barrosa Ridge would leave the whole Allied rear and flank unguarded and open to attack: some troops must be left on the ridge until the main body was safely across the Almanza. La Pêna reluctantly agreed that Graham could leave two British and five Spanish battalions on the ridge. Graham was leading the rest of the British force towards Bermeja when Spanish guerrillas, acting as scouts, brought him the news that two massive French columns were moving through the forest, one towards Barrosa Ridge and one towards the Allied flank. This was what Graham had feared.

The whole Allied army was now in danger of being cut off, surrounded and destroyed. Graham immediately turned the rest of his force about and ordered them to return to Barrosa Ridge with all speed. He himself galloped on ahead, and when he reached the ridge found that the Spanish troops had fled, and the few British were in desperate straits. Graham realised that the only way to avert disaster was by an immediate counter-attack. He galloped back to his two returning brigades, and it was said that he took three minutes to give out his orders for two attacks, one to recover Barrosa Ridge and one against the column threatening the Allied flank. As it would take time for the brigades to deploy, Graham ordered the two British 'flanker' battalions, which had been originally holding the ridge, to assault immediately.[1] One battalion, commanded by Lieutenant Colonel Browne, advanced up the Barrosa Ridge, while the other, commanded by Lieutenant Colonel Barnard, took on the French column attacking the Allied flank. Both battalions took terrible casualties, but they bought just enough time for the two brigades to mount their assaults. The fighting was fierce, but the personal leadership of the sixty-two-year-old Graham, who led the attack on Barrosa on foot when his horse was shot under him, and the disciplined volleys of the British infantry, won the day. Less than 5000 British and Portuguese infantry had taken on twice that number of French and had beaten them decisively. It was a great feat of arms, against all the odds. The French had 2500 casualties and lost four guns and an eagle (the first to be captured in the Peninsula), while the Allied casualties were 1700.[2]

The French were now in complete disarray. La Pêna's Spanish troops had played no part and were fresh. Now, thought Graham, was an opportunity to follow up and deal out yet more death and destruction. La Pêna refused to have any part of it, and Graham, almost incandescent with rage, had no alternative but to withdraw into Cadiz. Once there, Graham's castigation of La Pêna, whom he accused of having betrayed and deserted the cause, was such that Graham could no longer reasonably continue as commander of British troops there, and he asked to return to Wellington's main army. He would take over the 1st Division in August 1811. While as a Whig Graham had previously no great regard for Wellington, service under him turned him into one of his greatest admirers.

While the battle of Barrosa was being fought and won, Wellington's presence around Almeida inevitably attracted the attention of the French. Marshal Masséna, still smarting from his defeats at Busaco and his inability to force the Lines of Torres Vedras, moved from Ciudad Rodrigo with 50,000 men. Masséna's primary aim was to break the blockade of Almeida, something that Wellington had expected, and very soon the network of Spanish guerrillas, observing officers and local spies were reporting exactly where the French were. Wellington, who had arrived back at Frenada on 28 April, had known that Masséna would be bound to come to the aid of the garrison in Almeida, the only French troops remaining on Portuguese soil, and once again resolved to give battle on ground of his own choosing. Six miles east of Wellington's headquarters at Frenada and just on the Spanish side of the frontier was the village of Fuentes de Onoro. The village sat astride the main road from Ciudad Rodrigo and was on the forward, eastern, slope of a ridge that ran north from the village for about six miles. Wellington placed around half of his army, the 5th and 6th Divisions, along the reverse slope of the ridge, with only the artillery and the skirmishers forward. Around and behind the village were the 1st, 3rd, the newly formed 7th and the Light Divisions, while one battalion and the light companies of the other infantry battalions (twenty-eight companies or 2500 men in all) held the village itself. Forward of the village, and running parallel to the ridge, was the River Dos Casas, only a stream and no obstacle in front of the village, but which turned into a deep defile further north and protected Wellington's northern flank.

One might have expected the French to have learned the lessons of Talavera and Busaco, and to have avoided frontal attacks on defending British infantry, but, true to form, on the afternoon of 3 May 1811 Marshal Masséna attacked straight up the main road towards Fuentes de Onoro, with fourteen battalions. While the more junior French officers, who had taken the brunt of the Allied volleys in previous encounters, were becoming wary of attacking positions where they could not see the waiting British infantry, the generals had yet to be convinced that the *Furia Francese* and the Revolutionary *élan* of their columns could not sweep aside the numerically inferior British. The village was a veritable rabbit warren of small, one-storey, stone houses, each with a small patch of walled garden. Streets were winding and narrow. Fighting in the village was fierce. As tended to happen in built up areas and trenches, where a cornered defender could not run away, bayonets were used for their primary purpose, rather than for fishing or stirring stew. Eventually, when the light companies in the village were about to be overrun, Wellington, watching from the high ground above, ordered reinforcements in. The fighting in and around the village went on all day, but just before nightfall the French withdrew, leaving the strong point of the defence in Allied hands. The French lost around 700 men and the Allies 250. Some of the courtesies of the age still held, for when the next day dawned in thick mist it was observed as an armistice, with wounded being recovered and both sides washing and drinking from the river. In the afternoon the French held regimental parades, in full view of the Allies, while the British played football.

Both armies were still on the field, and Wellington was of the view that the French were unlikely to try another frontal assault but might try to outflank his position instead. While the left flank was well protected, the right was not, and so the 7th Division was sent five miles south south west, to Poco Velho, while the cavalry, so far hardly troubled, was sent a further four miles south to Nave de Haver where they could support a force of Spanish guerrillas against any wide French move to the south. Masséna now had to do something: he could not just stay where he was. Having learned from Busaco the folly of failing to reconnoitre a British position, and while his regiments were

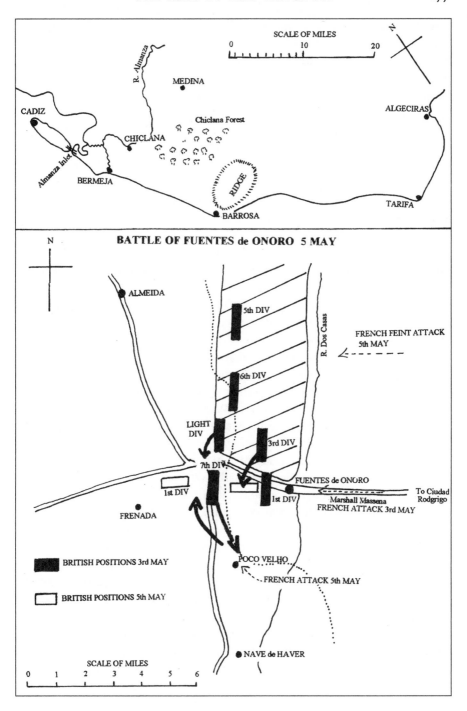

SCALE OF MILES
0   10   20

R. Almanza

MEDINA

CADIZ

Chiclana Forest

ALGECIRAS

CHICLANA

Almanza Inlet

BERMEJA

RIDGE

TARIFA

BARROSA

BATTLE OF FUENTES de ONORO 5 MAY

N

ALMEIDA

5th DIV

R. Dos Casas

FRENCH FEINT ATTACK
5th MAY

6th DIV

LIGHT
DIV

3rd DIV

7th DIV

1st DIV

FUENTES de ONORO

To Ciudad
Rodrigo

1st DIV

Marshall Massena
FRENCH ATTACK 3rd MAY

FRENADA

POCO VELHO

FRENCH ATTACK 5th MAY

BRITISH POSITIONS 3rd MAY

BRITISH POSITIONS 5th MAY

NAVE de HAVER

SCALE OF MILES
0   1   2   3   4   5   6

15. Barrosa and Fuentes de Onoro.

parading on 4 May in an unsuccessful attempt to overawe the Allies, Masséna and his staff rode around the area looking for possible lines of approach. All this was seen by Wellington himself, and by the guerrillas who hovered on the French flanks ready to snap up any unwary straggler. Wellington later admitted that he had made a tactical error, in that the 7th Division was now too far away from the main body to be supported: when Masséna threw a feint attack at Wellington's northern flank, and then attacked the 7th Division at first light on 5 May with three divisions of infantry and over 3000 cavalry, the situation became serious. The 7th Division could not hold, but Wellington sent the Light Division to cover its retreat back to the main position. Fortunately General Crauford had just arrived back from leave, taking over from the unfortunate Erskine (who assumed command of the 5th Division). Under Crauford the Light Division fought a brilliant rearguard action, supported by the British cavalry and a battery of horse artillery under Bull. The area was flat and open and good going for cavalry. The Light Division stood its ground while the 7th Division made good its escape, and then began to move backwards itself. The French cavalry would charge the British infantry, which would form squares on the march, going backwards, while the rifle regiments sniped and skirmished. Forming square on the march was a movement that was included in Dundas's *Regulations*, but it could only be done by highly trained troops. The French, in accordance with accepted practice, would bring up their artillery to blast the squares, but the enemy guns would be driven back by short, controlled charges by Cotton's cavalry, while Bull's galloper guns would unlimber, fire at the French and then gallop back to the safety of the Light Division's squares. It was probably the Light Division's finest hour, proving that all the tactical innovation, sweat, toil and blisters of Shorncliffe had been worthwhile.

The British cavalry too performed well. Hitherto such actions that they had undertaken had not been crowned in glory. The British cavalry had the best horses in the Peninsula and their men were better riders than the French; the problem was lack of control. British cavalry tended to be a fire-and-forget weapon, delivering a magnificent charge and then disappearing over the horizon in search of loot, not to be seen again until the end of the battle. Wellington thought that Cotton was the only cavalry officer present with the army who was capable of commanding more than a squadron, but the man who should have been commanding all the Allied cavalry, Henry Paget, was not there. Paget had shown his ability as the commander of Sir John Moore's cavalry during the Coruña campaign, but there were problems which prevented his employment now. Paget had been divorced by his wife on the grounds of his adultery with Lady Charlotte Wellesley, the wife of Wellington's brother Henry.[3] Charlotte's incensed brother challenged Paget to a duel, in which Paget 'deloped', that is deliberately fired wide. It was generally believed that Wellington refused to have Paget in the Peninsula, but it was more to avoid embarrassment for Henry, the British Ambassador. What appears to be the main reason for Paget's not having a command in the Peninsula was seniority. Wellington and Paget had both been promoted to lieutenant general on the same day, 25 April 1808, but Paget was four places higher up the list, and so senior to Wellington. He was not prepared to serve under his junior. Later, when Wellington had been promoted to general and then field marshal, the two served happily together during the Hundred Days in 1815, when Paget (now Earl of Uxbridge) was Wellington's second-in-command.

While the Light Division was covering the retreat of the 7th Division and then withdrawing itself, Wellington was redeploying his army to face the main French threat, now on his southern, right, flank. Nearly always a commander who succeeded in anticipating his enemy and then reacting more quickly, he now swung the 1st and 3rd Divisions around to face south, so that Fuentes now became the centre of his position rather than the right. The situation was still critical, as Wellington was in danger of having his new right flank rolled up and of being cut off from Frenada, and things got worse when, two hours after the attack on the 7th Division, Masséna hurled ten battalions, including three of the Imperial Guard, at the village of Fuentes. Once again the fighting was fierce. French cavalry, supporting their infantry, fell on the 1st Battalion of the 3rd Guards, in the 1st Division, who could not form square quickly enough and had many soldiers sabred by the French. The French advanced half way through the village, but Wellington fed in reinforcements and drove them out. A further eighteen French battalions attacked, and again they were repulsed. At last, at about two o'clock in the afternoon, a final attack, using battalions which had already been driven back at least once, came on. The French soldiers were now disheartened and the attack was not pressed home. Wellington's men stood to all night, and trenches were dug around the village and on the approaches to it. Wellington rarely dug his army in during this war, as he thought it would restrict his ability to move men to threatened areas, but in this instance, when dawn broke on 6 May, the French could see that any further attempts on the village were doomed to failure. Masséna had now had enough. He could make no progress around to the south until he captured Fuentes de Onoro, and that he had manifestly failed to do. If he could not move south then he could not relieve Almeida. Masséna ordered the rations which were being carried for the Almeida garrison to be distributed to his own men, and sent a message to the commander of Almeida telling him to blow up the fortress and escape as best he could. Three volunteers were sent with the message, dressed as

Spanish peasants. Two were captured and shot as spies by the guerrillas, one got through. On 7 May both armies watched each other warily, and on the 9th Masséna withdrew back to Salamanca. Wellington let him go.

At Fuentes de Onoro Wellington had lured Masséna into attacking him exactly as he had hoped, and the fighting on 3 May had gone as the Allied commander had expected. On 5 May Wellington had expected an attack to the south, but had not anticipated it in such strength or in such ferocity. The battle was nearly lost in the early morning, but by swift reaction Wellington snatched back the advantage. He sent the Light Division to the rescue of the beleaguered 7th, which had been placed too far away in the first place, and swung his line around to counter the fresh threat. Once again the fighting qualities of the Allied infantrymen in the village had held the crucial point of the battlefield, and Wellington's astute reading of the situation as it developed, and his feeding in of reinforcements just in time and in just enough numbers, gained a major victory for the Allies. The butcher's bill was more equal than the result of the battle: 1500 Allies to 2200 French, mainly because of the losses of the 7th Division on 5 May. The Light Division suffered only around fifty casualties during their epic retreat on the same day. For once Wellington had more artillery pieces than the French, and a long-range duel had managed to keep the French artillery from pounding the Allied positions in the village. The horse artillery had performed magnificently, and there was much grumbling in the bivouacs of the Royal Artillery when Wellington made no mention of them in his despatch after the battle.[4] Wellington did, however, note that the village had been virtually destroyed, and in his despatch recommended that seed and building materials should be given to the villagers to allow them restore their property.[5]

Napoleon was once asked what was the most important quality in a general. 'Luck', he replied. Wellington was lucky at Fuentes de Onoro, and he knew it, albeit that it was luck tempered by skill in handling his troops. He said that if Napoleon had been present the Allies would have been beaten, and he considered that the public announcement of the battle should not be accompanied by celebrations.

While the battle at Fuentes de Onoro was being fought, Beresford began his siege of Badajoz. He had been given wide discretion by Wellington, a necessary delegation when the two armies were a hundred miles apart. Short of proper siege artillery, he was making little progress when he discovered, on 12 May, that Marshal Soult was moving up from the south to the relief of the city with 25,000 men. Beresford packed up his siege and moved south east to the village of Albuera, where on 15 May his army of 23,000 was joined by 14,000 Spanish troops under General Francisco Castanos, now Captain General of

Estramadura and one of the less useless Spanish commanders. Beresford therefore had 37,000 men and fifty guns, considerably more than Soult believed him to have. The battle of Albuera was fought on 16 May 1811. Beresford was an excellent administrator and a loyal subordinate, but he was only a moderate field commander. All sorts of things went wrong: Beresford's orders were unclear and he did not check that they were being carried out; divisional commanders did not do what they were told to do; a sudden rainstorm at a critical moment made the Allied muskets misfire; Beresford seemed incapable of reacting as the battle developed; and the whole affair degenerated into a slogging match, with Allies and French pouring volleys into each other at ranges as short as fifty yards. Beresford himself was charged by a Polish lancer, brushed aside the lance and throttled the wielder. When both British and Spanish were able to deploy their lines against the French columns, it was the French who quit the field, but it was a Pyrrhic victory for the Allies. The French lost more than seven thousand men, the Allies six thousand, including over half of the British infantry strength. Nothing happened for two days, and on 16 May the exhausted French withdrew, with Soult declaring that the British had been beaten but did not know it and would not run. Beresford's nerve was shaken by the casualties, and his despatch to Wellington was truthful but gloomy. Wellington reassured him, saying that occasionally affairs like Albuera had to be undertaken, and later telling him to rewrite his despatch to show the battle as a victory, to avoid upsetting the public at home. Wellington never lost confidence in Beresford – largely because Beresford obeyed orders without question – but he never again gave him such leeway in independent command.

The 1400 strong French garrison of Almeida was commanded by General Antoine Brennier, who now realised that, with Masséna's relief column having been stopped and driven back at Fuentes de Onoro, he could no longer hold the fortress. He could not blow the defences up, as he had been ordered to do, but he did what he could and then slipped out and away on the night of 10 May. Wellington was furious, blaming his divisional commanders for allowing the French to escape unnoticed.[6] This was somewhat unfair: the troops were spread too thinly to cover every escape route and the French knew the country well. Wellington realised that he had been overambitious. When news came of yet more French reinforcements hurrying to the relief of Badajoz, he abandoned that operation to concentrate all his resources on Ciudad Rodrigo. Beresford was now sent to watch the Tagus against any French push from that direction, while Wellington settled down to invest Ciudad Rodrigo.

In July Wellington received promotion to full general, but in Spain and Portugal only. He was still a lot younger than other senior officers of the army, and there were many who were jealous of him. The promotion was political as well as being a recognition of merit, and gave him the British rank that he already held in the armies of Portugal and Spain.

Even with no French army in the area Wellington had insufficient engineers, and no proper siege train, and so little could be achieved other than to keep the garrison of Ciudad Rodrigo bottled up and watch for any opportunity to 'give a knock' to either Soult or Masséna, whose armies were now separated, should an opportunity arise. No opportunity did arise and when in September a French army of 50,000 men made a half-hearted advance towards the British lines, Wellington had no option but to withdraw back to the Portuguese frontier, where he took up a defensive position on the high ground around Fuenteguinaldo, south west of Ciudad Rodrigo and about eight miles inside Spain. Masséna, having failed to make any headway against the British, had now been recalled and replaced by Marshal Auguste-Frédéric-Louis Marmont. Marmont had been in Spain since early 1811, when he had succeeded Ney in command of the Sixth Corps. The son of a minor nobleman, he had been commissioned into the artillery in 1792, served in Malta and Alexandria and had contributed greatly to the victory at Marengo, where he had commanded the artillery. He became a marshal in 1809 when in command of the Army of Dalmatia. Marmont may have intended to attempt yet another invasion of Portugal, but an order to detach 10,000 men to Marshal Suchet for the pacification of Catalonia and Valencia, and small, though significant, actions fought by Wellington's rearguard at El Bodon, and by Hill (under Beresford) at Arroyo Molinos in October, dissuaded him. In late September, however, Marmont personally led a relief column to Ciudad Rodrigo. Wellington was outnumbered and had no choice but to let the column reach the town. Marmont entered Ciudad Rodrigo bringing supplies and ammunition, and destroyed what siege stores Wellington had been unable to take away with him. After a few days, when Marmont's men began to consume the rations intended for the garrison, the marshal withdrew back to Talavera. Wellington immediately renewed his investment of the town, and on 15 October the Spanish guerrillas had a major propaganda success when they observed that the cattle belonging to the garrison were taken outside the walls each day to graze. In a lightning raid the guerrillas not only managed to capture and drive away the cattle, they also bagged the governor – General Renaud – as well: he had chosen that moment to make an inspection of his cattle. Neither Wellington's troops not his guerrilla allies could surround the town completely, however, and in November a small French column managed to get into the town bringing some further provisions and the new governor – General Barrié. Leaving the garrison of Ciudad Rodrigo in place, the French went into winter quarters around Salamanca.

At home, the Duke of York had returned as Commander-in-Chief of the British army in May 1811, and more reinforcements began to arrive in the Peninsula. Although the numbers of men being sent out increased their general condition had not improved, for many of the soldiers still suffered from Wallcheren fever, contracted two years before. Wellington was particularly short of cavalry; at Fuentes the British cavalry had been outnumbered three or four to one, and most were light cavalry. These troops were excellent for reconnaissance and outpost duty, but the men were too lightly armed and the horses, while speedy, were too small for shock action. The Duke of York promised to send heavy dragoons, big men on big horses, armoured front and back, who could charge through the swarms of French cavalry. In general, though, the Allied army was in good order. The French no longer treated it with disdain, the Portuguese infantry were every bit as good as their British counterparts, and the Allied skirmishers, fighting in open order, were far more proficient than the French *tirailleurs* and *voltigeurs*. Provided that the disparity in numbers could be compensated for, by astute judgement of ground and selection of defensive positions which restricted the numbers of men who could attack them, the Anglo-Portuguese army was by now more than the equal of the French. French soldiers were generally very experienced, and fought well, but a higher standard of education and a genuine patriotism were no match for steadiness under fire, inculcated by drill and discipline, and the regular aimed volleys produced by years of hard training. The commissariat too had improved. As in India, Wellington's plan was to have a series of depots across Portugal, from where regular convoys could supply his forces. At the end of 1811 there were thirty of these depots, containing rations, military stores and, sometimes, ammunition. If there was a road then supplies were carried by bullock cart, and Wellington frequently had to remind officers that these must not be overloaded. More often supply was by mule train, with locally hired mules and handlers. A mule could carry 200 pounds twelve miles in a day, and troops up to fifty miles from a depot had no problems receiving supplies.[8] Rations were basic: beef, 'biscuit', tea, such green vegetables as could be obtained locally, rice, sugar, wine or spirits and occasional luxuries such as fresh milk. 'Biscuit' was actually bread baked twice, in order to keep it edible for longer, although some biscuit purchased from America was very similar to today's dog biscuit and was said (probably wrongly) to stop a musket ball at a hundred paces. As Portugal produced little more food than was needed to feed its own population, rations for the troops were increasingly imported from England, delivered to Lisbon or Cadiz by the Royal Navy. Beef was kept on the hoof for as long as possible, and often not slaughtered until it was actually in the encampment of the unit that was to consume it. This had the advantage of the ration being self-propelling, but also meant that, where cattle had been driven a long way with poor grazing, the meat was tough and stringy by the time it was butchered and eaten.

While the discipline of the army had improved somewhat during 1811, Wellington's general orders continued to thunder against misbehaviour and abuses. Most admonitions related to looting, in some cases of growing crops, in others of portable property including furniture. Units were ordered to place sentries in villages to prevent plundering, and the articles of war in relation to violence towards sentries (a capital offence) were ordered to be read out to all regiments. One battalion, guilty of cutting and taking away a field of Indian corn, was ordered to parade, with officers, every hour until further notice.[7] The cavalry were reminded that, while they were entitled to plunder the enemy, they were not permitted to seize cattle and other animals, belonging to the civilian population, which they might happen across while engaged in pursuit.[9] The Portuguese, despite being in their own country, were also guilty of plundering and were warned that if it did not cease (and, incidentally, if their appearance did not improve) offending regiments would be dismissed from the army.[10] As the Portuguese troops were generally several months in arrears with their pay, and there was little money for uniforms anyway, this was hard on them, but Wellington was adamant that such behaviour could only serve to turn the inhabitants against the Allies. Wellington also deplored the practice of regiments on the march catching up the supply convoy of a regiment ahead of it and appropriating those supplies for itself.[11]

In March troops were reminded of the reasons for their being required to witness punishments – floggings and executions – but there was to be one exception. In the previous two years the Brigade of Guards had not had a single man brought before a court martial, or even confined in the battalion guardroom, and so men of the Guards regiments were excused from parading to witness punishment.[12]

In August Wellington announced that a soldier, while searching for wine without permission, had recently been taken prisoner by the French. The Commander of the Forces hoped that this incident would serve to remind soldiers to be satisfied with the ration of wine provided, rather than risk being made a prisoner of war or of being posted as a deserter. This stricture evidently had little effect, however, for a month later Wellington promulgated a further general order saying that being taken prisoner while foraging for wine, and then accepting service with the enemy hoping to escape, was 'a dangerous experiment' which might lead to the man being in action against his own countrymen.[13]

In October there was an outbreak of burglary of civilian houses, while in December Wellington waxed indignant about the practice of 'embargoing' carts. Soldiers would demand a cart from its owner on the grounds of military necessity, all too often then extracting money to forgo the requisition. Pointing out that during the month of October 1811 three soldiers had been killed and two wounded in scuffles resulting from attempted extortion, Wellington reiterated that any officer or soldier requiring a cart for military purposes was to apply to an officer of the commissariat, or if none was present to the local magistrate. If the magistrate refused to requisition the cart then the matter was to be reported to superior authority. No one was to take the law into his own hands.[14]

Previously it had been accepted custom that any soldier capturing property from the enemy was entitled to its value when sold at auction under commissariat arrangements. Wellington noted that far too many men were interested in plunder to the detriment of their primary task of engaging the enemy, and from June 1811 a new system was introduced whereby the value of captured property was shared out amongst all those who were present, regardless of who actually captured it.[15]

As usual, officers were not exempt. Far too many of them were outstaying their sick leave, and henceforth any officer who considered himself to be sick, and whose leave had expired, was to parade in front of a medical board set up at each military hospital three times a month. The behaviour of some officers in Lisbon was causing concern, and they were reminded that for supposedly sick officers to appear at the theatre boisterous and drunk, often on stage, was unacceptable. Later sentries were placed in theatres and officers on sick leave banned from attending.[16] A commissariat officer based at Peniche was ordered to be suspended from duty without pay for his ill treatment of the civilian inhabitants, and all officers, but especially those of the medical and commissariat departments, were reminded as to the rules regarding billeting.[17] Remarking that officers were only entitled to basic accommodation for themselves and their horses, Wellington went on to say that the provision of officers' billets was the responsibility of the quartermaster general's department or the regimental quartermaster. If no such official was present then officers needing lodging must apply to the local magistrate and accept without question what they were allotted. One officer, supposedly sick, was reprimanded for borrowing his company's funds to finance a riotous lifestyle while in Lisbon – funds which he had not yet paid back.[18]

Training and tactics also occupied Wellington's mind while around Almeida and Ciudad Rodrigo during the latter half of 1811. Troops marching in column of route were now ordered to form in three ranks, not four, due to the narrowness of the roads, and not to straggle least those at the rear became exhausted by having to run to catch up.[19] Regiments not involved in the blockade were to carry out regular route marches and practise tactical evoloutions two or three times a week.[20] In the heat of the summer this training was to be over by eight o'clock in the morning.[21] A number of orders emphasised the importance of hygiene and cleanliness: sentries were to be placed on all drinking water fountains to prevent them being contaminated; every regiment was to have two or three latrines, which soldiers were to be made to use; and 'slack' lime (slaked lime) was to be used to disinfect them. Offal from the rations was to be buried or treated with lime, and all streets were to be swept daily and the resultant refuse burned or limed. Soldiers were to be reminded not to eat unripe fruit: the old soldiers knew the danger to health; those recently arrived might not. Wellington also detected the usual military habit of empire building and officers commanding hospitals were warned not to detain fit soldiers to be used as ward orderlies once their period of convalescence had passed.[22]

Wellington was a strict disciplinarian – and given the composition of his army he had to be – but he could temper punishment with mercy and a number of his orders announced the pardoning of soldiers sentenced to imprisonment, flogging or even death when their regiments had done particularly well. After the battle of Busaco he ordered the commanding officers of the 43rd and 52nd Regiments and the 95th Rifles each to nominate one sergeant to be commissioned as an ensign.[23] The filling of an ensign's vacancy caused by death was one of the very few powers to promote that Wellington had. Otherwise he could only recommend to the Military Secretary in London, where patronage and a fear of accusations of corruption often prevented that officer from securing the promotions that Wellington wanted. In one letter to Colonel Torrens, who provided as much support as he could, Wellington said that ideally promotion should be by military merit alone, but he accepted that such a system 'cannot be, I believe, brought into any military establishment'.

All in all Wellington had good reason to be satisfied with the results of 1811, and on 26 October, with the permission of the Prince of Wales as Regent, he accepted the Portuguese title of Count of Vimeiro and Knight Grand Cross of the Tower and Sword of Portugal. His immediate task was the capture of Ciudad Rodrigo, about which he had thought long and hard.

As early as July 1811 Wellington had turned his mind to the capture of the two strategically important fortresses of Ciudad Rodrigo and Badajoz, should a blockade fail to force them to surrender. To capture them in the teeth of a determined defence he would need a siege train, which had hitherto been arriving in dribs and drabs at Lisbon and held aboard ship in the mouth of the Tagus. Wellington ordered the navy to move the siege train 200 miles north to Oporto, and in July he issued a detailed memorandum to his Commander

Royal Artillery, Alexander Dickson, instructing him to move the train to Almeida, in Allied hands since May. Wellington has been criticised for not moving his siege train up sooner, but to have done so before he was absolutely certain that Portugal was secure would have been to risk losing it, and as recently as the winter of 1810 Lord Liverpool had stated that the withdrawal of the British army from the Peninsula was still an option. Wellington can never have seriously hoped that Beresford's blockade of Badajoz would be left alone by the French long enough to breach the walls and capture the town, and if Beresford had had the siege train with him in March he would almost certainly have been unable to carry it away and would have lost it.

Alexander Dickson was aged thirty-four in 1811. He had served in Malta and South America before being sent to the Peninsula, where he first came to Wellington's attention as a brigade major at Oporto in 1808. He had then been attached to the Portuguese army under Beresford until asked for by Wellington. Dickson had been commissioned into the Royal Artillery in 1794 but, because of the system of promotion by seniority alone then prevailing in the engineers and artillery, he was only a captain. In order for him to be able to command all Wellington's artillery over the head of other artillery officers senior to him, he was given the British rank of major in Spain and Portugal only, and was appointed a lieutenant colonel in the Portuguese army. In order not to cause offence, he always wore his Portuguese uniform. He was a highly skilled gunner, and a master of organisation, whom Wellington trusted totally.

Dickson left Wellington in July 1811, going first to Almeida. There he gave instructions for the repair of the fortress. Although General Brennier had failed to blow the defences up when he withdrew in May, the French had piled a large amount of stores in the ditch, which they did blow in. The ditch had now to be repaired, and the debris searched for cannon balls. As a twenty-four pound ball of iron was very nearly impossible to destroy, any which could be salvaged would reduce the number to be transported from Oporto. Portuguese labourers were engaged to trawl the spoil in the ditch and 8000 balls were recovered – eighty tons less to be moved. Almeida's guns had nearly all been spiked by the French (an iron nail driven into the touchhole), making the guns useless. These had to be drilled out and new, cone-shaped, vents inserted from the inside. Once Dickson was happy that matters in Almeida were in hand he moved on to Oporto. His task now was to move the sixty-eight siege guns and all their ancillary equipment, with powder and shot, a distance of one hundred miles to Almeida. The siege train that the Master General of the Ordnance had assembled and sent out included thirty-four iron twenty-four pounders (iron guns were just coming into service), eight ten-inch mortars, two eight-inch 'brass' (bronze) howitzers and twenty

five-and-a-half-inch brass howitzers. In addition Dickson had to move thousands of barrels of powder and ammunition of various calibres. A twenty-
four pounder gun weighed almost three tons and the barrel was ten feet long.
The guns and the howitzers travelled on wheels, but the long stay aboard ship
had caused many of them to warp, and new wheels had to be made. The
limbers (which carried first line ammunition and behind which the guns
were towed) were designed for draught horses. As there were insufficient
heavy horses in the Peninsula, the limbers had to be adapted for pulling by
bullocks and oxen. It required eight pairs of oxen to move one twenty-four
pounder on level ground, more often twelve pairs were used; to haul the gun
uphill needed twenty pairs. The mortars, which each weighed one ton, had no
travelling carriages and so wooden sledges had to be made for them. As
Dickson intended to move the guns as far as possible by river, boats had to be
found and adapted for their new role. By August Dickson was ready to
despatch the first convoy, initially up the River Duoro as far as Lamego and
then overland to Almeida. There were no roads capable of taking such heavy
convoys, so the Portuguese militia travelled ahead, improving the tracks and
building new ones where necessary. Wellington had calculated that it would
take sixty-four days for the siege train to reach him. Dickson, by prodigious
efforts and the use of 1100 oxen, would have achieved that but for Marmont's
manoeuvring in September, when the convoys had to wait at Villa da Ponte
for ten weeks. As it was, the complete train was present with the army on 1
December, a creditable achievement when it is remembered that normal
movement tables allowed for siege guns to travel ten miles a day on good
roads.

If the garrison of a fortress could not be starved out, then the attackers had
either to go under, over or through the walls. The garrison of Ciudad Rodrigo
could no longer be starved out in the time Wellington had available; the town
was built on rock and tunnelling under the walls was not an option, even if
there had been sufficient skilled men to do it; going over the walls – by
escalade – was a possibility, but liable to cause horrific casualties. Wellington
decided to go through the walls, by breaching them with the guns of his siege
train. In order for the guns to be able to breach the walls reasonably quickly,
they had to be sited close enough for the shot to be effective – four to five
hundred yards from the walls. This would mean that the guns – placed in
batteries – would be subject to fire and sallies from the defenders.
Additionally the gunners and the supporting troops would have to be secure
from the attentions of any relief force which might appear. To ensure this, the
normal practice was first to establish a secure base under cover from both fire
and view. From this base a sap, or trench, would be dug towards the walls.
Once the sap had reached breaching range a further trench, called a parallel

(because it generally ran parallel to the walls), would be dug and the guns placed in it. The guns would then begin to batter the walls to create a breach through which men could assault.

Ciudad Rodrigo had originally been a Roman outpost north of the River Agueda, guarding a bridge. Fortifications had been added by the Moors, more had been built during the middle ages and more recently by the Spaniards and the French. The fortified area, outside which were modest suburbs, was 850 yards east to west, along the river line, and 400 yards from north to south. North west of the fortifications were two hills, the Great Teson and the Little Teson. The Great Teson was 700 yards from the walls at their nearest point and, closer in, the Little Teson was 300 yards from the walls. The Great Teson was above the height of the ramparts, while the Little Teson was roughly level with them. Between the Little Teson and the walls was a defile. Along the south side of Ciudad Rodrigo the fortress was protected by the river and the town walls, while the rest was surrounded by a wall, a ditch and a glacis, or slope of rock which was intended to bounce shot above the walls or to their top, and to ensure that attacking infantry had no cover under which to approach. The French garrison was somewhat over 2000 men, and although now short of beef they had ample provisions and plenty of guns, including those of the siege train of Marmont's Army of Portugal, left there as it was too slow-moving to accompany the troops on the withdrawal from Portugal. The French had fully appreciated that the two Tesons were ideal locations from which to assault the town – they had used them themselves when they had captured Ciudad Rodrigo in 1810 – and had taken measures to prevent them being occupied by an attacker. On the south-east side of the Great Teson they had built the Renaud redoubt, so called because it had been built during the tenure of Governor Renaud, before he had been unlucky enough to have been captured by the guerrillas. The redoubt was held by a company of infantry with two guns and a howitzer, and was expected to be able to hold out for three to four days without relief. East of the redoubt, 400 yards from it and about the same distance from the walls of Ciudad Rodrigo, was the convent of San Francisco, which could not only support the redoubt with fire but could bring flanking fire onto the Little Teson. The third outwork, 200 yards west of Ciudad Rodrigo, was the convent of Santa Cruz. These three strong points could all support each other and would make occupation of the Great Teson difficult, and of the Little Teson impossible.

Like all good plans, Wellington's was simple. First the fortress would be isolated from any movement in or out. Secondly, a safe area would be established behind the Great Teson, the Renaud redoubt captured and the first parallel dug. Thirdly, once batteries were established in the first parallel, he

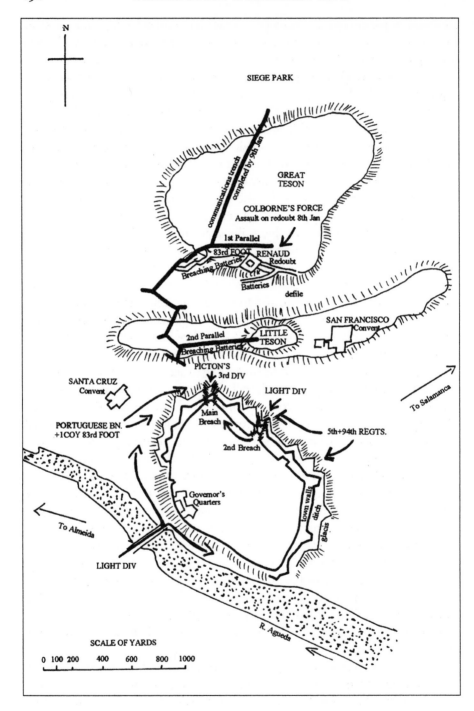

16. The Capture of Ciudad Rodrigo, 19 January 1812.

would sap forward to the Little Teson and dig the second parallel along it. Once the breaching batteries created a breach in the walls, the town would be stormed.

At around noon on a bitterly cold and frosty 8 January 1812 the Light Division crossed the River Agueda and took up positions surrounding the town and its outposts. This was unexpected by the French garrison: armies did not undertake major operations in winter. Although Napoleon held that military operations should continue all the year round, in Spain at least the French were unable to do very much in winter. The French system of living off the country meant that any form of concentration, or movement away from supply depots, was very difficult. There were no crops growing in the fields and, even more important, there was no grass for the horses and transport animals. Wellington's men were short too, but the British commissariat, with all its imperfections, was able to supply the troops, even if there were constant arguments as to the proper ration of hay for cavalry horses. Once the Light Division was in place, reconnaissance parties, including Wellington and his staff, rode all round the area hoping to confuse the French as to where the first blow might fall. At six o'clock that night it fell, when Lieutenant Colonel John Colborne, of the 52nd Regiment, with ten companies (four from his own regiment, two from the 43rd, two from the 95th Rifles and two of Portuguese *cacadores*) took the Renaud redoubt by a daring *coup de main*. His men got so close before the French sentries detected them that the guns in the redoubt could only fire one round apiece before the Allies were on them. The British and Portuguese surrounded the redoubt, and with musket and rifle fire swept the walls clear of defenders. In a matter of moments scaling ladders provided by the Royal Engineers were up against the walls and the Allies were in. The garrison's muskets were still piled and only a handful of men escaped back to Ciudad Rodrigo. It was a model example of what such an operation should be, with only six of the attackers killed and twenty wounded. Now the men began to dig furiously, in order to make a communication trench back to the Great Teson. Once the French realised what had happened, the guns on the north wall of Ciudad Rodrigo opened fire, but Colborne, anticipating such a reaction, had already pulled all his men out of the redoubt. By dawn on 9 January a trench ran all the way from the redoubt over the Great Teson to the siege park behind the hill.

Nothing could yet be done about the convent of San Francisco, and until guns could be in place to fire on the buildings the Allies would have to put up with artillery fire directed from there. Wellington, with Fletcher his engineer, had already decided upon the point of attack and during 9 January the Royal Engineers were able to examine the ground from the safety of the Great Teson. Once darkness came they went out and marked the locations of the first parallel, which was to be just behind and connected to the Renaud redoubt, and of the breaching batteries. When the engineers had pegged out the outline of the trenches, infantry fatigue parties, around a thousand men altogether, began to dig. It was originally intended to have four batteries of siege guns but, to the considerable anger of the engineers and digging infantry, when dawn broke it was clear that one of the batteries had been wrongly sited and its field of fire was restricted by the redoubt. Digging went on, and the 1st, 3rd, 4th and Light Divisions took daily turns as duty division, with the rest of the army in billets in villages some way behind the Agueda. The digging of the parallels (a second was begun even closer to the walls) was supervised by Fletcher and eighteen officers of the Royal Engineers, assisted by eighteen other ranks of the Royal Military Artificers. The actual digging was done by the infantry. It was an unpopular task – the infantry thought digging was beneath them – and made no easier by the constant fire from the walls, which went on into the night when the French dropped fireballs (bundles of straw soaked in pitch and lit) to enable them to see what they were firing at. Despite the cold, which forced a shift system to be introduced, and constant fire from the San Francisco convent, work proceeded steadily. During the night of 13 January the siege guns were manhandled into position, in batteries with ramparts twenty feet thick.[24] On the same night Santa Cruz fell to another *coup de main* when three companies of the KGL and one of the 60th Rifles took it by escalade. Next morning could have been a major embarrassment, when the French, noting that the men of the division being relieved were leaving the trenches before the division coming up had reached them, mounted a sortie from Ciudad Rodrigo. A battalion rushed out, got to the second parallel and began to push over gabions (wicker baskets full of earth) and break shovels. The few soldiers left in the trenches, mainly artificers, opened fire, and the relieving division arrived before too much damage had been done. On the afternoon of 14 January the siege guns opened fire. Their target was the site of the breach which the French themselves had blown in the north-west corner of the walls in 1810, as Wellington's engineers considered that new mortar would collapse more easily than that which had hardened over centuries. Two of the guns concentrated their fire on the convent of San Francisco, which was taken by yet another night raid the same evening by three companies of the 40th Foot. As all the siege guns were engaged in trying to breach the walls, and were not available to engage the guns of the fortress, from the night of 14 January riflemen from the 60th and 95th Rifles were sent out to dig individual positions close to the walls. Once in position, the riflemen sniped at any French sentry or gunner who showed himself on the walls or through an embrasure. The Baker rifle was highly accurate at this range and a combination of their efforts and of parties of engineers, standing by to extinguish fireballs with sandbags and buckets of earth, reduced the fire from the fortress.

Getting the siege guns into position and the control of firing was the responsibility of Alexander Dickson (although, as there was a major general of artillery present, Dickson was tactfully called the 'siege director'). There were no optical sights on guns of this period and aiming was carried out by using the dispart sight, engraved on the gun, for direction, and by an officer using a field clinometer for elevation. The new iron guns were far more accurate than their brass predecessors (whose barrels had a tendency to droop after constant firing), but the gun crews had no telescopes and only the naked eye to identify the target. The procedure was to drill two vertical lines right and left of the intended breach, by hitting the walls with successive balls one below the other, and then bombarding the base of the wall so that it collapsed. All this required skill of the highest order. Firing had to be kept up all day, or the defenders would repair the damage. At night, when the gunners could not see their target properly, fire could only be desultory, but Dickson manufactured his own version of grape shot (rarely used on land), using three-pound balls fired from twenty-four pounders, to keep the French away from the breach site at night.[25] Although the siege train contained mortars and howitzers, which fired at high angle and could drop shells over the walls, Wellington restricted their firing in the hope of minimising civilian casualties. With all the guns firing at the corner of the walls, a breach soon appeared and the gunners continued to enlarge it until it was a hundred yards wide, with the rubble extending forward to the ditch. By dawn on 18 January a further battery was established in the second parallel, only 300 yards from the walls, and fire was opened on a second breach site, a tower half way along the northern wall. The tower collapsed that same afternoon and a small but practicable breach could be seen. Prior to this war the defenders would almost certainly have surrendered, being allowed to march out with the honours of war. Napoleon, however, had made it clear that fortresses were to be defended to the last, with the attacker given no option but to assault. Wellington decided to attack at seven o'clock that evening.[26]

The main assault was to be carried out by Picton's 3rd Division against the main breach, while the Light Division would go for the secondary one. Prior to the main attack a Portuguese battalion of *cacadores* and the light company of the 83rd Foot were to clear a French outwork outside the walls, in which there were two guns, and the 5th and 94th Regiments would clear the approaches from there along the walls to the main breach. Just before seven o'clock the preliminary operations were successfully carried out and the 3rd Division prepared to assault. The 83rd regiment, less its light company, lined the first parallel to provide covering musketry fire on the breach, while the rest of the division waited in the second parallel. The signal to advance was given and the troops leaped out of their trenches and ran to the ditch. Picton had ordered that muskets were not to be loaded – there was too much danger of self-inflicted casualties in the dark – and the job was to be done with cold steel. Preceding the storming party were two engineer officers and a party of artificers carrying large sacks stuffed with hay. These were thrown into the ditch allowing the infantry to jump down and scramble across. By now the defenders had begun firing from the walls, and the first soldiers started to go down. The French had piled shells and barrels of powder in the breach and these now exploded; but, although the detonation was impressive, it was premature and caused few casualties. In the meantime the 5th and 94th regiments had been working their way along the wall and now came to the breach. They, along with the leading brigade of the 3rd Division, scrambled up and into the breach; five battalions intermingled with control impossible. The first men to reach the top of the breach were presented with a daunting sight: there was a sixteen-feet drop to the street below, and the defenders had sited two twenty-four pounder guns, one on each side of the breach. The guns fired two rounds of canister each, causing considerable carnage, but the British soldiers' blood was up and the survivors fell upon the gun crews. A mine just inside the breach blew up, killing Major General McKinnon, the leading brigade commander, but the stormers were in and there was now no stopping them. The soldiers jumped down into the street, many injuring themselves in so doing, and dashed after the French who were now withdrawing from the breach in disorder.

Further along the walls the forlorn hope of the Light Division was led by Lieutenant Gurwood of the 52nd Light Infantry.[27] Here too the order was to attack with the bayonet, leaving weapons unloaded. During the approach there was some confusion, for the engineer guides failed to turn up and the party supplying the bags of hay got lost. Somehow, despite having to cross the thirty-foot-wide ditch, the forlorn hope followed by the storming party got into the breach, but not without cost. Gurwood survived, but Major General John Vandeleur, commanding the leading brigade, Major George Napier (brother of William, the historian of the Peninsular War), commanding the stormers, and Lieutenant Colonel John Colborne of the 52nd were all badly wounded. General Crauford, the divisional commander, was mortally wounded. Once inside the breach the 95th Rifles turned right and worked their way along the walls to link up with the 3rd Division at the main breach, their appearance finally forcing the defenders to lose heart and withdraw. Gurwood immediately made for the governor's quarters, where he accepted Barrié's sword and his surrender. The commander of the 3rd Division forlorn hope, Lieutenant Mackie of the 88th Regiment, had to make do with accepting the surrender of the governor's ADC.[28] Pack's Portuguese turned a feint attack into a real one, and the French quickly gave up. They had suffered around 500 casualties and just under 2000 men were made prisoner.

Inevitably the successful storm of Ciudad Rodrigo now degenerated into a search for plunder and wine, a foray which some of the bad hats amongst the Spanish inhabitants, and even some French soldiers, joined. There are numerous accounts of the misbehaviour of British troops once into Ciudad Rodrigo, and almost as many accounts which say that order was quickly restored. General Picton was seen laying into his own men with a musket barrel and a number of British casualties were caused by exuberant and random firing in the town. Kincaid of the 95th Rifles, who was present, says that his regiment were quickly reformed and spent the night camped on the walls eating a good meal washed down with (presumably looted) wine.[29]

Whatever the truth about the actions of the troops after the storming, order had certainly been restored by the next morning, when fresh troops were marched in. The breaches were cleared, the dead buried and the wounded attended to. Marmont's siege train was incorporated into that of the British. On 20 January work started to repair the walls and trenches were dug on the Great Teson to defend the siege park. The butcher's bill had been comparatively light: nine officers and 169 other ranks killed and seventy officers and 748 other ranks wounded, of whom one hundred were killed and four hundred wounded during the actual storming; but the loss of General Crauford, who died of his wounds on 22 January, was a severe blow. For all his temper and hot-headedness, he was a first-class commander and he was buried at the foot of the breach up which he had gone at the head of his division. It was said that when the Light Division returned from the funeral they deliberately marched through every puddle and rivulet on the way, as a tribute to their feared but loved leader. At the same time, at the other end of the walls, six British deserters to the enemy, found inside Ciudad Rodrigo, were shot by firing squad.

Wellington was fulsome in his praise for the troops, both in his formal despatches and in his general orders after the battle.[30] A number of men under sentences of death or flogging were pardoned, with the caveat that those sentenced for stealing were to placed under stoppages of pay.[31] Once the news of Ciudad Rodrigo arrived in England there was jubilation. In February both Houses of Parliament passed a vote of thanks to Wellington for the successful capture, and he was created Earl of Wellington with a grant of £2000 per annum.

Wellington has been criticised for his siegecraft, it being contended that he was impatient, cut corners and did not pay enough attention to his artillery and engineer advisers. The great Vauban had pronounced that any fortress could be taken in forty-two days; Wellington had taken Ciudad Rodrigo in eleven days. He had not dug a third parallel closer to the walls, from where the troops could have assaulted with fewer casualties; the breaches were only just practicable when he decided to attack; and the artillery bombardment was only just long enough and made little use of the mortars and howitzers. Wellington, however, could not afford to take any more time. The greatest threat to any army besieging a town was the arrival of a relief in its rear. While the French would have found it difficult to move in winter, had Wellington taken as long as some of his critics would have liked, Marmont would have moved and the siege would have had to have been abandoned. The Royal Artillery and the Royal Engineers thought that Wellington had little time for them. This was not true: men like Dickson and Fletcher were highly valued, but gunners and sappers came from the Board of Ordnance, an organisation which Wellington disliked: it was the wretched artillery and engineer officers who had to explain to the Commander of the Forces why essential stores demanded of the board had not been sent, or were insufficient, or were damaged. While the artillery and engineer officers were there to advise, and their advice was carefully considered, it was the overall commander who had to make the final decision. Apart from Wellington himself there was hardly anybody with the army who had any practical experience of siegecraft. As it was, the whole operation was carried out swiftly and effectively. On 20 February Wellington handed over Ciudad Rodrigo to the Spanish and began to move the army south, divisions moving independently towards Badajoz. He himself did not move until 5 March, in order to keep the French guessing at his next move. In January, once its task at Ciudad Rodrigo was over, the siege train had been sent back to Oporto as, apart from the mortars, the guns were too heavy to be moved all the way south by road. Ciudad Rodrigo had been relatively lightly defended and was badly located to withstand a siege. Badajoz would be a harder nut to crack, but the army had gained much experience and confidence in their first serious attack on a fortified town.[32]

On 12 March 1812 Wellington arrived at Elvas, fifteen miles to the west of Badajoz, and by 16 March the army, now reinforced to a strength of around 60,000 British and Portuguese troops, was in position in and around Badajoz. The siege train, in another striking example of movement control by Alexander Dickson, arrived on 3 March. Wellington despatched Hill with 14,000 men north to watch Marmont, and Graham with 19,000 to watch Soult, who was still besieging Cadiz in the south. Wellington now had 27,000 men, fifty-two field and horse artillery pieces and the siege train to deal with Badajoz.

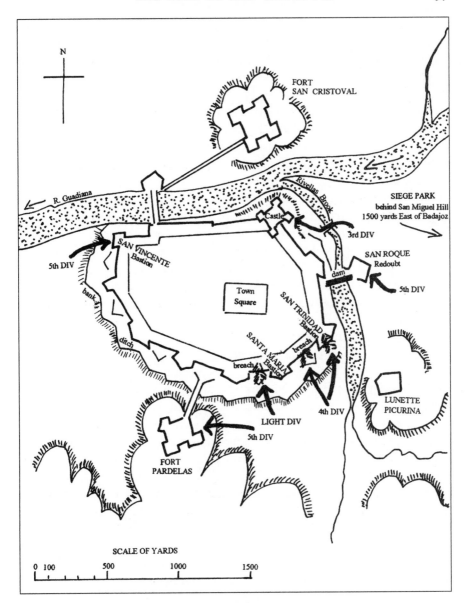

N

FORT
SAN CRISTOVAL

R. Guadiana

Rivellas Brook

SIEGE PARK
behind San Miguel Hill
1500 yards East of Badajoz

Castle

3rd DIV

5th DIV

SAN VINCENTE
Bastion

SAN ROQUE
Redoubt

dam

5th DIV

bank

Town
Square

SAN TRINIDAD
Bastion

ditch

SANTA MARIA
Bastion

breach

breach

LUNETTE
PICURINA

4th DIV

LIGHT DIV

5th DIV

FORT
PARDELAS

SCALE OF YARDS

0 100   500   1000   1500

17. The Capture of Badajoz, 6 April 1812.

Badajoz, the capital of Estramadura, lay just on the Spanish side of the frontier, 120 miles east of Lisbon and the same distance south of Ciudad Rodrigo. It was located on the left (south) bank of the River Guadiana on a fertile plain. The pre-war population had been around 17,000 but this had been much reduced since the war began. The town of Badajoz was surrounded by nine bastions linked by walls, outside which ran a ditch and a bank. To the north west was the Guadiana and to the north east and east ran a tributary of the Guadiana, the Rivellas, which the French had flooded. The fortified town was 1500 yards long, north east to south west, and 1100 yards deep, south east to north west. Inside the town was a strongly built castle, its own walls between twenty and forty feet high, which adjoined the town walls at the north-east corner and stood sixty feet above the surrounding plain. The French garrison, of 5000 men, including some German troops in the French service and a battalion of King Joseph Bonaparte's Spaniards, was commanded by General Baron Armand Philippon. Aged fifty-one in 1812, Philippon had joined the Bourbon army in 1778 and was commissioned after the Revolution. After service in Spain (1793–95), Germany and Switzerland, and at Austerlitz and Talavera, he was ennobled and promoted to brigadier general. He was appointed governor of Badajoz in March 1811, shortly after the French had taken the town from the Spaniards. After successfully resisting Beresford's and Wellington's half-hearted first siege, in May to June 1811, he was promoted to major general. Philippon was an astute, energetic commander, personally brave and a skilled administrator. The difficulties that Wellington would face in taking Badajoz were very largely of Philippon's making. Driven by their governor, the garrison had repaired the damage done by the siege of 1811, created more gun embrasures on the walls, ploughed the ground for 300 yards around the walls, flooded the Rivellas, and fortified and manned three outworks to the south east and another three to the north west, across the Guadiana. With the exodus of much of the population, increased when news of the Allied approach was received, the garrison had commandeered the gardens and lawns inside the town to grow crops to feed themselves. There were plenty of guns – about 150 altogether – but only enough powder to conduct a stout defence if carefully managed. The stores and magazine were established in the castle, which Philippon intended to use for a last stand should the Allies break into the town. The guns on the walls had a good field of fire all round and Philippon was confident that he could resist whatever Wellington might throw at him, although his efforts were somewhat undermined by the desertion to the British of an engineer non-commissioned officer who took the plans of the fortifications with him.

As with most of Wellington's Peninsular sieges, there was insufficient time available to go through all the accepted procedures for the conduct of a siege. Badajoz must be taken before the French could move to its relief. Wellington knew by now that the rumours circulating during the winter of 1811/1812 about Napoleon's deteriorating relations with Russia were true, and he was also aware that French troops and equipment were being withdrawn from Spain to built up the *Grande Armée* for the march on Moscow, but there were still around 200,000 French troops in Spain, and Wellington could not afford to dally.

On 14 March the Royal Engineers threw a pontoon bridge across the Guadiana five miles from Badajoz. On 16 March Beresford, with the 3rd, 4th and Light Divisions (the latter now under the temporary command of Colonel Andrew Barnard, who had commanded one of the flank battalions at Barrosa), began the investment of the town. An observation post was established on the heights of San Miguel, a hill about 1500 yards east of the town, from where Wellington and Fletcher could observe the walls. About a thousand yards from San Miguel and 300 yards from the town walls was a fort, the Picurina lunette. North of that, and much closer to the walls, was the San Roque redoubt, sited where the French had dammed the Rivellas. Wellington decided to establish his first parallel as close as possible to the lunette. He would then capture Picurina and sap forward, creating further parallels until he could get his guns within breaching distance, when the siege guns would concentrate on the area of the Santa Maria and San Trinidad bastions, on the south-east corner of the town walls. Initially two breaches would be made, with a third one created at the last minute so as to avoid the enemy digging flanking trenches as they had at Ciudad Rodrigo.

Having established a siege park behind the heights of San Miguel, Fletcher, with twenty-three officers of the Royal Engineers, 115 Royal Military Artificers, and 120 volunteer sappers and eighty carpenters from the infantry, began to prepare for the siege. The first task was to peg out and then dig a communication trench which zigzagged its way forward three quarters of a mile from behind San Miguel to a point 300 yards from Picurina. Work began on the night of 17 March. Despite heavy rain, which began that night and continued on and off for the rest of the siege, the communication trench and the beginnings of the first parallel were complete by daybreak on 18 March. Immediately guns were hauled up the communication trench and fire brought to bear on Picurina and San Roque, while digging, protected now by three battalions of infantry, continued. On 19 March the French made a sortie from Badajoz with three battalions and a squadron of cavalry, the infantry making for the parallel and the cavalry for the siege park. They were beaten off, but not before they had brought back 150 shovels, for which they had been promised one silver dollar apiece. Fletcher was wounded in the affair, but continued to direct the siege from his bed. From then on a squadron of Allied cavalry and a troop of horse artillery were posted behind San Miguel as a quick reaction force against similar forays. Despite the appalling weather, which caused trenches to collapse and men to go down with various fevers, and a brisk fire from the defenders, the digging was completed by 24 March and the siege guns hauled into position. Wellington had hoped to increase the number of siege guns at his disposal by borrowing from the Royal Navy at Lisbon. Admiral Berkeley, commanding the ships, said that he had no twenty-four pounders but would be delighted to supply eighteen-pounders. When Dickson went to Lisbon to collect them, he found that the offered guns were actually Russian, found in a store in Lisbon, and that the only English eighteen-pounders available there were those on the flagship, which the admiral had no intention of giving up. The Russian guns were old, rusty and of different calibre to either British or Portuguese equivalents, and the windage of such shot as existed for them was too great to obtain the accuracy needed for siege work.[33] Wellington was not pleased but accepted the situation, telling Dickson to sort out the different types of shot for British, Portuguese and Russian guns. Each shot then had to be gauged and painted in a colour indicating which type of gun it was for.[34] Portuguese Militia had carried much of the ammunition all the way from Lisbon up to the guns, each man carrying one twenty-four pound shot. On 25 March the siege batteries opened fire. On the same night the Picurina lunette was stormed by Major General Kempt and six companies of infantry supported by engineers. The fort was manned by a weak battalion, around 300 men, who had seven light guns, but as the attack did not come in until ten o'clock at night they had managed to repair much of the damage done by the Allied guns that day. It was a difficult operation and resulted in 60 per cent casualties to the attackers, who only managed to get in when the fort was completely surrounded and the garrison had fled in the direction of Badajoz. Only the French colonel commanding and eighty men got back; the rest were either killed, drowned trying to cross the flooded Rivellas or captured by the British. Three battalions were brought up to protect the lunette from a French counter-attack, which did not materialise.

Digging and battering went on; an attempt to blow up the dam on the Rivellas failed when, because of the flooding, the explosives had to be placed too far away to be effective, but gradually two breaches began to appear in the town walls. They were slow in forming because, although the stones and mortar were crumbling satisfactorily, the packed earth behind the stonework was not collapsing as had been hoped. Despite the artillery firing case, canister and shrapnel at the breaches throughout the night, the defenders, with great determination, were able to effect some repairs.

On 4 April Spanish guerrillas brought news that Soult was stirring, and seemed to be withdrawing some troops from the Cadiz area to move to the aid of Badajoz. Wellington decided to wait no longer and wanted to assault on 5 April, but was dissuaded by Fletcher: the existing breaches were strongly defended and only just practicable. Wellington then ordered all the guns to be turned on the proposed site of the third breach, between the Santa Maria and San Trinidad bastions, with the intention of attacking as soon as a breach appeared and before the garrison could repair it. On the morning of 6 April eight twenty-four pounder and six eighteen pounder guns were turned on the wall between the two bastions and by the end of the day there was a breach: not an easy one, but a breach nevertheless. Governor Philippon withdrew men of his reserve from the castle to cover this third breach, leaving only three companies still in the citadel.

Wellington had already prepared his orders for the assault on 5 April, and now amended them to take account of the third breach. The attack would take place on the night of Easter Sunday, 6 April. The 4th Division would assault the right-hand breach, at San Trinidad, and the new breach to its left. The Light Division would go for the left-hand, Santa Maria, breach and the 3rd Division would attempt to take the castle by escalade. The 5th Division would detail a brigade to each of three tasks: the storming of the San Roque redoubt; an attack on the San Vicente bastion by escalade (on the other, north, side of the town); and the capture of Fort Pardelas, an outwork to the south. Wellington considered his main point of attack to be the three breaches. He did not consider that the 3rd Division had much chance of getting into the castle, nor that the tasks of the 5th Division would contribute much to the overall plan, but by mounting attacks all around the town he would force the governor to split his forces and would at least have other options should the main attack fail.

The coordinated attacks should have gone in at half past seven at night, but the troops could not be assembled and preparations finished in time, so Wellington ordered a postponement until ten o'clock. Things began to go wrong from the start. The rain had stopped but the night was dark and over-cast, columns got lost and there was confusion as to who was to do what. The 3rd Division, responsible for the attack on the castle, began fifteen minutes early while the 5th Division, tasked with the diversionary attacks, was an hour late. When the two main breaches were attacked both 4th and Light Division's forlorn hopes were virtually wiped out. The French had placed all manner of obstacles in the breach, including mines, shells, fireballs, and rows of sword blades fixed to beams and chained in position. The French infantry lined the breaches, each man with three muskets, while impressed civilians and lightly wounded soldiers loaded for them. No progress could be made and after an hour the Allies had taken over two thousand casualties and were no nearer forcing the walls. The conterscarp, the bank on the attackers' side of the ditch, had not been blown in and the men had to jump into the ditch, where many of the 4th Division drowned in a flooded portion. Something between thirty and forty separate attacks were made on the breaches but to no avail. Further north the escalade on the castle by the 3rd Division met a similar fate. The ladders were too short and were pushed over by the French or broke with the weight of men trying to ascend them. The defenders hurled unexploded shells and improvised bombs down upon them and casualties here too began to mount. Again and again Wellington ordered his men to return to the assault. Eye-witnesses said that, for the only time during his tenure of command in the Peninsula, he was seen to be on edge and nervous. At last, at about half past one in the morning, when Wellington had seen the flower of his army destroyed on the breaches and was considering calling the whole operation off, a young officer galloped up to report that Picton's 3rd Division had finally got into the castle, one of the first officers in being Ned Pakenham, Wellington's brother-in-law. Wellington told the ADC to tell Picton that the castle must be held at all costs, and ordered the 4th and Light Divisions to make one more attempt at the breaches. At about the same time the 5th Division managed to get over the town walls to the north east, and their men swarmed through the narrow streets to attack the breaches from the rear. At this point the French defence, up to now conducted with great bravery and skill, began to crumble. Governor Philippon, realising that the castle, where he had hoped to make a final stand, was now in enemy hands, led a despairing charge with a troop of dragoons on the British columns entering the town square. When most of the horses and many of the troopers were killed by musket fire, he fled to the fort of San Cristobal, outside the town and to the north of the Guadiana. As more and more British and Portuguese troops flooded into the town through the now abandoned breaches the French lost cohesion and began to surrender in groups. The tricolour flying from the castle was torn down and replaced by a British officer's jacket. By four o'clock in the morning all resistance had ceased. The next morning Wellington was said to have wept when he surveyed the carnage in the breaches.

There now followed what is considered to be one of the most disgraceful episodes in British military history, for all control was lost and the soldiers gave themselves up to plunder and drunkenness. For two days officers tried to restore order, and some were shot by their own side in so doing. The full scale of the looting, murder, rape, burning and wanton vandalism has never been tabulated but it was considerable, and hardly a woman or a house escaped undamaged. When General Philippon surrendered on the morning of 7 April, his daughters had to be escorted to the British camp by two officers with drawn swords to prevent them from being seized and raped by the men of the Connaught Rangers.[35] It was appalling, but perhaps understandable. The troops had endured twenty days of siegework in dreadful weather and with constant casualties caused by cannonade and sniping from the walls, to which the infantrymen were unable to reply. The assault had been horrific, with a huge death toll and many more wounded. The population was believed to be anti-British, and when the town was finally taken the soldiers saw it as their right to exploit what they had won: they were, after all, lucky to have survived. The average British infantryman came from the dregs of British society and was kept to his duty by strict discipline. When that discipline was relaxed in the relief of victory, many of the men reverted to type. It was (and is) a common reaction after fierce fighting. On the 8th Wellington entered the town and ordered a gallows to be erected in the main square. Any soldier found in the town from the 9th onward was to be hanged. No one appears to have been hanged, and on the 9th the mayhem subsided, more due to the effects of overindulgence than to the threats of the provosts. Eventually the army was brought back to camp and cleaning up could begin.[36]

The siege of Badajoz cost Wellington seventy-two officers and 963 other ranks killed, and 306 officers and 3481 other ranks wounded, with sixty-three other ranks missing. Three thousand of the casualties were incurred during the assault. The reasons were a combination of a stout defence under an able leader, the inherent strength of the fortifications, the lack of British engineering skills in sufficient quantity, and the need to hurry. The lack of engineers would in future be remedied, at least in part. Wellington's recommendation to Lord Liverpool that a corps of sappers and miners be provided for the Royal Engineers was accepted, even if it would take some time for any to arrive in the Peninsula.[37] Wellington would not have attacked on 6 April if he could have taken a further week to enlarge the breaches, but he had no choice – the French were moving against him. As it was, he had taken the two strongest positions on the frontier, 120 miles apart, in under four months. Portugal was safe and it was now time to consider offensive operations in Spain.

9

Into Spain

On 7 April 1812, when order was still being restored inside Badajoz, Wellington sent his report of the capture of the town to Colonel Torrens, military secretary to the Commander-in-Chief in England, enclosing with his official despatch a copy of his written orders for the attack, and the reports from the divisional commanders as to its execution. The next day he wrote to Torrens again, explaining that, while he had sent the despatches by hand of one of his ADCs, Captain Canning, he would have sent them with Major Lord Fitzroy Somerset, had he been able to spare the services of that officer. The bearer of despatches subsequent to a successful action was usually promoted: would His Royal Highness the Commander-in-Chief, as a favour to Wellington, please consider promoting Somerset in this instance?[1] Promoted to major by brevet in June 1811, Somerset was the archetypal staff officer: conscientious, hard-working, with a good head for detail and – his chief quality in Wellington's eyes – never initiating anything without being told to. Accompanied only by an orderly and a Portuguese drummer, he had been sent to the fort of San Cristobal outside Badajoz on the morning of 7 April and had persuaded Governor Philippon to surrender his sword. On this occasion Wellington's request was met, and Somerset was promoted to lieu-tenant colonel.[2] Wellington also asked that something be done for Dickson, the siege director ('he deserves any favour which can be conferred upon him') but Dickson was in the Artillery, where promotion was rigidly bound by seniority, and it would be a long time before he was promoted.[3]

There were now two French armies requiring Wellington's attention. Soult had made a belated move to raise the siege of Badajoz, but had scuttled hastily back to his position outside Cadiz when it had become clear that the fortress would fall. The so-called Army of Portugal, under Marmont, was in Salamanca. The French main supply routes led from Bayonne, in southern France, through Salamanca and then to Cadiz and Madrid. If Marmont could be eliminated, not only would any remaining threat to Portugal be removed, but also, by taking control of the road to Bayonne, Wellington could strand Soult in Andalusia and make life difficult for King Joseph in Madrid. In May Napoleon reiterated his order that King Joseph was Commander-in-Chief in Spain. Joseph was essentially a decent man – even his Spanish enemies called him 'Tio Pepe' – but he was no soldier, and the marshals either ignored him or treated him with contempt. In any case the situation of the French was deteriorating. The removal of troops for the Russian venture had exacerbated the difficulties of maintaining order in French-occupied territory; and, with fewer troops to chase them, guerrilla activity had increased. There was a serious risk of the French losing control altogether in some of the coastal areas, where the Royal Navy could supply the guerrillas with arms and money. French supply problems increased; living off the country had never been a satisfactory system and now foraging parties had to be escorted by large numbers of cavalry to protect them from ambush. At last, but far too late, the French began to establish magazines and stores depots on British lines, but it was one thing to built these depots and quite another to fill them.

Wellington too had his problems, mainly of manpower. Casualties in the siege of Badajoz had been severe and there was constant wastage from disease. Part of the problem was that, although reinforcements were arriving, recruiting at home was still carried out under the voluntary system and the men were often in poor physical shape. Newcomers were not tough enough to endure rigorous campaigning, and the cold, wet winters and hot, dry summers took their toll. There was a shortage of horses and losses had to be made good by using those taken from the French, for which a bounty of £25 was paid to the captor. Many infantry battalions were under strength, and Wellington often combined two or more into a provisional battalion, or various sub-units into a battalion of detachments. This did not find favour with the Duke of York, who was a traditionalist in matters of regimental identity, but there was little choice. Some battalions had the gaps in their ranks filled by enlisting local Spaniards, but with this came language problems and a high desertion rate.

One of the ways of reducing wastage was by returning sick and wounded men to duty as soon as possible. Wellington started the war with a medical department which was inefficient, undermanned and antiquated. As with the commissariat, medical support, other than that integral to battalions, came not under the army but under a board in England. The Medical Board was headed by a triumvirate of the Physician General, the Surgeon General and the Inspector General of Hospitals. Below them came a variety of officials of varying competence or none: the Apothecary General's appointment had been an hereditary office since the reign of George I and the holder did not necessarily have any training in the manufacture and provision of medicines. The three heads of the board were civilians with large and profitable private practices. When he was asked to go to Walcheren to investigate the very high rate of sickness the Physician General refused, saying that he knew nothing of the diseases to which soldiers were subject. This at least provoked a reconsti-

14. Napoleon and his brothers. Left to right: Joseph, King of Spain; Louis, King of Holland; Lucien, Prince of Camino; and Jerome, King of Westphalia.

15. Marshal André Masséna, thwarted by Wellington at Torres Vedras.

16. Marshal Nicholas Soult, Wellington's long-term opponent.

17. The Lines of Torres Vedras. French troops under fire
from one of the earthwork redoubts.
(*National Army Museum*)

18. The early stages of the battle of Fuentes d'Onoro, 3-5 May 1811. The Allied line
faces the River Dos Casas, in the middle distance.
(*National Army Museum*)

19. The storm of Badajoz, 6 April 1812. The main attack on the breaches, which actually took place at night, is otherwise not unrealistic.
(*National Army Museum*)

20. The Allied army marches into Salamanca from the south, fording the River Tormes, a few days before the battle of Salamanca, 22 July 1812.
(*National Army Museum*)

21. Gebhardt Leberecht von Blücher,
Prince of Wahlstadt.

22. Marshal Michel Ney.

23. Waterloo, 18 June 1815. Fighting around the south gate of Hougoumont farm.
(*National Army Museum*)

24. French heavy cavalry attacking a British infantry square on the Allied right at Waterloo.
(*National Army Museum*)

25. 'Mein lieber Kamerad! Quelle affaire!', was Blücher's greeting to Wellington when they met at La Belle Alliance after the battle.

26. Thomas Graham, Baron Lynedoch.
(*National Portrait Gallery*)

27. Sir Thomas Picton.
(*National Portrait Gallery*)

28. Sir Galbraith Lowry Cole.
(*National Portrait Gallery*)

29. William Carr Beresford, Viscount
Beresford.
(*National Portrait Gallery*)

30. Wellington's office at the Horse Guards.
(*Malcolm MacGregor*)

31. Apsley House, Wellington's London residence.
(*Malcolm MacGregor*)

32. Wellington by Alfred, Count d'Orsay, 1845.
(*National Portrait Gallery*)

tution of the board, but even so conditions were deplorable, with shortages of
medicines and overcrowded hospitals. Medical science in the early years of
the century was primitive, and while some surgeons had university degrees
many had not. As a military doctor was paid about a third of what he could
earn in civilian practice, it was difficult to find medical men prepared to
accompany the army to war. Eventually they were advertised for in the press,
the qualification being to pass an elementary examination in medical lore
after which they were granted a free commission. Within battalions things
were slightly better. Prior to the war the provision of regimental medical officers was the responsibility of the colonel of the regiment, and battalion
surgeons generally purchased their commissions. The surgeons were assisted
by regimental medical mates, who were either soldiers detached from their
companies or impecunious doctors who served as other ranks until they
could either save the purchase price or were given a commission free of
purchase as the war went on. Each battalion had a surgeon, who ranked as a
captain, and two assistant surgeons with lieutenant's rank. Men who could
not be cured by the battalion's surgeons were sent to Lisbon to recover in
hospital, where unsanitary conditions and neglect ensured that many never
did. Wellington was concerned about the treatment of wounded, not so
much for humanitarian reasons but because of his shortage of manpower. On
one occasion he rode thirty miles at night, accompanied only by an ADC,
Captain Alexander Gordon, to check a report that wounded men had been
left outside on the ground while their officers were comfortably billeted in
houses. Arriving at the scene, he ordered the officers out of their accommodation and the wounded into it. Knowing his army as he did, Wellington
returned the next day to find the officers once more inside with the wounded
back on the ground. The officers were arrested and court martialled.[4]

Eventually, in January 1811, Wellington obtained as his inspector general of
hospitals – his senior medical adviser – Dr James McGrigor. McGrigor, aged
forty-one in 1812, had qualified as a surgeon and joined the army in
September 1793, as surgeon to the 88th Foot, the Connaught Rangers. He had
served in the Netherlands in 1794/95 and in India while Wellington was there.
He had accompanied Major General Baird's expedition to Egypt before being
appointed Deputy Inspector General of Hospitals for the British army in
1805, and Inspector General after the reorganisation of the board in 1809.
McGrigor was a far-sighted, energetic and humane man who went through
Wellington's medical services in the Peninsula like the proverbial dose of
salts. He dismissed the totally incompetent and managed to arrange for the
supply of ambulances with sprung wheels. The French had used this type of
vehicle for the wounded since their arrival in Spain, but the British had only a
few. Sprung ambulances were expensive, but they were far better than the

previous mode of casualty evacuation on bullock carts or on the back of a mule. One of McGrigor's major improvements was to design portable hospitals, consisting of prefabricated wooden huts which could be transported with the baggage train and then erected close behind the troops. These probably saved thousands of lives of men who would either have died on the way to a permanent hospital or while they were there. The portable hospitals also had the advantage of dispersing the great mass of sick and convalescent soldiers concentrated in Lisbon, about whose discipline Wellington frequently had cause to complain.

Restoring casualties to fitness was always difficult in an age before antibiotics and antiseptics, and there were many wounded after the siege of Badajoz. A low velocity musket ball would not kill if it did not strike a vital organ, but infection leading to gangrene would. The immediate action was to remove the ball and, equally or more important, to remove the detritus driven into the wound. Letters written by officers of the time frequently ask their relatives to send out a dozen or so white linen shirts. A clean shirt donned before battle lessened the risk of infection from wounds, but the common soldier was only issued with two shirts, and he had probably lost one, or sold it for drink. As complete removal of all the dead tissue caused by the energy of the missile was not possible, tetanus often set in. Frequently the only solution to a bullet or splinter wound in a limb was amputation, carried out as quickly as possible to obviate shock, which would cause a sudden drop in blood pressure and kill the patient. Military surgeons became experts at removing arms and legs – thirty seconds was the standard – usually with the only available anaesthetic being a tot of rum. The life expectancy of wounded soldiers was less than that of officers, although most amputees survived. Loss of an arm would not necessarily lead to discharge from the service, but loss of a leg would, and there were no pensions. Wellington felt that recruiting would be made considerably easier if wounded men received a pension and if the state took some responsibility for the care of soldiers' families, but it would be long after Wellington's time that a miserly Treasury would accept the expenditure involved. Stomach wounds were nearly always fatal, either because the bleeding could not be stopped or because the patient contracted peritonitis. There is some evidence that surgeons practised what is now known as 'triage', the separation of wounded men into three categories: those who could be quickly patched up and returned to duty; those whose lives could be saved given time; and those whose treatment would take a long time and who might not survive anyway. As resources were scarce, men were treated in that order of priority.

The establishment of three surgeons to a battalion as against one today is indicative of the general health of the army, even when it was not engaged with the enemy. Medical inspection of recruits was rudimentary; tuberculosis was endemic in the civilian population, and was exacerbated by the damp and cold Spanish weather in winter. Intestinal complaints from contaminated water were rife, and dysentery was a frequent visitor. Typhoid fever and cholera were not unknown but did not devastate the army as they had done a century before – possibly because of Wellington's insistence on water hygiene. Heat exhaustion was understood, but the link between it and heat stroke – nearly always fatal – was not. It was not uncommon for 30 or 40 per cent of a battalion to be on the sick list and surgeons had little with which to cure their patients. Apart from a box of medical instruments – saw, forceps, probe, scalpel, drill – which surgeons had to buy out of their own pockets, there was little in the way of pills or potions. Sabre and bayonet wounds were stitched up by the regimental mates, often using unsterilized needles and twine, and maggots applied to remove rotting flesh (this, at least, worked). Opium (laudanum) was administered to relieve pain, and bleeding was the universal nostrum for most ailments. Desperate remedies were sometimes resorted to and, as quinine ('Jesuits' bark') was in short supply, for a while the fashionable procedure applied to malaria cases was to shave the head and douse the patient with freezing water from a great height. It was claimed to be efficacious, but as the type of malaria prevalent in Spain and Portugal was recurrent, rarely leading to death but causing a high fever which lasted a few days and then subsided to reappear later, the patient's symptoms would presumably have cleared up anyway. Nursing was rudimentary and care sporadic, although wives and locally acquired girlfriends helped the surgeons and mates when they could.

Despite his difficulties, Wellington now, for the first time, commanded a combined army larger than any of the individual French armies. His numbers would increase as the sick returned to their units, and Spanish help, for what that was worth, was promised. He decided that his immediate target should be Marshal Marmont and the Army of Portugal. Intelligence sources said that Marmont had around 20,000 troops in Salamanca. Marmont was still in a position to threaten Ciudad Rodrigo and Wellington had doubts as to the ability of the Spanish governor and garrison of the fortress to withstand an attack if it came. Marmont could, of course, call for reinforcements, but this would be a long process. French intelligence was poor; communications between the marshals was sketchy and intermittent at best; coordination was difficult, and much of their correspondence was captured by the guerrillas and decoded by Wellington's staff. In order to ensure that the other marshals did not move, Wellington sent Hill, with 20,000 British, Portuguese and Spanish troops, off to Almarez, where they captured the bridge carrying the main road over the Tagus. This meant that if Soult did stir from outside

Cadiz, and wished to move north, he would have a difficult and arduous march around and through the mountains. Soult was in any case fully occupied with trying to maintain the siege of Cadiz, while fending off the probes and raids of the Spanish regular army under General Ballasteros in Andalusia. Quite apart from wanting to keep Soult from helping Marmont, Wellington had no wish for the siege of Cadiz to be raised: only here, and around Gibraltar, could French armies be tied down at so little cost to the Allies. At the same time Hill could occupy General d'Erlon, who commanded a weak French corps supposedly controlling Estramadura. To prevent any transfer of French troops from northern Spain, Admiral Sir Hope Popham, whom Wellington knew well from Copenhagen, in conjunction with the guerrillas, ensured that the French got no rest there. By his ability to land and embark men anywhere along the Biscay coast, Popham, with only two battalions of British marines and a battery of artillery to support the guerrillas, was able to convince the French that the forces opposed to them were far larger than they actually were. Eastern Spain might be a problem, for here the governor was Louis-Gabriel Suchet, promoted to marshal in July 1811 and a humane administrator who realised the importance of appealing to the hearts and minds of the occupied Spanish. As a result of his policies Suchet faced less resistance than French governors elsewhere, and so had to be prevented from assisting his brother marshals further west. To achieve this Lieutenant General Sir William Bentinck, British commander in Sicily, would, in conjunction with the Royal Navy, demonstrate along the east coast with British, Spanish and Neapolitan troops. In the event they achieved little militarily, but at least prevented Suchet from sending a single soldier into central Spain.

Marmont was now effectively cut off from other than purely local reinforcement. On 13 June 1812 Wellington and his army of seven infantry divisions, two Portuguese brigades (commanded by Pack and Bradford) and fifty-four guns – nearly 50,000 men – marched from Ciudad Rodrigo towards Salamanca, seventy miles away. The morale of the army was good, and most of the officers and men saw going out to find and beat the French as preferable to defensive battles and sieges.

Salamanca lies on the northern side of a bend in the River Tormes. The river flows north from Alba, turns west ten miles east of Salamanca and then flows north west from the town. With the river as a defensive barrier to the south, Marmont had renovated and manned three forts in the western suburbs. Knowing that he was outnumbered, Marmont evacuated Salamanca and took up a position at Fuentesauco, to the north east, leaving the garrisons of the forts in place. Wellington gave the task of taking the forts to the 6th Division, under Major General Henry Clinton. Clinton, three years younger than Wellington, had served in the Netherlands and in India, and as British liaison officer to the Russians. He had been Moore's adjutant general in the Coruña campaign and assumed command of the 6th Division in February 1812. While Wellington was occupying Salamanca itself, it became clear that, far from having 20,000 men, Marmont had more than twice as many, making his army only just smaller than that of Wellington. Now began a series of manoeuvres, with Marmont hoping to delay contact until called-for reinforcements arrived, and Wellington trying to bring about a battle on his terms.

Unexpectedly, on 20 June, Marmont made a move back in the direction of Salamanca, and Wellington abandoned his siegework and concentrated the army on the ridge of San Cristobal, north of Salamanca. Marmont paused at the foot of the ridge, and each army looked at the other. For two days there were artillery duels and minor skirmishes between outposts. As Marmont was known to have at least two further divisions on their way to join him, called in from the outlying areas, on the morning of 21 June Wellington came under pressure from some of his staff to attack before French reinforcements arrived. Wellington declined: the positions of the opposing armies were not to his liking and he would wait. Marmont, when the two French divisions arrived on the afternoon of the same day, wanted to attack Wellington on the 22nd, but was dissuaded by two of his best divisional commanders, Clausel and the newly arrived Foy. Attacking a British army in a defensive posture on a ridge with a reverse slope would not be a wise move. On the night of 22 June Marmont moved east and the manoeuvring began again, with each side trying to entice the other into a battle. The investment of the outlying forts of Salamanca was restarted. Despite Wellington's army having no siege train and very few guns capable of battering walls, one fort was breached and the other two set on fire. All were quickly taken on 27 June with 430 British casualties, two hundred French killed and wounded and six hundred prisoners.

Despite Napoleon's orders that no French troops were to leave northern Spain, Marmont had one further reinforcement on its way. His own 8th Division, seven thousand strong and commanded by General Bonnet, had been summoned south. Also summoned had been a division under General Caffarelli, but that officer had decided that he needed all the infantry that he had, and sent only cavalry and artillery, to Marmont's considerable annoyance. On the arrival of Bonnet on 1 July, Marmont knew that he could expect no further increase in his forces – pleas to Soult and Suchet had been answered by polite refusals. Marmont nevertheless now disposed of more than 50,000 troops, more or less equal to Wellington's resources. Marmont lacked reliable intelligence, however, and was unsure what Wellington might do. He also feared a descent by Hill's corps, although in fact Hill was still in

Estramadura and there were no plans for him to move. Meanwhile, in Madrid, King Joseph and his military adviser, Marshal Jourdan, were concerned as to what might happen should Marmont be beaten, or even if a battle ended in a draw with Marmont having to withdraw from the Salamanca area. Such a result would leave the route to Madrid open, and that could not be countenanced. Joseph and Jourdan decided to strip all the French garrisons in Castile, except for those in Toledo and in Madrid itself, which should give then around 13,000 men to assist Marmont. Unfortunately for Marmont, French communications were so bad that he knew nothing of this plan, although Wellington, whose staff had decoded the captured French despatches, did.

At this point Marmont's army was at Tordesillas, fifty miles north east of Salamanca, while Wellington was concentrated at Medina del Campo, eighteen miles away to the south east. Manoeuvring by both sides went on. Marmont crossed and recrossed the Douro trying to threaten first Wellington's left flank and then his right. Wellington moved to check him. Skirmishes, but no battle, took place. On 15 July Marmont began to move south, towards Salamanca. Wellington moved in the same direction, parallel to and initially about three miles away from the French. Wellington began to fear that he had lost control of the situation, particularly when he heard next day that Joseph and Marmont had managed to gather over 13,000 men in Madrid and were preparing to march. He did not know whether Marmont also had this information. The routes between Marmont and Madrid were well covered by the guerrillas, but whether or not Marmont knew that Joseph would shortly be on his way was irrelevant: if the two French armies joined, Wellington would have no choice but to withdraw back to Ciudad Rodrigo without a decisive battle.

As the two armies fell back, the British to the west and the French to the south of the Guarena rivulet, often only a few hundred yards apart, Wellington was constantly on the move, watching for any sign that Marmont might try to dart to his right and cut the British off from Salamanca. Theoretically the British should have been faster marchers than the French; the standard British pace for marching in column of route was thirty inches at 108 paces per minute, the French a twenty-five and a half inch pace at 100 per minute, but in fact the reverse was the case. The British soldier had to carry his rations and personal kit in his pack and, even after Wellington's strictures on unnecessary baggage, regimental carts, private mules and wives slowed the columns down. The French foraged for much of their food and had much less regimental baggage. On 20 July Wellington placed his army on the heights of San Cristobal, where they had been a month before. His options were still open, but a retreat to Ciudad Rodrigo was looking increasingly likely.

On 21 July the Allies entered Salamanca and crossed the River Tormes that night. There was a violent thunderstorm with heavy rain: horses panicked, men were struck by lightning and the whole army received a thorough soaking. Later such a storm would be seen as an omen of a great British victory, but for the moment it only added to the army's discomfort.[5] The French crossed the Tormes further to the east, at Huerta, and continued south. On the morning of 22 July Wellington ordered the baggage train to move west, back along the road to Ciudad Rodrigo, while the army continued to march south west. The area into which the Allied army now moved was broken and had many small valleys and reverse slopes where troops could be positioned without being seen by the French. A low, broken ridge ran roughly north to south to the village of Los Arapiles, about six miles south of Salamanca. To the east of the village were two hills: the Arapil Chico, which was an extension of the ridge although separate from it; and the Arapil Grande. Wellington occupied the Arapil Chico and the village. He did not occupy the Arapil Grande, which was forward and to the east of the area where the army now was. It has been suggested that Wellington deliberately chose not to occupy the Arapil Grande because if he had done so his position would have been impregnable. Marmont, rather than attack it, would have waited until King Joseph's reinforcements came up when Wellington, greatly outnumbered, would have been forced to retreat without a battle. Good as Wellington was at predicting what his enemies might do, this is to credit him with more precognition than even he could muster. Wellington did not occupy the Arapil Grande because he could not have supported the troops there without exposing the rest of the army. He was still poised to retreat back to Portugal if he could not bring the French to battle on his terms.

As Marmont moved south, now about two miles east of where Wellington's army was, he came to the village of Calvarassa de Arriba. From there he could see the 7th Division (commanded by Major General John Hope) on the hills about two miles away. By now Marmont had learned not to attack British infantry in a defensive position, but he had assessed Wellington as being essentially a defensive general, who would not risk an attack and who could not manoeuvre in open country. At the same time he could see clouds of dust away to the west. This, he assumed, was Wellington retreating to Ciudad Rodrigo. The troops on the hill could only be a rearguard. Even a rearguard in such a position would be difficult to take on frontally, but a wide sweep to the south could avoid the ridge and cut the road to Ciudad Rodrigo, trapping Wellington between Marmont's army and Salamanca. In this more open ground Marmont felt more than a match for the British. The French divisional commanders agreed, and French troops occupied the Arapil Grande.

Unfortunately for Marmont, the dust which he could see along the Ciudad Rodrigo road was only the baggage train, the mobile hospitals and the ammunition carts; the 7th Division was not a rearguard but just one division of the whole of Wellington's army, the rest of which was concealed by the ground from Marmont's gaze. Marmont ordered three divisions to swing west, to cut off what he thought to be the retreating Allies. General Thomières' division, followed by those of Generals Macune and Brennier, set off in column of route. The French had now occupied the Arapil Grande and were hauling their guns into position, but they were spread out over four miles, and Marmont had extended his left flank without pulling in his right. Wellington moved his divisions to conform, watching the French movements from the Arapil Chico. At about half past three in the afternoon Wellington was in the village of Los Arapiles, having a snack lunch of a chicken leg. An ADC galloped up and reported that the French were marching along the British front. Wellington called for his telescope and put it to his eye. 'By God, that will do', he exclaimed, and threw the half-eaten chicken leg over his shoulder. Mounting his horse he galloped up the hill and confirmed what he could see from lower down. It may not have been the moment that Wellington was waiting for, but it was a moment that he seized. Galloping to the 3rd Division, now commanded by his brother-in-law, Ned Pakenham, while Picton recovered from the wound sustained at Badajoz, Wellington gave brief orders: 'Carry all before you', he said. 'I will, my lord', said Pakenham somewhat dramatically, 'if you will but give me your hand.' The handshake executed, Wellington now galloped half a mile to General Leith, commanding the 5th Division, and gave him similar instructions.

The three French divisions were making best speed westwards, separated now in their hurry to reach the Ciudad Rodrigo road, when the 3rd Division, supported by Colonel D'Urban's Anglo-Portuguese cavalry, suddenly debouched from woods to their right front and fell upon Thomières' column. Within minutes the leading French division was scattered and Thomières had been killed. A few more minutes later Leith's 5th Division erupted over the ridge and crashed into General Macune's division, which stood no chance. Leith was supported by Stapleton Cotton's cavalry, which began to sabre the scattered French infantry. One of Cotton's brigades, commanded by Major General John Le Marchant and consisting of around a thousand heavy dragoons, sent out to the Peninsula as a result of Wellington's importuning the Duke of York, rode on and charged the head of the third French division, that of Brennier. The French had no time to form and they too were routed. Brennier was badly wounded, later to die in British hands. Within thirty minutes a quarter of Marmont's army was incapable of action; Marmont himself, on the Arapil Grande, was wounded by shrapnel, and his second-in-

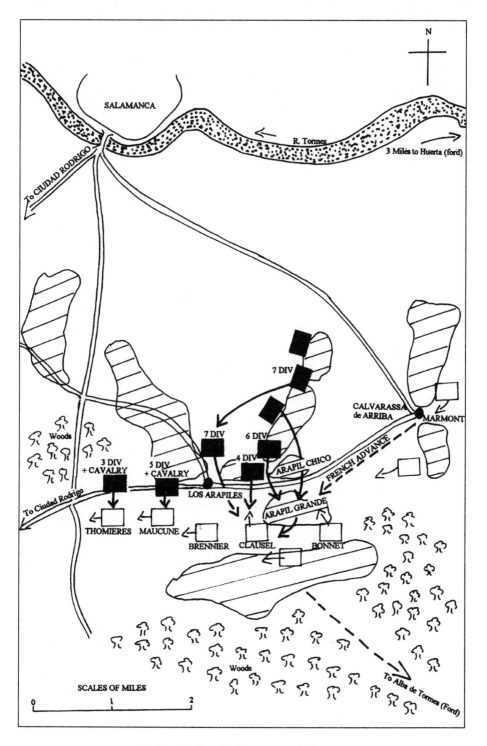

18. The Battle of Salamanca, 22 July 1812.

command, General Bonnet, killed. General Clausel, commanding the next French division, which had not been the object of the sudden British attack, attempted to retrieve the situation. He was a brave and experienced officer, and at about half past five he launched a counter-attack straight through the centre of the British positions, swept aside Lowry Cole's 4th Division and Pack's Portuguese brigade, and reached the outskirts of Los Arapiles. It was of no avail: Wellington brought up Clinton's 6th Division to seal off the northern end of the French salient, and placed artillery and Portuguese infantry where they could bring down a telling crossfire on the French. Once the British 1st and 7th Divisions, so far unused, came up Clausel's fate was sealed and, despite furious fighting, he was forced to cede the ground won. By now only one French division – that of General Foy – was still intact and it fought a stubborn rearguard action to allow the remainder of the battered and defeated army, now under Clausel, to flee.

It was a great victory, but it should have been even greater. The French army had disintegrated and now was the opportunity to pursue the remnants and destroy them utterly. The Allied cavalry set off in the direction of the fords at Huerta. It was only at Huerta, Wellington thought, that the French could cross the Tormes, as the only other crossing point, a bridge at Alba de Tormes, eight miles to the south east, was held by a strong Spanish garrison placed there on Wellington's orders. Or, rather, it should have been held. General Carlos José d'Espignac España commanded a Spanish division attached to Wellington's army. Well before the battle of Salamanca, during the manoeuvring phase, Wellington had ordered España to place a strong garrison on the bridge at Alba de Tormes. Espana had never seen the point of this task, and had, without telling Wellington, removed the garrison. Now he was far too frightened of Wellington's wrath to admit what he had done, and it was midnight on 22 July before Wellington discovered from reports by his pursuing cavalry that the bulk of the French soldiers were making not for Huerta but for Alba, and that they were crossing the bridge unopposed. Wellington was furious. The pursuit went on for three days, and did considerable damage to French bodies of soldiery that it managed to catch, before Wellington called it off.

One notable event took place at Garcia Hernandez, five miles north east of Alba de Tormes, on 23 July. Major General Eberhardt von Bock, a Hanoverian officer and a major general in the British army since July 1810, was commanding the heavy cavalry brigade of the KGL during the pursuit when he caught up with a French regiment of infantry, which promptly formed three battalion squares. Von Bock's eyesight was poor and he asked his assistant adjutant general to show him where exactly the French were. Once he had been led to where he could identify his enemy, he ordered a charge. This was contrary to all accepted tactical doctrine – unsupported cavalry should not waste time charging infantry in square – but, possibly for the only time in the war, the cavalry broke the squares and killed or captured most of the French infantry. What appears to have happened – and von Bock, with his poor eyesight, was himself unsure – is that a KGL horse, of what we would now describe as the heavy hunter type, was killed by a musket shot and the momentum carried the dead animal into the face of the square, creating a gap. Other cavalrymen seized the opportunity and jumped their horses into the square, which was unable to close and was destroyed. This seems to have unsettled the other squares, which began to waver. Gaps in their lines appeared and the whole thing was over in minutes.

During the pursuit Dr McGrigor received the rough edge of Wellington's tongue. Medical support was important, Wellington was glad to have McGrigor and trusted him totally, but there was to be no doubt as to priorities. When he discovered that McGrigor had altered the route allotted to the commissariat, so that the ambulance convoys could use it, Wellington, who was being sketched by Goya at the time, rounded on the unfortunate doctor: 'Who is to command the army, sir, I or you? As long as you live, sir, never do so again; never do anything without my orders.'[6] Wellington's rages rarely lasted long and McGrigor was invited to dinner that same night

Total Allied casualties were 5200, with the Portuguese taking a slightly higher proportion than the British, and including nearly seven hundred officers, British and Portuguese, killed. Beresford, Cole and Leith were all injured, Wellington himself was hit by a spent musket ball which went through his cloak and pistol holster bruising his thigh, and Cotton was wounded by one of his own sentries. French losses are not known, but something like 30 per cent of their men were killed, wounded or captured in the battle, a further 30 per cent of the army was scattered far and wide. Wellington had also captured twenty guns. Altogether Marmont probably suffered in the region of 15,000 casualties. Wellington's most serious loss was General Le Marchant, who had been killed in the latter stages as he directed his heavy cavalry against the imperfectly formed French squares. John Gaspard Le Marchant, like many British officers, was of Huguenot descent and was a far-sighted and thinking officer. He had designed the sabre carried by all British light cavalry and the current cavalry tactics manual had been written by him. He was a great reformer and was the founder of the officer training schools at High Wycombe and Marlowe, forerunners of the Staff College and Sandhurst. He came to the Peninsula in June 1811, where, unusually for a cavalry officer, he understood the importance of keeping cavalry under tight control. Had he lived, he would surely have been an outstanding cavalry leader. His death was caused by his being far too far forward, and being conspicuous in continuing to wear his old regimental uniform of blue, rather than conforming to the rest of his brigade which wore red.

Salamanca was an encounter battle in the classic mode. It demolished for all time the notion that Wellington was capable only of defensive battles. The French General Foy, one of the more capable and perceptive of Marmont's divisional commanders, wrote 'hitherto we had been aware of his prudence, his eye for choosing a position and his skill in utilising it. At Salamanca he has shown himself a great and able master of manoeuvres ... it was a battle in the style of Frederick the Great'.[7] Wellington had kept his troops hidden all day, had waited until Marmont had extended his line and was vulnerable, and had then launched a devastating attack at just the right moment. French morale would never be the same again, and despite Allied reverses that were to come, Salamanca was the turning point in this war. The victory had considerable military and political impact. King Joseph, who had finally left Madrid to go to the aid of Marmont on 23 July, heard about the battle and its result while on the road. There was now nothing that his men could do; they were not even strong enough to defend Madrid. Joseph abandoned the capital and marched off to the south east, to the protection of Marshal Suchet at Valencia, on the east coast. This worried the French marshals: occupation of Madrid was symbolic of French rule in Spain and its evacuation made them forget their personal rivalries long enough to realise that Wellington's army really was a threat, and that the only solution was to concentrate all available French armies in Valencia and mount a combined offensive against him.

On 12 August Wellington entered Madrid unopposed, the garrison of the citadel surrendering when threatened with an artillery bombardment. The Allies were received with wild acclaim by the populace. Wellington received this jubilation with barely concealed scepticism, as by now he almost despaired of the Spanish army and of the politicians who controlled it. The Spanish Regency Council remained suspicious of British long-term intentions, with some justification, and feared that Wellington's determination to make the Spanish army into a professional, properly led and competent body, as had been done with the Portuguese, might create an army which would in time overthrow the government. Wellington realised that the Spaniards would never accept British officers in command of their troops, on the Portuguese model, but he wanted the military effort in Spain to be coordinated under one supreme command – his own. After his triumphant entry into Madrid the Spanish did agree to make Wellington a Generalissimo, the highest rank in their military hierarchy, but while the rank carried intimations of supreme command this was yet to be offered. General Ballasteros, Captain General of

Estramadura, thought that the appointment was a slight on the honour of Spain, and such cooperation as he had been able to provide grew less.

At home there had been political changes. In May 1812 the Prime Minister, Spencer Percival, was shot dead in the lobby of the House of Commons by a deranged bankrupt, the only British Prime Minister ever to have been assassinated. As with previous cabinet changes, there were fears that the Prince Regent would turn to the Opposition (as before, Wellington said that in that case he would continue to serve) but he did not. Lord Liverpool, a staunch supporter of Wellington, was appointed in Percival's stead, while the rehabilitated Castlereagh became Foreign Secretary, and Henry, 3rd Earl Bathurst, assumed the office of Secretary for War and the Colonies. Wellington did not know Bathurst, and at first his letters lacked the intimacy that he could express to Liverpool, but Bathurst was to be a solid proponent of the war in Spain and provided much assistance and support. Shortly before the reshuffle Marquess Wellesley resigned as Foreign Secretary. It was said later that he had done this in protest at the lack of support for his brother in Spain and the slow pace of progress towards Catholic Emancipation. Although Percival had been accused of being only lukewarm towards the war, the fact was that by 1812 Wellington retained the complete confidence of the government for his efforts in Spain. The truth appears to be that the marquess had become increasingly neglectful of his duties, his considerable intellect having been distracted by womanising. Wellington certainly thought so: 'I wish Wellesley would be castrated', he confided.

On 18 August 1812 Wellington was further advanced in the English peerage and created Marquess of Wellington, while the Regency of Portugal, not to be outdone, made him Marquess of Torres Vedras. Wellington, normally appreciative of marks of the King's favour, regarded his latest elevation with some scepticism: living in Madrid was costing him a great deal of money, as he explained to Lord Bathurst:

> I have been going on for more than three years upon the usual allowance of a commander-in-chief, that is ten pounds per diem, liable to various deductions, among others income tax, reducing it to about eight guineas; but it will be necessary that the government should now either give me an additional pay under the head of table money, or any other they please, or that they should allow me to charge some of the expenses, such as charities etcetera, which I am obliged to incur in the existing state of this country, or I shall be ruined ... I should not have mentioned the subject knowing that the public in these days expect to be well served at the lowest possible rate of expense, if I did not find that I was in a situation where I must incur expenses which I cannot defray without doing myself an injury.[8]

Financial succour would come. In the meantime Wellington decided that his next step should be to follow up Clausel's retreating army, which might allow him to capture Burgos, strategically placed on the junction of the main roads from Salamanca and Madrid to the French base in Bayonne

Wellington left Hill with 20,000 troops to hold Madrid and marched himself on 31 August. He was glad to leave the cloying atmosphere of the capital with its constant balls, receptions and dinners, but the two-week sojourn there had been useful in allowing the army to rest and replenish. One of the reasons Wellington had not been able to follow up Clausel further than Madrid was a deterioration in staff work at his headquarters. The excellent Quartermaster General, Colonel (with what was officially termed local rank he was a major general in Spain and Portugal) George Murray, had returned to England at the end of 1811 to recover his health, which had broken down under a combination of climatic conditions and overwork. His replacement, foisted on Wellington by the Horse Guards, was Colonel James Gordon, a thirty-nine-year-old officer of great ambition but less competence. Gordon's inability to coordinate the various moves of the army and its commissariat was to pile even more work onto Wellington's shoulders. The Commander of the Forces managed to sack him (on the grounds of health) at the end of the year and persuade Murray to return, but in the meantime Gordon had to be endured.

Madrid contained one of the major French military depots, with guns, muskets, ammunition and two eagles. The muskets were handed over to the Spanish army and the guerrillas. Also found in Madrid were stocks of French uniforms. The Royal Artillery took the opportunity to adapt blue French tunics and issue them to their own gunners, whose British uniforms, also blue, were by now distinctly shabby. No one else seems to have bothered very much about outward appearances. Numerous contemporary accounts relate how Wellington cared little how his men were dressed, provided they were produced at the right time and at the right place with sixty rounds of ammunition. By now the British troops presented a ragamuffin appearance. The cheap serge tunics had faded from their original scarlet to a dull brick red, and many soldiers wore brown Portuguese peasant's trousers rather than the issue blue grey. Wellington did, however, insist that the men wore their issue shakos, dented and battered though most now were, as the silhouette of the headgear was often the only way to distinguish British from French troops in bad light or at night. Boots (known then as shoes, to distinguish them from cavalry riding boots) were another matter. British boots were identical, that is there was no right and left, and soldiers had to make their own lace holes, punching holes in the leather with a nail or a bayonet. Boots were provided by contractors at home, who produced the cheapest article that they could get away with, and which rapidly wore out with the strain of marching. On one occasion a consignment of boots was found to have been soled with cardboard, painted black, which disintegrated in the first shower of rain. Soldiers shod themselves as they could, with looted French boots, local clogs or even by wrapping their feet in rags. In an age when many of the recruits would have spent the formative years of their lives barefoot, this was not as great a hindrance to movement as might be expected, and foot injuries do not seem to have been very common. Large stocks of boots found in Madrid were quickly snapped up.

A source of constant complaining was the British issue pack. Designed by a Mr Trotter, it was made of wood covered by felt and looked very smart on parade. It was hopelessly impractical for campaigning, being too small to carry everything that the soldier needed to have with him, and attached to the man by a series of straps which constricted the shoulders and interfered with breathing. A common affliction of old soldiers was 'Trotter's Chest', or pains in the chest and difficulty in breathing after exertion. The French pack was made of goatskin, capacious and comfortable to wear. The first item to be taken from a looted French body was its pack. Wellington himself dressed modestly and practically, generally in a dark blue frock coat and a grey cloak. On his head he wore a plain cocked hat, devoid of the plumes and braid favoured by the French generals. It was perhaps as well that he did, for his habit of being constantly at the point of crisis would have drawn French fire had they been able to recognise him.

Wellington crossed the River Douro unopposed on 6 September, and reached Burgos on the 18th. Burgos had been an important town in the middle ages, when it was on the main pilgrimage route to Santiago de Compostela. Since then it had declined in importance. The town lies on the junction of two rivers, the Arlanzon and the Vena. It is 135 miles north east of Salamanca and the same distance north of Madrid. Bayonne is a further 135 miles north east of Burgos, through the western Pyrenees. The town was dominated by its castle, which stood on a hill to the north. The castle had been occupied as a royal residence until 1736 when a fire destroyed most of the interior. It had then lain derelict until Napoleon, during his one visit to Spain, ordered it repaired and garrisoned. This had been done in a half-hearted manner. While perfectly capable of withstanding attacks by guerrillas and Spanish armies lacking siege guns, the castle should not have posed much of a problem to a British army properly equipped. It was not very large, perhaps 400 yards by 250 yards, and the approach from the south, where the castle overlooked the town, was very steep and impassable to an attacker. To the north, and about 400 yards from the outer wall, was a hill, the heights of San Miguel, the same height as the bottom of the wall and separated from it

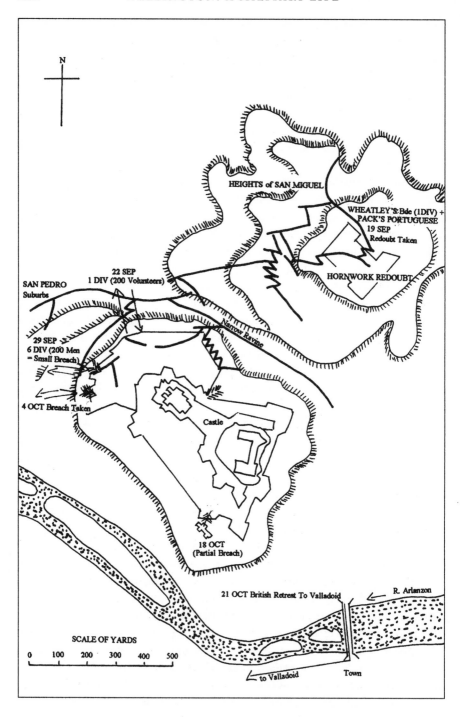

19. The Siege of Burgos, 18 to 22 October 1812.

by a deep but narrow ravine. The governor of the castle, General Dubreton, had seen that the obvious approach for an assault was from the north, and had built a strong redoubt on the heights of San Miguel. Known as the Hornwork, the redoubt was equipped with a number of guns and manned by 200 soldiers, although they had little cover and had to bivouac in the open.

The French had evacuated the town completely and there were now 2500 men in the castle, well supplied with food and ammunition, although short of water, which had to be rationed. The Hornwork was attacked on the night of 19 September by Wheatley's brigade of the 1st Division and Pack's Portuguese, using the tried and tested tactic of using a battalion to sweep the top of the banks with fire while an escalade was mounted from the front, and a feint attack went in from the rear. In the event the frontal assault failed, but the feint, three light companies commanded by Major Somers Cocks of the 16th Light Dragoons and one of Wellington's most talented intelligence officers, succeeded. There was criticism of the Portuguese involved in the main attack, and the Allies sustained over 400 casualties, compared to 200 French. Wellington blamed the heavy casualties on the fact that the 1st Battalion of the 42nd Regiment, who provided the covering fire, were new to the Peninsula and would not take cover by lying down. So far, however, all had gone reasonably well and for the rest of the night soldiers supervised by engineers and artificers dug furiously to prepare a position for the guns which would try to breach the walls of the castle itself. The Hornwork was the only feasible location for a battery of guns to bombard the walls of the castle, but Wellington had no siege train and the only suitable guns were three eighteen pounders which had last been used to batter the forts in the suburbs of Salamanca. The guns were known to their crews as Thunder, Lightning and Nelson, the latter so named because it was missing a trunnion, the iron projection on the side of the barrel which fitted into the gun carriage.

Things then began to go wrong. Wellington has been criticised, then and since, for not bringing up his siege train, and much has been made of the fact that the Royal Navy could have landed the guns and equipment at the port of Santander, only 120 miles to the north. A cursory glance at a map indicates that this was indeed a feasible option, but an examination of the ground shows that, even given reasonable weather and unlimited labourers, it would have taken a minimum of thirty days and more likely six weeks for the siege train to reach Burgos. The weather was not favourable, and in any case Wellington did not have six weeks, for he was well aware that the French were now determined to destroy him and were on the move. If the British could capture Burgos castle and garrison it themselves, or put a half-way competent Spanish force in it, then not only would the main routes in and out of Spain for the French be blocked, but no French commander would risk moving south with an unfriendly garrison in his rear. Once again Wellington was forced to cut corners and get the siege over and done with as quickly as possible. He hoped to do this by a combination of breaching and mining, so tunnelling started from the suburbs of San Pedro, to the west.

On 22 September Wellington decided to mount a *coup de main* without waiting to breach the walls first. Two hundred volunteers from the 1st Division were to escalade the north face, under covering fire of musketry and howitzers. At the same time the division's Portuguese *cacadores* would put in a diversionary attack from the south. Lessons from the siege of Badajoz, where congestion on the ladders had led to many casualties and had slowed the attack, had obviously been taken note of, and the orders for the ladder parties were specific. Men in the storming party were to be divided into sections of twenty, each under an officer; once the ladder was up, the section was to run up it in single file and the following section was not to leave cover until all the men in front of it were up the ladder. Once on the wall the men were then to hold their position and break down the masonry to create a small breach up which further troops would be sent.

The attack was launched at midnight and was an unmitigated disaster. The Portuguese, unusually, would not move from cover and achieved nothing. The covering force, instead of providing covering fire, joined the stormers, and the ladder parties were blown away with canister and musket fire from determined defenders. The few men who actually got up the ladders were bayoneted and the rest dispersed with grenades and lighted shells being tossed down amongst them. The officer in command of the storming parties, Major Laurie of the 79th Foot (the Cameron Highlanders), was killed early on and the ensuing argument about who was next senior prolonged the agony before the attack was called off. Most British officers blamed the Portuguese, and they do seem to have behaved with more than normal caution. Although the plan has a surprisingly modern ring about it, putting officers in command of men whom they did not know, and who did not know them, at night, and in small groups of twenty who must have felt horribly exposed, was a mistake.

Despite having only three guns and a few howitzers, the British now began to run short of powder, and on 24 September Wellington wrote to Admiral Popham at Santander, asking for any he could spare. The efficient Popham could spare some, and immediately despatched a mule train of forty barrels, which arrived at Burgos on 5 October. The siege went on, with the weather showing no signs of improvement and the fire of the guns of the castle unabated. Tunnelling against the north wall was stepped up. While the tunnellers were fortunate in that the clay through which they were digging did not need shoring up, progress was slowed because the picks and shovels available were of civilian pattern and far to big to be wielded efficiently in the confined space of a tunnel four feet high and three feet wide. Eventually the miners reported that they had come up against masonry, which was assumed to be the bottom of the wall. The miners began to ferry barrels of powder along the tunnel. The next attempted assault took place on the night of 29 September when the mine, containing 1000 pounds of explosive, was detonated under the north wall at midnight. The assaulting parties were ordered forward, led by the forlorn hope and followed by two hundred men of the 6th Division. First into the resulting very small breach were a sergeant and four men who found it deserted – the defenders having fled. The rest of the forlorn hope was called forward, went too far to its right, and returned to the trenches reporting that there was no breach. The attack was called off and the defenders quickly returned to the breach, driving off the gallant sergeant and his little party. Control in the dark and in driving rain was of course difficult, but a contributory factor was that shortage of engineers, and, contrary to normal practice, the forlorn hope had not been accompanied by an engineer officer to guide them.

The requirement to conduct the siege did not lessen the paperwork with which Wellington had to deal. The Archbishop of Burgos offered the use of his palace as a residence and Wellington set up his headquarters there, riding up the hill to the castle each day to direct operations. On 2 October he finally received a formal letter from the Spanish Regency Council offering him command of all Spanish forces. Wellington knew very well that, whatever his title on paper, there was political and military resistance to an Englishman being given any real power over the Spanish army. He did not want to accept the appearance of command – which would allow the Spanish to blame him for their reverses – without the substance of power. Wellington believed that it would only be by radical internal reform of the Spanish military system that the Spanish army could be made into an effective participant in the war, but it was this power to direct changes that the Spanish were reluctant to give him. The correspondence between Wellington and the Council went on. That the situation was sensitive was reinforced in Wellington's mind when General Ballasteros (who had offered no assistance whatsoever during the siege of Burgos), stung by the offer of supreme command to a foreigner, attempted a *coup d'état*. In the event Ballasteros found no support within his own army and was arrested and imprisoned in Spanish North Africa.

On the morning of 4 October Wellington's few guns opened fire on the west wall of the castle, while tunnellers hastened to place explosives in another mine which had been dug under the same wall. By early afternoon the guns had managed to create a breach, and it was decided to attack at 5 o'clock in the evening. The mine was duly blown, and half a battalion assaulted each breach. At last there was some success: both breaches were taken and the British were now in possession of a two hundred feet long section of the outer defences. As there was a further defence line thirty yards away, into which the defenders had retired, the stormers now had to hold what they had gained until a further attack could be made. It was intended that this attack on the second line of walls should be made on the night of 5 October, but General Dubreton, who had been watching preparations carefully, launched a sudden sortie, driving off the besiegers from the outer wall, and destroying a quantity of stores and digging tools before they withdrew back to the second line in the face of a British counter-attack. The rain got worse and trenches became flooded. There was now a stand off, with the besiegers directing most of their energy to baling out the fast-filling trenches. On 8 October the French launched another sortie, and drove off the British once more. Once more a counter-attack was launched and the French withdrew, but not before the officer leading the counter-attack, Somers Cocks, was killed. His death was a severe blow to Wellington, who normally did his best to hide his anxiety when presented with the butcher's bill. He attended the funeral personally and looked so mournful that Colonel D'Urban, commanding the Anglo-Portuguese cavalry, attempted to say a few words to him. Wellington rounded on his interlocutor and snapped: 'D'Urban, had Cocks outlived the campaigns, which from the way in which he exposed himself was morally impossible, he would have become one of the finest generals of England'.

The French continued to mount small sorties and showed no signs of becoming short of ammunition, unlike Wellington, who, despite the supply of powder from Popham and more which arrived on 10 October, now had to ration artillery fire and even restrict the firing of musket cartridges to clearly identified targets. The final British attack took place on the afternoon of 18 October, when a partial breach had been made in the second line of defence. A mine was detonated under the garrison church, which went off in the wrong place and only encouraged the French to set off their own mines, under what was a store but not an important part of the defences. The Portuguese then occupied the resultant debris, while 300 men of the KGL and a similar sized party from the Guards went through the breach. At first some progress was made. The Guards and the KGL reached the second line, and got over it in places, only to come under fire from the third, inner line. Both attacking groups were driven off, each with about a third of their force casualties.

The siege had gone on for over a month, had cost the Allies over 2000 dead and wounded, and Wellington had now run out of time. In the south Marshal Soult had finally given up the siege of Cadiz, on 24 August, and intelligence suggested that he was withdrawing from Andalusia altogether, confirmed when a British force under Major General Skerrett captured Seville on 27 August. The good news that the Tagus valley was now free of the French was more than overturned by the realisation that Suchet, King Joseph, Soult and d'Erlon all seemed to be making for Valencia. On 9 October Wellington received reports that their armies had joined, about fifty miles west of Valencia. On 18 October, the day of the final abortive attack on Burgos Castle, news arrived from Hill: the combined French armies were marching from Valencia towards Madrid. Added to this were the activities of French generals nearer Burgos. General Joseph Souham, another ex-ranker of the Bourbon army elevated by the Revolution, had recently returned to Spain from leave and had taken over command of the Army of Portugal from Clausel, who had been in temporary charge since the wounding of Marmont at Salamanca. Souham had joined with General Caffarelli, who had finally shaken off Popham and his guerrillas, and their combined armies, of around 50,000 men, were now marching towards Burgos and Wellington's 34,000 British, Portuguese and Spanish. On 20 October a French probe was repulsed without difficulty, but it was time to go. On the night of 21 October the Allied army began to slip away, through the town and away to the west. By first light on the 22nd the army was ten miles away and heading for Valladolid. Much equipment which could not be transported rapidly had to be destroyed, and during the next few days Thunder, Lightning and Nelson had to be made inoperable and dumped, as there were insufficient bullocks to move them at the pace of the columns.

As we have seen, retreats were not the British army's forte, and the year that had started so promisingly at Ciudad Rodrigo, and had continued in a string of victories, looked like ending in defeat. In fact Wellington knew what he was doing: while a retreat to Portugal was inevitable, he knew that, provided he could keep his army together, he was in no real danger as long as he kept ahead of the French. Morale plummeted, however, and grumbling about the Commander of the Forces recurred. Burgos was not one of Wellington's finest hours, and it was one of his very few failures. Nevertheless the plan was imaginative, and had it succeeded it might have forced a French withdrawal from the Peninsula a year early. As it was, the lack of siege guns, the need to take the castle quickly, Ballasteros's refusal to help, and a stout defence by a determined commander all conspired to rob Wellington of yet another victory. He can, perhaps, be criticised for not using enough men in the various attacks on the castle. He had in his army three battalions of Guards and three battalions of KGL. Had he assaulted on 18 October with all six battalions, his best infantry, instead of with only six companies, they might have been able to go straight on against the second and third lines of defences, and have overwhelmed them by sheer weight of numbers.[9] To have done that would inevitably have incurred heavy losses (even if these might have been worth it) but the heavy casualties at Badajoz had made Wellington chary of throwing men against walls. Britain had only one army and Wellington knew he had to preserve it.[10]

The army moved at an average speed of twenty-five miles a day, the rear-guard of cavalry, horse artillery and Halkett's brigade of the KGL and the Brunswick Oels Regiment keeping the French at bay. The Duke of Brunswick was one of the few German princelings to have no truck whatsoever with Napoleon. He had formed the 'Black Legion' to fight in the Austrian army, and when Austria was defeated and Brunswick occupied by the French, the duke marched his regiment, the Oels, across Germany, had it evacuated by the Royal Navy and placed it at the disposal of the British. Inevitably, they were known to the British soldiers as the Brunswick Owls. Hill too was having to retreat from the combination of Soult and King Joseph. On 1 November the French re-entered Madrid, and on the 8th, after a series of minor skir-mishes with the pursuing French, both British armies were united in a strong position around Salamanca, running from the heights of San Cristobal as far as Alba, where they stayed for a week. The French made several minor probes, but at no stage was there any likelihood of a major action. Wellington knew that the French had left Madrid again, and that Soult was now intending to join up with Souham. The French would not have evacuated the whole of southern Spain for no good reason, and their combined armies would total at least 80,000 men. Given the difficulties that the French faced when concen-trating armies, it was inconceivable that they would not attempt to force a decisive battle, and it was clear to Wellington that a further retreat, to Ciudad Rodrigo, was now called for, before Soult got around his rear and cut of his route to Portugal.

The move from Salamanca to Ciudad Rodrigo, a distance of sixty miles, began on 15 November and took four days. While the French were success-fully kept at arm's length, it was a trying experience. The heavy rain continued, and many soldiers went without rations, having to eat whatever they could find along the way. For once this was not the fault of the commis-sariat, but of the Quartermaster General, Colonel Gordon, who had ordered the ration convoys to move by routes which bore no relation to those which he had designated for the troops. On one occasion three divisional comman-ders thought they knew better than their commander and decided to pick their own routes. Two got lost and the third was blocked on a road that had already been allocated to the Spanish army. Wellington had personally to ride across country to find them and direct them onto the correct road, leaving the crestfallen generals in no doubt as to their error in deviating from orders. Once again discipline broke down and Wellington became angrier and angrier at what he saw as officers' unwillingness or inability to control their men. The retreat from Salamanca to Ciudad Rodrigo cost the Allies three thousand casualties, considerably more than had been lost in the attempt to take Burgos castle, although only 367 were from that part of the British army directly under Wellington's command. Most were caused not by enemy action but by men straggling, or leaving the line of march to plunder, and being captured. Some got drunk and fell unconscious by the wayside, at least one man was drowned in a barrel of wine. Some were killed by Spanish peasants whom they were trying to rob. While on the march to Ciudad Rodrigo, on 16 November 1812, Wellington issued a general order:

> The Commander of the Forces requests the General Officers commanding the divisions will take measures to prevent the shameful and unmilitary practice of soldiers shooting pigs in the woods ... he has this day ordered two men to be hanged who were caught in the fact of shooting pigs ... The number of soldiers straggling from their regiments, for no reason excepting to plunder, is a disgrace to the army...The Commander of the Forces considers the commanding officer of any regiment from which there are men absent on a march, to be responsible; and he now desires that the Hon. Lieutenant General Cole will put in arrest the commanding officer of the –rd Regiment for having allowed soldiers to straggle form the ranks of the –rd Regiment, on the marches of yesterday and this day.[11]

By the evening of 19 November the Allied army, British, Portuguese and Spanish, was safely under the protection of the walls of Ciudad Rodrigo, warm, dry and fed. The French did not risk approaching and pulled back east and north. On 28 November Wellington, still simmering over the deficiencies of the retreat, wrote a long, 1200 word, letter to all divisional and brigade commanders pointing out the faults of the army. He would have preferred to talk to them in person, but as they were spread out over many miles a letter was the only way to get his views across to all:

> I must draw your attention, in a very particular manner, to the state of discipline of the troops ... I am concerned to have to observe, that the army under my command has fallen off, in this respect, in the late campaign, to a greater degree than any army with which I have ever served, or of which I have ever read ... the officers lost all command over their men. Irregularities and outrages of all descriptions were committed with impunity; and losses have been sustained which ought never to have occurred ... I have no hesitation in attributing these evils to the habitual inattention of the officers of the regiments to their duty ... I am far from questioning the zeal, still less the gallantry and spirit of the officers of the army; and I am quite certain, that when their minds are convinced of the necessity of minute and constant attention to understand, recollect, and carry into execution the orders which have been issued for the performance of their duty, and that the strict performance of this duty is necessary to enable the army to serve the country as it ought to be served, they will give their attention to these points ... The commanding officers of regiments must enforce the orders of the army, regarding

the constant inspection and superintendence of the officers over the conduct of the men of their companies in their cantonments; and they must endeavour to inspire the non-commissioned officers with a sense of their situation and authority; and the non-commissioned officers must be forced to do their duty, by being constantly under the view and superintendence of the officers. By these means ... soldiers will not dare to commit the offences and outrages, of which there are too many complaints, when they know that their officers and their non-commissioned officers have their eyes and attention turned towards them.

Wellington went on to remind officers that the only way to prevent soldiers from losing equipment and selling ammunition to Spanish civilians was to hold daily inspections of the men and their kit. He also complained as to the length of time it took for soldiers to prepare and eat their meals. A laid-down system, properly enforced, would reduce the time needed for this aspect of personal administration. Officers were also to use the time now available to ensure that soldiers did not lose the ability to make long, hard marches, and regular route marches were to be carried out by all. In conclusion:

I repeat that the great object of the attention of the general and field officers must be, to get the captains and subalterns of the regiments to understand and to perform the duties required from them, as the only mode by which the discipline and efficiency of the army can be restored and maintained during the next campaign.[12]

This letter was supposed to be for divisional and brigade commanders only, but it was widely circulated and caused great offence. Officers insisted while some regiments might have behaved as Wellington alleged, their particular unit had been faultless. The letter was even published in the English press, where the readership was divided between those who thought it was sound common sense and those who considered it a slur on the names of famous British regiments. One can only speculate as to what the French generals thought – many were avid readers of the English newspapers. If the army was the shambles that its own commander averred, why was it constantly beating them with their larger numbers? The answer was that the army was a shambles, until it was asked to fight a battle, when it shook off its normal quasi-criminal tendencies and did what it was told with considerable ferocity.[13]

In his letter Wellington had mentioned the problem of getting the non-commissioned officers to do their duty. He had long campaigned to enhance their status, and in June 1812 he had written to Lord Liverpool pointing out that while the pay of private soldiers had been increased from 6d. per day to 1s. od. per day, that of corporals had gone from 8d. to 1s. 2d. and that of sergeants from 1s. to 1s. 6d. Differentials were thus eroded and 'the non commissioned officers not only feel no inclination to preserve a distinction between them and the private soldiers, but they feel no desire to incur the responsibility, and take the trouble, and submit to the privations of their situation for so trifling difference in their pay ... and they are indifferent whether they continue non-commissioned officers or not'.[14] Wellington was of the opinion that only the Guards met the required standards, and he would in time achieve improvements in the lot of non commissioned officers, but as with anything involving money and the Treasury, it would take a long time.

For the present, with the army in winter quarters and the French well away from the frontier, Wellington could consider his plans for the year 1813.

10

The Year of Victory

Despite ending in retreat, discomfort and indiscipline, the year 1812 had in fact been a highly successful one for Wellington. Admittedly he would spend the winter where he had been in the spring, but the situation was now far more favourable for the Allies than it had been nine months before. The French had been driven out of Madrid and Salamanca, even if they would briefly reoccupy them; Ciudad Rodrigo and Badajoz had been taken; and, even by concentrating half their total forces in Spain, the French had not been able to corner Wellington and defeat him. Most of southern Spain had been liberated, and despite the need to retreat back to Portugal the Allied army could recover far more quickly than the French. Logistics and administration might not be glamorous, but they were the key to the survival of Wellington's army. His careful management of the commissariat and his clear and unequivocal instructions to his heads of departments, combined with England's mastery of the seas, ensured that the British and Portuguese soldiers were soon able to make good the losses of November. The French, short of rations in an already impoverished country, found it impossible to press Wellington once he had reached the walls, guns and stores depots of Ciudad Rodrigo, despite their being able to deploy twice the number of men. Elsewhere too, things were not going well for Napoleon. Throughout the winter of 1812/13 Spain abounded with rumours of disaster in Russia. Napoleon would need a new *Grande Armée*, and began to withdraw cadres of officers and NCOs from Spain to train it. These men would be replaced, but no overall increase in the French forces in Spain was likely.

One coup that the French had managed during their pursuit was the capture of the commander of the 1st Division, Sir Edward Paget, who had only just returned to the Peninsula after losing an arm at the crossing of the Douro in 1809. Wellington wrote to his captor, General Macune, sending £200 for Paget's subsistence. Burgos had been an abject failure, but it is a measure of Wellington the man that he neither tried to conceal the facts, nor attempted to place the blame anywhere but on his own shoulders. 'a disposition already exists to blame the government for the failure of the siege of Burgos', he wrote to the Prime Minister in London, 'the government had nothing to say to the siege. It was entirely my own act'.[1]

As there were now no French troops south of the Tagus, the Allied army could stay in the area around Ciudad Rodrigo and Wellington could spend the winter restoring the health and discipline of his army and planning his moves for the new year. His badgerings of the Horse Guards and the British Government ever since his appointment to command in the Peninsula had not all fallen on deaf ears, and early in 1813 tents for the soldiers began to arrive at last. Previously soldiers who could not be accommodated in Spanish or Portuguese houses had had to make do; at best sleeping in a 'hut' – actually a makeshift shelter made of branches of trees with leaves and sods of earth for a (generally very leaky) roof – or at worst on the ground wrapped in a great-coat. Sleeping on wet and sometimes frozen ground with little shelter from the elements led to endemic rheumatism, 'agues', 'fevers' and all manner of arthritic complaints, which in turn led to a constantly high sick rate during bad weather and a consequent reduction in the number of able-bodied soldiers whom Wellington could field. The tents, of the bell variety and each sleeping twenty men in a clock formation with their feet to the centre pole, were a major improvement, particularly as they were to be carried on govern-ment mules rather than by the men themselves. With the arrival of the tents the soldier's load could be lightened by the withdrawal of greatcoats into central stores. Now a blanket and a light waterproof groundsheet would suffice. Also withdrawn were the heavy cast-iron camp kettles, carried on mules and used for communal cooking. They were replaced by lightweight tin pots, which could be carried easily by the men and which speeded up the preparation of meals, delays in which had already attracted Wellington's ire. There was no money to meet Wellington's recommendations as to improve-ments in the pay and status of sergeants, but one in each company received an increase and a new rank badge: a single chevron on the right arm, surmounted by the royal crown over crossed union flags with crossed swords. With the extra pay came responsibility, and the new colour sergeant, as the senior NCO of the company, was the forerunner of the company sergeant major, although this latter rank would not be instituted for another seventy years. Previously the term colour sergeant had been applied to those sergeants detailed as escorts to the regiment's colours, the six feet square silk banners on ten feet long poles, one representing the King and one the regi-ment, carried into battle as rallying points. The colours themselves were carried by junior ensigns and were inevitably the focal points of enemy attacks, for to capture a colour was glory indeed. Contrary to received opinion, the sergeants detailed for the dangerous task of escorting the colours were not the bravest, the best, the smartest or the tallest, but those who had in some way offended the sergeant major, the senior NCO of the battalion. It was not a popular job, nor was it conducive to long life.

Rank badges in the British army were only now being formalised. Prior to the outbreak of war officers' rank was denoted by the number and type of epaulettes worn on the tunic, the lace on the cuffs and a sash of crimson silk worn by all officers round the waist. As the army grew and the war went on it became necessary to be able to distinguish rank at a glance, and by 1812 rank for officers was indicated by badges on the epaulette. A colonel wore a star surmounted by a crown on both epaulettes, a lieutenant colonel a crown and a major a star. Captains wore two plain epaulettes, ensigns and lieutenants one. Even this was not standard throughout the army, and in some regiments field officers (majors and above) wore gold epaulettes while those of captains and subalterns were silver, with the captain sporting a crown and star, the lieutenant a crown and the ensign nothing.[2] General officers wore no specific badge of rank, but could supposedly be distinguished by cockades on hats and gold aiguillettes. This was supposedly because, as we have seen, Wellington dressed plainly and many senior officers wore either their regimental uniforms or, like Picton, civilian clothes. As there were few generals and as those in command were well known to their men, this did not create problems of recognition.

Non-commissioned officers had previously been distinguished by the sergeant's sash, similar to the officers but of coarser cloth, and by carrying a halberd (a type of poleaxe) instead of a musket, while the corporal wore a simple aiguillette. The Guards were the first to standardise badges of rank for NCOs, originally by copying the French chevrons but reversing the point, and this was now extended to the whole army. The sergeant major (one in each battalion) wore four chevrons, point downwards, the colour sergeant his newly instituted one chevron with badge, the sergeant three chevrons and the corporal two. The rank of lance corporal did not yet exist in the British army, but it was evident that some sort of (unpaid) stepping stone was needed to prepare a man for corporal's rank. He was generally known as a 'chosen man', wearing either a white armband or, in some regiments, a single chevron.

In gentler times NCOs learned their trade by doing it, but now Wellington ordered the setting up of NCOs' schools in order that the many newly promoted corporals and sergeants could be properly trained in their duties. While this was happening the battalions were being drilled and practised in their weapon handling and firing. In an age when drill was essential to tactical deployment, this 'square bashing' was designed to ensure that a battalion could move from column into line, from line to column and from line or column into square within thirty seconds. Individual drill was very different from that seen today: the arms were not swung but held at the side; there was no stamping; the toe was pointed downwards while marching; the salute was

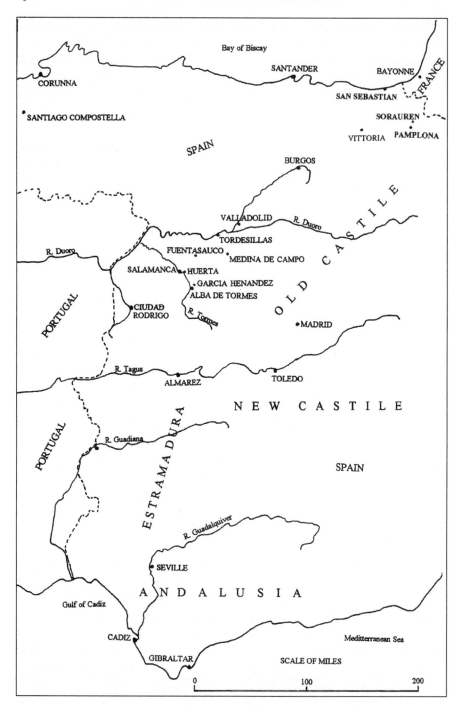

20. Spain: Area of Operations, 1813.

simply the hand raised to the cap. Soon the new reinforcements, and the veterans, began to take on the appearance of a healthy and seasoned fighting organisation once again.

Meanwhile Wellington was, as usual, engaged in all the myriad tasks of a Commander-in-Chief, ranging from international relations to the minutiae of daily administration. On the one hand, the negotiations for his assumption of supreme command of the Spanish army continued, and he finally agreed to become their Captain General on 22 November. He wrote to his brother to tell him of his intention to go secretly to Cadiz as soon as possible to persuade the Spanish generals and politicians that a major reform was necessary if their army was to be effective. Wellington laid down five stipulations which he saw as vital if he was to be an effective Commander-in-Chief of the Spanish forces: the sole authority for promotions and appointments to command in the Spanish army must be his; he must have the power to dismiss Spanish officers; the Regency council must supply the money required to pay the troops and purchase their supplies; a Spanish Army chief of staff with the necessary staff officers must be located at Wellington's headquarters, as orders to the Spanish Army would be issued through them; and no Spanish officer was to address the Spanish government except through Wellington, the reverse also to apply. All these demands were reasonable common sense, but they were accepted only grudgingly and half-heartedly. While Wellington knew very well that the Regency Council might only follow his suggestions with reluctance, Spanish hatred of the French, inflamed with the annexation as departments of France of Aragon and Catalonia, the two Spanish provinces bordering on the Pyrenees, would at least keep them in the war. The most effective Spanish resistance was provided by the guerrillas. Their leaders, previously regarded by the Regency Council as little more than brigands, were now given formal commissions in the Spanish Army. Francisco Espoz y Mina (originally an officer of the Spanish army), whose band operated in Aragon and Navarre, and Francisco Longa (originally a gunsmith), the commander of irregulars in Cantabria, both became generals. Others too were awarded ranks from colonel to general and did their best to obey the orders of the new Generalissimo, who repeatedly stressed that they should avoid open battles, sticking to what they did best: raids, ambushes and keeping the countryside in a state of insurrection where it was unsafe for the French to venture except in large numbers.

While in Cadiz Wellington had once more to curb the ambitions of his Adjutant General, Charles Stewart. Stewart had written to Wellington suggesting that the Allied cavalry should now be organised into two divisions, one commanded by Stapleton Cotton, as now, and the other by Stewart himself. Wellington made it clear that all the cavalry would remain under

Cotton, with brigades detached where necessary: 'although it might be more agreeable to you to take a gallop with the Hussars, I think you had better return to your office'.[3]

At the other end of the scale, Wellington expressed his annoyance that horses landed at Lisbon for the Household Cavalry were in poor condition, and that no curry combs or other grooming equipment had been sent. Bureaucracy does not wither in war, indeed it thrives, and on 30 November Wellington had occasion to ask the British Government to pay the customs dues demanded by the Portuguese authorities, who had seized a consignment of cloth landed in Lisbon for the purpose of making uniform trousers for the soldiers.[4] Despite the reservations of the Duke of York, Wellington managed to retain his understrength battalions, combining them into provisional units, rather than sending them home to recruit, and the retention of these experienced and acclimatised soldiers would pay dividends in the year to come.

In a long letter to Lord Liverpool at the end of November, Wellington accepted that the government and the public might have thought that the campaign of 1812, ending as it had in retreat, had been an unsatisfactory one.[5] On the contrary, he explained, it had been the best year yet for the British in Spain. Despite their best efforts the French had, apart from the Burgos affair, been consistently worsted. Arrangements for command of the Spanish armies were proceeding satisfactorily. They and the guerrillas would, provided they adopted the measures Wellington recommended, be of much use in the coming year. As for 1813, Wellington was cautious in what he wrote - he was well aware of leaks in high places - but he was optimistic that he could take the offensive in the spring and that he could produce valuable results.

In December 1812 Wellington was addressing the ticklish question of his second-in-command. If anything happened to him, would the Allied army be commanded by Beresford, a marshal in the Portuguese army (Wellington was a marshal general), or by the officer appointed by the Horse Guards to be second-in-command of the British army, who might be senior to Beresford in the British, but not the Portuguese, service? Wellington had no use for seconds-in-command: 'It has a great and high-sounding title, without duties or responsibility of any description ... excepting in giving opinions for which he is in no manner responsible'.[6] Wellington was, however, quite clear that, should he be killed or incapacitated, the command-in-chief should be given to Beresford. Wellington had no illusions about Beresford: he knew him to be liable to panic in sole charge of a battle, and there were other generals in the army – Hill, Picton and Graham – who were better commanders of troops on operations. Beresford, however, had shown by his energetic reform of the

Portuguese army, which by now was every bit as good as the British, that he took the broad view and understood the strategic and political aspects of the war. He could handle allies and understood the international dimensions of coalition warfare. Next to himself, thought Wellington, only Beresford had the ability to prosecute the war using all the assets available.

One major improvement in the manning of Wellington's headquarters came in December, when the Quarter Master General, Colonel James Gordon, returned to England on health grounds. Wellington was glad to be rid of him. Gordon was not only incompetent – many of the difficulties of the retreat from Burgos were directly attributable to his lack of planning and his inability to understand the necessity for detail in the administration and movement of an army – but he was suspected of passing military secrets to the Whig press in England. With Gordon gone, Major General George Murray, whose abilities had been proved in earlier campaigns in the Peninsula, could now resume his appointment as Quarter Master General, relieving Wellington of much of the day-to-day burden of managing the army.

Wellington intended to resume the offensive in the spring of 1813. The French still had around 200,000 men in the Peninsula. Suchet, between Valencia and the French border, had between sixty and seventy thousand, and Clausel, with the Army of the North, disposed of around thirty thousand. In central Spain were Gazan and the Army of the South, d'Erlon and the Army of the Centre and Reille who commanded the so-called Army of Portugal. All this was known to Wellington from his by now highly sophisticated intelligence network. Apart from the French troops in the north of Spain, there were around 45,000 men spread out over 200 miles between the Tagus and the Douro. Wellington's outline plan was to make a wide sweep to the north, bypassing the main French garrisons one by one, and cutting them off from France. The French did not believe that this was an option, knowing that Wellington's army drew its supplies from Portugal, but the Royal Navy's command of the seas and the coasts allowed a switch of supply bases and ports from Portugal to northern Spain. When the time was ripe Wellington would shift his logistic effort to Santander and Bilbao. The army could march north and still be fed and supplied.

In order to keep the French guessing as to his intentions, Wellington planned a two-pronged advance. He, with Rowland Hill and 30,000 men, would march straight for Salamanca. The French would assume that Wellington's presence indicated the main thrust, but meanwhile Thomas Graham would take the rest of the army on a wide swing north, over the Douro, and then cut in behind the French defences. Major General John Murray and the Sicilian contingent would keep Suchet on the east coast of

Spain, while the guerrillas in conjunction with the navy would occupy the attentions of Clausel's Army of the North. Once all this was accomplished Wellington would shift his attentions to the north.

Before leaving the relative security of the Portuguese frontier area, Wellington needed to be sure that his rear would be safe. He was unhappy as to the conduct of the Spanish garrison of Ciudad Rodrigo, and on 30 November 1812 he wrote to General Vives, commanding the troops there:

> I am by no means satisfied with the conduct of the officers and troops composing the garrison of Ciudad Rodrigo, particularly in respect to the mode of performing the duties which they have been called upon to perform, [and] in escorting prisoners etc. I hope that ... when I shall have an opportunity of reviewing the garrison of Ciudad Rodrigo, which I propose to do at an early period, I shall find all the troops in a good state of discipline, and their arms, accoutrements and clothing in good order. [7]

The Commander of the Forces went on to say that he expected every gun in the outworks to have twenty rounds of ammunition placed by it, each outwork to be manned by an officer and twenty men, and a flying piquet of 200 men ready to move to any threatened point.

On 3 February 1813 Wellington wrote to Arthur Gore, now a colonel but still (after eleven years) in command of the 33rd Foot. Wellington explained that, having been appointed colonel of the regiment of the Royal Horse Guards, he must relinquish that of the 33rd. Wellington had little choice but to accept the colonelcy of the 'Blues', it having come as a direct offer from the Prince Regent, but he was not entirely happy, especially once he discovered that the expense of maintaining a regimental band had been met by the previous colonel, the Duke of Northumberland: 'Let the expense of the band be paid as it has hitherto by the Duke', he wrote to the regimental agent, but hinted darkly that he would look into it 'as it would be absurd in me to incur permanently such an expense because the Duke of Northumberland did'. [8]

Inevitably the Commander of the Forces was much involved with matters of discipline, ordering presidents of courts martial to review their findings where he thought they had been too lenient, and complaining to the home government that the new regulations allowing written depositions to be accepted in evidence at trials – something that Wellington had asked for – were rendered useless because of the rule that the accused must be present when the deposition was taken: often impossible because the witnesses had moved on and were scattered all over Spain and Portugal. He noted that some officers who had been awarded Spanish and Portuguese knighthoods were styling themselves 'Sir' as a result, and instructed that the Prince Regent be asked to rule on this thorny point of protocol. He was required to decide whether or not the accounts of Guards regiments could be inspected by their divisional commander, should that officer not himself be of the Guards (they could be); and replied, briefly but politely, to numerous requests from people in England seeking preferment for their relatives (mostly knocked into the long grass of military procedure).

Throughout the spring of 1813 British reinforcements continued to arrive, despite the difficulties in America where the United States had launched an attack on Canada.[9] Wellington had hoped to advance on around 1 May, but had to wait until the spring grass was sufficiently grown to provide forage on the move. On 20 May the British and Portuguese troops were ready to march. Wellington and Hill advanced directly on Salamanca, with three divisions including the Light Division, three British cavalry brigades and a Spanish contingent. On 26 May Salamanca was captured after a running scuffle with the French garrison, which escaped with 500 casualties and having lost most of its baggage. By the evening of that day the Allied force was in position on the well-known San Cristobal and Arapiles position. By spreading his troops out Wellington endeavoured to give the impression that the whole of the Allied army was there. This was what the French wanted to believe: they had assessed that when the Allied attack came it would be from the west. A larger than normal British cavalry contingent had been included to ensure that the French could be kept at a distance and prevented from reconnoitring the Allied position, when they might well have discovered that this was but a feint. In fact Wellington had accompanied only about one third of the field army. While Salamanca was being restored to Allied hands, Graham, with around 60,000 men, had crossed the Douro inside Portugal and was pressing north east.

At first light on 28 May Wellington left Hill at Salamanca and, accompanied by only a few ADCs and a small escort of guerrillas, rode the fifty miles to Miranda do Douro, crossed the river by bosun's chair, then rode a further thirty miles to Graham's headquarters south of Bragança, reaching there on the evening of 29 May. To ride eighty miles in two days, over rough country, crossing one river and numerous ravines, was a near incredible feat; but four years of campaigning and attention to health and physical fitness had made the Commander of the Forces as lean and as tough as any man in his army.

Wellington found Graham on the west side of the River Elvas, a tributary of the Douro, awaiting the arrival of the pontoon train last used to cross the Douro in Portugal. During the night the last elements of the pontoon train arrived and at first light on 30 May Wellington pushed a force of cavalry and infantry across the swollen and fast-flowing river. The infantry waded across hanging onto the stirrups of the cavalry and captured a French observation post which was supposed to be watching the Elvas to give warning of any approach. Soon a secure bridgehead was established, although not without the loss of a number of cavalry horses swept away by the current and some soldiers drowned. For weeks afterwards men found without items of clothing and equipment, which they had sold to Spanish civilians, were able to plead 'lost in the Elvas'. Wellington now ordered the engineers to place the pontoon bridge in position, and soon the bulk of the army began to cross. By last light the whole force was safely on the east side of the Elvas and the advance guard was moving on Zamora, which the French evacuated without a fight.

Wellington now sent a message to Hill telling him to move on Toro, thirty miles east of Zamora and sixty miles north of Salamanca. Hill moved fast and by the evening of 3 June the whole Allied army was reunited. The French had been taken by surprise: they had expected an attack from the west, and when Wellington moved on Salamanca they had assumed that to be the main effort. They had now been outflanked and the Allied army was north of Douro, which could have been a serious obstacle had the French defended it against the 70 per cent of Wellington's army which had comprised the northern pincer.

The French cause had not been assisted by the recall to Paris, for employment in Germany, of Marshal Soult (replaced as commander of the Army of the South by General Honoré Gazan, previously a divisional commander) and General Caffarelli, both competent but uninspiring commanders. Napoleon's habit of trying to direct strategy in Spain from a distance continued to cause problems for the commanders on the ground. King Joseph, advised by Marshal Jourdan, had already abandoned Madrid on 27 May, and now ordered a concentration at Valladolid. Once there, the French army withdrew in the direction of Burgos, followed by the Allies in three columns, led by Wellington, Hill and Graham, spread out over a front of thirty miles. For nine days, over a distance of a hundred miles, the Allied columns harried the French, who at last, on 12 June 1813, halted in a defensive posture just west of Burgos and appeared to be ready to give battle. Wellington sent Hill's column directly at the French position while the Light Division slipped round the flank, making for the French rear. The French retired, realising that they were about to be cut off from the road to France, and there was no contact other than skirmishing by cavalry patrols and desultory artillery duels. On the morning of 13 June the French blew up Burgos castle and withdrew back towards France. Wellington's advance had taken them completely by surprise and they were caught flat-footed.

The road from Burgos to the French border ran through rocky defiles, any of which would have provided the French with a good blocking position had they chosen to use it. If the French could hold Wellington on the road, or at least impose a delay, then Clausel's Army of the North would be given time to disengage from the guerrillas and join King Joseph and Jourdan. In fact Jourdan had sent a despatch to Clausel on 9 June, ordering the Army of the North to march to join the King as soon as possible. Such was the threat from the guerrillas that the despatch rider was escorted by a brigade of cavalry. It eventually reached Clausel in Pamplona on 15 June, but the reply acknowledging receipt never got through. Wellington knew exactly what was going on and had no intention of allowing the French to make a stand. He ordered a brigade of Spanish cavalry, under Julian Sanchez, to follow the French along the main road from Burgos, while the rest of the army swung north to get round the French flank. They moved over rough tracks and through hills that the French considered impassable for an army accompanied by artillery and baggage, but by the night 15/16 June all three Allied columns had reached Villarcayo, forty miles north of Burgos. The British army had learned from its experiences of moving artillery and wheeled vehicles, and personal baggage was now reduced to the essential minimum. The French, on the other hand, were slowed by the vast amount of transport carrying plunder, military stores removed from depots, and large numbers of wives, mistresses and sundry other women who encumbered the combat troops.

Wellington's columns now turned east, moving parallel to each other and three to four miles apart. The 6th Division, under the trusted Pakenham, was left at Medina de Pomar, twenty miles east of Villarcayo, to safeguard communications with Portugal and the Spanish coast. To begin with there was no sign of the French; then, on the evening of 17 June, scouting British cavalry skirmished with their French opposite numbers. On 18 June Graham's column, travelling east, was about to cross the road running from Miranda de Ebro north to Bilbao when it ran into a French column hurrying north – presumably to prevent the French flank from being turned. At roughly the same time Wellington's column, four miles to the south of Graham's route and about five miles short of the Miranda to Bilbao road, came upon a French division in and around the village of San Millan. Wellington took personal command and deployed the Light Division with cavalry in support. The riflemen skirmished forward while the two light infantry battalions attacked in line. There was confused fighting; the French attempted to get off the road into the hills and one French brigade found itself in rear of the 52nd Light Infantry, now in column of companies in open order and pursuing another French brigade. In a manoeuvre which only trained regular soldiers could have carried out, the 52nd formed line at the double, faced their rear rank about and drove off the enemy behind while still pursuing those in front – what Oman described as 'charging in reverse'. The French division was scattered, losing 400 casualties and most of its baggage and supplies. Having taken San Millan and dispersed the French, Wellington immediately rode north to Graham, where he arrived just in time to see that Allied column put its opponents to flight. It was now clear to Wellington that the French had intended to defend along the line of the River Ebro, which runs north west to south east along the neck of northern Spain. It would indeed have posed a formidable obstacle to the Allies, but Wellington had turned the French flank and was north of the river and behind the French right.

Wellington now ordered Graham to head north and then east, while he himself with his own and Hill's column marched south. The French were still to be kept guessing, and Wellington was keeping his options open as to where he might move next. On the evening of 18 June Wellington and Hill had reached Espijar (modern Espejo) to find that there were some French troops in a defensive position overlooking the valley of the River Bayas to the east. Wellington did not wish to give battle on the 19th: his army was still dispersed and tired after nearly a month of hard marching, so he halted short of Subjiana de Morillos, on the Bayas and twelve miles south west of the town of Vittoria. During the night intelligence came in from Wellington's 'correspondents' to the effect that the number of French vehicles, mostly containing the plunder of the past six years, flooding into Vittoria was such that it would take days to clear them all back along the road to France. As there was complete gridlock inside Vittoria, King Joseph had no option but to hold the town until the baggage could be cleared, or until Clausel with his 30,000 men could come to the rescue. Wellington knew that Clausel had received his marching orders on 16 June. Assuming that he marched as soon as his army was concentrated, he could arrive at Vittoria on 22 or 23 June. Wellington must therefore attack Vittoria before 22 June, and this he determined to do.

Although it was June, the weather for the past few days had been unseasonably cold. On 20 June, as Wellington rode out from his headquarters in the village of Subjiana to reconnoitre the French positions, there was a low-lying mist and intermittent rain. The significance of Vittoria was that it lay on the 'Great Road' to the coast, over the French border and to Bayonne. If this road was cut off, not only would the French in Spain be unable to receive reinforcements and supplies (not that much was in the offing anyway), but they would be unable to withdraw to France should they fail to hold their present position. If the Allies could defeat the French armies at Vittoria and get behind them, the war would be over, as those French armies not engaged would be too small to reassert French control.

The road ran roughly north west from Burgos to Vittoria, and then east before turning north for the border. The town of Vittoria lay at the head of a

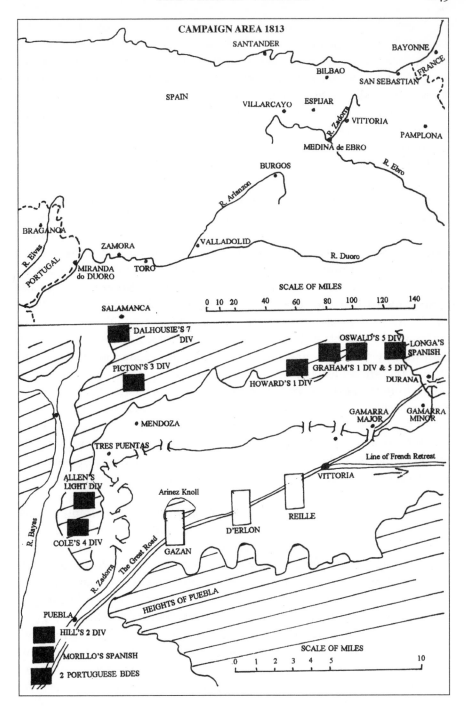

21. The Battle of Vittoria, 21 June 1813.

horseshoe-shaped valley about ten miles long west to east, and about seven miles wide. Along the valley ran the Zadorra river, which flowed south west to Miranda, where it joined the Ebro. On either side of the river and in the valley west of Vittoria were a number of small villages, each with perhaps thirty or forty houses, all of which could be defended. From the French perspective Vittoria was protected by the Zadorra to the north and west, and by rocky hills to the north and south. An attack, if it came, would most likely be from the west, so Jourdan advised three lines of defence to cover that approach, each line having its left, or southern, flank anchored to and protected by the Heights of Puebla.

French forces available to King Joseph and Marshal Jourdan numbered about 70,000. The first line of defence, seven miles west south west of Vittoria, was manned by the Army of the South under Gazan, with four and a half divisions of infantry, whose line ran over a knoll, the Arinez, which dominated the ground to the west, and ended on a loop of the Zadorra. Behind, and one and a half miles to the east, was d'Erlon's Army of the Centre, with two infantry divisions. A further two miles nearer Vittoria stood the Army of Portugal, under Reille, consisting of two infantry divisions. Although the Heights of Puebla offered some protection to the French left, they were by no means impassable, but the French did not place any troops there, other than a few piquets. Additionally, the position was vulnerable to attack from the north, provided an attacker could get across the Zadorra. In reserve, held just west of Vittoria, was most of the cavalry, six divisions or about 12,000 troopers, and the King's Spanish army. This latter organisation, about 6000 infantry and cavalry, had not hitherto been highly regarded by friend or foe. Now, however, the men could be expected to fight well, as if they were captured by the Spanish loyalists they were likely to be killed out of hand.

Wellington's aim was not confined to the taking of Vittoria: simply to drive the French out of the town would still leave them with an army in being. He wanted to cut them off from France and finally destroy French power in Spain. To achieve this he had available seven British and one Portuguese divisions, ten brigades of British and Portuguese cavalry and a Spanish contingent of five small infantry divisions (really brigades) and two brigades of cavalry. Thanks to the progress made in the reconstitution of the Portuguese army, in addition to the wholly Portuguese division, the system of incorporating Portuguese battalions in British brigades had moved on, and most British divisions now included a Portuguese brigade. Of the seven British divisions, four (the 2nd, 3rd, 4th and Light) were commanded by tried and trusted generals: Hill, Picton, Cole and Charles Alten (originally of the KGL). The 1st Division was now commanded by Major General Kenneth Howard, whose previous appearance had been as a brigade commander under Spencer at Fuentes de Onoro in 1811; the 5th by Major General John Oswald, who had arrived to take over temporarily from Leith; and the 7th by the recently promoted Lieutenant General Charles Ramsay, seventh Earl of Dalhousie, who had arrived in the Peninsula in October 1812.

For once Wellington had a reasonable amount of artillery: seventy-eight British and twelve Portuguese guns, compared to the French total of 138. Wellington has been criticised for his use of artillery, it being averred that he failed to use his guns other than as infantry support weapons. The facts are that he was usually so outnumbered in guns that he had little choice but to spread them among his infantry battalions. British batteries (troops in the horse artillery, companies in the foot artillery) had five guns and one howitzer; French batteries had eight guns. The British, in general, had six pounders for the horse artillery and nine pounders for the foot gunners; the French a proportion of twelve pounders in their foot batteries. This meant that Wellington rarely allowed counter-battery fire - the engagement of enemy guns by guns – as the greater range of the French twelve pounders made this impractical. Similarly, and unlike the French, Wellington rarely made use of massed artillery batteries, except during sieges; there were not enough guns to concentrate them without denuding his divisions of the essential artillery support needed, particularly in defence. As with the engineers, the Royal Artillery were convinced that Wellington did not like them and did not give them the credit they deserved. This was untrue: what Wellington disliked was the Board of Ordnance, which often failed to produce the guns and ammunition that Wellington wanted. For the coming battle Wellington had more guns than ever before, and he could make use of at least some of it to suppress French artillery.

Altogether Wellington could call on the services of 71,500 British and Portuguese troops and 25,500 Spaniards, in addition, of course, to the guerrilla bands in the countryside. This was considerably more than the French total of 70,000, but far from the three to one superiority considered necessary for an attack on a defended position. Had Wellington attacked from the west, as the French expected, he would indeed have faced a formidable task, but Wellington was far too experienced a general to do what his enemies expected: he intended to attack on both flanks and to the rear, making full use of the weaknesses in the French position. From a hill to the west Wellington could see, through his telescope, King Joseph, Marshal Jourdan, General Gazan and their staffs. During the night of 20 June Allied intelligence reported that Clausel and the Army of the North had marched from Pamplona, heading west. He could arrive at Vittoria on the 22nd. Wellington would attack on the 21st.

Contemporary accounts of the battle vary, and French and British reports give different timings for each phase, but Wellington's plan seemed simple enough. The Allied army would be divided into four columns. To the south Hill, with the 2nd Division and Morrillo's Spaniards, would climb the Heights of Puebla and demonstrate against the French left. The purpose of this operation was to persuade Jourdan to reinforce that flank, thus distracting attention from the right. On the French right (north) the Earl of Dalhousie would take his own 7th Division and Picton's 3rd Division and attack the French right flank. Picton was unhappy about this arrangement – he felt that as the more experienced general he should have been in command – but Wellington never trusted the impetuous Picton with an independent command, and in any case Dalhousie was (just) senior. In order to cut off the French line of retreat, Graham, who did not have his own division and was used by Wellington to command detached columns where required, would take the 1st and the 5th Divisions, two Portuguese brigades and Longa's Spanish and make a wide sweep round the French right, to emerge to the east of Vittoria and cut the road to Bayonne and Clausel's expected line of advance from Pamplona.

As expected by the French, there would indeed be an attack from the west, to be carried out by the Light and the 4th Divisions, but this would be a fixing operation, rather than an all-out attempt to push the French back, and would be controlled by Wellington himself. Wellington emphatically did not wish Gazan to be able to retire in good order, for if he did then the flanking attacks would come to nothing. The plan was simple in appearance, but only a well trained and experienced army could have carried it out: the necessary co-ordination of the various columns and the movement of the supporting artillery were highly complex. Great trust had to be placed in the column commanders, and any operation which requires a fixing of an enemy position, or a demonstration against it, requires careful control if it is not to develop into an all-out attack to the detriment of the overall plan.

On 21 June the morning dawned in rain and mist, which cleared as the day wore on. All the Allied columns had long approach marches to make before they could close with the enemy. Despite starting before first light, it was eight o'clock in the morning before Hill's men began to climb the Heights of Puebla. To reach the hills they had to cross the Zadorra, but although some of the many bridges were defended none had been blown up, possibly because the river was hardly a serious obstacle anyway, having numerous fords and shallow stretches along its length. Jourdan had obviously had second thoughts about his left flank, and during the night the piquets on the Puebla had been reinforced by *voltigeurs* and *tirailleurs*. Hard fighting followed.

While Hill was engaged in demonstrating against the French left, Dalhousie should have been falling upon their right. As yet, however, there was no sign of him. The two divisions under Dalhousie's command had to move by circuitous routes across difficult and broken country. The route laid down for the 3rd Division, under Picton, was to the south of that allotted to Dalhousie's 7th Division, and Picton had reached the position from where the assault on the French right was to be launched on time. Dalhousie, however, was still struggling through the hills.

Wellington, realising that his carefully though out plan was in danger of falling apart, despatched an ADC at the gallop to find Dalhousie, and decided that now was the time to launch his frontal attack. Just as he was issuing orders to the Light and 4th Divisions, which included their having to wade across the Zadorra, something that was perfectly possible but would inevitably be slow and would also have to be carried out in full view of the French, a Spanish civilian was brought in. He was able to tell General Alava, Wellington's Spanish liaison officer, that a bridge across the Zadorra at Tres Puentas, a mile away to the north east and just short of the French right flank, was not only unguarded by the French, but not even observed by them. With his usual ability to seize the moment, Wellington ordered Kempt's brigade of the Light Division to launch an immediate attack on the bridge. Moving along dead ground the light infantrymen got to the bridge at the double, unobserved by the French until they began to cross. They went across at the rush, closely followed by the 15th Hussars, and took post on the far side. A few cannon shot came their way, doing little damage but killing the unfortunate Spanish informant, and Wellington had a bridgehead over the river.

At about this time the ADC sent to find Dalhousie arrived at Picton's position. The irascible Welsh general had observed the taking of the Tres Puentas bridge, and the deployment over the river by the Light Division, and was himself anxious to get involved in the fighting. He demanded from the ADC what orders were being carried to Dalhousie. The exchange has been widely reported. When told that Dalhousie was to attack and capture a further bridge, south of the village of Mendoza and behind the French right flank, and would be supported in doing so by the 4th and 6th Divisions, Picton angrily retorted that his own 3rd Division would capture the bridge in ten minutes, and the other divisions could support if they wished.[10] Waving his furled umbrella Picton urged his division forward, his orders liberally punctuated with his customary foul language. Within ten minutes the 3rd Division had captured the bridge and were behind the French flank.

It was now about two o'clock in the afternoon and Graham, who had been sent on the twelve-mile flank march to cut off the French retreat, had been poised north of Vittoria and the Zadorra since about ten o'clock. By midday

Longa's Spaniards had cut off the road to Pamplona, ensuring that, even if Clausel arrived earlier than expected, he could not assist King Joseph. Longa pressed on and attacked the villages of Gamarra Minor and Durana on the main road to France, both now defended by Spanish troops in the French employ. Other brigades from Graham's command attacked the villages of Ariaga (and a further bridge a mile west of it) and Gamarra Major. These three objectives were critical, as they not only controlled the main escape roads leading away from Vittoria but also provided crossings of the Zadorra north of Vittoria. The fighting here grew in intensity, for General Reille, originally commanding the third line of defence with his men positioned roughly north to south, had seen Graham's columns moving round the French flank and redeployed his two divisions south of the Zadorra to face the new direction of attack. Reille's initiative was too late to save the day. To the east there was now the best part of two divisions assaulting the French north, while they were being pressed by Hill in the south, and by Wellington in front. Gazan's men began to fall back. By around three o'clock Wellington had captured the Arinez knoll, and the French Army of the South was pushed back into d'Erlon's lines farther east. Wellington sent the 4th Division straight up the road; it met the French where Gazan and d'Erlon were trying, ineffectually, to form their men into line. The 4th Division hit them at the join. Now was the turning point of the battle.

Up to this point the French soldiers had fought bravely and well. Their dispositions had been faulty from the start, but they mounted a stiff resistance. Experienced though many of the French officers and men were, and imbued with patriotism and belief in their cause as most were, they were not the seasoned professionals of the British army. Morale, ostensibly high, was in fact brittle. Even the least well informed French infantry private had realised by now that the war was not going well, and that France and home must be the next backward step. The battle was by no means lost yet, but, quite suddenly, as if a wave of defeatism had swept through the ranks, the French army began to disintegrate. Those who could began to edge towards the rear and safety. At about four o'clock, with his troops assailing the French from all sides, Wellington ordered a general advance towards Vittoria. Despite a skilful rearguard action by Reille, all cohesion was lost as French soldiers, individually and in groups, began to stream down the Great Road towards the French border, King Joseph well to the fore. Panic was catching, and even those units which had not yet been engaged withdrew from their defensive positions and made for the road to France. Allied troops began to press into the suburbs of Vittoria and the last French resistance crumbled. Despite poor French morale, Jourdan's illness and the inability of any French general other than Reille to grip the situation, Vittoria was a great victory.

Wellington had planned and executed a manoeuvre battle, striking at four points in the French defences spread out over a distance of twelve miles. Vittoria is the further proof, if such is needed, that Wellington could fight other than defensive battles.

Now should have been the culmination of all Wellington's tactical skill. The escape routes were cut and the French army was surrounded: it should have been destroyed utterly. Unfortunately, in the moment of triumph, the British army, enthusiastically aided by the Spanish, reverted to type. The cavalry led the way. Being mobile, it was the horsemen who first entered Vittoria to find the town and the area for miles to the east littered with French baggage wagons carrying the plunder accumulated throughout the war. All order and discipline broke down as the cavalry troopers abandoned their primary mission and began to loot the wagons. The infantry, arriving later, soon joined in: there was plenty for all. Inevitably, stores of French brandy were uncovered and drunkenness fuelled the frantic scramble for riches. The officers were completely unable to prevent it, and some even joined in. Jewels, gold and silver plate, women's dresses from the salons of Paris, candlesticks, stocks of medals and the contents of the French army's pay chest, all disappeared into knapsacks, pockets and shakos. Spanish muleteers festooned the necks of their animals with the ribbon and insignia of the *Légion d'Honneur*, and someone ate Marshal Jourdan's lunch. The 14th Light Dragoons almost captured Joseph, the King escaping from one door of his carriage as a cavalry officer opened the other. The regiment lost the King but they did liberate Joseph's silver chamber pot.[11] There could now be no question of a pursuit, the army simply could not be persuaded, coerced or cajoled into taking the road again. The French had lost eight thousand men, mostly taken prisoner, but over sixty thousand escaped, mostly down the road to Pamplona. The French would eventually reform the refugees from Vittoria and use them to stiffen the defences of the Pyrenees.

Clausel knew nothing of the disaster that had befallen Joseph until his cavalry patrols reported the area of Vittoria covered with British troops engaged in looting. Realising that he could do nothing, he turned south east and began a circuitous march in the direction of the Pyrenees and France. Foy, also hurrying to assist, did the same, although he was almost caught on the road by Graham a few days later.

Wellington was, of course, incensed. He calculated that over one million pounds in coin alone had been appropriated by the soldiery, as compared to the relatively trifling 275,000 francs which came to the Allied military chest. In his official despatch after the battle he said nothing of yet another breakdown in discipline, but writing to Bathurst on 29 June he pulled no punches:

up to the day of the battle nothing could get on better; but that event has, as usual, totally annihilated all order and discipline ... The night of the battle, instead of being passed in getting rest and food to prepare them for the pursuit of the following day, was passed by the soldiers in looking for plunder. The consequence was that they were incapable of marching in pursuit of the enemy and were totally knocked up ... this is the consequence of the state of discipline of the British army. We may gain the greatest victories; but we shall do no good until we shall so far alter our system as to force all ranks to do their duty.[12]

Wellington felt that the regiments lately arrived from England were the worst, and considered one cavalry regiment to be 'a disgrace to the name of a soldier'. If he could not get the better of them any other way, he said, he would take their horses from them and send the men home.

It was not only bullion and portable property that changed ownership after Vittoria. The French had been accompanied by large numbers of women, ranging from *bona fide* wives of officers to Spanish mistresses and prostitutes from Paris. With Joseph's withdrawal from Burgos back towards France, every local girl who had formed an association with a French officer or soldier was desperate not to be left behind to the tender mercies of the guerrillas or the church authorities. There were so many of them at Vittoria that the French had erected stands for the women to watch the battle in comfort. When the French army broke and ran, most of the women were left behind. Officers' wives were, by and large, treated well and sent home, but all others were regarded as the spoils of war. Many simply changed their allegiance; exchanging the favours of a French dragoon for those of an English hussar, and the prostitutes carried on as before, even if they were less likely to be paid.

The sex life of the common soldiery in the Peninsula is generally ignored in contemporary British accounts. The French were far more realistic and established official brothels, some of them mobile. In Wellington's army there were few courts martial for rape, and the incidence of that offence seems to have been slight, except in the aftermath of a siege, like that of Badajoz. Wives who were on the strength and whose husbands were killed found no difficulty in a swift remarriage, often only days after burying their previous husband. One account tells of a particularly pretty widow of a private soldier bursting into tears when proposed to by a sergeant the day after her husband's funeral. The tears were not of remorse for her lost spouse but because she had already accepted the proposal of the corporal in charge of the firing party on the way back from the funeral. The sergeant would have been a better catch. As Spaniards and Portuguese were Roman Catholic, British soldiers would promise marriage in order to persuade the girls to live with them on campaign. In most cases the soldiers had not the slightest intention of marrying them, which caused considerable distress when the girls, often with a child, were eventually sent back home rather than being transported to England. It was estimated that by early 1813 there were no less than 4500 Portuguese and Spanish girls attached to and travelling with British soldiers, a figure that increased after Vittoria. That there was no shortage of sex for the rank and file is indicated by an outbreak of syphilis in England in 1818 when the troops eventually returned from the wars, but whether this was contracted in the Peninsula or later in France is uncertain.[13]

Despite the reversion of the army to a horde of looters, the battle of Vittoria was of huge significance.[14] The Allied casualties were relatively light – only 750 killed, 501 of them British – and not only the French baggage but all of their guns except two had been captured. Wellington was careful to give due credit to the Royal Artillery this time: 'The artillery was most judiciously placed by Lieutenant Colonel Dickson. It was well used, and the army is indebted to that corps'.[15] Relations with the royal regiment were not, however, improved by the unfortunate case of Captain Norman Ramsay. At one stage of the battle Wellington had personally ordered Ramsay to position his battery of horse artillery on a ridge and not to move until told to do so by Wellington himself. The Commander of the Forces moved on, but sometime later a staff officer (no one ever discovered who) galloped up to Ramsay and told him to advance. Ramsay did so, Wellington returned and found the battery gone. The exasperated Wellington ordered Ramsay's arrest. The matter would probably have been resolved amicably enough had Wellington not then totally forgotten the incident (he had a battle to fight and an army to command), until reminded some three weeks later that Ramsay was still under arrest. Ramsay was released, and continued to be a highly competent battery commander, but the incident rankled and continued to do so with the Royal Artillery long after the wars were over.

One piece of French property that did not end up in a soldier's knapsack was Marshal Jourdan's baton. Wellington had it sent to the Prince Regent, who replied by having Wellington promoted to field marshal and sending him the (first ever) baton of a British field marshal. Wellington had already been made a Knight of the Garter in March 1813, and this latest promotion was gazetted on 3 July, backdated to 21 June, the day before the battle. The Commander-in-Chief of the British Army, the Duke of York, objected to the promotion because of Wellington's relatively junior position in the army list (he was a general in Spain and Portugal only, and his substantive rank was lieutenant general). Wellington was of course aware of this, and wrote to York to say that he fully understood that the objections were not personal but made because of the Duke's concern for seniority and military procedure. Even the Spanish government was delighted with Vittoria and awarded Wellington estates in Granada, which are still in the possession of the family.

The significance of Vittoria went far beyond the confines of the Iberian Peninsula. The subject peoples of Europe saw that Napoleon could be beaten, and this, coupled with the French disaster in Russia, gave new impetus to the coalition. Austria, currently neutral since Napoleon had married Marie-Louise, daughter of the Emperor Franz I, announced its intention of renewing the struggle against France. There was an upsurge of German nationalism and the British, the paymasters of the coalition but not seen by others as contributing very much on land, could pose as the liberators of Spain. Renewed German enthusiasm for the war had a direct bearing on Wellington's army. Before the outbreak of war with the United States in 1812, most of the grain for the Peninsular army was imported from America. Once war broke out this source was no longer available. Previously stocked supplies lasted for a time, but from now until the end of the war British and Portuguese soldiers would live on grain imported from the German plains.

At home the population was jubilant at yet another victory. Colonel Torrens, Military Secretary to the Duke of York, even thought that popular support for the war was now such that 'conscription would be acceptable'.[16] Fortunately Torrens's enthusiasm soon subsided to a more realistic level, as conscription in Britain would have been regarded as the utmost tyranny and was never seriously considered, although the bar on soldiers of the Militia volunteering for regular service had been lifted and this did somewhat alleviate the army's manpower problems.

Wellington and the British government had to consider what to do next. Suchet was still on the east coast of Spain, but while he seemed to be beginning to get the better of the Anglo-Sicilian contingent opposing him, his 30,000 men were in no position to reassert French control of the Peninsula. Suchet could be left to wither on the vine. Politically an invasion of France would offer more in the way of bringing the war to a successful conclusion, but this must be carried out with care. Wellington has been criticised for not following up the retreating French immediately he had restored order in his army. It was developments in northern Europe which persuaded him not to do so. Napoleon had returned to Paris from the debacle in Russia and had managed to raise another field army of 200,000 men, many of them filched from Spain. In May 1813 he had beaten the Russians and the Prussians twice, at Lützen and again at Bautzen, and an armistice had been at agreed at Pleischwitz on 4 June. Had Wellington mounted a ruthless pursuit in June, he would undoubtedly have got into France and would almost certainly have defeated the French forces immediately opposed to him. If the armistice held, however, Napoleon would have been able to take troops away from the north and Wellington's relatively tiny army might have been cornered in southern France, unsupported by the navy, and destroyed. Wellington would wait.

While the members of the coalition had never been able to agree to a common statement of war aims, the results of Vittoria were making it clear to all that Napoleon could – and must - must be toppled. Twice in 1813 he had been offered reasonable terms and twice he had used the negotiations as a cover to gain military advantage. Wellington considered that Napoleon could not be trusted and that he must go, and this meant an invasion of the French homeland. Vittoria ensured that the French armistice with the Russians and Prussians would not endure.

Before Wellington's Allied army could venture into France, one or two obstacles to movement must be removed. San Sebastian, on the Biscay coast, and Pamplona were still held by the French. In France Marshal Soult was known to be reorganising the refugees from Vittoria and might yet attempt to return to Spain. Wellington ordered San Sebastian to be put under siege, while Pamplona was blockaded by the Spanish, and British divisions were placed to cover any French move out of the Maya and Roncesvalles passes through the Pyrenees. Wellington established his headquarters at Lesaca, about twenty miles south east of San Sebastian. While this was not in the centre of the area of operations, it allowed the Commander of the Forces to keep an eye on what was happening at San Sebastian and also to be only fifteen miles away from the pass at Maya, the more northerly of the two possible approaches for the French. The headquarters was on the main road leading north from Pamplona, so Wellington could be kept informed of the situation there, while the guerrillas would ensure that information from Roncesvalles would reach him quickly.

Wellington continued to wax ever more furiously about the inability of the soldiers to behave, and of the officers to control them: 'We have in the service the scum of the earth as common soldiers, and of late years we have done everything on our power, both by law and by publication, to relax the discipline by which alone such men can be kept in order'.[17] Ever with an eye for the smallest detail of army administration, Wellington pointed out to Lord Bathurst that while British losses in the battle of Vittoria had been 3164, by 1 July they had lost a further 2733 gone looking for plunder. This at least had some effect. Parliament in England hurriedly passed a series of amendments to the Articles of War. While these did not grant Wellington all the powers that he wanted, they did allow the cumbersome procedural niceties of courts martial to be speeded up, with less room for delay caused by the need to collect all the relevant witnesses to an offence. The 'bloody provost' was expanded into what was effectively a corps of military police, and the time between the findings of the court and the carrying out of the sentence was reduced. Slowly the army was returned to its allegiance, but not without an upsurge in desertion, presumably by men who had been successful plunderers at Vittoria and wished to enjoy their new-found riches.

Wellington now had to capture San Sebastian and Pamplona and guard the frontier over a distance of fifty miles. It was a situation fraught with risk, as Wellington recognised, and he did it by holding the bulk of his troops back where they could be deployed to counter any French stroke. On 25 July the first assault on San Sebastian, under the direction of Graham, failed. San Sebastian had been garrisoned by General Foy, on his retreat from Spain. The town was commanded by General Rey, a competent officer, and could be supplied by coastal shipping from France. The Royal Navy were short of the small boats needed for inshore operations (most had gone to America) and the guns of San Sebastian had a range of over a mile out to sea. Wellington left his headquarters, galloped to San Sebastian and ordered that the town was not to be assaulted again until sufficient ammunition had been stockpiled for the siege guns. While Wellington was on the road the French blow fell. Soult had taken command of the newly constituted 'Army of Spain' and been named as Napoleon's lieutenant. He intended to launch a two-pronged attack through the passes and out of the Pyrenees.

In the north the Allied covering force was commanded by Rowland Hill, who had given the task of guarding the egresses from the Maya pass to his own 2nd Division, commanded by Major General William Stewart, normally a brigade commander in that division but who had frequently been placed in charge of the division when Hill had taken more troops under command. The forward brigade, covering the pass itself, actually a plateau about two miles wide, was commanded by Major General Pringle, who had arrived from England only the previous day and who knew neither the ground nor his troops. Pringle had placed one company on a rocky outcrop, supposedly covering the approaches, with the remainder of his brigade further back. His intention was, presumably, that the forward company would give warning of an enemy approach and the battalions further back would move to meet the threat.

At first light on 25 July 20,000 French troops under d'Erlon debouched from the Maya pass, catching Pringle by surprise. Stewart, the divisional commander, was away investigating reports of firing to the south. Pringle took command of the division but the forward British positions were overrun and, despite Pringle's mounting of a series of counter-attacks, the British could not hold and were forced back. Stewart now reappeared, and, having grasped the situation, regrouped the division further back, stopping any further French advance, at least for the moment. By five o'clock in the afternoon the French were in possession of the pass. The British had taken around 1500 casualties, and had lost four Portuguese guns, a rarity in battles of Wellington's army.

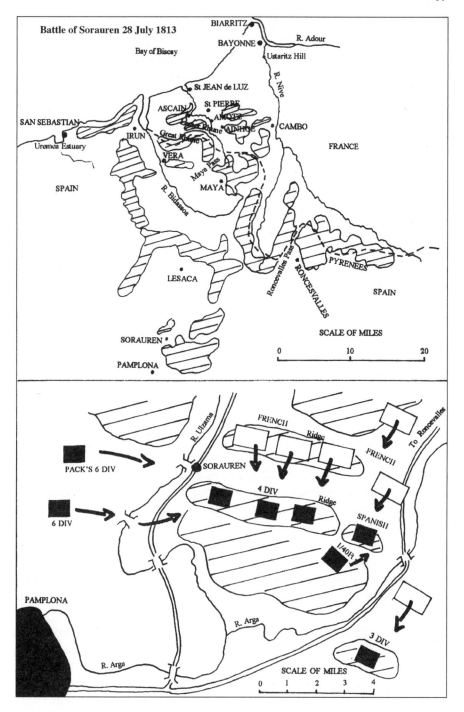

22. Battles of the Pyrenees, 1813-14.

Meanwhile, further south, the passes at Roncesvalles were the responsibility of a mixture of 13,000 British, Portuguese and Spanish troops under Sir
Lowry Cole of the 4th Division. Here Soult had allocated the forcing of the
passes to Generals Reille and Clausel, with 40,000 men between them. Soult
himself accompanied this force, his aim being to break through and reach
Pamplona. The attack was launched at six o'clock in the morning, but the
British, although outnumbered, managed to hold. Attacks and counter-
attacks went on until around four o'clock in the afternoon, when a thick mist
arose, reducing visibility to a few yards and bringing the fighting to an end.
Lowry Cole had never commanded so many troops before; he had not had
any sleep for two nights and was undoubtedly suffering from stress. Greatly
outnumbered as he was, he feared that he would be outflanked in the mist
and his force destroyed in detail. Despite orders from Wellington that he was
to hold at all costs, he decided to withdraw. As night approached Cole and his
men fell back in the direction of Pamplona. After retreating for two nights
and a day, with Soult snapping at his heels, he reached the village of Sorauren,
six miles north east of Pamplona, on the morning of 27 July, where he took up
a defensive position on a ridge running south east from the village. It was a
strong position but the French had the advantage in numbers. Clausel urged
Soult to attack at once and break through to Pamplona. Soult, naturally
cautious and with considerable experience of attacking British troops on
defended ridges, hesitated.

Wellington, away at San Sebastian, only heard of Cole's reverses late on 26
July. On 27 July, with Fitzroy Somerset the military secretary and a few guerrillas, he rode south at top speed. Wellington now had to act swiftly if all the
successes of the Vittoria campaign were not to be snatched from him.
Reaching the left flank of the British lines he assessed the situation, scribbled a
few lines to the Quarter Master General, Murray, who was following up, and
rode into the lines of a Portuguese brigade, who immediately started cheering
him. Wellington disapproved of cheering, 'if you let them cheer, then next
time they might boo', he said, but he now employed psychological warfare. If
the British thought that his presence was better than a reinforcement of ten
thousand men, as Captain Kincaid of the 95th Rifles averred, then the French
thought much the same. Wellington knew that Soult was by nature careful, so
he stationed himself on a prominent hill and openly regarded the French
marshal through his telescope. He needed time for further Allied divisions,
ordered to march by Murray, to arrive. If he could delay the French attack for
twenty-four hours he would be safe. Sure enough, despite the urging of the
increasingly angry Clausel, once Soult saw that Wellington was present in
person he would not attack without further reconnaissance: indeed he spent
most of 27 July asleep. That night there was a fierce thunderstorm and heavy

rain, but, as dawn broke on 28 July, Wellington thought that Soult might attack at any moment. It was not until after midday that the French finally moved, and by then it was too late. A further British division, the 6th under Denis Pack, had arrived and was in position. The battle, when it came, was in the classic Wellingtonian mode. The French advanced; Wellington moved his troops to meet the threat and managed to obtain local superiority. The disciplined British volleys drove the French back, and while the Spanish on Wellington's right flank eventually broke, the 1st Battalion 40th Foot, judiciously placed to their rear, saved the situation. On the other side of the position, when the French captured the chapel in the village Wellington was on the spot and sent two battalions in on the French flank. By four o'clock in the afternoon the French were back in their original position and Soult had to recognise that his plan had failed. He had suffered four thousand casualties and had not reached Pamplona. With further Allied reinforcements arriving on the field he could not now do so. Next day, the 29th, Wellington redeployed his artillery onto his ridge and on 30 July launched a powerful, coordinated attack of his own. The French were driven back in disorder, and pulled back to France under Foy. Soult fought one rearguard action against Hill and then he too withdrew from Spain.

At San Sebastian more siege guns had arrived. Some were from a siege train which had been assembled in case the siege at Burgos was extended, some were borrowed from the Royal Navy. By 29 August a breach in the walls was declared practicable and the town was assaulted on 31 August at low tide (eleven o'clock in the morning). Wellington was not present; he was away to the east, worried about the security of the frontier where his spies told him Soult might make yet another foray into Spain to relieve San Sebastian, and had left Graham in charge of the siege operations. At first the attack, against a one hundred yards long breach, did not go well: almost all of the forlorn hope were killed. While some Portuguese volunteers got in through a smaller breach by wading across the estuary of the River Uremea, they could not break into the main fortifications. Eventually Graham tried a brand new tactic. He ordered Dickson, in charge of the artillery, to provide overhead fire while his men charged the breach once again. This had never been done before – artillery fire control simply was not developed to that extent, nor were there any range tables for overhead fire – but it worked. The Allies were in and bitter fighting began inside the town. Then the French powder magazine blew up, and the tide of battle turned. By two o'clock in the afternoon the survivors of the garrison withdrew to the central keep (where they held out for over a week before surrendering) and the Allies, with nine hundred killed and 1500 wounded, had the town. The most serious loss, and one which Wellington grieved, was that of Richard Fletcher, the Chief Engineer. The holder of such an office should not have had personally to involve himself in an assault, but there were too few engineers available, and no option but for most of the officers of that corps to accompany the attacking troops. The depressingly familiar routine now followed: the troops sacked the town, got drunk and sacked some more. Eventually the town was set on fire, whether deliberately or by accident is not known, and there was much work for the provosts before the army was eventually brought back under control. Madrid was furious, and London was unhappy: San Sebastian was an Allied city, yet the inhabitants had been treated as if they were the enemy. The Spanish government even accused Wellington of deliberately setting fire to the town to cover up the depredations of his soldiers and to damage Spanish trade with France.

On the day that San Sebastian fell at last to the Allies, Soult made one more despairing sortie into Spain, as Wellington had suspected he might. At Vera, on the River Bidassoa, four French divisions under Clausel were persuaded to withdraw when it was clear that they were about to be outflanked and attacked in rear by the Light Division and elements of the 4th and 7th Divisions. After a day of confused fighting in heavy rain, including a gallant but unsuccessful attempt by a company of the 95th Rifles to prevent the French retreat across the only bridge over the now swollen Bidassoa, Clausel retired back into France, leaving twelve hundred dead and wounded, to an Allied toll of eight hundred. Ten miles farther to the north west, Soult led three divisions against the San Marcial feature near Irun on the west side of the Bidassoa estuary. This position was held solely by Spaniards. They defended the position stoutly. When they asked Wellington for reinforcement, he refused to send any: 'They have won already, let them have all the glory for themselves', he said. Wellington was right, and here too the French withdrew. Pamplona was still holding out, but its garrison was starving, and would have to ask for terms soon. The Allied army could move on, and the way was clear for an invasion of France when the time was ripe.

11

France

By the end of September 1813 Wellington was ready to press on into France. It had taken time to reconstitute the army after months of campaigning, and in late August Wellington estimated that one third of the British troops and one seventh of the Portuguese were unfit for duty, either recovering from wounds, sick or absent seeking plunder. Nevertheless, there were now no French troops anywhere in Spain with the capacity to do anything other than defend themselves and their line of retreat to France. Pamplona still held out, and could pose a threat to Allied communications, but no help was at hand and it would be only a matter of time before its garrison would have to surrender. Suchet still held on in eastern Spain, but he too was under pressure and could do little but defend himself. The Allies could move anywhere in the Peninsula virtually unhindered, and the import of 90 per cent of the army's food meant that Wellington was no longer dependent upon the broken promises of the Spanish government. After the string of victories British Exchequer bills were now more acceptable, but with a view to an eventual invasion of France the British government had coined a supply of guineas, minted from gold from India and from French gold coins which had not been appropriated by the soldiery or which had been smuggled out of France by Rothschild's bank.

Soult had now gone onto the defensive, placing his 48,000 troops behind the River Bidassoa, running from Maya twenty miles north west to the sea. This was a very long front to defend: Soult could not hold everywhere in strength, nor could he cover all the possible approaches. His assessment was that the estuary of the Bidassoa, on the French right flank, could not be crossed by a force of any size, and he considered that Wellington would probably attempt an outflanking sweep round the French left. Soult based his defence on the Greater Rhune, a three thousand-foot high feature, north east of Vera and roughly in the centre of his position. Taking the example of Wellington's own defences in northern Portugal, the Lines of Torres Vedras, Soult ordered the building of redoubts and the construction of lines of entrenchments and fortifications, but he had neither the skilled engineers nor the time even to begin to emulate Fletcher's creation.

While awaiting a suitable opportunity to move, Wellington received a letter from the French General Gazan, who requested that the families of French officers left behind during the retreat from Vittoria should be repatriated to France. Wellington replied that he would indeed allow those families to present themselves at the French outposts, as had been the custom between their nations for the past twenty years, but he reminded Gazan that there were a number of Spanish families (belonging to guerrilla leaders and loyalist officers) who had been detained in France against their will. 'Leur detention ... ne peut influer nullement sur les opérations de la guerre.'[1]

By now Wellington's intelligence operatives could move almost anywhere in Spain, and both guerrillas and officers in observation moved backwards and forwards behind the French lines, while information came in from 'correspondents' resident in French-controlled territory. Wellington knew almost to a man where the French were: three sectors from north west to south east commanded respectively by d'Erlon, Clausel and Reille, with a small reserve of 8000 men under Vilatte. Wellington realised that Soult considered the Bidassoa estuary to be relatively safe for the French. If he could cross the river there and pierce the French lines he would not only achieve surprise but could also keep in contact with the navy, which could supply him as he moved up the coast. The intelligence department discovered, from local shrimpers, that the estuary was in fact passable by men on foot at low tide, and the next low tide was 7 October 1813. This was when the Allies would make their move. On 1 October Wellington rode over to Roncesvalles, on the French left flank, and carried out an ostentatious reconnaissance of the area. This was reported to Soult and fitted in exactly with what the French thought – the British would attempt to turn the French eastern flank. More French troops were moved to cover that possibility.

Wellington's plan was for the 2nd Division at Maya and the 6th Division at Roncesvalles to demonstrate to their front. To 'demonstrate' means to occupy the enemy without actually doing very much, and the aim was to keep the troops on the French left busy, thus preventing them from being moved to where the real attack would come. This latter would be carried out by the 1st and 5th Divisions, supported by two (under strength) Spanish divisions under Freyre and two Portuguese brigades under British commanders, who would cross the estuary. This would be coordinated with the movements of the Light Division, which, supported by two Spanish divisions under Longa and Giron, would attack the Greater Rhune.

At twenty-five past seven in the morning of 7 October 1813 the Allied infantry, guided by Spanish fishermen, plunged into the water of the Bidassoa as it reached the sea. It was low tide, but the water came up to the waists of most men and up to the chests of others. Some, a few, were drowned, but as the early morning mist cleared and three batteries of Allied guns opened up on the French positions at Irun, the battalions had waded across the five hundred yard stretch of water, their muskets and cartridge pouches held above their heads, and were on the opposite bank before the French knew what was happening. In this sector the French were outflanked and could not hold. By half past nine Reille's troops had been forced out of their positions and by half past eleven the Allies had established a bridgehead on the east bank of the river. Soult, arriving from his headquarters at Ainhoe, could do nothing and ordered a withdrawal.

Farther south east, at first light, the Light Division drove in the French piquets along the river and pressed up towards the heights. Fighting through the partially constructed redoubts, by midday the light infantrymen and riflemen were on the crest of the Pyrenees and could look down into France. Once again Wellington had achieved a neatly executed two-pronged attack against superior numbers in a defensive position of their own choosing. Allied casualties were around 800, compared to the French figure of 1300. The French abandoned their guns and most of their baggage. Perhaps as important, they had once again been reminded that the Anglo-Portuguese army could attack them where and when it liked. Wellington did not order a pursuit: to send men off into France with no real idea as to what might await them was just too risky; Napoleon might be able to disengage in the north and send troops against the Allies, and in any event Pamplona was still holding out. A tactical retreat in Spain was one thing, but the political repercussions of a reverse on the soil of France itself would be quite another. Now that the navy could dock unmolested anywhere on the northern coast of Spain, resupply was no longer a major problem; and while Britain might have the smallest army of the coalition partners, it had the longest purse. British soldiers were badly paid by civilian standards at home, but they received twice as much as any European conscript, and they were rarely more than a few months in arrears. Only 8 per cent of the in-country war expenditure went on pay, however: 56 per cent was spent on supplies; 9 per cent on transport – hire of carts, bullocks, mules and drivers – and the rest on subsidies to the Spanish and Portuguese. The army was soon ready to go onto the offensive again, and in late October the garrison of Pamplona surrendered rather than starve. The French commander of Pamplona had originally sought terms, from the mainly Spanish besiegers, which would have allowed then to withdraw into France with all their baggage and six guns, on the undertaking that they would not serve against the Allies for a year and a day. The Spanish commander rejected this offer, and four days later accepted the surrender of the garrison as prisoners of war.

Earlier in the month Wellington had tendered his resignation as Commander-in-Chief of the Spanish army, while retaining field command of the whole Allied force. The Spanish had never wholly accepted Wellington's proposals for reform, and rumours had reached him that the liberals in the Cortes, frightened lest a reformed army would become too powerful, were agitating for his removal. Wellington had in any event been reducing the numbers of Spanish troops attached to the army. Having himself used the Spanish insurrection to great effect, and knowing that it was kept alive not just by British money but also by the behaviour of French troops in Spain, he was determined not to face a similar situation himself once he entered France. As early as July he had issued a general order reminding the army that they were at war with Napoleon, not with the French people. Looting in France would be punished as harshly as it was in Spain: it was vital to secure at least the tolerance of the inhabitants, if a general uprising was to be avoided. 'The Commander of the Forces is particularly desirous that the inhabitants should be well treated, and private property must be respected, as it has been hitherto.'[2] While British and Portuguese soldiers might be kept in line by strict discipline, it was clear that the Spanish could not be. The French had looted and pillaged all over Spain, and their rule had been harsh towards those who did not support them. The Spanish were, not unreasonably, looking forward to taking revenge on the French population.

Also late in October Wellington received news that the armistice between Napoleon and the Austrians, Prussians and Russians had broken down. British victories in Spain and Napoleon's refusal to agree a permanent peace that would meet the coalition's terms had encouraged the huge armies of the continental Allies to move again. On 19 October 1813 an army of almost 300,000 Austrians, Russians, Prussians and Swedes, with 1300 guns, defeated and routed a French army of 200,000, including their Italian and German allies, at Leipzig. British participation was limited to a rocket battery, but only a third of Napoleon's army escaped unmolested, and his last German allies now deserted him. The news filtered down to the men of Soult's army and could only serve to further lower morale, already shaken by the series of retreats into France.

When Soult had been outmanoeuvred along the Bidassoa he had not withdrawn far. Only a few miles back he was defending along the River Nivelle with his troops, made up to around 60,000 by further drafts of conscripts, trying to hold a front of twenty miles. Once again it was far to long to be defended properly throughout, and once again redoubts and fortifications had been hastily constructed. When defending the Bidassoa Soult had been deceived by Wellington's assault across the estuary. He was determined not to be caught twice and assumed that the Allies, dependent upon naval support, would try the same tactic again. This time Soult would defend forward, west, of the river with three divisions and a fourth in reserve

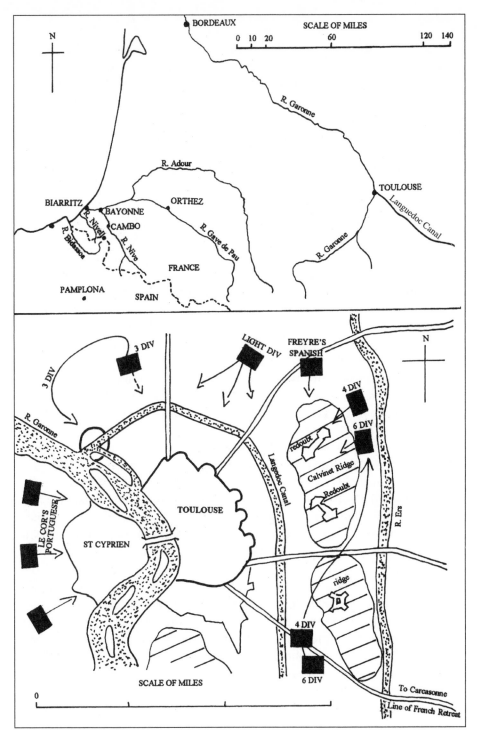

23. France: Area of Operations 1814 and the Battle of Toulouse, 10 April 1814.

committed to the five-mile stretch between St-Jean de Luz, on the coast, and Ascain. The whole of the rest of the front, fifteen miles of it, was held by only five divisions, based on the Lesser Rhune, a ridge parallel to, and three quarters of a mile north of, the Greater Rhune which the Light Division had taken in the attack across the Bidassoa.

Wellington had no intention of conforming to Soult's wishes. He now had 82,000 troops to Soult's 60,000, although 22,000 of these were Spanish who, while willing, were inexperienced and not entirely reliable. In a deviation from his normal methods, Wellington actually discussed his plan with his divisional commanders before taking them to the top of the Greater Rhune to look at the French positions. Perhaps success had mellowed him or, more likely, he felt that his subordinates were now sufficiently experienced in his way of warfare to be taken into his confidence. One weak link in the command structure had recently been removed: General Skerret, originally a brigade commander in Lowry Cole's 4th Division, had been placed in temporary command of the Light Division for the crossing of the Bidassoa. Unused to command of anything more than a brigade, when the company of the 95th Rifles had attempted to block the French retreat across the only bridge over the swollen river, Skerret had refused to reinforce the position – indeed he had seemed incapable of any movement at all. His standing within the division was now so low that Wellington had removed him from command and sent him back to England, where he retired from the army. Officially, the reason for his departure was for reasons of health, but the Light Division was now back in the capable hands of Charles Alten.

Having seen that Soult expected another attack along the coast, Wellington resolved to launch his main thrust in the centre. If he could capture the Lesser Rhune, then the position held by the French would become untenable and they must withdraw or be destroyed piecemeal. At first light on 10 November the attack began. On the Allied left General Sir John Hope with the 1st and 5th Divisions, Freyre's two Spanish divisions and fifty-four guns pinned down the four French divisions watching the coast. Beresford commanded the main assault, by the 3rd, 4th, 7th and Light Divisions, Giron's two Spanish divisions and twenty-four guns, against the French centre. The Light Division stormed the Lesser Rhune, not from the obvious southern approach but along the ridge, from the west, and by nine o'clock in the morning they had taken the last French redoubt on the ridge. Two hours later the French force was split in two by the capture of the bridge at Amotz by the 3rd Division. A gallant counter-attack by General Foy, to the east of the Allied advance, caused some difficulty but that too was halted and driven off. Some French positions surrendered to the British when told they were surrounded by Spaniards, who were unlikely to observe the customs and usages of war in regard to French prisoners, and by two o'clock in the afternoon the French were in full retreat back to the next river line, that of the Nive. Allied losses were 2400. Wellington might, at this point, have managed to cut off the retreating French, but there were only a few hours of daylight left and ever since Seringapatam, fourteen years before, he had eschewed night attacks over ground that had not been reconnoitred.

It was a week before Wellington could march again. The farther into France he advanced, the more cautious he had to be, and the longer his supply lines became. He had to balance the wish to reduce the proportion of Spanish troops, who might embark upon an orgy of looting, against the need to retain enough soldiers overall to ensure that he could not be driven out of France. Soult, his losses of 4300 on the Nivelle once more made up by drafts, had withdrawn back to Bayonne, defending along the River Nive. Having driven in the French outposts at Cambo, on the west bank of the Nive, on 16 November, Wellington hoped to advance on Bayonne on two fronts, from the east and from the south, with the intention of manoeuvring the French out of their defence lines and out of the city, or risk having their withdrawal route cut off. A difficulty was that the army was now held up by the River Nive, which heavy rains had turned into a serious obstacle to movement. Three weeks later the waters had subsided enough for Wellington to risk sending Beresford and Hill across the Nive, with instructions to advance north along the east bank, while Hope would advance along the coast to protect the Allied left flank and to give the impression that Bayonne was to be attacked frontally.

At dawn on 9 December 1813 Beresford and Hill, with five British, two Spanish (under Morillo), and one Portuguese divisions between them, crossed the Nive on a five-mile frontage, using fords and a pontoon bridge. At the same time, the movements of all being coordinated by beacons, Hope with three British divisions and one British and two Portuguese independent brigades drove up the coast. East of the Nive Soult's men found themselves outnumbered and withdrew into Bayonne. On the coast Hope's divisions pushed steadily forward, met little opposition and by nightfall were five miles from Bayonne. They posted piquets and settled down for the night.

Soult had a trick or two left, however, and during the night he moved nine divisions to the south of Bayonne. At nine o'clock in the morning he launched an attack, under d'Erlon, on Hope's unsuspecting pickets and drove the whole line back two miles. The Light Division found themselves having to withdraw as far as Arcangues, where they found a strong defensive position on a ridge, their flanks protected by flooded ground. An augmented battery of French artillery began to bombard them from a range of 450 yards, but such was the marksmanship of the riflemen of the Light Division that the gunners eventually had to abandon their guns, perhaps the only example in this war of artillery being defeated by long-range rifle fire alone. Shortly after midday the French attack ground to a halt. It was raining heavily, many of the troops were new recruits and only hastily trained, and morale, not high to begin with, sank further when an attempt to outflank the Light Division position was thwarted by the arrival of the British 7th Division. Along the coast General Reille had made some progress and Hope's men had been pushed back as far as Biarritz, but here too the timely arrival of more Allied divisions forced the French to break off their attack. By early evening the French had withdrawn back into Bayonne and its environs. Soult tried again on 11 and 12 December: both times he achieved immediate and local surprise, but both times his moves were countered by Wellington's swift redeployment of his divisions and the ability of the seasoned Allied army to react far faster than the largely inexperienced French. The battle petered out on 12 December. In the sense that casualties were about even (roughly 1500 on each side), the battle was a draw. The French might even be said to have won on points, in that they had surprised the Allies and inflicted delay, but only a decisive victory could save them now, and that they had not achieved.

On the night of 12 December the Nive suddenly rose again, swollen by heavy rains inland. All the pontoon bridges across the river were swept away save one, at Ustaritz. Hill, with his 14,000 men and fourteen guns positioned about three miles south east of Bayonne, found himself isolated from the rest of the army. Soult took his chance and at eight o'clock in the morning of 13 December seven French divisions, with an eighth in reserve and the whole supported by twenty-two guns, sallied out along the three roads leading to Hill's position. Hill knew that he was outnumbered (by about three to one, as it happened) and that, although gallopers took the news to Wellington immediately, it would be several hours before reinforcements could reach him across the pontoon bridge. The fighting was desperate: Hill's right was driven back, his centre was threatened from behind, a British battalion fled to the rear, the Allied guns were almost taken and the last reserves had been committed.[3] The line was holding, but only just. Hill headed a last desperate counter-attack with a mix of men from different battalions led by a lone piper of the Gordon Highlanders with a broken leg, which saved the Allied guns for the moment, when the 6th Division, led by Wellington himself, hove into view to the rear. They had crossed the river at Ustaritz and had been marching for four hours. Close behind them came the 3rd, 4th and 7th Divisions, who had also crossed the river, at Villefranque this time, where the engineers had managed to repair the bridge. Wellington having arrived, Hill offered to step down as commander of the battle. Wellington declined: the day could now be won and Hill should have the glory. With the balance of numbers now swinging in favour of the Allies, Hill went onto the offensive, although the ADC sent to tell the forward brigade (Byng's brigade of Guards) to advance found himself in command when he discovered that all the officers of the brigade headquarters were dead or wounded. By two o'clock in the afternoon the situation was stabilised and Hill could order a general advance. By three o'clock the French began to withdraw and the battle was over. What became known as the Battle of St-Pierre (from the name of the nearest village, St-Pierre d'Irube) had been a near thing: ferocious fighting had caused nearly 2000 Allied and over 3000 French casualties in the space of half a day, and showed that, despite their divisions being largely composed of half-trained boys led by officers well aware of the overall war situation, the French were still capable of fighting well on their home ground. It was a rare example of Wellington delegating command to a subordinate, as he knew that if the Nive flooded then a French attack, if it came, would fall on Hill. Hill was, however, totally reliable, and the orders he had received were simple and clear: hold until reinforced. That is exactly what he had done.

Soult now left a garrison commanded by General Thouvenot in Bayonne, and withdrew the bulk of his troops to the east, to another river line, that of the Gave de Pau, which runs roughly west to east through the town of Orthez. The French took up position on a ridge, running parallel to and north of the Gave, with the centre about two miles north west of Orthez. It was potentially a good position, and, had his army not now been reduced to about 36,000 men with forty-eight guns, Soult might have elected to make the position a very hard one to crack. As it was, Soult was desperate to keep a French army in being: the war could not last much longer, but forces in the field meant a stronger hand when negotiations began. He would fight at Orthez if he must, but it would be only a delaying action to allow him to make a further withdrawal with his formations intact.

It was late February before the Allies could move again, the intervening time being spent in establishing a line of communication which, by the time Wellington left the Bayonne area on 24 February 1814, ran for almost one hundred miles to the Atlantic coast. He left only one battalion to guard it. With Bayonne bottled up and the French problems farther north, there was little risk of the supply columns being interfered with by the French, but the convoys would now have to travel much farther than the fifty miles that Wellington had endeavoured to make the norm in Spain. On the 27th February the Allies occupied Bordeaux with elements of the 2nd and 7th Divisions, while on the same day Wellington took five divisions and two cavalry brigades, or about 30,000 men, north of the Gave, while Hill with the remaining 13,000 remained on the south bank to occupy the attention of the garrison of Orthez. That morning, just as it began to get light, the main attack began. The 4th Division attacked the ridge from the west, getting as far as the village of St-Boes before being checked. Picton's 3rd Division attacked the French centre from the south west before they too were held up. Wellington paused, redeployed his divisions and attacked again. The 6th, 7th and Light Divisions attacked from three sides; Hill threatened Orthez itself and shortly after midday the French, with their line of withdrawal now at risk, began to disengage and retreat off to the north west. Soult had lost 4000 men and six guns to the Allies' 2200 men. Wellington kept up the pursuit, and by nightfall Soult had been forced back ten miles, to Sault de Navailles.

Once again Wellington halted to resupply and consolidate, and in the meantime Soult withdrew further, to Toulouse, 140 miles east of Orthez. While swift Allied action might have ended the war sooner, Wellington simply could not afford to press on into hostile country with an ever lengthening supply line without thorough preparation and with his men fully equipped and with ample supplies of ammunition and rations. To do otherwise would have run the risk of being cut off inside France and of throwing away all that had been won. Wellington was not by nature cautious, but he was careful, as indeed he had to be. The total of Allied infantry was less than 50,000, of whom 10,000 were Spanish, and the cavalry barely 4000. Wellington had only fifty guns. Soult was still being reinforced, albeit by the rawest of raw recruits, but he had almost as many men as Wellington, twice as many guns and he was fighting in his own country.

Letters from London telling Wellington of the progress of the war usually took ten days to reach the Allied headquarters. Despite the enormous forces ranged against him, Napoleon still sought a way to end the fighting to the French advantage. A quarter of a million Prussian, Austrian and Russian troops had now entered the borders of France on three fronts, and there were no more than 60,000 French soldiers to oppose them, many of them hastily embodied levies and reservists, young boys and old men. Negotiations were opened at Châtillon sur Seine, as much a cover for Napoleons preparations for another offensive than in any genuine intent to make peace. It is a mark of the awe in which Napoleon was still held by his enemies that he was actually offered – and refused – a settlement based on the pre-1792 frontiers of France. Then he launched a series of lightning attacks, frightened the Prussians badly and forced the Austrians to retreat. It bought time, but not much. The Coalition now vowed to offer no more terms to Napoleon but to fight him to the end. The northern Allies regrouped and returned to the advance.

All this had implications for Wellington. If Napoleon could hold in the north then he might be able to despatch troops to the south. Suchet was extricating himself from eastern Spain and might turn west to aid Soult. Wellington's worst fear was a national uprising in the south, leading to guerrilla warfare and the isolation of his tiny army. The situation was not helped by the recent arrival at Wellington's headquarters of the Duke of Angloulême, nephew of the Bourbon claimant Louis XVIII and later himself Charles X. The Duke made extravagant offers of the assistance of a largely non-existent Bourbon resistance army, which Wellington tactfully declined. The Allies had not yet decided their intentions towards Napoleon. Personally Wellington probably favoured a Bourbon restoration – he was no absolutist but he was a believer in legitimacy – but he was well aware that any expressed French sentiment in favour of the Bourbons was brought on more by war weariness than by any genuine affection for this corrupt and incompetent dynasty. It was not beyond the bounds of possibility that the Coalition might allow Napoleon to remain if the terms were right, or at least allow him to abdicate in favour of his infant son, the King of Rome. Until the governments made a decision, Wellington would concentrate on winning his part of the war.[4]

Toulouse was a formidable proposition for an attacker. Protected on the west by the River Garonne, five hundred yards wide in places, to the east by the River Ers, a tributary of the Garonne, and to the north by the Languedoc canal, its walls were strong and in good repair. Soult had time to construct redoubts and to place his guns where they could cover the likely approaches. Wellington's siege train was not with him, and would take weeks to come up from Santander. Given the size of the garrison, the walls could not be taken by escalade and there was not the time to starve the defenders out. The town was overlooked by a ridge, the Calvinet, which was about a mile east of the town, one and a half miles long and 600 feet high. This was the weak spot in the defences; if an enemy could take the ridge then they dominated the town and could prevent reinforcements arriving or the garrison departing. Soult was well aware of the importance of the ridge, placing half his force there, well entrenched and protected by earthworks, redoubts and guns.

Wellington hoped to manoeuvre the garrison out of the town, but before he could mount any offensive operation against Toulouse he had to cross the Garonne, and on 27 March 1814 the engineers duly began to built a pontoon bridge about seven miles south of the town. By now the Royal Engineers were skilled in obstacle crossing, the wagons carrying the pontoons were soon up and work began. Unfortunately the Garonne was, apart from the Douro, the widest river that Wellington's engineers had yet had to tackle, and there were insufficient pontoons to stretch all the way. The bridge had to be dismantled and all the equipment moved to another site, a mile farther south. On 30 March the river was bridged, and Hill, with 13,000 men, began to cross. Having got his force over, Hill found that the roads were so bad that even the cavalry could barely move along them, much less the artillery. Wellington abandoned the idea of an attack from the south and recalled Hill and his men.

This would not have happened in Spain, where the intelligence department was fully acquainted with the ground over which the army intended to move, but in France the observing officers could not move freely behind the enemy lines, and the flow of information from locals which had been so helpful – vital even – in the Peninsula was here but a trickle.

After much personal reconnaissance on horseback Wellington decided to cross the Garonne about fifteen miles downstream, north of Toulouse, and on 4 April the engineers duly bridged the river. Beresford, with the 4th and 6th Divisions, was first across, but then the river flooded and the bridge was washed away. Fatigue parties with draught horses and bullocks, and led by engineers, were sent downriver along the bank and by 7 April all the pontoons had been recovered and the bridge rebuilt. Soult knew very well what was going on, the French floated logs down the river in the hope of smashing the pontoons, and dead horses in the hope of causing disease amongst the troops, but with the curious paralysis which seemed to affect Soult – and many of the French marshals – whenever he was opposed to Wellington in person, he did nothing more. Had Soult launched a sortie against Beresford when the latter was cut off, without reinforcement the two British divisions might well have been destroyed. Now that the rest of the army, except for Hill's two divisions (the 2nd British and Le Cor's Portuguese), could cross the Garonne, Wellington intended that Hill would demonstrate against Toulouse and the suburb of St-Cyprien, which was on the west side of the river. While Hill kept the enemy looking west, the 3rd and Light Divisions, with Freyre's Spanish division, would feint from the north. The real thrust would be launched by Beresford, who would take the 4th and 6th Divisions, or about 11,000 men, around the east side of the Calvinet ridge and attack it from the south east.

To begin with all went well. Hill demonstrated as ordered, but Soult was too old a soldier to take his main force off the ridge. Beresford's flanking march took longer than intended because of marshy ground made worse by flooding; and, when he ordered his guns to open up at long range against the French artillery harassing his men, Freyre took this to be the start of Beresford's attack, and promptly launched his own division in a supporting foray against the north of the ridge. Predictably, with the French able to devote all their attention to Freyre, this assault was a disaster and the Spanish were driven back in disorder. The headstrong Picton, supposedly advancing along the riverbank to hold the attention of the French without actually attacking them, could contain himself no longer and hurled his division directly at the outer defences of Toulouse. As might be expected, he too recoiled with heavy losses. At last, however, Beresford got into position at the end of the ridge and began to advance up and along it. The French, with great bravery but great foolishness also, launched a counter-attack in column; but, as so often in this war, the steady British line firing their synchronised volleys saw them off. Beresford's men now began to fight their way along the ridge, although against stout resistance. Along the river bank to the north west Picton launched yet another attack and was again brought to a halt with considerable loss, mainly to the Spanish who had agreed to support him. This did at least relieve the pressure on Beresford, and by early evening the fighting had swung in favour of the Allies. The French began to withdraw off the ridge and back into Toulouse, and by last light the Allies had the ridge. It was a victory, but hardly a satisfactory one: Wellington had lost 4500 men, the French just over 3000; the Allied infantry had fired off most of its ammunition and Soult might yet counter-attack.[5] As it was, Soult decided not to make a stand, and during the night he withdrew in the direction of Carcasonne. Next morning, 12 April 1814, Wellington rode into Toulouse, now suddenly transformed into a Bourbon city with white cockades everywhere to be seen. It had been an unnecessary battle, for that evening a British cavalry officer on a sweat-lathered horse galloped into the city to inform the Commander of the Forces that the war was over: Napoleon had abdicated the previous day.

Despite Napoleon's last-ditch resistance, and the diversion of troops intended to reinforce Soult to aid the Emperor in the north, he could prosecute the war no longer. The steady advance into France by the northern Allies and the expulsion of French troops from Spain and Portugal had dented the imperial magic. There were now very few territories outside France from which the army could be paid and fed, and the supply of manpower was drying up. On 30 March 1814 Marshal Marmont surrendered Paris and on 3 April the French Senate declared that the Emperor had forfeited the government. A provisional government was appointed and negotiations with the Allies began. An attempt to secure agreement to the provisional government ruling in the name of Napoleon's son, with the marshals as regents, was turned down, and the provisional government then declared for the Bourbons. Napoleon, in his palace at Fontainebleau, was still moving imaginary or greatly under strength armies when his marshals confronted him on 11 April and persuaded him that he had no option but to abdicate.

The war might be at an end, but the fighting was not. Wellington sent one British and one French officer with a letter to Soult telling him the news, and the marshal promptly ordered General Thouvenot, in command at Bayonne, to surrender. Pierre Thouvenot was aged fifty-seven in 1814 and had been an engineer officer in the old Bourbon army. Declining to serve the Revolution he went into exile, before being reconciled to the new regime in 1800 and returning to the French army. His career was competent if undistinguished, and he had become somewhat of a professional town governor and garrison commander, rather than a leader of troops in the field. Thouvenot refused to accept that the war was over, and declined all offers to surrender. The Allied troops besieging Bayonne under Lieutenant General Sir John Hope had not yet been told officially that hostilities had ended, but rumours abounded and there can be little doubt that vigilance was considerably relaxed from 12 April onwards. During the night of 13/14 April two French deserters from the garrison arrived opposite the British piquets. They were brought before the duty brigadier, Major General Hay, for questioning. There were numerous Hays in Wellington's army: this one was Andrew Hay, fifty-two years old in 1814 and normally a brigade commander in the 5th Division. Described varyingly as 'a most energetic and capable officer' or 'a fool and an arrant coward', depending upon which obituary one reads, Hay could not speak French and so Major General Hinüber, of the KGL, who did speak French, was sent for.[6] The deserters said that the garrison was planning a sortie at first light. Hay did not believe them, but Hinüber did. Thouvenot, the desertion having been reported to him, now ordered the sortie to be brought forward, to three o'clock in the morning. It was launched just as Hinüber was standing his own men to and passing the news to Sir John Hope.

General Maucomble and three thousand men burst out of the citadel and attacked north. Overwhelming the Allied piquets they plunged into the outlying village of St-Etienne, half a mile from the walls, and killed Hay who had just galloped up shouting that the village must be held come what may. The fighting became confused, and Sir John Hope, the overall commander, was awoken. Throwing on civilian clothes (easier and faster than a uniform) and accompanied by an ADC, Lieutenant William Moore of the 52nd Foot (nephew of Sir John Moore), and a staff officer, Lieutenant William Herries, with a small escort, he rode up to St-Etienne to assess the situation. Moving up by a sunken road, Hope and his party were ambushed by a party of twenty French soldiers led by a warrant officer named Pigeon. Hope was wounded by a shot and his horse killed, trapping the general underneath it. The accompanying officers were wounded, Moore mortally and Herries losing a leg, while the general was carted off to Bayonne as a prisoner, being wounded yet again on the way, probably by a British musket shot fired at his captors. Pigeon was awarded an immediate field commission. Wellington cannot have been surprised by Hope's fate. Only the previous December, after the battle of the Nive, he had written to Colonel Torrens on the subject:

I have long entertained the highest opinion of Sir John Hope, in common, I believe, with the whole world, but every day's experience convinces me of his worth. We shall lose him, however, if he continues to expose himself in fire as he did in the last three days; indeed his escape was then wonderful. His hat and coat were shot through in many places, beside the wound in his leg. He places himself among the sharpshooters, without, as they do, sheltering himself from the enemy's fire. This will not answer; and I hope that his friends will give him a hint on the subject ... I will see Sir John Hope himself if I should find a favourable opportunity; but it is a delicate subject.

It was General Hinüber who saved the night for the Allies, rallying his own men and counter-attacking. Eventually other units responded and by dawn the French were driven back into the citadel. The escapade had cost the French nearly 1000 casualties, and the Allies 800, of whom 230 were prisoners. It was embarrassing for the Allies and totally unnecessary, being regarded by both sides as not only a waste of lives but bad form to boot. Still Thouvenot held out, and it was not until a fortnight later, when emissaries from Soult were admitted into the citadel on 26 April to confirm that the war was indeed over, that he finally agreed to lay down his arms. Quite why Thouvenot behaved as he did is a mystery. He was a sober professional officer, not a hot-headed patriot, but he may have been encouraged to make one last dramatic gesture by some of his younger officers who still believed in the Napoleonic legend.

The Peninsular War was over. In six years Wellington had driven the French, the greatest military power of the age, from Portugal and then from Spain. Opposed by most of the greatest names of the French marshalate, he had defeated them all. He had done it with a tiny British army augmented by Portuguese and Spanish soldiers, had never allowed the far larger French armies to corner him, and had used the guerrillas to great effect. He had turned a corrupt and creaky commissariat into a slick, efficient organisation capable of supplying not only the British but the Spanish and the Portuguese too. He had built up excellent relations with the navy, whose ability to land men and stores anywhere along the coast Wellington had made full use of; and despite his problems with his Allies he had always retained the respect and admiration of the Portuguese and Spanish governments, even if, for their own reasons, they could rarely give him all that he wanted. It was a war fought skilfully and economically by a commander who not only had to manage and lead the army but who had to keep the home and Allied governments happy too. Rarely in British history has one man held so much power and been allowed, eventually, such unfettered discretion, and rarely has it been used so well. Wellington learned much but he taught his army more. From simple frontal battles like Rolica and Vimiero the army had developed to a point where it could carry out complicated battle of manoeuvre such as Vittoria and those of the Pyrenees campaign. Personally he had risen from relative obscurity, appointed to command in the Peninsula because there was no one else, to Field Marshal, Marquess and England's foremost general. His fame had spread: the Peninsula may have been a sideshow in the greater scheme of things, but it was there, and only there, that the French had consistently been beaten since 1808.

Napoleon debated fleeing to America, where he had been offered sanctuary by the United States, still at war with Britain, but instead found himself exiled to the island of Elba in the Mediterranean. He retained the rank of general and was granted the title of King of Elba, with 1200 men of the Imperial Guard as an escort. Most of the marshals and senior generals, anxious to retain their titles and estates, turned their coats and accepted positions under the Bourbons. Soult became Minister of War; Masséna continued to be the governor of Toulon military district; Marmont accepted a peerage and became governor of the Paris military district; d'Erlon, Suchet, Reille and Foy accepted command of corps and divisions of the much-reduced army, now stripped of its eagles, without the Guard and with most of the Napoleonic regulars discharged without pensions or hope of employment; and Thouvenot, commander of the last French offensive in the Peninsula, carried on as governor of Bayonne.

It was not only the new French government which was anxious to rid itself of the burden of military expenditure. Now that the war was over, the British army too could be much reduced. Within days the finely-tuned instrument that had faced and beaten the flower of the French nation found those battalions not wanted for garrison duty in Europe being transported to England for disbandment, or sent to America. A priority was the return to Spain of the Spanish units, which regarded committing outrages on French civilians as a matter of national honour. Then there was the question of wives. Those wives who were 'on the strength' were of course entitled to free passage to England, but the hordes of Spanish, Portuguese and French girlfriends, common law wives and prostitutes, many with children sired by British soldiers, were entitled to nothing: they were to make their own way home as best they could. Many was the tearful farewell, and there were the inevitable desertions by men who thought France, or Portugal, or Spain might be a better option than soldiering on in peacetime.

At one stage it was suggested that Wellington should be offered the command in America, but he made clear he would decline. He thought it a pointless war in a continent where, apart from the defence of Canada, Britain had no strategic interest other than trade.[7] George Murray, the erstwhile Quarter Master General, went instead and Wellington advised him to make sure that he retained complete naval supremacy on the Great Lakes, as being essential to the defence of British territory. Having set in motion the arrangements for the repatriation of the army, Wellington hastened to Madrid, where there was some final tidying up to be done. Included amongst this was the return to Spain of those paintings and treasures which had been found in King Joseph's baggage and which had not been appropriated by individual soldiers after Vittoria. Wellington wryly noted that, as most of the paintings appeared to be of the Italian school, they had presumably been looted from there in the first place.

On 21 April Wellington agreed to accept the ambassadorship to Bourbon France. He had already been showered with foreign orders and decorations, even before the war had ended, and now could add the Grand Crosses of the Imperial Military Order of Maria Teresa (from Austria); the Imperial Russian Military Order of Saint George; the Royal Prussian Military Order of the Black Eagle; and the Royal Swedish Military Order of the Sword to his uniform – should he chose to wear them (which, apart from formal receptions and when posing for paintings, he rarely did). When Wellington assumed command of the Peninsular army he had been only a humble Knight of the Bath. Now, on 3 May 1814, having become successively a baron, viscount, earl and marquess, he was elevated to the highest rung on the peerage that can be held by a man not of royal blood – that of duke. Parliament voted the Duke of Wellington a grant of £400,000 to maintain a standard of living commensurate with his rank, and, on 23 June 1814, having handed the arrangements for the dispersal of the army over to Lord Dalhousie, he landed in England for the first time in over five years. A quiet period of leave with his family was not allowed him, even if he had wanted it, which he probably did not, and he was plunged into a round of royal audiences, receptions, banquets, bestowals of honours and consultations with government. On 28 June he finally took his seat in the House of Lords, as baron, viscount, earl, marquess and duke, and two days later replied from the bar of the House to an address by the Commons. On 5 July his appointment as ambassador to France was announced, and on 9 July he was the guest of honour at a banquet given by the Lord Mayor and corporation of the City of London. In between all this, he saw his wife, grumbled at her mismanagement of household accounts, and put in train the search for a suitable estate.

Within a few weeks Wellington was in Paris, where he found himself flung into a maelstrom of political manoeuvring. The Treaty of Chaumont, agreed by the Allies before the war ended, had decided that Napoleon was to be exiled and Louis XVIII recognised as the King of France. The question now requiring immediate settlement was what shape France should be, before moving on to a wider European settlement. The Treaty of Paris was signed on 30 May 1814 by the victorious powers – Britain, Austria, Prussia, Russia, Spain, Portugal and Sweden – and by the new government of France. It was a generous settlement, which did not attempt to ignore all the effects of the French Revolution. The French frontiers were defined as those of 1 January 1792, thus allowing the retention of some of the Revolutionary conquests; Britain would return most of the French colonies captured in the West Indies; the legal system introduced by Napoleon – the *Code Napoléon* – would remain; France would return the archives and documents removed from conquered territories but not the looted art treasures; and Belgium, the former Austrian Netherlands, would be incorporated into Holland under the King of the Netherlands. The details, and a Europe wide settlement of all outstanding problems, would be threshed out at a congress of the powers to be held in Vienna.

The Congress of Vienna began in September 1814, with Great Britain represented by Castlereagh. It attempted to achieve two things: a barrier to further French aggression; and a structure for Europe which would provide lasting peace and – that age old aim of British foreign policy – a balance of power. In many ways the Congress was the first of the modern settlements, with the powers trying to move on from the old dynastic European politics to a system based on the recognition of national aspirations and the balancing of opposing interests. One of the basic contentions was that any power affected by a part of the settlement had the right to be consulted: now and later.[8] It soon became apparent that the two main players at Vienna were Russia and Great Britain. Both had worldwide strategic interests, and while Russia had produced the largest armies, Britain had dominated the seas and was the richest member of the Coalition. The futures of Belgium and Italy were not difficult to solve. Italy would return to being a plethora of states dominated by Austria, albeit complicated by the presence of the ex-Napoleonic marshal, and brother-in-law of Napoleon, Joachim Murat as King of Naples (he was overthrown in May 1815 when he was defeated by the Austrians after attempting to arouse Italian nationalism against foreign occupation). It was when the future of the German states came to be decided that difficulties arose. Russia's long-term aim in the west was to establish a barrier against invasion. To this end it wished to retain the Napoleonic Grand Duchy of Warsaw, with some adjustments, coupled with a miscellany of German states strong enough to resist French expansion but not strong enough to pose a threat to Russia. Prussia, hoping for parts of Saxony, the only German state to remain loyal to Napoleon throughout the war, leaned towards Russia. Britain was unhappy that the Napoleonic Confederation of the Rhine was to be replaced by much the same thing dominated by Russia, and was suspicious of Prussian ambitions. The resultant disagreements over the future of Saxony allowed that consummate French politician, Talleyrand, who had served Bourbons, Revolution, Directory and Consulship, and now the Bourbons again, to ensure some French influence in the Congress.

While discussions in Vienna were continuing, Wellington was immersed in the diplomatic round in Paris. There had been no British official diplomatic accreditation to France for over twenty years, and there was much to discuss. As far as possible Wellington attempted to curb the returning émigrés' wish to extract revenge for the Revolution, but he was involved in much discussion and correspondence. Matters requiring resolution ranged over many matters including pre-war debts; the French constitution; fortification of the Netherlands; the size of the French army; the movement of French subjects to and from American ports blockaded by the Royal Navy; courts martial hanging over from the Peninsular War; whether or not an officer of the army on board ship off the Spanish coast should have the medal for the siege of San Sebastian (he should have the naval one); a refusal to allow the French government to import building materials from the United States (they could be imported from Canada instead); and negotiations for the abolition of slavery in the French colonies. This latter issue seems to have been one about which Wellington felt strongly. He was in regular correspondence with William Wilberforce, the anti-slavery campaigner, and he did his best to persuade the French King of the need for abolition. At the same time he suggested to Lord Grenville, the British government minister responsible, that anti-French and pro-abolitionist tirades in the English press only inflamed French public opinion, which was ignorant of the issues and thought that British pressure to abolish slavery was motivated by a desire to bankrupt the French colonies rather than by any genuinely humanitarian motive. During his time as ambassador in Paris, Wellington was also involved in persuading the Portuguese to abolish slavery in their territories, provided that Britain paid compensation for the slaving ships which had been seized by the Royal Navy.

Many of Wellington's letters to Lord Liverpool in England and to Lord Castlereagh in Vienna consisted of intelligence summaries of the state of affairs in France. He was well informed as to Murat's activities in Italy and warned both ministers that the French population were largely ambivalent as to the Bourbon restoration, citing a riot in Rennes when a royalist commission, set up to award compensation to the widows and wounded of the royalist uprising in the Vendée, was set upon by a mob encouraged by the local prefect.[9] He pointed out that many of those in secure employment under the empire were now penniless, and that the large number of ex-officers sent back to their villages to subsist on half pay could be a source of future discontent. Wellington also reported the strange case of Mme Raucourt, an actress of note, who died in January 1815. The entire company of the *Théâtre Française* descended upon the church of St-Roch, with the body, and demanded that it be given a Christian burial. As this theatre and anyone connected with it had been excommunicated *en bloc* by the Pope long before the Revolution, the curate refused to oblige, whereupon a riot ensued. The situation was only defused by the arrival of royalist troops and a chaplain from the King, who agreed to perform the service, with the result that cries of *'Vive le Roi!'* replaced those of *'à la Lanterne!'*. This sort of incident, Wellington thought, served to illustrate how volatile public opinion was.

Inevitably much of Wellington's correspondence during this time was answering pleas for preferment from those who had served him during the war, or who felt that they had been hard done by in the allocations of medals, titles or promotion. As was his way, Wellington was not prepared to advance the claims of anyone who did not, in his view, merit it. To one Spanish general he wrote:

> I did not recommend you to the King of Spain for promotion, not from any doubt of your zeal and gallantry in His Majesty's service and cause, of which I had witnessed so many instances, but from having known that you had not made the military profession your study, and from having observed that you paid but little attention to the discipline and good order of the troops ...[10]

In the same letter, Wellington summarised his views on promotion generally, a view which he expressed to many who sought his favour:

> Zeal and gallantry are indispensable qualities for an officer, and you possess both, and activity and intelligence to an extraordinary degree; but it is my opinion, and I have always acted on that opinion, that an officer appointed to command others should have other qualities; and I cannot with propriety recommend for promotion one who, in my opinion, does not possess them.

Castlereagh, in Vienna, was reliant on Wellington for advice on how to deal with the contending issues being discussed there. It was not that Wellington had any greater knowledge of European politics, but simply that he had a cool head and could see the vital issues, untrammelled by emotion or short-term advantage. In November 1814 he went to Vienna and played a major role in advising the British contingent on the Saxony question, and towards the end of the year Castlereagh suggested that Wellington take over from him as the British plenipotentiary to the Congress. There were domestic reasons for this: Parliament in England was due to sit at the beginning of 1815 and there were pressing issues – such as the repeal or otherwise of income tax – which the government felt needed Castlereagh's presence. Wellington was reluctant to leave Paris for Vienna until he was quite sure that both the home government and Castlereagh had decided what should be done; he also felt that Castlereagh had done such a good job so far that he should be allowed to see it to fruition. By January 1815, however, Lord Liverpool had decided that

Castlereagh was needed at home and that Wellington should go to Vienna. He left Paris on 24 January and by early February was fully involved in the Congress. His reputation had preceded him: as the only general in Europe who had kept up the battle against Napoleonic France for six years without being routed, and with his experience of dealing with Allied and his own governments, the representatives of the other powers respected his views and sought his advice. Even the Tsar deferred to him. On 3 January 1815, prior to Wellington's arrival in Vienna, Talleyrand had managed to negotiate an arrangement that ranged Britain, Austria and France against Russia and Prussia, designed to curb the ambitions of the latter. The details were left to Wellington to arrange, and this and all the other aspects of the European settlement began to absorb most of the Duke's time.

Then, on 26 February 1815, everything was suddenly thrown into the melting pot: Napoleon escaped from Elba.

12

Napoleon's Return

When King Louis XVIII eventually deemed it safe to return to Paris in 1814 he was sixty years old and had been in exile for twenty-three years. He was said to weigh over twenty stone. Had he accepted that French society had changed, he might have been able to rally the country, where a whole generation had grown up knowing nothing but war. He initially refused to accept the Charter, a constitution drawn up between the Allies and the provisional government under the aegis of Talleyrand, on the grounds that the French Senate was an illegal body. Pressured by the Tsar he agreed 'to grant his people a constitution', and then signed it 'in the nineteenth year of our reign', thus ignoring everything that had happened since the Revolution.[1] He had already annoyed Talleyrand, who wanted a constitutional monarchy on the British model, by appointing his brother, the Comte d'Artois, as 'Lieutenant General of My Kingdom', or supreme commander of the armed forces. Talleyrand rejected the appointment, then had the Senate offer Artois the very same position. To replace Napoleonic imperial insignia on uniforms and coats of arms was fair enough, but to ban the flying of the tricolour and replace it with the white Bourbon flag was, to many people, an indication that the old feudal ways were returning.

The Bourbons began to whittle away at the Napoleonic legal system, and to tinker with the genuinely good things that had been introduced since the Revolution: promotion by merit in the professions and in the army; education for the poor; hospitals for veterans and homes for their widows. The middle classes and skilled artisans were to be disenfranchised, and more and more power was to be concentrated in the hand of the King, and effectively in those of the returning exiles and their adherents. As the prisoners of war and the foreign garrisons came back to France, they found officers placed on half pay (which arrived months in arrears or not at all), and men discharged, or, like the Guard, reduced to the status of the line. Even the marshals and generals who served on under the new regime found their humble origins sneered at and their titles ridiculed. The influence of the church, curbed by Napoleon's concordat with the Pope, increased, and Parisians were particularly incensed by the priests' ordering of the closure of cafés on Sundays and their holding of religious parades and services to commemorate royalist 'martyrs'. The *Légion d'Honneur*, the highest military award for bravery and open to all ranks, was downgraded to a civil decoration, and regiments of Swiss mercenaries were raised while French regular regiments were disbanded.

For the first time since the wars began France had to pay her way from internal revenues: there were now no other countries from which to levy forced loans or acquire plunder. The end of the war had led to a recession in the manufacturing industries and taxes were increased, which particularly affected the rural peasantry, nearly three quarters of the population. Much of the money raised was spent on ostentatious glorification of the Bourbons. Bad faith was alleged when Louis refused to pay the agreed two million francs a year (£80,000 at the then rate of exchange) for the upkeep of Napoleon's court in exile and his 1200 man army, or to pay the pension agreed for the ex-Empress and her son. All in all, it was not a good start for a monarch hoping to rule over a stable, peaceful, united and contented country.

When Napoleon left France for exile as the sovereign of Elba, he declared that he would return before the violets bloomed in spring. He landed on Elba on 3 May 1814, to a twenty-one-gun salute from a British man-of-war. While a Royal Navy ship remained on station and Colonel Sir Neil Campbell, the British commissioner charged with looking after Napoleon's person, was based on Elba, this was as much for Napoleon's protection as to keep an eye on him. Under the terms of the Treaty of Fontainebleau he was not a prisoner and, only 120 miles from the coast of France and five miles from the Italian coast of Tuscany, he was kept fully informed about what was going on at home. By February 1815 Napoleon's officers on Elba were feeding false information to known Bourbon agents: the English were coming to spirit the Emperor away; the Emperor would land in Italy to support Murat in his resistance to the Austrians; the Emperor was intending to move to Corsica. It was all a smokescreen. On 26 February 1815 Napoleon and his 1200 troops, two guns, a travelling carriage and forty horses slipped out of Elba in the *Inconstant*, a frigate allowed him under the treaty, and two smaller ships, the *Saint-Esprit* and the *Caroline*. Narrowly avoiding the patrols of the French and British navies, he headed for the coast of France.

In Vienna the representatives at the Congress, on hearing of his escape, thought Napoleon would land in Italy, and declared him an outlaw. This was an unusual proscription, for it meant that Napoleon himself could be killed by anyone, in any way, without legal sanction. In Westminster there was disapproval. Samuel Whitbread MP, that constant thorn in the flesh of governments throughout the wars, demanded to know why the Duke of Wellington, as Britain's representative, had put his signature to a document which advocated assassination, making him, Wellington, a potential murderer. As the declaration was in French there now ensued a long-running argument as to the exact meaning of the words used. To his brother, William, Wellington wrote that the sentence in the declaration that described Napoleon as having placed himself *hors la loi* had been inserted at the behest of supporters of Louis XVIII, and that the word *vindicte* meant justice, not vengeance.[2] It was bandying words: the Congress was not only worried, it was frightened; and there was panic in Paris.

On 1 March 1815 Napoleon landed not in Italy, but between Cannes and Fréjus (where he had embarked for Elba the previous year), and headed for Grenoble. On 5 March the news was delivered to the King in Paris in the form of a telegraph, and Marshal Soult, the Minister of War, was called into hurried conference with the court at Versailles. Soult's advice was that the troops already stationed in the south of France, as a precaution against any trouble from Murat in Italy, would suffice to deal with Napoleon and the vestigial Imperial Guard. This force, Soult suggested, should be divided into two, to attack Napoleon from the front and from the flank. One group should be commanded by the Comte d'Artois, the King's brother, with Marshal MacDonald as his adviser, while the other should be under the Duc de Berry, Artois' son and the King's nephew, with Marshal Ney as adviser. As this involved a total of 60,000 troops, it might have been thought sufficient to deal with 1200, but just in case, advised Soult, the King could call up 120,000 reservists and station them south of Paris. The King agreed at once, and orders for mobilisation were dispatched. While there is no direct evidence, it is a reasonable presumption that Soult, knowing very well that the army would return to its old allegiance, and intending to do so himself, wanted the maximum numbers of men to be available at the disposal of the returned Emperor in due course. Marshal Ney, the erstwhile commander of the rear-guard in the retreat from Moscow and now commander of the Bourbon cavalry, announced that he would leave immediately and bring Napoleon back in an iron cage. It was a statement that was later to cost him his life.

Initially, the French population along Napoleon's route waited to see what would happen, but then at Gap, sixty miles inland, the inhabitants greeted Napoleon enthusiastically. At Laffrey, on 7 March, came the first confrontation, between a battalion of the supposedly Bourbon 5th Regiment of the Line and Napoleon's forty Polish lancers with the regimental band of the Old Guard, marching under the flag of Elba with imperial bees sewn onto it, and followed by Napoleon himself. There was a brief moment of tension and then the men of the 5th began to cheer.[3] Napoleon's tiny army was instantly doubled in size and now the other battalions of the 5th came marching down the road under their old tricolour and eagle, hidden during the Bourbon reorganisation. The same evening, at Grenoble, the local military commander, General Marchand, found that his artillery was unwilling to fire on the Bonapartists, and the populace demanded that the gates be opened to the Emperor. Here too Napoleon added the garrison to his growing army. On 10 March Napoleon entered Lyon, to the acclaim of the populace, and acquired yet another increment of soldiers. The Comte d'Artois, finding neither soldier nor civilian to support him, left hurriedly for Paris with a handful of royalists. Even Marshal MacDonald had to flee, pursued by a troop of hussars.

From Lyon Napoleon issued the first imperial decrees of his new reign: the returned *émigrés* were banished; the changes in the laws were nullified; Bourbon titles, commissions and promotions were cancelled; the return of lands confiscated by the Revolution was reversed; the Bourbon insignia were to be replaced by those of the Revolution; the Swiss mercenary regiments were abolished; and a provisional government was nominated. Napoleon's progress gathered momentum. He now had eleven infantry and two cavalry regiments, along with fifty guns and a horde of discharged soldiers and offi-cers, about 60,000 men in all, at his back. Everywhere the people and the army were declaring for the Emperor. Those regiments despatched to stop the usurper merely went over to him, and a Napoleonic wag pasted up a placard in Paris, which said 'From Napoleon to Louis XVIII: there is no need to send me any more soldiers – I have enough!' On 11 March Marshal Ney reached Besançon, and, claiming to have just learned of the way in which the King had ignored the terms of the treaty of Fontainebleau (to which he, Ney, had been a signatory), declared for Napoleon, taking his troops with him.[4] Royalists began to liquidate their interests and leave Paris, as did many of the British diplomatic corps and their families, including the Duchess of Wellington, who had remained in the British ambassador's residence when her husband left for Vienna. Napoleon was now unstoppable, and at midnight on Sunday 19 March Louis fled Paris for Ghent. Napoleon reached Fontainebleau that day and then pressed on to Paris. By nine o'clock that night he was once more Emperor of the French. He had reconquered France in just under three weeks, without firing a shot.[5]

At Vienna the powers were cobbling together a military response. Initially they thought that there would be civil war inside France, Royalist versus Bonapartist, and that Allied troops would act in conjunction with the Bourbon army. All those at Vienna wanted Wellington to command the forces in Flanders, but Castlereagh offered him the choice of remaining in Vienna as the political and diplomatic representative of Great Britain or of taking command in the field. To Wellington the choice was clear. On the morning of 29 March 1815 he left Vienna, arriving in Brussels on the evening of 4 April.

Having realised that there would be no Royalist resistance to Napoleon, the Allies resolved to position troops on the French border, ready for a coordinated invasion when the time was ripe. The Russians, Austrians and Prussians would field 700,000 men between them, with the British contributing 150,000 men and £5,000,000 in cash. The Russians and Austrians would mass on the eastern and south-eastern frontiers of France, while the Prussians would cooperate with a British-commanded Anglo-Dutch army in Flanders. Meanwhile Napoleon was reconstituting his army and issuing decrees (including the immediate abolition of the slave trade, a contrast to Louis' reluctant promise to Wellington to abolish it in five years time), while writing placatory letters to the Allied sovereigns. Napoleon wanted – indeed he needed – peace, but the powers would have none of it. Prince Metternich returned Napoleon's letter to the Emperor of Austria unopened, while even the Tsar, disliking and distrusting the Bourbons as he did, issued orders for the movement of troops.

The army that the Duke of Wellington found at his disposal in Flanders was a polyglot one. Britain was supposed to provide 150,000 troops; but, even if the whole of it had been available, the British army would not have reached this number. The battalions had been sent to America or disbanded, and while a peace settlement with America had been signed in January, the troops were still on the high seas and would only arrive in Flanders in dribs and drabs. On arrival in Brussels Wellington found that his command consisted of 23,000 British and Hanoverian troops (these latter separate from the KGL), 20,000 Dutch-Belgians, and sixty guns. In addition he had 13,400 men in garrisons in Mons, Tournai, Ypres, Ostende, Nieuport and Anvers.[6] It was a far cry from the 150,000 which Britain had agreed to find. On 6 April Wellington wrote to Lord Bathurst:

> Although I have given a favourable account of ours [the British troops] to General Schwarzenberg [the Austrian commander] I cannot help thinking, from all accounts, that they are not what they ought to be to maintain our military character in Europe. It appears to me that you have not taken in England a clear view of your situation, that you do not think war certain, and that a great effort must be made, if it is hoped that it shall be short. You have not called out the militia, or announced such a measure in your message to Parliament, by which measure your troops of the line in Ireland or elsewhere might become disposable; and how we are to make out 150,000 men ... appears not to have been considered. If you could let me have 40,000 good British infantry ... and 150 pieces of British field artillery fully horsed, I should be satisfied, and take my chance for the rest, and engage that we would play our part in the game. But, as it is, we are in a bad way.[7]

Once again the British resorted to paying for the use of troops from the German states. Some of these would come directly under British command, some would come under the Prussians. For those men not directly employed under Wellington, the British would pay the other Allies £11 per man per year, up to the shortfall from the 150,000 which they had contracted to supply. Over the next two months the German contingents that would serve under Wellington assembled in Flanders. Hanover, liberated from Napoleon in 1813, was once more an independent state, closely linked to Britain. It produced eight regular and fifteen *Landwehr* (militia) infantry battalions, three regiments of cavalry and two batteries of foot artillery. Brunswick, whose Duke had consistently opposed Napoleon (one of his battalions, the Brunswick Oels, had served in the Peninsula but was not present in Flanders), found six battalions of infantry, a regiment of hussars, half a regiment of lancers and two batteries of artillery, one foot and one horse. The Nassau contingent consisted of seven regular battalions and one *Landwehr* battalion. The King's German Legion was still, just, part of the British army, although a number of officers and NCOs had been detached to train the new Hanoverian army. It provided eight regular battalions, three cavalry regiments and two horse batteries and and one foot battery of artillery. Apart from the KGL, most of whose officers and men had served in the Peninsula and were hardened and competent troops, the majority of the soldiers of the German contingents were recent recruits, half-trained militia or men previously in the service of Napoleon.

Virtually all of the Dutch-Belgian troops had been in the French service, and many still wore their French uniforms, with an orange cockade to distinguish them as Allies. The Netherlands made available to Wellington ten regular and sixteen militia battalions, seven regiments of cavalry and four foot and one horse battery of artillery. In addition there were two West Indian and one East Indian battalions in the Dutch service, although they played no part in the fighting. Wellington's own view was that Portuguese troops should be included: they were as good as British troops, could be mixed in with them and still had their complement of British officers. He recommended this course to the home government and also wrote to the Prince Regent of Portugal, but events were to overtake any possibility of reinforcement from that source.

The purely British contribution, available for operations and not tied up in garrison duty, would (eventually) total thirty infantry battalions, nineteen cavalry regiments, ten foot and eight horse artillery batteries, or about 24,000 men, only 15,000 of them infantry. The infantry were not all the experienced veterans of the Peninsula. Twenty-one of the battalions had indeed served there, some only arriving from America shortly before hostilities began, but some were without many of their most experienced officers and NCOs, who had been discharged following the peace of 1814. Of the rest, many were second battalions, filled with recruits or under strength. Of the nineteen British cavalry regiments, eleven had served in Spain or Portugal. Some of the others had not seen recent, or even any, overseas service (the Scots Greys had not been abroad for twenty years), although most of the artillery had. It was no wonder that Wellington described them as 'an infamous army', although here he was using the term in its original meaning – not famous – rather than in a pejorative sense.

While trying to put some semblance of good order into his heterogeneous command, Wellington was constantly irritated by the unwillingness of the Horse Guards to allow him to choose his subordinates. As he wrote in a letter to the Adjutant General of the Forces, Torrens (now a major general), on 14 April, 'I am very much distressed about the numerous staff we have got here'; and again on 21 April, 'before you send any more General Officers let me see more troops'.[8] The fact was that every unemployed officer in England wanted to serve in the coming war. Even General Sir John Craddock, from whom Wellington had assumed command in the Peninsula in 1809, wrote asking for a command, alluding to the (in his view) unfair circumstances of his super-session. The reply was terse: 'at present this arrangement is out of the question; as we have scarcely more English troops here than we have Generals in the list'.[9] Even the Duke of Kent, son of King George III, received a dusty answer to a list of officers he wanted promoted: 'the promotion of those offi-cers would occasion applications from the whole army, which could not be granted. I hope that your Royal Highness will pardon me if I request you to excuse me from applying now for promotion for those officers'.[10]

Busy as he was with military matters, Wellington had little choice but to participate in the social round in Brussels, where he had his headquarters. As the victor of the Peninsula he was lionised by local and expatriate society, and rumours as to his amours persisted. He was already believed to have availed himself of the services of Harriette Wilson, a high-class London courtesan well known to members of the aristocracy, on his return from India and before his appointment to command in Portugal. This at least may be true, but when Wilson eventually wrote her memoirs, in which the Duke featured, she alleged numerous meetings in London at times when the Duke was actu-ally in the Peninsula. Her claims bear little credibility.[11] He was also supposed to have had liaisons with Portuguese and Spanish ladies; but again there is no hard evidence. Given the prodigious amount of work which daily fell to the Commander of the Forces, it is difficult to see when he could have found time for affairs. He certainly attended balls and dinners while in the Peninsula, and was noted as attentive to the ladies, but he always seems to have returned to his headquarters, often riding twenty or thirty miles in the small hours of the morning to get there. His favourite relaxation in the Peninsula was hunting, which he pursued with vigour, rather than amorous dalliance.

In Paris, when British Ambassador, Wellington was alleged to have had affairs with, among others, Pauline Borghese, Napoleon's sister. The impropriety of conducting an affair with the sister of his late enemy was something that Wellington would never have countenanced, particularly when Kitty, his wife, was also in Paris. Their relationship was almost certainly a matter of business only: the new British embassy was in a building purchased from Pauline. He was certainly taken with the singer Madame Giuseppini Grassini, as had been Napoleon, and he did attend her theatre performances and often met her socially in Paris, but the attraction, at least on his part, was almost certainly due to his love for, and appreciation of, good music. In Brussels he was said to have had affairs with a singer, and with the young daughter of the British Minister, the Duke of Richmond. While Kitty was not in Brussels, Wellington's mother, the redoubtable Anne, dowager Countess of Mornington, was, and there is no reliable evidence whatever that such attention as he may have paid to the ladies was other than social.[12]

Wellington was certainly sexually normal. Homosexuality was condemned in society and sodomy a capital offence in both civil and military law. Wellington had plenty of enemies, and if there had been any indication of unnatural practices it would have been used to bring him down. It is nevertheless reasonable to wonder how he could have remained celibate for all the years he was in India, unmarried, and in the Peninsula without seeing his wife for over five years. The answer is surely that Wellington was motivated throughout his life by a concept of duty, and loyalty to the public interest, and this included his personal behaviour and private life. To have openly taken a mistress, or indulged in sexual activity that might have drawn criticism, particularly when he was attempting to impose good order and discipline on the army, would have been unthinkable. Certainly he enjoyed the company of intelligent, witty and socially confident ladies – none of which Kitty was – but if there were any affairs, they were conducted with the utmost discretion.[13]

As the troops that would form his army arrived in their cantonments, from America, England, the German states and the Netherlands, Wellington, as Commander-in-Chief of the Anglo-Dutch army, examined the various military options open to the Allies. He had already struck up an excellent working relationship with the Commander-in-Chief of the Prussian army, Field Marshal Blücher. Gebhard Leberecht von Blücher, Prince of Wahlstadt, had been a soldier since the age of fourteen, initially in the Swedish cavalry and then in the Prussian service of Frederick the Great. He was now seventy-three years old and, unusually for a professional soldier, had a personal hatred of the

French in general and Napoleon in particular. In no sense a great military thinker – his troops called him 'Marschall Vorwärts' – he led from the front, literally, but had a lot of sound common sense and an indomitable spirit. Blücher did have one or two idiosyncrasies. He lived largely on a diet of onions, gin and coffee when in the field, and on occasion he would announce that he was pregnant. On one occasion he told an embarrassed Wellington that he was not only expecting, but that the foetus was actually that of an elephant, fathered by a grenadier of the French Imperial Guard![14] Despite this, and the fact that their only common language was French, the two commanders got on excellently, an important fact given that it was largely due to Blücher's loyalty to Wellington that the campaign ended in the Allies' favour. The King of Prussia, who well knew of Blücher's intellectual limitations, had appointed as his chief of staff the fifty-five-year-old General August Wilhelm Anton von Gneisenau. Gneisenau had a good record as a field soldier and, with Scharnhorst, had been one of the leading lights in the reform of the Prussian army after its defeat by Napoleon in 1806. He had considerable intelligence, was a master planner and had long experience and understanding of staff procedures. It was unfortunate that Napoleon found a copy of the secret treaty of January 1815, ranging Bourbon France, Britain and Austria against Prussia and Russia, and made it public. Relations between Blücher and Wellington were not soured – both saw themselves as soldiers first – but Gneisenau's suspicions of English motives, and of Wellington's, were aroused.

Wellington was now beginning to get his way in at least some of the appointments to his army. Sir Hudson Lowe (later to be Napoleon's gaoler on St Helena) was suggested by Torrens as Quarter Master General. Wellington, who knew Lowe, and considered him to be an incompetent ditherer, dug his toes in. He could not have his old Peninsular Quarter Master General, Murray, now in America, but he did get Colonel Sir William de Lancey, who had proved his worth as a staff officer in Spain. Stapleton Cotton wrote offering to command the cavalry, and Wellington would have welcomed him, but the Prince Regent had promised the appointment to the Earl of Uxbridge (previously Lord Paget, who had eloped with Wellington's brother's wife but had been the highly regarded commander of Sir John Moore's cavalry). Wellington was happy to accept Uxbridge, who was now unquestionably his junior in rank. On being told by the Adjutant General at Horse Guards the name of the officer appointed as Provost Marshal, Wellington replied:

> This officer was latterly, and is now, utterly unfit for the situation he is named to fill, and I apprehend that on any movement of the army I shall be under the necessity of leaving him in the rear, as I did in the Peninsula.[15]

Some of Wellington's wishes were met. To command brigades and divisions he managed to obtain the services of some of his old Peninsular commanders. Alten, Barnes, Byng, Clinton, Colville, Halkett, Hill, Kempt, Lambert, Maitland, Pack, Picton, Ponsonby, Somerset, Vandeleur and Vivian all appeared and would be put to good use. Fitzroy Somerset rejoined as the Military Secretary. He could not have Larpent as his Judge Advocate (on a government mission to Vienna) or James McGrigor as his chief medical adviser (now Director General of the Medical Department in England). Lowry Cole wanted to come but begged a postponement, as he was about to be married. Ned Pakenham, Wellington's brother-in-law, had gone to America and been killed at the battle of New Orleans. As for the others: 'I shall do the best I can with the instruments sent to assist me'.[16]

In Paris Napoleon realised very well that he could not simply sit still. Despite his endeavours, there was no hope of the Allies coming to terms with him. If he did nothing then the ponderous but mighty Russian army, assisted by the Austrians, would concentrate on the French frontier, invade and destroy him. Time was of the essence and the Emperor's only hope was to split the coalition and defeat his enemies one by one. To do this he needed an army. The unemployed soldiers and half-pay officers were recalled, the Guard reconstituted, and conscription – the 'blood tax' – reintroduced. This latter was not entirely successful: it was widely evaded and there was also a production bottleneck in the production of muskets, but by the end of May Napoleon had assembled the *Armée du Nord*, of 125,000 men, mainly veterans, in northern France. It would take time for the Russians to muster, and in the meantime something might be done in the Low Countries. Belgium had a network of good roads, the terrain was well suited to the Napoleonic way of manoeuvring, the population were thought to be pro-French and, despite Wellington's remonstrances, there had been little attempt to fortify the frontier. The recapture of Belgium, which had been French since it had been taken from the Austrians in 1794, would enhance Napoleon's standing internally but, more to the point, it might drive Britain out of the war. Napoleon was well aware that the British public were not whole-heartedly in favour of going to war all over again. There was a peace party in Westminster (said to include Richard, Marquess Wellesley) and, Napoleon reasoned, it was only British money that held the alliance together. If the British could be defeated then they might leave the war, and the coalition would fall apart. That yet another British scuttle from the Continent might have been more likely to intensify British belligerence, rather than reduce it, is irrelevant: Napoleon saw the British as the linchpin of the combination against him, to be knocked out by a swift blow. It was of course a gamble, but Napoleon had always been a gambler. He decided to chance all on one decisive stroke.

The quality of Allied intelligence from within France varied. There was plenty of it, but it was difficult to separate disinformation, rumour and mistaken reports from hard truth. Blücher had been in favour of mounting an invasion of France by the Anglo-Dutch and Prussians as soon as they were ready – perhaps in May. There were political objections to this: the Allies were theoretically at war with Napoleon, not France, and did not want to appear to be the aggressor. Wellington, knowing that his own army was neither complete nor ready, advocated caution. He wanted to wait until all the Allied contingents were in position – the Russians, with the farthest to come, would take longest – and then mount a coordinated invasion, perhaps in July. In the event, Napoleon got his blow in first.

By the second week in June 1815 it was clear that Napoleon was intending to move in the direction of the Prussians and the Anglo-Dutch: the question was where. To the British the Channel Ports, and the routes to and from them, were vital. It was from Antwerp and Ostende that supplies and reinforcements would come, and through those ports that a British withdrawal could be effected should that become necessary. Wellington insisted that the garrisons of those towns could not be left to the Netherlands army; they must be composed of British or Hanoverian troops. Shortly after his arrival in Brussels, Wellington had organised the Anglo-Dutch army so as to use the talents of the better units and compensate for the weaknesses of the less good. He had, for the first time, organised the army into corps, rather than, as in the past, commanding divisions directly himself. This was necessitated more by Dutch sensitivities than by any need to have an extra layer of command. One of the conditions under which Wellington was appointed a field marshal in the Netherlands service, and the Netherlands army placed under him, was that the Prince of Orange, heir to the throne of the Netherlands, should be given a senior command. The Prince was only twenty-three in 1815. He had been an ADC to Wellington during the latter stages of the Peninsular War, when his father was in exile in London, and had been considered by Wellington to have 'a very good education, his manners are very engaging and he is liked by every person who approaches him; such a man may become anything; but, on the other hand, he is very young and can have no experience in business'.[17] He was enthusiastic, well meaning and personally brave. Not everyone had a high opinion of him, however, and to the British officers of the army he was known as 'The Young Frog', to distinguish him from his father, 'The Old Frog', or, to those who actively disliked him (and whatever Wellington thought, there were some), 'Stinking Billy'. By now he was a lieutenant general in the British Army.

Wellington formed his army into three corps, the 1st Corps commanded by the Prince of Orange, the 2nd Corps led by Rowland Hill (Lord Hill since the peace of 1814) and the 3rd Corps, called the Reserve Corps, commanded by Wellington himself. Each corps had a mixture of British and Allied troops: the 1st and 2nd Corps had British and Dutch-Belgian divisions, the 3rd British, Brunswick and Nassau divisions. Within the divisions too there was a mix: experienced with inexperienced, old with young, trusty with unreliable. In the two months during which the Duke had been in command, standards improved as training programmes were enforced and veteran units began to arrive. Morale too improved and, in the minds of the British soldiers at least, there was no doubt that, whatever 'Nosey' asked them to do, they would be victorious once again.

As early as May 1815 Wellington and Blücher had agreed that their armies would cooperate closely. The boundary between the Anglo-Dutch and the Prussians was the old Roman road running from Bavay to Maastricht. The Prussians would concentrate to the south of it with the Anglo-Dutch to the north. At this stage the Allies were still intending to mount an invasion of France, and it was agreed that when this began the Prussians would advance by Charleroi and Mauberge, and Wellington by Mons and Cambrai. It must be remembered that this initial concentration was designed to facilitate an invasion of France from north east to south west, not to defend against what actually happened. By June it was clear to both Wellington and Blücher that it would be Napoleon who would do the invading. While the two armies' areas of responsibility were not altered, both commanders agreed that Ghent and Brussels were the obvious targets should Napoleon move.

The Prussian headquarters was at Namur, with two corps forward, one back and a fourth in reserve. Forward left, in the area of Ciney and Dinant, was the 3rd Prussian Corps, commanded by Lieutenant General von Thielemannn. Forward right was Lieutenant General von Zieten's 1st Corps, around Charleroi, Châtelet and Fosse, and centre rear was the 2nd Corps of Major General von Pirch I, east of Gembloux and north of Namur.[18] In reserve, and in cantonments to the west of Liège, was von Bülow's 4th Corps.[19] Wellington had his headquarters in Brussels with, in the surrounding area, Picton's 5th Division, Cole's 6th Division, the Duke of Brunswick's contingent and the Nassauers. Picton had very nearly not come at all: he had a presentiment of death and had insisted that he should not be placed under command of anyone but Wellington. He only arrived on 15 June and all the preparatory work and training was carried out by the divisional staff, supervised by Wellington himself. Lowry Cole was rarely present, being heavily committed in the arrangements for his forthcoming nuptials, but both divisions had a sound leavening of British veteran units to balance the young recruits and the inexperienced Hanoverians. The 1st Anglo-Dutch Corps was forward left, with the Prince of Orange's headquarters at Braine le Compte. The 3rd Dutch-

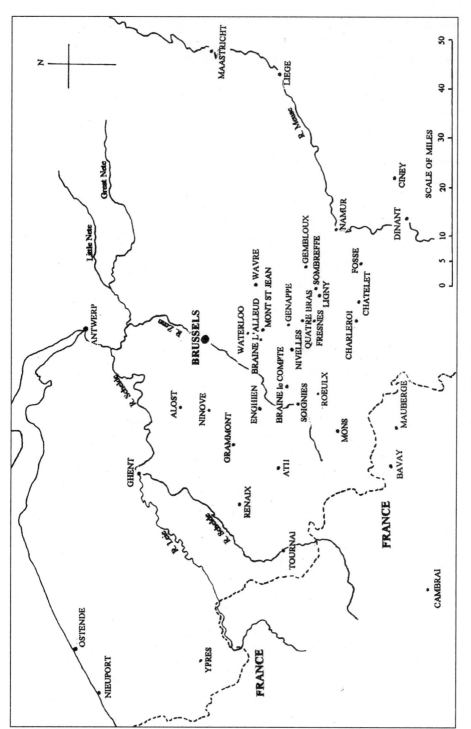

24. Area of Operations, 1815.

Belgian Division (Lieutenant General Chassée) was at Roeulx; Alten's 3rd British Division (actually a mix of British and Hanoverians) at Soignies; Cooke's 1st Division (composed entirely of Guards battalions) at Enghien; and the 2nd Dutch-Belgian Division, under Lieutenant General Perponcher, were in the area Nivelles – Quatre Bras – Genappe. The 2nd Corps was forward right, with its headquarters and the 2nd British Division (Clinton) at Ath; the 1st Dutch-Belgian Division under Lieutenant General Stedman at Grammont, the Dutch Indian Brigade at Alost and the 4th British Division (Colville) at Renaix. While there was a cavalry screen to the front and right of the two forward corps, the bulk of the cavalry was concentrated between the 1st and 2nd Corps, with Uxbridge and his headquarters at Ninove.

Each army commander attached a staff officer to the other. Blücher sent Major General von Muffling, an experienced staff officer and a good English speaker whom Wellington liked and respected, while Wellington detached Lieutenant Colonel Henry Hardinge, who had been a most competent staff officer during the Peninsular War, notably as Assistant Quarter Master General of the Portuguese army. These two officers were charged with keeping open communications between the two armies, and of representing their own commander at the other's headquarters.

If Napoleon attacked – and by 10 June it was becoming obvious that he would – there were three avenues of approach open to him. He might attack from the direction of Mons, which lay on the main road from Paris to Brussels; he might come by way of Tournai, which would be particularly dangerous for Wellington, as it would threaten his lines of communication back to England; or he might come via Charleroi, which was not the most direct route but which would allow the French to make use of a good road system leading across the frontier and on to Brussels. A French advance from Mons or Tournai would fall first upon the Anglo-Dutch, one through Charleroi on the Prussians. Wherever the blow fell, the two commanders agreed that they would support each other, and Wellington was sure that he could concentrate his army ready to operate in the threatened area within forty-eight hours. Both Blücher and Wellington were well aware of Napoleon's propensity to launch feint attacks, to use surprise and to strike at the junction of two enemy armies.

Napoleon's abilities as a general stemmed not merely from his leadership: he was an avid student of military history, a voracious reader and a genuine military innovator. His development of the *corps d'armée*, anything between 6000 and 40,000 men strong, with its own integral cavalry, artillery and logistical back up, was a major advance in the science of making war. Despite disposing of vast armies – far greater than anything Wellington ever commanded – Napoleon rarely had overall superiority over his combined enemies. He had two major tactical ploys that made him master of European warfare: the manoeuvre of envelopment and the manoeuvre of the central position. The former involved pinning an enemy against a frontal attack or a line of defences, while then attacking in flank or rear; the latter enabled him to insert his army where he could defeat two enemy armies, one after another, before they could join. It was the manoeuvre of the central position that he was attempting in 1815.

Napoleon had, for all his great strengths, a number of personal weaknesses that were to affect his performance in 1815. While he could be ruthless in battle, he had a soft spot for those who had been loyal to him, and he tended to give his political enemies the benefit of the doubt. Ney was a bad choice as second-in-command in 1815. He had offended Napoleon greatly, first as the moving spirit behind the marshals' demand that the Emperor should abdicate in 1814, and secondly with his 'iron cage' comment. Ney was, however, brave and had impressed the Emperor as commander of the rearguard during the awful retreat from the snows of Russia. He was rehabilitated, but then given a responsibility that he was incapable of discharging. Soult, good soldier though he was, was unsuited for the vital post of Chief of Staff; there were others (Davout or La Bedoyère, despite his junior position in the list of generals) who would have been better choices. Napoleon should also have had the Minister of Police, Fouché, executed in 1815; instead he left this royalist agent at the very centre of power in Paris.

Napoleon could also be spiteful: when his brother-in-law, Murat, had attacked the Austrians from his base in Naples in May 1815 he had acted prematurely, been defeated, surrendered his army and fled to Marseille. Napoleon was furious: Austrian troops, which would have been retained in Italy to face Murat, were now available for operations against France. Napoleon refused even to see Murat, and rejected out of hand his offer to command the cavalry. As Murat was the best commander of cavalry in Europe, this was an error of judgement.

Napoleon had never met Wellington, nor faced him in battle, and was contemptuous of him. What could this 'sepoy general' know of war on the grand scale? Wellington might have beaten most of Napoleon's marshals, but that was because they were frightened, or because of the special circumstances of Spain – only a minor theatre anyway. The English were bad soldiers, little more than mercenaries, and one short, sharp shock, aided by the Emperor's twelve pounders, would soon blast this rag-tag army out of the way. In contrast, Wellington admired Napoleon, and recognised his abilities as a statesman and as a soldier. He was not, however, overawed by him, and always maintained that he could be beaten: it was only a matter of time before legitimacy triumphed.

Napoleon left Paris by coach, escorted by cavalry of the Imperial Guard, at half past three in the morning of 12 June and, having stopped briefly at Laon to issue instructions to the various military district commanders, arrived at Avesnes on 13 June. That night the suspicions of the soldiers of von Zieten's 1st Prussian Corps were aroused by the reflection in the clouds of hundreds of camp fires – the French army had concentrated near the border. At about five o'clock in the morning of 15 June Napoleon and the Army of the North crossed the border in three columns and fell upon the Prussian piquets around Charleroi. Gneisenau, on Blücher's authority, ordered the Prussian army to concentrate in the area of Sombreffe. The message to Zieten, Pirch I and Thielemannn was clear and unambiguous, and their units started to move as ordered. Bülow, commanding the reserve corps away at Liège, was senior to Gneisenau, and the message to him was couched in such obsequious and flowery language that Bülow was not at all clear what was meant. He did not reach the battle area until much later than his fellow corps commanders.

There now ensued a period of muddle and misunderstanding, which gave rise to argument that continues to the present day. Once the Prussians were engaged, a message was sent to Wellington telling him of a French attack. Wellington has been accused of having received this message in the morning of 15 June and of doing nothing until late in the afternoon. It has even been suggested that Wellington deliberately allowed the Prussians to fend for themselves because of some nefarious British plot to weaken the Prussians militarily, and thus reduce their post-war influence on the future shape of Europe.[20] Everything that we know about Wellington's life and character belies this: with his firm belief that a gentleman's word was his bond, he simply was not the sort of man to leave an ally in the lurch. It may be that despatch riders were slow, or got lost, but in any case there is no evidence in the surviving records of Wellington receiving any intelligence from the Prussians about the French attack until about three o'clock in the afternoon of 15 June. Even if Wellington had received the information earlier, it was hardly in sufficient detail to persuade him to concentrate his army against what might only be a reconnaissance in force or a feint. Wellington's primary responsibility was for the two routes from Mons and Tournai: to move away from those approaches on scanty information, which did not confirm that the attack on Charleroi was the main French offensive, would have been foolish – and dangerous – in the extreme. Whatever the truth of the time of receipt of the Prussian despatch, subsequently augmented by reports from the Prince of Orange, whose corps was nearest to the threatened area, Wellington sent out orders telling all divisions to concentrate in their laid-down areas. He gave no orders for movement beyond the corps areas, there being insufficient evidence to convince him beyond doubt that this was the main thrust: until he was so convinced he dare not move his army.

Sometime in the late evening of 15 June, Wellington received news from the commander of the cavalry brigade covering Mons, Major General von Dörnberg, previously an officer in the Prussian but now in the British service, that the whole of the French army had moved in the direction of Charleroi and that there were no enemy to his front. Here too there had been delay and misunderstanding, but at last Wellington was convinced that the attack on Charleroi was indeed being carried out by the whole of the Army of the North. Orders went out, at around eleven o'clock at night, for the whole army to move left, to its east. Divisions were to concentrate at Nivelles and Quatre Bras. By concentrating at these two points Wellington could help to stop the French advance – Quatre Bras was on the main route from Charleroi towards Brussels – and he could assist the Prussians if they were attacked in their concentration area around Sombreffe. By nightfall on 15 June Napoleon had good reason to be pleased with his progress so far. The French had achieved almost complete surprise and had advanced eighteen miles, severely disrupting Allied communications and causing a mixture of panic and jubilation among the civilian population.

That night Wellington, along with many of his senior officers, attended a ball given by the Duchess of Richmond, wife of the British Minister in Brussels. There could be no question of his not attending, or of cancelling the ball: to do so would only have encouraged the pro-French elements in the city, and in any case it gave Wellington an opportunity of quietly briefing officers in person as to their future movements. While the ball was going on, battalions and regiments in Brussels were standing to, being issued with ammunition and rations, and moving off on foot or horseback. All night the infantry tramped out of the Brussels and the jingle of the artillery harness could be heard during the pauses between tunes played by the military bands. Wellington himself, having gone to bed at around two o'clock, left Brussels on horseback at around seven o'clock in the morning of 16 June. He had arranged to meet Blücher at Brye, and on the way he inspected the positions at Quatre Bras. Quatre Bras was a small hamlet, little more than a cluster of houses at a crossroads formed by the Roman road, running south east to north west from Namur to Nivelles, and the main Charleroi to Brussels road, running south to north. Now that the Prussians were concentrating around Sombreffe and the British at Nivelles, this Roman road was important, as it was the main communication route between the Prussians and the Anglo-Dutch. Quatre Bras had to be held, not only to keep this route open but also to prevent the French from making straight for Brussels, or outflanking the Prussians, or both.

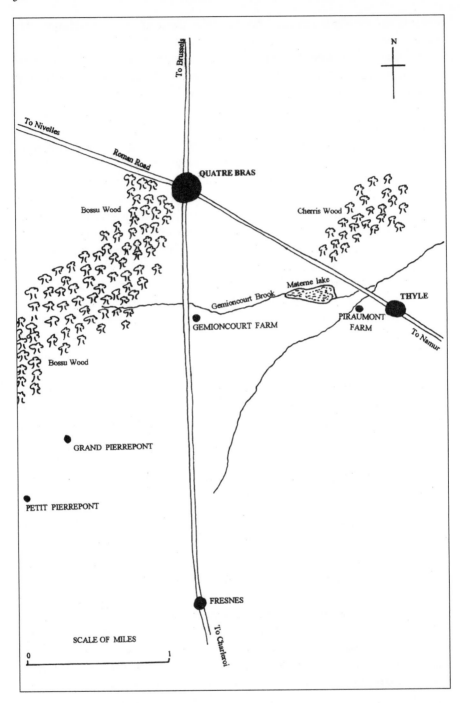

25. The Battle of Quatre Bras, 16 June 1815.

The Prince of Orange had been allowed limited authority in regard to the two Dutch-Belgian divisions in his corps, and what Wellington found at Quatre Bras satisfied him. The previous evening, south of Quatre Bras, a brigade of Perponcher's division, composed of Nassauers in the Dutch service and commanded by Prince Bernhard of Saxe-Weimar, had met French cavalry and held them off, and early on the morning of the 16th they had prevented French skirmishers from approaching the crossroads. The Prince of Orange, who arrived at Quatre Bras from the ball at about eight o'clock in the morning, had good reason to be pleased. Saxe-Weimar's men were one of the few Dutch units to be wearing the new uniform of the army of the Netherlands, blue-grey with orange facings. Beneath the smart appearance, however, there were problems: two of the four battalions were equipped with French muskets, retained from their former employment under Napoleon; and the other two battalions had a mixture of rifles of four different calibres. Each man had only ten rounds of ammunition and resupply would not be easy. By about ten o'clock in the morning, when Wellington arrived at Quatre Bras, Perponcher's division was spread in a semicircle towards the south, centred on the crossroads. In Bossu wood, to the west of the main north/south road, and in the villages beyond, was Saxe-Weimar's brigade, while the second brigade of the division, that commanded by Major General Bylandt, held the east with its left flank on the hamlet of Thyle. The farm of Gemioncourt, actually a large manor house, built in the middle ages as a bishop's residence and with stout walls, formed a strong point in the centre of the position, about a mile south of Quatre Bras. The divisional artillery, two batteries or eighteen guns, was spread around the semi-circle.

Wellington inspected the position accompanied by the Prince of Orange, declared himself satisfied and rode on up the Namur road to meet Blücher at Brye. He rode the seven miles to Ligny, and found that Blücher had concentrated three of his four corps on rising ground north of the Ligny brook, with the hamlets and the village of Ligny itself forming part of the line of defence. The Prussians were drawn up in column, on the forward slopes, awaiting the French assault. Wellington thought this was unwise: the French artillery could pound the waiting infantry from a range at which they could make no reply.[21] Wellington suggested that the men should be moved back onto the reverse slope, but Blücher was adamant that his men liked to see their enemy. The Prussians were, not unnaturally, anxious about the coming battle: they were outnumbered and their fourth corps had not arrived. They would have liked Wellington to detach part of his army, or even to bring the whole of his army to the Ligny position. Wellington knew very well that such a manoeuvre could not be completed in time; but even if it could be, he dare not risk putting all his eggs in one basket. If he did, then the French might well slip round by the west and pounce on Brussels. He did, however, promise to come to Blücher's aid 'provided I am not attacked myself'. This remark is the source of controversy, it being suggested that Wellington promised to come to the aid of the Prussians without any caveat. As both Muffling and Dörnberg, who were present, recorded the words used, there can be little doubt that it was Wellington's intention to help the Prussians if he could, but not at the expense of abandoning his own forward positions should they come under attack.[22] Wellington now rode back to Quatre Bras, where he was to find that the situation had taken a sudden turn for the worse.

On the evening of 15 June Napoleon, well satisfied with the progress made that day, issued orders for the next day, the 16th. These orders were issued through Marshal Soult, who was now the Emperor's chief of staff. Soult was a fine soldier and a good tactician, but he was unsuited for the post as chief of staff and lacked the precision in the issuing of orders in the Emperor's name that had distinguished Napoleon's long-term chief of staff, Marshal Berthier. Berthier, who had always held residual royalist sympathies, and had declined to rejoin Napoleon in 1815, met his death on 1 June of that year by falling from a window in Bamberg, just as Russian troops were marching past on their way to join the invasion force. Whether Berthier jumped or was pushed has never been established.[23] Napoleon's plan was to attack at the junction of the Prussian and Anglo-Dutch armies and smash them individually before they had time to join together. For 16 June he divided the army into two: the right wing under Marshal Grouchy, and accompanied by Napoleon himself, would take on the Prussians; while the left wing, under Marshal Ney, would head for Brussels. When the Prussians had been dealt with, the whole army would concentrate once more and deal with the patchwork Anglo-Dutch army. Napoleon assumed that, if he could defeat Blücher, the Prussian army would retreat along their lines of communication, back to Namur and the Rhine, thus drawing farther away from Wellington, who would be left without Prussian support when Napoleon turned on him. It was a classic Napoleonic strategy, but, unfortunately for its inventor, both Wellington and Blücher knew a lot about Napoleonic strategy after twenty-three years of war.

The first orders received by Ney instructed him to go straight up the Brussels road, capture Quatre Bras and destroy anything coming up from the direction of Brussels or Nivelles. To do this he would have two corps, those of d'Erlon and Reille, elements of the cavalry of the Imperial Guard, with Kellermann's 3rd Cavalry Corps, heavy cavalry, following up. Altogether Ney's wing of the army would total 40,000 men, with sixty-four guns. The right wing, which would descend on the Prussians, would have Grouchy's own Reserve Cavalry Corps, the 2nd and 4th Cavalry Corps, Vandamme's 3rd

Corps, Gérard's 4th Corps, and most of the Imperial Guard. Ney, for a man who had a reputation for fire and energy, had been dilatory. He did not hasten to move on the morning of 16 June, and he had not ordered any reconnaissance of the Quatre Bras position. Napoleonic armies did have a tendency to be late starters, largely because of the time it took them to prepare breakfast, which was often obtained by forage, even in France. At around two o'clock in the afternoon Ney reached the Quatre Bras position, with 19,000 men of Reille's corps supported by 3500 cavalry and most of the guns. The 18,000 men of d'Erlon's corps brought up the rear, a few miles back. The men of Bylandt's division could not hold. They were bustled out of Gemioncourt farm and the buildings to the east of the Charleroi road and retreated back towards Quatre Bras in some disorder. The Prince of Orange only escaped capture by being on a faster horse than his pursuers. To the west of the road, however, Saxe-Weimar's brigade, although driven out of the two farms of Petit and Grand Pierrepont, managed to withdraw into Bossu wood, where they were holding, although ammunition was running low.

It was at this point that Wellington, with his uncanny knack of being at the right place at just the right time, arrived at the crossroads of Quatre Bras. A few minutes later, at about three o'clock, the first brigade of Picton's division, Kempt's Peninsular veterans, ordered to move the fifteen miles from north of Brussels the previous day, began to arrive. Wellington now took over the battle, and as Picton's units began to arrive on the field he fed them into the fighting. The 1/95 Rifles were ordered to go left and into Piraumont, about 300 yards south of the Nivelles/Namur road. This they could not do (Piraumont was full of Frenchmen); but instead they occupied the hamlet of Thyle and Cherris wood, both on the Namur road. This anchored Wellington's left flank and, except for one brief period, the riflemen, supported by a battalion of the Brunswick contingent which arrived shortly after Picton, were to hold the position for the next five hours. The superiority of rifles against muskets at long range was well proven here: the French skirmishers could not get anywhere near the riflemen lining the hedge and ditch, and sniping from the trees.

Bylandt's brigade, which had retreated from the first French onslaught, was now arriving at the crossroads. Bylandt and the Prince of Orange having rallied the men, Wellington ordered them to advance back up the road and retake Gemioncourt Farm, with the 1/28 Foot from Picton's division following them up to garrison the farm once taken. Bylandt's men were unable to get within striking distance of Gemioncourt, but they did buy some precious time, which Wellington used to good purpose. He sent Kempt's brigade, now down to two battalions after the detaching of the 95th Rifles and the 28th Foot, to the edge of Materne Lake, an artificial pond about 300 yards

south of the Namur road and a mile south east of Quatre Bras. As Picton's
second brigade, that of Dennis Pack, arrived at the crossroads, its four battalions were sent to form a line running diagonally from the crossroads to join
up with Kempt. The two artillery batteries of the division, one of the Royal
Artillery and one Hanoverian, were stationed either side of the crossroads.
This was the first artillery available to Wellington, as most of that belonging
to Perponcher's Dutch-Belgian division had been overrun by the French. The
leading troops of the 6th Division, a Hanoverian brigade commanded by
Colonel Carl Best, arrived and were stationed along the Namur road. For the
moment the situation was stabilised, then, looking south to the high ground
beyond Gemioncourt Farm, the cluster of officers on horseback at the crossroads saw a mass of French infantry come over the crest. Three French
columns, each of brigade strength, were heading north, between the
Charleroi road and Materne Lake, while two more, farther back, marched
west of the road. At the same time groups of *tirailleurs* swarmed around the
southern edges of Bossu wood, where it was clear that Saxe-Weimar's men
were in difficulty. A galloper darted from the crossroads with Wellington's
orders for Picton: the division was to advance and attack the oncoming
French columns. Wellington himself rode up the rear of the line telling individual commanding officers to get their men up and on. The orders were
transmitted by beat of drum and voice; the soldiers stood up, formed line and
moved forward.

At first the men could not see very much: the field was sewn with unharvested rye and only the officers on horseback and the tips of bayonets told the
watchers where the six battalions were. Then, about three hundred yards
short of Gemioncourt, the rye ended. The battalions emerged, brought their
muskets to the present, took aim and waited. The French columns came
closer, driven on by the beat of drum and cries of *Vive l'Empereur!* It could
have been any of the Peninsular encounters between line and column, and
the result was the same. The British volleys began. Although the French
stepped over the bodies of their own front ranks, they could make no
progress against the storm of musket balls being directed at them. The French
withdrew and the British pressed on, as far as Gemioncourt brook.
Wellington had now returned to the crossroads, where he found the Duke of
Brunswick, who had just arrived with the bulk of his contingent. The infantry
was sent into Bossu wood, to help the Nassauers.

Now, with the French disordered, was the time to launch the Brunswick
horsemen, the only Allied cavalry present at this point.[24] Led by the Duke of
Brunswick, the cavalry headed north, between Bossu wood and the Charleroi
road. They had just under a mile to go. Cavalry drill books directed that the
first quarter mile was to be at the walk, the second at the trot, the third at the

canter and the final quarter mile at the gallop. In this case, as was usually the case with most British and Allied cavalry, walking, trotting and cantering were forgotten, and the two regiments, about 900 men in all, took off at the gallop. It was too late; the French battalions formed square and, with no artillery to support them, the troopers were driven back. The Duke of Brunswick tried to rally them near the crossroads, only to be shot dead by a French sniper. Some Dutch-Belgian cavalry was arriving and the Prince of Orange now tried to lead them and the survivors of the Brunswick horse in another charge either side of the road. They had got almost as far as Gemioncourt when they found a French cavalry brigade formed up to meet them. The Dutch-Belgians were reluctant to charge home and the whole lot turned about and made off back to the crossroads, pursued by French cavalry. Wellington, endeavouring to prevent them leaving the field, found that they simply streamed past. He was now in danger of capture himself and galloped for the crossroads. There the 92nd, the Gordon Highlanders, knelt in the ditch. Wellington shouted to them to drop their musket barrels and putting his spurs to his horse, cleared the rank of Highlanders just before they fired a volley into his pursuers. Some of the French cavalry got through and emerged behind the lines of Picton's battalions. The 42nd Foot, the Black Watch, were caught in the act of forming square and some French cavalrymen got inside. The square closed and they were all killed. The rear rank of the 44th faced about and began their volley fire. A French lance pierced the jaw of Ensign Christie, carrying the regimental colour, and the lancer seized the colour. Christie hung grimly on and his escort cut the lancer down. After confused scrimmaging the French were driven off, but at the left of Picton's division things were not going well. The British had reached Gemioncourt brook and, although they lay down, they had formed square and had to remain in that formation because of the presence of French cavalry. There was no reverse slope, the French gunners could see them, and round shot and canister ploughed into the massed ranks. Eventually they pulled back, into the rye grass, where they could at least get some cover from view if not from fire. The stubble in front of the brook had caught fire, probably from burning cartridge wads, and many of the British wounded, who could not be brought back when the line retired, were burned to death.

Back at the crossroads more Allied soldiers were coming onto the field. There were now five batteries of artillery, two British, one from Brunswick and two Dutch-Belgian. They could fire canister at the French cavalry but the range of their six pounders did not allow them to do much about the French artillery, a mile away. The Dutch-Belgian cavalry were still reluctant to charge the French, but they did take up position in a line behind the Namur road: while posing little actual threat, they did at least look formidable.

By now Kellermann's heavy cavalry had come up, and Ney ordered the *cuirassiers*, big heavy men on big heavy horses, in a headlong charge up the Charleroi road. It was a brave sight, but volleys from the 92nd at the cross-roads, directed by Wellington personally, and supporting fire from the men in Bossu wood, and the battalions of Picton's division to the east, cut them down. Although they wore steel breast- and back-plates these could not stop a musket ball, and soon the road was choked with dead, dying and fleeing horses without their riders and riders without their horses. Those who remained mounted and unwounded did not pull up until they had got back to Fresnes, two miles to the French rear. Kellermann, who led the charge, had his horse killed under him and had to catch a loose horse to make his own way back. All in all the *cuirassiers* did little damage to the Allied infantry, but they did catch a number of the skirmishers and some of the gunners, who had not been swift enough in making their way back to the protection of the infantry when they had fired their last canister round at the approaching cavalry. Once their cavalry had got out of the line of fire, the French artillery opened up again, and, unusually for a Wellingtonian battle, the French skir-mishers were harassing the British line. More French cavalry came pouring down the Charleroi road, and yet again they were repulsed. Wellington ordered Picton to send two battalions – the 3/1st and the 1/28th – to advance in mass column to chase off the French *tirailleurs*, which they did, then forming a two-battalion square alongside the Charleroi road. This was prob-ably the low point of the battle from Wellington's viewpoint. He had to defend an area where he would not normally have chosen to fight a battle; there was no reverse slope; some of Picton's battalions had lost a third of their strength; the Rifles had just been driven out of Thyle and were holding grimly onto Cherris wood; and all were short of ammunition.

All was not going as well, however, as the French had hoped. The initial orders sent out by Soult had not got through to all the addressees – Soult sent only one courier with each message, whereas Berthier had always used three – and one of the divisional commanders of Gérard's 4th Corps, General de Bourmont, deserted to Blücher taking the corps plan with him. Although the information was too late for the Prussians to react, it increased suspicions in the French army, where any military reverse tended to be equated with treachery. The French right wing attacked the Prussians at about half past two in the afternoon, shortly after the fighting at Quatre Bras had started. Napoleon now changed his orders to Ney, instructing him to hold the British at Quatre Bras, and sent an order direct to d'Erlon, up to now Ney's reserve, ordering him to move across to his right, east, and fall on the Prussian flank. It was at about this point that Ney ordered Kellermann's charge, which was repulsed in some style. All Ney's attacks so far had been beaten off, and he came to the conclusion that Wellington had far more troops opposite than he really had. Ney recalled d'Erlon, and the result was that d'Erlon's corps spent the day of 16 June marching to and fro across the battlefield without ever firing a shot.

At Quatre Bras it was about five o'clock, and two brigades of Charles Alten's 3rd Division were arriving from Nivelles. Wellington immediately sent one brigade, Hanoverians commanded by Major General Kielmansegge, to help the 95th Rifles get back into Thyle, which they did, and then told them to advance on Piraumont. The second brigade, Halkett's British brigade, he gave to Picton to stiffen up his line, which was still holding but short of ammunition and taking heavy casualties. Picton took the four battalions and put them across the Charleroi road in square, where they could support both Picton's other battalions and the Brunswickers and Nassauers in Bossu wood. These battalions had full ammunition pouches and would make a significant difference to the British defence line. It was unfortunate, while Wellington was on his left flank, directing the retaking of Thyle, that the Prince of Orange, unsupervised, decided to take a hand in affairs on the right. The Prince rode up to Halkett and ordered him to move his four battalions out of square and into line. The Prince's logic was, presumably, that more fire support could be delivered by battalions in line, and that a line was a less inviting target for the French artillery round Gemioncourt. The French cavalry appeared to have withdrawn, at least for the moment. Both the experienced Halkett and Picton were furious: it was bad enough having to take orders from a boy, but this, they thought, was tactical madness. The Prince was, however, the son and heir of an Allied sovereign and the two generals had no option but to obey. It was exactly what the French had been waiting for. Mounted cavalrymen were posted in folds in the ground, with only their heads visible. As soon as they saw the battalions form into line, they struck. Three of Halkett's four battalions had little experience of fighting the French. The first line of French horsemen hit the 69th and scattered them, taking their regimental colour (the only colour ever lost by a British battalion under Wellington's command); the 33rd, Wellington's old regiment, and the 2/73rd simply ran for the wood, the French spearing and sabreing them as they fled, all cohesion lost. Only the 2/30th stood their ground. A Peninsular battalion, they had seen it all before: the rear rank faced about, the battalion continued to fire its steady volleys, the drums beat to form square when the first furious rush of horses had passed, and the battalion, now horribly exposed, retreated in good order, joining the rest of the brigade in the wood.

As soon as Wellington returned from his left flank and saw what had happened, he galloped to the edge of Bossu wood, threw the reins of his horse to an ADC and walked up the lines of the shaken soldiers, now being reorganised by their officers. He reminded the 33rd that he had been their colonel for ten years, and that he expected better of them. Wellington had seen British soldiers run before, and Gurwood remembers him once saying at the dinner table:

> The fellow may, for a moment, in the hour of hot battle, feel half-disposed to go to the rear. Yet there is still an innate or an educated feeling which excites him immediately to resume his sense of duty, not only to efface the transitory fault, which is really not in his nature, but to induce him by increased energy, to regain his character with his comrades and to make greater efforts to retrieve the errors of his imagination.[25]

In this instance all was by no means lost, for when Wellington returned to the crossroads he found that two more Brunswick infantry battalions had arrived, and he sent them up the Charleroi road in two columns. A string of ammunition carts now rumbled up, and they were sent forward to resupply the troops in the forward line and in the wood. Each fresh division had brought its two batteries of artillery, and more Brunswick guns were also on the field. At last, at some time between six o'clock and half past six, the British 1st Division, four battalions of the Guards, came down the Nivelles road. They had marched twenty-five miles from Enghien, and had covered the last four at the double. Although only two of the four Guards battalions had been in the Peninsula (3/1st and 2nd Coldstream), these were the flower of the British army; battalions fully up to strength, with the pick of the recruits and with the best NCOs in the world. As they arrived at the crossroads by companies Wellington threw them straight at and around Bossu wood. Wellington now had superior numbers to Ney in every arm except cavalry. Despite the Anglo-Dutch losses, the French had been unable to gain any ground and the vital crossroads was still in British hands.

It was now time to order a general advance. In the woods there was confused fighting but, within half an hour, the Guards emerged at the northern end and went on to recapture the two Pierrepont farms. On the left, the Hanoverians and the Rifles had retaken Piraumont and pressed on up the left flank. In the centre, two hundred yards down the Charleroi road, was a small house still occupied by the French. Wellington ordered the 92nd, the Gordon Highlanders, to charge and take it. The charge was actually led by Major General Edward Barnes, who was the army's Adjutant General and had no business to be there at all, but he had always been of a fiery temperament and could not resist the temptation. Barnes was lightly wounded but the Gordons' commanding officer, Colonel Cameron of Fassiefern, was killed. Suddenly, the whole tempo of the battle changed, and Ney, with d'Erlon's corps still miles away, had no more troops to throw in. Everywhere the now numerically stronger Allies were making progress, the French gave way and by dark Ney was back at Fresnes, where he had started the day. It had been an untidy battle, but Wellington's ability to remain cool and collected, and his Frederician talent for feeding units into the fray as they arrived, had saved the day at Quatre Bras. He had been unable to offer any assistance to Blücher, however, and his losses were heavy. The 3/1st Foot had lost 200 men killed and wounded, the 42nd, the 79th and the 92nd around 300 each, the 32nd 200 and the 1st Guards 500 men from their two battalions. Altogether Wellington reported 2275 British casualties, 879 Brunswickers and 369 Hanoverians. The Dutch-Belgians reported 1500 casualties, from a strength of around 9000, and these may have been overstated. The French total is not known with accuracy but was probably slightly fewer. As night fell the weary soldiers tended the wounded, many now suffering from heatstroke having been lying out in the blazing sun all day, and cooked their evening meal. Wellington pushed out piquets, who exchanged a desultory fire with their French opposite numbers.

Information from Ligny was fragmentary. All day Wellington could hear the noise of artillery and musket firing five miles to his east. When the fighting at Quatre Bras was over, a patrol of British hussars found the area covered with French skirmishers and Thielemann's corps fighting a desperate rearguard action while the rest of the Prussian army got away.[26] Napoleon and Grouchy had defeated the Prussians, but they had not routed them. Blücher ordered counter-attack after counter-attack as the French artillery pounded his infantry and the French columns pressed ever nearer, but the Prussians, outnumbered, could not hold and began to withdraw. Blücher himself had been unhorsed and ridden over by a French cavalry charge and had to be carried unconscious off the field. Gneisenau issued orders for the retreat, which Napoleon expected to be to Namur and the Rhine, back along the Prussian lines of communication. Although Gneisenau would have preferred exactly that course – he was still smarting over the British failure to come to the Prussians' aid, and he distrusted the British (whom he thought might make for the Channel Ports), he obeyed Blücher's earlier instructions to him. He ordered a withdrawal back to Wavre, to the north and back along the route to Brussels, where the army would remain in contact with Wellington, rather than moving farther away from him as Napoleon had hoped. There had been desertions from the Prussian army – up to 7000 men according to some sources – but Blücher was unconcerned: if they did not want to fight, he was better off without them. As soon as he heard that the Prussians had withdrawn, Wellington knew that he had no alternative but to follow suit. To remain at Quatre Bras would have left him isolated, in a position difficult to defend and liable to be outflanked and destroyed once the two wings of the French army were reunited. Wellington's first inclination was to withdraw that night, difficult though this would have been given the exhausted state of the troops and the clogging of the roads caused by reinforcements still coming up. It was Muffling, the Prussian liaison officer, with his long experience of fighting Napoleon, who assured him that he could safely wait until the morning: Napoleon liked to ensure that his men had their breakfast before moving, and the French were unlikely to launch a night attack given the two battles they had fought that day.

During the night Wellington issued orders for the withdrawal, back to the ridge of Mont St-Jean, ten miles to the north. This was a position that Wellington had looked at earlier in the year, as being one of the features from where Brussels could be defended should the French invade by way of Charleroi. The withdrawal began at ten o'clock in the morning, and, contrary to some of the impressions of those who were there – particularly the junior officers and the soldiers – it was a masterpiece of tactical handling by Wellington. Those marching with the battalions, hurrying to get away from the French, naturally thought all was chaos, but in fact the withdrawal was carefully planned and brilliantly executed. In order to make the French think that they were still opposed by the bulk of the Allied army, those in the rear moved first. Wellington had not issued orders to stop troops still on their way to Quatre Bras. Had the regiments and battalions been told to turn about it could have caused then to believe that Wellington had been defeated. The British would not have worried overmuch, but rumours might have caused panic amongst the inexperienced Allied contingents, and to try and reverse the movement of supply columns, particularly at night, would have created an almost insoluble traffic problem. As the fresh battalions arrived in the area they were fed into the front line, while those battalions previously in position slipped away up the Brussels road.[27]

Napoleon still believed that the Prussians had retreated towards Germany, and ordered Ney to take Quatre Bras if it was held only by a rearguard. If the whole Allied army was still there then he, the Emperor, would come to Ney's assistance. Ney did indeed think that all of Wellington's army still faced him: whatever might be seen in the front line, his Peninsular veterans knew that Wellington usually concealed his main body. By the time that Napoleon marched down the Namur road to Quatre Bras, at about two o'clock in the afternoon, it was too late: the Allied army had gone. A clean break was helped by violent thunderstorms and heavy rain, which slowed up the eventual pursuit by restricting the move of French cavalry and artillery to the road. The Allied rearguard, of the 95th Rifles, horse artillery and cavalry, had little difficulty in keeping the French at arm's length, and the total casualties in the withdrawal were only ninety-six, mostly in the cavalry. Not all the British cavalry had adjusted to the requirements of all-out war. Captain Kincaid, adjutant of the 95th Rifles, was organising an ambush during the withdrawal when he saw a trooper of the Life Guards trotting peaceably up the road towards him. The man had clearly fallen from his horse at some stage, for his tunic was covered in mud, but he seemed unharmed. Kincaid demanded to know where he was going, whereupon the trooper, indicating his mud-stained tunic, explained that he had been sent to rear as being unfit to be seen on parade.[28]

13

Waterloo

During the afternoon and evening of 17 June the Allied army, wet, cold and hungry, began to arrive at Mont St-Jean. Most came from Quatre Bras but others arrived from Brussels and from other concentration areas round about. Wellington now knew the full extent of the Prussian defeat at Ligny, but he also knew that the Prussians, true to their word, had withdrawn north, and were now concentrating at Wavre, six miles to the east of Mont St-Jean, where they had been joined by their fourth corps, that of von Bülow. Communications between the two armies had now been restored, and Wellington sent a message to Blücher telling him that he would fight on the Mont St-Jean position provided Blücher could support him, even if that support was but a single corps. At about two o'clock in the morning of 18 June Wellington learned from Blücher that two Prussian corps would move to his assistance at dawn. Wellington's mind was made up: he would fight where he stood.

Napoleon too was gathering more information as to the true situation regarding the Prussians. He now knew that they had moved north, not east, but he considered that this did not matter very much: he could beat the Anglo-Dutch and then hand out another trouncing to the Prussians. To make sure that the Prussians did not attempt to help Wellington, Napoleon detailed Marshal Grouchy to take Vandamme's and Gérard's corps, with the two cavalry corps of Pajol and Exelmans, and follow up the Prussians, keeping them on the run and preventing them from joining up with Wellington. This was a total of 33,000 men, or nearly a third of Napoleon's army. To Napoleon the 18th of June 1815 must have seemed the climax of his career. He had launched his army into Belgium on 15 June, accompanying its right-hand column, and fought and won the battle of Ligny on 16 June. He had had little rest for four days, but a lifetime of campaigning had inured him to that.

As the Allied units arrived at Mont St-Jean during the evening and night of 17 June staff officers directed them into position. The later arrivals, stumbling about in the dark, trying to keep their cartridges dry and still being rained upon, had little opportunity for sleep, even if there had been any cover for them to shelter under, which there was not. Some soldiers managed to light fires, which burned fitfully, but many, unable to cook, had nothing to eat but the biscuit they carried in their packs. There was at least an issue of spirits, mostly Dutch gin, and despite the weather and the after effects of the battle of 16 June, few realised the precarious position they were in. Bylandt's brigade was detailed as the piquet brigade and their men scurried down off the ridge, where they found themselves only a few hundred yards from their French opposite numbers.[1]

The French too had a difficult time of it. Following up the Allies, they arrived on the ridge of La Belle Alliance (named after an inn which stood on the centre of its summit). Patrols and the camp fires indicated that Wellington was indeed intending to make a stand, and Napoleon ordered his chief engineer, General François Haxo, to discover whether Wellington had entrenched (he had not, possibly to discourage Napoleon from manoeuvring). The night was even more uncomfortable for the French troops than for their opponents. Unlike the British, they wore their great-coats (many of them British-made) on the march, rather than carrying them on top of their haversacks or leaving them in the regimental transport carts. The coats became soaked and great globules of mud stuck to them. They too straggled into their positions on the ridge opposite to the British and spent the night trying to make themselves presentable for the Emperor's review on the morrow.

The ridge that Wellington had chosen for his position was in many ways archetypal of his defensive battles. It was just over a mile long, with a reverse slope. A lateral road, sunken in places and with a hedge running along most of its length, ran along the ridge. It was bisected south to north by the main road to Brussels. Three miles behind the ridge, in the Brussels direction, was the village of Waterloo, from which the coming battle would take its name. On Wellington's left flank was a fortified manor, Papelotte, and a farm, La Haie. Further to the east were the hamlet of Smohain and the château of Fischermont. The ground to the east was marshy, made worse by the heavy overnight rain, and with numerous sunken farm tracks. In the centre of the position and 200 yards forward of it, alongside the Brussels road, was the stoutly built farm of La Haye Sainte (not to be confused with La Haie). To the right of the ridge, 400 yards from the summit and in the valley, was the château and farm of Hougoumont, like La Haye Sainte built around the early 1600s and intended to be used for defence as well as agriculture. Just west of the position was the village of Braine l'Alleud, and six miles farther west Tal and Hubize. Running south from the ridge of Mont St-Jean the ground sloped gently down before rising to La Belle Alliance, about 1200 yards away. Wellington was not overconcerned about his left flank: it was from that direction that the Prussians would come, and the swampy ground and sunken

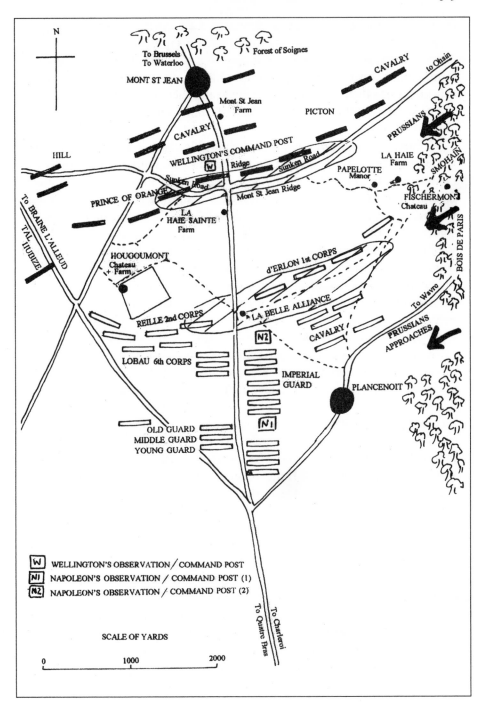

26. The Battle of Waterloo, 18 June 1815.

tracks would make any major movement by the French in that direction very difficult, particularly for cavalry and artillery. He instructed Bernhard of Saxe-Weimar, whose brigade had fought well at Quatre Bras, to occupy the farms and hamlet. These positions would be supported by two cavalry brigades, one (British) commanded by Major General Sir John Vandeleur, and the other (combined British and KGL) commanded by Major General Sir Hussey Vivian.

Wellington was, however, worried about his right. While he hoped that Napoleon would attack straight up the middle, the Emperor's fondness for manoeuvre and the indirect approach might tempt him to carry out a left flanking movement, round to the west of Wellington's position, where there was no Allied army and which, if successful, would endanger his lines of communication and possibly reach Brussels. To guard against this possibility Wellington placed two brigades of infantry, one British and one Hanoverian, with two British artillery batteries, in Tal and Hubize, while an entire division of Dutch-Belgians, that of Chassée, was placed in Braine l'Alleud. Both these formations were ordered to patrol constantly to give early warning of any French attempt to outflank the main position, while Rowland Hill kept a watching brief on the whole Allied right flank. To the right of Wellington's battle area Hougoumont farm was critical, as whoever held it could dominate that part of the battlefield; if the French did so then they would find it relatively easy to move round the Allied right flank. On the night of 17 June the light companies of the Guards were sent into Hougoumont; it was as well that they were, for they got in just before some French *tirailleurs* who were trying to do the same thing. The French were driven off, and early on the morning of 18 June Wellington reinforced the farm with a battalion detached from Saxe-Weimar's brigade and some Hanoverian riflemen.

As Hougoumont was the key to the right of Wellington's position, so was La Haye Sainte to the centre. Here the defence was entrusted to the 2nd Light Battalion of the KGL, 375 men armed with Baker rifles and commanded by Major Baring. During the night they prepared the buildings for defence and placed a roadblock of carts and farm equipment across the road, although it was perhaps unfortunate that they took down the stout wooden door to the courtyard and used it for firewood. To give the defence further firepower a detachment of the 95th Rifles was placed in an old sand quarry on the east of the road and a hundred yards forward of the crest.

With the left, centre and right anchored, Wellington placed the main body of his troops along and slightly to the rear of the ridge. His own command post was in the centre, where the lateral road crossed the main Brussels highway. To the left, running from the crossroads to just short of the cavalry above Papelotte, was Picton's division. Picton now had six brigades: he had absorbed the two brigades of Lowry Cole's 6th Division (Cole was still away on his honeymoon), and had also taken Bylandt's brigade under his wing. This division, two British brigades, two Hanoverian and Bylandt's, covered a front of about a thousand yards. Picton's British brigades were veterans, Bylandt was sandwiched between two of them, and the less experienced Hanoverians were on Picton's extreme left, a relatively safe area. Immediately to the right of the crossroads stood a KGL brigade which was not involved at Quatre Bras but had fought in Spain, then Kielmansegge's Hanoverians, who had performed well on 16 June. On the other side of Kielmansegge was Halkett's brigade, still shaky after having been ridden down and carved up at Quatre Bras, and on the right flank stood Cooke's Guards, where they could see and support their light companies in Hougoumont. This right flank was nominally under the command of the Prince of Orange, although Wellington himself would direct their movements. The Brunswick and Nassau infantry were placed in reserve, slightly to the rear. Two cavalry brigades, those of Major General Sir Colquhoun Grant (no relation to his namesake of Peninsular intelligence fame) and Major General Dörnberg, took post behind the Guards on the right, while the bulk of the rest of the cavalry was held in the centre rear. The heavy cavalry, of two brigades, was just behind the centre; the Household Brigade, consisting of the two regiments of Life Guards, the Royal Horse Guards (Blues) and the 1st (King's) Dragoon Guards were west of the Brussels road, while the Union Brigade (Scots Greys, Inniskillings and Royal Dragoons) were to the east, behind Picton's division. The artillery, as was Wellington's practice, was in support of the infantry, spread along the front and on the crest or the forward slope, as it had to be when indirect fire was not a practical proposition and there was insufficient to use it in mass. Wellington had guarded against an outflanking march to the west, placed just enough troops to the east to hold that flank until the Prussians should arrive, and stiffened his centre with his experienced men interspersed with those less experienced or less reliable.

Under a mile away, on the ridge to the south, Wellington and his staff could see Napoleon reviewing his troops. They were drawn up in conventional formation. The corps of d'Erlon, which was reasonably fresh, having not taken part in the battles of 16 June, was on the French right, with four divisions stretching from the farm of La Belle Alliance to a few hundred yards short of Papelotte. Reille's corps, of three divisions, was on the left. On Reille's left was a division (fifteen squadrons or the equivalent of five small regiments) of cavalry, but the bulk of the horsemen were divided into two groups, stationed behind the two forward corps. In reserve, and held back on either side of the Brussels road, was Lobau's 6th Corps, and behind them the three divisions of the Imperial Guard. The Guard was the pick of the French army. Divided into the Old, Middle and Young Guards, with its own cavalry and artillery, its men were paid more and its officers held higher rank than their equivalents in the line. To be considered for the Old Guard, officers and NCOs had to have completed a minimum of twelve years service, and soldiers ten years (which might be in the Young and Middle Guards), which had to include active service. The Young Guard were *voltigeurs* and *tirailleurs* while the Middle and Old Guards were the equivalent of line infantry. The Guard was usually held in reserve; once committed it had never been beaten. Napoleon's artillery was allocated to corps and divisions, but, as was his normal practice, he had formed a massed battery of eighty guns located on the forward slope of the centre of his line.

The French outnumbered the Anglo-Dutch in infantry and cavalry – around 73,000 to 68,000 – which was not a marked superiority when it was the French who must attack, but they greatly outnumbered Wellington in number of guns: 246 to 156. It was not only in numbers that the French artillery was superior, but also in type. The Allied foot artillery consisted of nine pounders, with a maximum effective range of 700 yards, whereas amongst the French batteries were twenty twelve pounders, with a range of 950 yards. Despite having a superiority of only 5000 men in cavalry and infantry, the French army had considerable strengths denied to Wellington. It was a homogenous body: while not all the men were French, they all wore French uniforms; they spoke the same language; they had all been trained in the same way; and they all used the same equipment, weapons and ammunition. This was not the case in Wellington's Allied force. Against this, morale in the French army was brittle: there was internal dissension and suspicion, particularly of many of the officers who had now switched loyalties twice. Any misfortune was likely to be blamed on treason. Whereas, if Wellington was defeated, his army, or at least the British portion of it, would retain its cohesion, the French officers well knew that only a victory could keep their army in being.

The battle of Waterloo started sometime in the early morning of 18 June when the skirmishers of Durutte's division, on the French extreme right, drove in those of Saxe-Weimar, but this private war was hardly noticed by most of the men on both sides, who were either being inspected by the Emperor if French, or lying down on the reverse slope if Allied. The first major action of the day took place at about eleven o'clock in the morning, when the French massed battery opened fire on the Allied centre. There is doubt as to exactly when the first shot was fired: no soldiers had watches and only some of the officers. Those who did have watches set them by the sun, but there is no indication that watches were synchronised. Contemporary accounts vary by up

to an hour, but in any event battle commenced later than the nine o'clock
that Napoleon had intended. One of the reasons for this late start was that
some units of the French army were still arriving on the field well into the
morning: they had marched through a stormy night and had to find breakfast
in areas already passed through twice by the Allies, clean their weapons and
generally prepare themselves for action. The other main reason for the delay
was the state of the ground. While the morning of 18 June was clear, it had
rained for most of the previous day and night. The manhandling of guns into
position was difficult, and the soft ground meant that a round shot would
sink into the mud where it first hit, instead of skipping along the ground and
killing more men with each bounce. Common shell too would sink in the
mud, and either not explode at all or have its force muffled. In order to allow
the ground to dry out Napoleon had perforce to delay his opening bombardment. In any event the massed battery, including all the twelve pounders, did
little damage to the Allied infantry, who were all on the reverse slope, except
possibly for Bylandt's brigade who may have been forward at that stage.[2]

Shortly after the artillery opened up on the Anglo-Dutch centre, the
extreme left-hand division of Reille's corps moved on Hougoumont. This
was originally intended to be a diversionary attack: Napoleon was well aware
that Wellington's right would be his main concern: if he could threaten that
right then Wellington must move troops to support it, thus weakening his
centre which could then be attacked. Once in possession of Mont St-Jean, the
battle would be won. The division which now attacked was commanded by
Prince Jerome Bonaparte, Napoleon's younger brother, failed King of
Westphalia, failed army commander and now working his way down the
French military hierarchy. His first brigade pushed through the wood to the
south of the farm, drove back the Hanoverian and Nassau sharpshooters, and
emerged from the wood to face the north gate of the farm across a thirty yard
wide strip of cleared land. Facing them they could see only levelled musket
barrels pointing at them through loopholes in the wall and the roof of the
farm. The French soldiers rushed the gate. None got anywhere near it: the
British guardsmen could not miss at such a range and Boudoin, the brigade
commander, and most of his first line were blown away. More men struggled
out of the wood and lapped around the wall of the orchard and garden. Here
too the Guardsmen had made loopholes and the few who got as far as the wall
without being shot were bayoneted as they tried to climb over it. Now began a
battle that would last all day, sucking more and more French soldiers in,
eventually absorbing the attention of most of Reille's corps. No wonder
Wellington later said that Hougoumont was the key to Waterloo, for while
there were some tense moments, a relative handful of the Guards held off
many times their number all day. If the light companies were pushed back,

their parent battalions on the hill got them back in again; and, in a rare example of overhead fire, the British howitzers fired over the farm at the Frenchmen crowding to it. Why Napoleon, or Ney, to whom the Emperor had effectively delegated the tactical handling of his army, did not call off this wasteful attack, once it was clear that the farm could not be taken by a *coup de main*, may be explained by the fact that from La Belle Alliance, the French tactical headquarters, it was not possible to see the farm at Hougoumont.

The next phase was the launching of the whole of d'Erlon's corps against the Allied centre (unweakened, despite Hougoumont) and left. This began at some time between half past eleven and one o'clock, when 8400 men, in echelon of divisions and with cavalry on the flanks and guns in support, came marching down the hill, the bands playing in the rear, the drummers battering their drums and the troops cheering to keep their spirits up. In sixteen battalions they covered a frontage of 1200 yards, and their left lapped around La Haye Sainte and up to the sandpit, from which the 95th Rifles wisely retreated to the relative safety of the high ground behind them, from where they continued to snipe at officers, buglers, drummers and colour bearers. The Allied gunners fired perhaps three or four rounds each at the oncoming mass before running back to the protection of the infantry, the horse artillerymen removing a wheel to prevent their guns being taken away. Picton had ordered his men to stand up, dress forward and line the hedge along the lateral road. Thirty yards from them the French halted to deploy into line, always a difficult moment: to deploy too far away made it difficult to maintain the line, while to deploy too close invited exactly what happened. Picton's front rank infantry fired a volley that could not miss, then, as they reloaded, the second rank fired. The French, caught in trying to change formation and still packed thirty-five yards deep, found great holes torn in their ranks, and the verve with which they had started their attack evaporated. The British infantry clambered through the hedge, with Picton, sitting on his horse and waving his umbrella, urging them on. At that moment a French musket ball went through his top hat and he fell, mortally wounded.[3] Picton's death did nothing to quell the ardour of his men, most of whom would not have seen him fall, and they pressed through the hedge to close with the French. As often happened when a bayonet charge took place, the defenders did not stand to receive it and the French columns began to disintegrate. At least one battalion simply dropped its muskets and fled. The right-hand French division, that of Durutte, which, because of the advance in echelon was farthest away from the British line, simply stopped when they saw what was happening and withdrew back onto their ridge. On the Allied side only Bylandt's brigade, already unsteadied by the effects of the artillery bombardment, left the line, heading for the rear.

With the French disorganised, now was the time to strike and Wellington ordered the heavy cavalry to charge and sweep all before it. Later, Uxbridge was to claim that it had been his decision to send in the heavies at this point, but in this situation it is inconceivable that Wellington would have delegated command of his heavy cavalry to anyone. The two brigades, Household and Union, cantered up to the hedge and forced through or over it, while those on the right came diagonally across the crossroads. Contrary to what is depicted in the many paintings of the action, they would not have been in the gallop: the ground was far too heavy and it is unlikely that they were in more than a steady canter or a brisk trot. It made no difference: these troopers had spent hours every day developing their sword arms; as they passed a fleeing French soldier they swung their sabres backhanded causing fearful wounds to faces and the upper body. The only hope of escape for an encumbered infantryman was to lie down, where only a lance (which the British did not have) could reach him, but panic prevented many from saving themselves in that way. D'Erlon's corps was scattered and the British had taken two eagles. Now was the time to rally the cavalry, reform them, return them to the ridge and hold them until needed again. Bugles blew and commanding officers shouted, but the horsemen's blood was up. 'On to Paris', shouted one officer as he cantered down into the valley, and most of the two brigades spurred their horses on up to the French-occupied ridge ahead. Some even got into the French massed battery but, inevitably, disaster struck. Arriving in front of the French lines, where d'Erlon's men were trickling back and forming up, the British came under musket and artillery fire. Control was abandoned and individuals or small groups of cavalrymen were attacking such targets as they could find. A regiment of Polish lancers in the French service now charged in from the flank. The British, their horses blown and all formation lost, had no option but to engage in duels with the Poles or flee for the safety of Mont St-Jean. Only about half of the 2400 got back, rescued by the Life Guards. By no means all were killed or wounded, but a heavy cavalryman without his horse is useless on a battlefield, and once unhorsed many had no option, other than being butchered, but to surrender. The heavy cavalry played but a minor role for the rest of the day.

At La Haye Sainte Baring's men had held out, but only just, and the Prince of Orange sent a KGL battalion to retake the sandpit, while he dispatched a Hanoverian battalion of Lüneburgers to help Baring around the farm. Once again the Prince insisted that the men attack in line, and once again the French cavalry supporting d'Erlon took the opportunity to charge and destroy the Lüneburgers. Despite all this, and the fighting still going on around Hougoumont, the Allied line was holding, at least for the moment. Over at Wavre, Gneisenau had submitted his plan for the move to Mont St-

Jean to Blücher. Grouchy's scouts were in contact, and Thieleman's corps was to hold Wavre against him, withdrawing away from Mont St-Jean if necessary, and forcing Grouchy to follow him, away from Napoleon's battle. The move to join Wellington would be led by von Bülow's corps. It had arrived too late to fight at Ligny and was therefore fresh and up to strength. This made sense, but, as it was the rear corps when it got to Wavre, it had to pick its way through the regiments, and their baggage, in front. The Prussian army had maps of the area, made by the British Royal Engineers, but the maze of tiny sunken roads, lined with hedges, made progress slow, and the move was not assisted by the village of Wavre catching fire as Bülow's men passed through. The Prussians were on their way, however, although it would take much longer than Blücher thought or Wellington hoped.

From the French perspective, the attack on Hougoumont had not forced Wellington to weaken his centre, and d'Erlon's attack had failed. Visions of Eylau and Borodino must have passed through Ney's mind at this point. He was temporarily without his Emperor, who had retired to rest at Rossomme, and he decided that if the attack on the Allied left had failed, then they must surely be vulnerable to a mass cavalry attack on their right. All along the line the French artillery opened up, concentrating on the Allied centre and right, while the cavalry formed up in the valley between the road and Hougoumont. On the right the Allied infantry formed square, while the Netherlands cavalry formed up behind. Most of the squares were on the reverse slope, but even so round shot and shell coming over the ridge could not fail to hit something, and the interior of the squares began to fill up with wounded and dead men, while the sergeants grew hoarse with giving the constant command to close up. To charge steady infantry in square with cavalry unsupported by infantry or guns was as much against French tactical precepts as it was against the British, but Napoleon had removed the horse artillery batteries from the cavalry to strengthen the artillery bombardment, and no attempt seems to have been made to add infantry behind the horsemen. It may be that the wagons and colours moving back on the western side of the ridge deceived Ney into thinking that the Allies were withdrawing, but these were only ammunition carts going back to replenish, and colours being sent to the rear, a normal practice in time of danger. It was at about this time, half past three in the afternoon, that the French saw the advance guard of the Prussians, several miles away to the north east. Prussian black and French blue are hard to distinguish at a distance, particularly when visibility is much reduced by cannon smoke and musket fire, and it was said to those who asked that the troops in the distance were those of Grouchy. The French could still win the battle, provided the decisive blow was struck soon.

By now around five thousand horsemen had formed up in the valley, including regiments which had not been ordered to participate but were determined not to miss the glory that would surely be theirs. Ney led them personally, as they advanced at a slow trot up the hill. As they came over the ridge, just in a slow canter, they saw the chequer board of infantry squares, which began to fire their volleys by ranks. Even a lancer had to get very close to a square before he could do any damage, and very few did. Those cavalrymen equipped with carbines or pistols rode up to the squares and fired, but it is difficult to be accurate on a plunging horse, and reloading had to be done in the rear. The clouds of horsemen could do little but mill aimlessly around the squares, hoping that one might panic and break. None did. Again and again the French withdrew, reformed and charged, and again and again they were driven off by the steady fire from the squares or short charges by the Dutch cavalry. As they withdrew, the gunners darted out back to their guns and fired into the retreating mass. No attempt was made by the cavalry to spike the guns, an error which cost them dear. The old soldiers were happy: as long as there was cavalry to their front they were spared the artillery, and some described the sound of musket balls hitting breastplates as being like a hailstorm on a slate roof. As long as the men in the squares stood tightly packed they were safe from cavalry, but each time the French lancers, dragoons and cuirassiers drew back to reform, the artillery from the ridge of La Belle Alliance would start again. All – alive, wounded or dead – had to remain in the square, and while dehydration from the heat ensured that there was little need to urinate, the haphazard rationing of the past few days left many men with mild dysentery. The soldiers defecated where they stood, and the smell of faeces mixed with vomit and the blood of the wounded made one participant liken the inside of his square to 'a perfect hospital, full of dead and dying and mutilated soldiers'.[4] With each charge the French numbers were getting fewer; their horses could now barely get into trot, and even Ney, with three horses killed under him, saw the pointlessness of it all. Even the last cavalry reserve, a regiment of carabiniers left around Hougoumont, had been thrown in to no avail. The squares stood, and eventually, about half past four in the afternoon, Napoleon, returned from Rossomme and, horrified by what Ney was doing, ordered a division of infantry to the support of the cavalry. It was too late. Six thousand men started to move down into the valley, but, as the cavalry recoiled, with thirteen generals killed or wounded, the Allied gunners, firing double shot now, raked the infantry ranks, causing at least 1500 casualties.

The Dutch-Belgian and Hanoverian cavalry had stood their ground and had fought well, with the exception of the Cumberland Hussars. This was a regiment of gentleman rankers raised in Hanover (the Duke of Cumberland, fifth son of George III, was King of Hanover). When the French cavalry attacked, their courage deserted them; refusing to charge, they turned tail, making for Brussels. Their arrival there with tales of doom, gloom and defeat caused some mild panic amongst the British and encouraged a faction of the city authorities in their preparations for a banquet to greet Napoleon. By now, however, at Mont St-Jean Wellington could hear cannon fire way over to the east, beyond the French right flank. The Prussians were beginning to take a hand.

Still Wellington's line was intact, but there were many casualties in the squares and amongst the troops around the crossroads, where the reverse slope was more of a plateau. By now Napoleon was fully aware that the Prussians were on their way. Lobau, with elements of the Guard and of his own 6th Corps, had already been sent behind the French right flank to block their approach. Napoleon could still win the battle, but only if he could defeat Wellington very quickly and then fall upon the Prussians on the line of march. It was now the Allied centre that became the objective of the French. They had already been repulsed twice from La Haye Sainte: once when they had attacked as part of d'Erlon's advance; and then at about half past three, when they had again been driven off by Baring's men supported by the right hand two brigades of the late Picton's division. On that occasion the farm buildings had been set on fire, but the flames were extinguished by the organisation of a bucket chain using the cooking pots of a Nassau regiment which had been stored at the crossroads. Now, at about six o'clock, came another assault, by infantry supported by guns this time. A swarm of *tirailleurs* rushed through the orchard and threw ladders against the walls. Baring and his men fought grimly, using the bodies of dead Frenchmen to barricade the entrance where the wooden gate had been used for cooking fires the previous night.

The Prince of Orange ordered Colonel Christian von Ompteda, commanding the KGL brigade stationed to the west of the crossroads, to send two battalions in line to drive off the *tirailleurs* attacking La Haye Sainte. An experienced Peninsular veteran, Ompteda protested vigorously: there was French cavalry about, the men should advance in column or square. The Prince was adamant, and the 5th and 8th line battalions tramped down the hill. They succeeded in driving off the French, at least for the moment, but then the French cavalry struck. The 8th line virtually ceased to exist and Ompteda was killed. The 5th managed to form square and retire, covered by the remnants of the Household brigade who rode to their rescue. It was at around this time that the Prince of Orange was wounded and carried off the field, perhaps to the relief of the KGL and Hanoverian contingents.[5] Still the French came on again, and their guns were now north of the farm, firing into the Allied centre at a range of not much more than a hundred yards. Baring and his men were slowly being overwhelmed. They were fast running out of ammunition, and repeated requests by runners sent to the top of the Allied ridge failed to provide any. Baring's battalion was armed with the Baker rifle, which fired a different cartridge from the line infantry. The battalion's ammunition wagon appears to have overturned in a ditch during the day, but it is difficult to understand why it could not have been resupplied from the 95th Rifles, armed with the same weapon. Perhaps the 95th too were running short, or perhaps Baring ran up against an archetypal British quartermaster who would not issue stores to any but his own unit, whatever the circumstances. In any event, Baring got no more cartridges, and had no option but to withdraw his men back through the farm, eventually escaping through a door to the rear. The Germans did not give up the farm easily; of the 375 men with whom Baring began the day, only he and forty-two emerged from La Haye Sainte.

Now was the crisis of the battle. La Haye Sainte had been taken and the French were poised to smash through Wellington's centre. On the Allied left many battalions had now formed two-battalion squares, such were their losses, while on the right the troops were by no means unscathed by the cavalry attacks which had gone on for most of the afternoon. Ammunition was running low, every gun was now in the firing line and there were no more reserves of any arm to be had. True, Saxe-Weimar with his Nassauers and the cavalry still held on the extreme left, although he had long given up Frischermont as being of little tactical significance and too expensive in manpower to hold. On the extreme right, the Guards held at Hougoumont. The Prussians were heading for the French right flank, but if Napoleon could burst through the centre, and he now had the springboard of La Haye Sainte from which to do so, then Wellington's position must collapse.

Wellington was, as always, where the fighting was most furious. Calmly he rode up and down the line, making no attempt to conceal himself, here speaking a few words to a divisional general, there encouraging a battalion commander. To Halkett's ADC, who brought a message asking permission for his brigade to retire to the rear to reorganise, Wellington replied: 'He and I, and every Englishman on this field, must stand and die on the spot which we now occupy.' Although Wellington may not have known it at the time, Napoleon was already facing real trouble from the Prussians, who were streaming onto the field, both on the French right flank and on the Allied left – where they initially fired on Saxe-Weimar's troops, assuming their blue uniforms to be French. Bülow's cavalry had entered Plancenoit, a village behind the French right, and although bustled out again by the Young Guard, more and more of Bülow's men were coming up and there was now a serious threat of the French being taken in flank and rear. Grouchy, still skirmishing with the Prussian rearguard at Wavre, had been unable to interfere with the forward Prussian' corps move to Mont St-Jean. Marshal Gérard, one of Grouchy's two corps commanders, suggested that they should move to rejoin the Emperor, as the noise of the firing coming from the direction of Mont St-Jean indicated that a major battle was taking place. Grouchy refused: he had his orders and, unless they were countermanded by the Emperor, he must continue to obey them. Frantic messages from Soult to Grouchy, ordering him to come to the aid of the Emperor, did not get through.

It was time for Napoleon to play his last card: the Imperial Guard. Some of the Guard had been sent with Grouchy and some were involved in the fighting around Plancenoit, two battalions were left at La Belle Alliance and one further back as a final rearguard if needed. Napoleon led his last reserve, eight battalions, with the band playing *Ça Ira,* down the hill to the valley floor, where he handed over to Marshal Ney.[6] It was not very much, but it was the invincible Guard. At about seven o'clock in the evening two columns, one of six battalions the other of two, began to advance up the hill towards the British line. They probably moved in *ordre mixée,* a sort of hollow square with the rear side missing. The obvious line of advance was straight up the Brussels road, via La Haye Sainte, which was now firmly in French hands with artillery well forward. This would have taken them straight into the Anglo-Dutch centre, now Wellington's weakest point and to where Wellington was directing every available battalion – by now not many. It may be that the road was blocked by artillery and by the remains of Baring's road block, or it may be that the men carrying the small marker flags on the leading edges of the columns got lost in the smoke and dust of battle, but in any event the Guard veered left, coming up the ridge between La Haye Sainte and Hougoumount.[7] They brushed aside the British and Hanoverian skirmishers, and emerged onto the ridge. The men in the French left-hand column found themselves facing Maitland's British brigade of Guards. The two battalions of the 1st Guards had been lying down, just behind the crest in four ranks. Wellington sat on his horse, Copenhagen, just behind them. 'Now, Maitland, now's your chance', said Wellington loudly but calmly, and the Guards stood up and fired a volley from twenty yards. The results were predictable. Three hundred French guardsmen were killed in that first volley, but still the Guard came on. The other three ranks of British Guardsmen fired their volleys in quick succession: no soldiers could stand in the face of such a tightly packed blast of musket balls. Byng's brigade, of the 2nd Coldstream and 2/3rd Guards, joined in from the British right, firing obliquely into the French column. Farther to the east the right-hand French column ran up against the brigades of Halkett and Kielmansegge, and the 33rd foot redeemed themselves for Quatre Bras.

At La Belle Alliance the watchers could see little: Prussian canon balls were bouncing off the road around them and the Guard had disappeared into the smoke half a mile away. The sound of volley fire could be heard. Then they saw a few men run back out of the smoke, then groups and then whole battalions – *'La Garde récule!'*. Brave men though they were, eight battalions was simply not enough to force a way through the steady volleys of the British and Hanoverian infantry. As the Guard recoiled, the 52nd Light Infantry, on the initiative of its commander Colonel Colborne, left the line and wheeled round to face the French left flank, hitting them with more musket fire as the poured back down the hill. From the watching French troops the cry of *'Trahison!'* went up. The Prussians were now finally in possession of Plancenoit and were round the French right and rear. More and more black-clad Prussians were coming onto the field, both here and on the Allied left. It was Napoleon's last chance and it had failed. The French army, all hope gone, broke and began to flee the field. Wellington rose in his stirrups, waved his hat in the air and ordered a general advance. Looking around he saw that one battalion appeared to be still on the east of the crossroads, failing to move. He asked a staff officer who it was: it was the men of the 27th Inniskillings, dead in square. Two battalions of the Old Guard formed square at La Belle Alliance to allow Napoleon to escape on his horse, later transferring to a coach at Rossomme. At around nine o'clock at night Wellington and Blücher met at La Belle Alliance. *'Quelle affaire!'* said the old marshal. It was Wellington's last battle.

In examining why the Allies won at Waterloo and Napoleon lost, it is necessary to cut through French myths that surround the Emperor to this day. It was said that Napoleon failed because he was betrayed; because of the incompetence of others; because he was tricked into fighting the battle; because of the weather; because he was ill. There is some truth in all of these claims. There were royalist agents inside France, and within the French army, who were working against him. Ney was incompetent in that he failed to force a way through at Quatre Bras and allowed his aggressive nature to overrule military prudence at Waterloo. Grouchy had not been able to drive the Prussians away from Wellington, but his attempts to do so deprived Napoleon of 33,000 men, cavalry and artillery. Napoleon might have fought Waterloo differently had he been fully aware of what was happening with the Prussians. The weather and hence the state of the ground hindered Napoleon's ability to move his artillery, and reduced its effectiveness when it was used. The Emperor was certainly not at his best during the campaign: he left the field of Waterloo on at least one occasion to rest; long years in the saddle and sitting on the a wooden seat of his coach may have given him piles, as has been alleged, although no mention of them is made in the post-mortem carried out after his death in 1821.

For all this, Napoleon was the head of state and the commander of the *Armée du Nord*. It was Napoleon who had promoted his marshals, and who had selected and briefed his subordinates. Despite the presence of individual royalists with the army, and a few individuals who did desert to the Allies, far too late for their information to be of any use, the soldiers fought with their usual *élan* and bravery. That the army's collapse was sudden and complete was not unusual with French revolutionary armies, which for all their patriotic fervour lacked the dour, dogged determination of British troops. Napoleon had created this army and it is he who must be held responsible for its character, its actions, its victories and its defeats.

To French historians the battle of Mont St-Jean was an unlucky defeat. If Napoleon had been able to destroy the Prussian army completely on 16 June; if Grouchy had managed to prevent the Prussians from coming to Wellington's aid on 18 June; if Napoleon had not, by his absence, allowed Ney to throw unsupported cavalry at infantry squares; if enough infantry had been available to take advantage of the capture of La Haye Sainte, then the result might have been different. All this, however, is speculation. The facts are that Napoleon was defeated and in assessing that defeat we must judge by what actually happened, and not by what might have been.

As for Wellington, Waterloo was his most remembered battle but was not his most skilled. As he said in a letter to Beresford: 'Napoleon did not manoeuvre at all. He just moved forward in the old style, in columns, and was driven off in the old style.'[8] The Anglo-Dutch army contained a mix of nationalities: orders were given in four languages; many of the troops were inexperienced or of doubtful reliability; the French artillery was better handled and there was far more of it. Any ideas of manoeuvring or the use of clever tactical devices had to be abandoned – the army was simply not capable of them. Wellington had selected the ridge of Mont St-Jean because it lay across the main route to Brussels and it had a reverse slope. What Wellington had to do was hold his position, keep his army intact and wait for the Prussians. This involved little finesse, but it was what was needed, and it is what Wellington did.

Given the nature of his army, probably only Wellington, imbued with the respect in which he was held by all the Allied troops, could have kept the disparate contingents on that ridge. He rode up and down, from threatened point to threatened point, maintaining, as was his wont, a calm and unflurried appearance. He was many times in great personal danger, but to retain the confidence of the Dutch, Belgians and Germans, and of his own raw battalions, he had to be seen by them, and this meant being far closer to the fighting than would have been wise, or necessary, in a different situation. If Wellington was on edge underneath it never showed, not even in his writing during the battle. Written messages were sent by galloper or ADC, written in pencil on a strip of goat or donkey skin, which could be erased and used again. Not many of Wellington's battle messages survive, but those that do show that, even at moments of extreme crisis, his instructions were clearly expressed, in a firm, legible hand employing correct grammar and punctuation. Much of this was, of course, a deliberate pose honed over many years on campaign, but his outward confidence, whatever doubts he may have felt inwardly, communicated itself to the troops and to their officers.

Wellington had slept for perhaps four hours on the night of 15/16 June, and about the same during the night before Waterloo. He was never one for wasting too much time in bed, and always said that when it was time to turn over, it was time to turn out.[9] Despite what some of his staff thought was fool-hardy courting of death or wounds, the closest Wellington came to serious injury was when the battle was over. Dismounting from his charger, Copenhagen, which had carried him all day, the Commander of the Forces gave the animal an affectionate slap on the rump, whereupon the previously impeccably behaved chestnut lashed out with both hind hooves, narrowly missing splitting his owner's skull.

In the aftermath of Waterloo Wellington, naturally, regretted the cost in dead and wounded, and particularly mourned the death of his ADC, Alexander Gordon, who had been badly wounded and died in Wellington's own quarters in the village of Waterloo, while the Duke was writing his post-battle despatch. There was little time for introspection, however. There was still business to be done and there is no indication in Wellington's subsequent career of any lasting psychological effects.

Arguments as to whether or not the Prussians, rather than Wellington, won the battle are irrelevant: had Wellington not relied upon Blücher to come and join him, he would not have fought the battle at all. As it was, the two commanders trusted and respected each other and the result was to the credit of both.

The price of the Anglo-Dutch-German victory was a heavy one. Total Allied casualties, Anglo-Dutch and Prussian, were 23,665. The small British contingent alone suffered 6729 casualties, or 34 per cent, the highest of any of the participants, and a percentage higher than at the Somme a century later. Of the 840 British officers present, eighty-five were killed, 365 were wounded and ten were returned as 'missing', most later discovered to be dead. The Prussians had 28 per cent casualties; the Dutch-Belgians 17 per cent; the Hanoverians and Brunswickers 16 per cent. The highest butcher's bill for any one battalion was that paid by the 27th Inniskillings. They had been sent to America the previous year and only arrived on the field of Waterloo late in the morning of 18 June 1815, 740 strong. That night there were only 157 all ranks left alive and unwounded. Of their fifteen officers only one escaped unscathed. The generals too had not shirked danger: of the commanders, Picton, Posonby, du Plat and Ompteda were killed, as was de Lancey, the Quarter Master General, hit by a roundshot while a few yards away from Wellington. Uxbridge, Alten, Cooke, Kempt, Pack, Adam and Halkett were wounded, as were the staff officers Barnes and Fitzroy Somerset. The French lost around 25,000 and another 8000 taken prisoner. About 10,000 horses were killed, or had to be put down later as a result of wounds sustained. It took three days to collect all the wounded. Wellington is reported as having said that next to a battle lost, there was nothing so bad as a battle won. The Anglo-Dutch were in no state to follow up the French, so the pursuit was mounted by the Prussian cavalry, accompanied by drummer boys of the infantry (who, as non-riders, had to be tied onto the saddles of cavalry horses). Whenever the exhausted French tried to halt to rest and regroup, the drummer boys would beat a sharp tattoo. The French, thinking they were about to be attacked by Blücher's infantry, struggled on.

Waterloo was not the end of the war, but its result destroyed forever Napoleon's chances of re-establishing his rule. By 21 June the British army was in France, moving via Mons and Bavay, passing over Marlborough's old battleground of Malplaquet. Napoleon had reached Malmaison, south of Paris. He abdicated as Emperor for the second time, in favour of his son, on 22 June, but he was still officially a general, and he still hoped to beat the Allies. Grouchy's wing of the army, 33,000 men, had withdrawn skilfully and relatively unscathed from Wavre, and had collected a further 30,000 from garrisons on the way. He was now making for Paris, where there were a further 70,000 troops, including men of the National Guard. Paris was reasonably well fortified and could be expected to hold out against a lengthy siege. As the Prussians and the British advanced they had to reduce forts and towns along the way, which in turn had to be garrisoned. The numbers of Napoleon's enemies were getting less all the time; surely there was one more chance of a decisive battle which could yet, at the eleventh hour, turn the tide? The French deputies would have none of it: Blücher reached the outskirts of Paris on 29 June with Wellington hard on his heels. Negotiations began, with the French insisting that the Allies had repeatedly said that they were at war with Napoleon and not with the French people. Napoleon had abdicated, they argued, so the war was automatically at an end. This was disingenuous, as Wellington pointed out: the people of French had helped Napoleon and it was France which must surrender. On 4 July the provisional French government did surrender, and the Allies occupied Paris. Blücher wanted to execute Napoleon but was persuaded by Wellington not to. He also wanted to blow up the victory column in the Place Vendôme, and the Pont de Iéna, so called after the Prussian defeat in 1806. Wellington posted a British sentry to protect the bridge, but Blücher's men blew it up anyway. Fortunately Prussian demolition expertise was rudimentary and little damage was done, except to the sentry.

The powers, with the exception of Britain, had no wish to reimpose Louis XVIII on France: they had seen the results of one Bourbon restoration, and discussions ranged from an acceptance of Napoleon's son to the import of a foreign monarch. The British, for their own reasons, insisted that Louis was the rightful ruler and once more he was returned to Paris.

Napoleon planned to escape to America, but when that failed he threw himself on the mercy of the Prince Regent. He left the French port of Rochefort aboard HMS *Bellerophon* on 15 July, and the ship anchored off Torbay on 24 July. Napoleon hoped that he might be permitted to retire to England, but at forty-six, and still with a large following inside France, he was far too dangerous to have anywhere near Europe. On 7 August he was transferred to HMS *Northumberland*, which set sail just in time to evade an order of Habeas Corpus, ordering Napoleon to be produced in the High Court of London.[10] Napoleon, to be accompanied by three French generals (none posing any military threat to peace), a small staff and a handful of servants, was exiled to the remote Atlantic island of St Helena, and reached there after a voyage of sixty-seven days. His chief gaoler was Sir Hudson Lowe, to whom Wellington had refused an appointment in the army of 1815, there was a garrison of three thousand British soldiers, and four frigates were kept on station. Napoleon was housed in five rooms at Longwood, a modest but comfortable house in the centre of the island. All his mail, incoming and outgoing, was censored by the British and he had little to do but brood on what might have been, and dictate his memoirs and commentaries to his staff. He died there on 5 May 1821. The cause of his death is still uncertain, and theories abound. Was he murdered by a Bourbon agent? Or by the British? The post-mortem showed that the stomach was ulcerated, and the cause of death was given as cancer. Later it was suggested that he died from poisoning by arsenic, which could either have been administered or came from the wallpaper in Napoleon's bedroom.

Whatever the truth about his death, Napoleon's glory lives on. On 15 December 1840 the British permitted his remains to be repatriated, and they were laid to rest in a magnificent tomb in Les Invalides in Paris, the ceremony presided over by Napoleon's nephew, Emperor Napoleon III. The tomb remains a site of inspiration to the French military, and a place of pilgrimage, to this day.

On 3 August 1815 Bourbon agents arrested Marshal Ney, who was duly tried for treason before a court of peers on 4 December. Found guilty, he was sentenced to death. Ney's wife appealed to Wellington to intercede. Wellington privately deplored the 'white terror' that was now unleashed by the Bourbons, egged on to an extent by the British government, but he felt that he could not interfere between a legitimate ruler and his people. Ney was shot on 6 December, giving the orders to the firing squad himself. He was a brave, if headstrong, man, but his promise of March, to bring Napoleon back in an iron cage, sealed his fate. Murat, whom Napoleon had refused to employ in 1815, was captured by the Austrians, court martialled and shot on 13 October. A number of other Bonapartists were tried and executed, or exiled, or imprisoned. Many more fled France, but in due time many of the Emperor's marshals would be restored to favour and would carry on very much as they had done before, whether under Napoleon or the Bourbons.

14

The Later Years

With the war over, the Congress of Vienna reassembled. This time the terms imposed on France were much more severe than those demanded before June 1815. The Prussians and the German states wanted France broken up and reduced to bankruptcy, but Wellington realised that such draconian impositions would only fuel resentment and stock up future enmity. France, thought Wellington, must be brought back into the family of nations. The final result was that France was to pay a war indemnity of £28,000,000 and bear the costs of an Allied army that would occupy France for five years until it was paid. The obvious Commander-in-Chief of the army of occupation was Wellington. He was now a duke in four countries, a prince of the Netherlands, a field marshal in every major European army, and held a score of knighthoods and other honours showered on him by grateful heads of state.

On 26 June 1815 the House of Commons voted the sum of £200,000 in order to settle an annuity on the Duke and his successors, and to purchase an estate commensurate with his rank in the peerage. In return, he and his heirs were to present a tricolour flag annually, to the monarch at Windsor Castle.[1] Now he was appointed as British Ambassador to France as well. Wellington divided his time between his diplomatic headquarters in Paris and his military headquarters in Cambrai, this latter presided over by his Chief of Staff, George Murray, now returned from Canada. It was a difficult time, calling for all Wellington's diplomatic skills and prestige. The army of occupation was fixed at a strength of 150,000, made up of contingents from nine countries. While most of Wellington's time was spent in negotiating the settlement of war debts, he did not neglect the old problem of discipline in the army. He could not do very much about Prussian swaggering and the tendency of Prussian, Cossack and Austrian soldiers to help themselves to anything they fancied, but he could ensure that the British troops, at least, behaved. As early as July 1815 Wellington ordered that officers were to cease forcing the owners of theatres to open private boxes for them; and reminded officers that if they appeared in the streets of Paris they were to be properly dressed and carrying side-arms.[2] In November, Wellington noted that much of the game on the estate of the French King had been wiped out by unauthorised hunting parties, and officers were ordered not to shoot game on private land without the permission of the landowners.[3] Wellington was concerned that the behaviour of the soldiers must not be such as to cast any aspersions on the character of the army or of the British. In an order circulated to all corps and divisional commanders in November 1815, after ordering that any mutinous assembly by the local inhabitants against the military was to be fired upon, he made clear that: 'The service must be respected. The general officers are to take care that the good conduct and discipline of the troops merits the respect demanded.' Wellington's insistence on condign punishment for the usual offences of looting, drunkenness and absence, though necessary, was not popular in the ranks.

At the same time Wellington understood the difficulties faced by French agriculture in recovering from the war:

> The Field Marshal is desirous of giving every assistance in his power to reap the harvest, and accordingly authorises commanding officers of regiments to allow the soldiers to assist in reaping it, upon the application of the inhabitants. The owners of the harvest will make their own bargain with the soldiers for the payment they are to give them; but ... the commanding officer must know exactly where to find the soldier, and he must return to his regiment every night if possible, or at all events at least twice a week.[4]

Despite the peace, the Duke was much engaged with the aftermath of war. The question of honours for officers took up much of his correspondence, including a recommendation to the Duke of York that the conferring of the Order of the Bath should no longer be confined to field officers (majors and above): 'many captains in the army conduct themselves in a very meritorious manner, and deserve it; and I never could see the reason for excluding them either from the Order or the medal'.[5] Unlike the French, the British were parsimonious in the extreme in the award of medals. Gold medals were awarded to generals, and later to field officers, for many of the Peninsular battles, but there was nothing for junior officers and soldiers. As early as 28 June 1815 Wellington was recommending that a medal be struck for all officers and soldiers present at the battle of Waterloo. This was agreed to: a silver medal with the head of the Prince Regent on the obverse, and a winged figure of victory with the words 'Waterloo' and 'Wellington' on the reverse, was struck and issued between 1816 and 1817. It was bestowed on all who had been present at Quatre Bras and Waterloo. A medal for all ranks to cover the other battles of the wars took much longer to appear. The Military General Service Medal, issued with a bar for each battle between 1793 and 1815, was eventually authorised in 1847, by which time many of those entitled to it were dead.

As for the battle of Waterloo itself, Wellington considered that what he had said in his despatches was history enough, and that enquiries into the conduct of individuals should not be pursued. In regard to one officer, who had left the field claiming to be wounded but whose name was not included in the surgeons' list, Wellington felt that after making his own private enquiries he doubted whether anything could be proved before a trial. 'I confess that I feel very strong objections to discuss, before a General Court Martial, the conduct of any individual at a battle such as Waterloo', he said in a letter to the Duke of York, 'It generally brings before the public circumstances which might as well not be published; and the effect is equally produced by obliging him who has behaved ill to withdraw from the service'.[6]

Amateur historians received short shrift. In a remarkably candid reply to one such, Wellington wrote:

> The object which you propose to yourself is very difficult of attainment, and if really attained is not a little invidious. The history of a battle is not unlike the history of a ball. Some individuals may recall all the little events of which the great result is the battle won or lost; but no individual can recall the order in which, or the exact moment at which, they occurred, which makes all the difference as to their value or importance. Then the faults or the misbehaviour of some gave occasion for the distinction of others, and perhaps were the cause of material losses, and you cannot write a true history of a battle without including the faults and misbehaviour of part at least of those engaged. Believe me, that every man you see in a military uniform is not a hero ... it is better for the general interests to leave those parts of the story untold, than to tell the whole truth.[7]

To another letter asking for details he replied: 'I regret much that I have not been able to prevail upon you to relinquish your plan. You may depend upon it you will never make it a satisfactory work.' Even Wellington himself was not – could not – be aware of all that had happened at Waterloo; for in answering a series of written questions about the battle, he attributed the loss of La Haye Sainte to 'the neglect of the officer commanding on the spot'. This was, of course, a gross injustice to Major Baring, who had only been forced to give up the farm when he had run out of ammunition and most of his men were dead or wounded.

While the administrative details of keeping the army of occupation in being did not tax the field marshal (as general orders now styled him) overmuch, conflicting claims by the victorious nations did. In 1815, shortly after the end of the war, an Allied commission was set up to negotiate war debts, those sums owing between all participants of the war, some dating back to the 1790s. After two years the commission had got nowhere and eventually, in 1817, Wellington was asked to take over its chairmanship. His prestige was enormous and he was transparently honest; within months he had resolved all outstanding questions and had even negotiated an international loan to France to allow her to repay her debts quickly. There was no longer a requirement to keep an army in France as security for the indemnity, and in any case Wellington was concerned that the troops might be drawn into factional disputes in France. There were increasing physical clashes, and a battle of pamphlets, between Bonapartist sympathisers and supporters of the restored Bourbon regime, for which Wellington largely blamed the intransigence of members of the royal family. In 1818, after only three years of its projected five-year lifespan, the army of occupation, on Wellington's recommendation, was broken up, and the troops returned to their respective home countries. In a final general order, the British troops were thanked for setting, by their conduct, a good example to others.

On Wellington's return to England in 1818, the government of Lord Liverpool was under pressure, both from within Parliament and in the country. The end of the war had led to industrial decline, and bad weather had caused a series of poor harvests. Urban unemployment was now swollen by the hordes of discharged soldiers and rural unrest was on the increase. There was increased clamour for parliamentary reform and the government had lost seats in the election of June 1818. Wellington had been involved in none of this, and his personal popularity amongst all classes throughout the country was such that, ministers felt, his presence, if properly exploited, would have a stabilising effect. Although Wellington was no stranger to politics, he still saw himself as a soldier first. The obvious post for him was that of Commander-in-Chief of the British army, but that post was not available, being held by the Duke of York. In any case, the Prime Minister wanted Wellington in the Cabinet, and offered him the post of Master General of the Ordnance. That post too was filled, by General Lord Mulgrave, but that officer was persuaded to step aside, being retained in the Cabinet.[8] It was not a post that Wellington coveted: he had too much experience of the inefficiencies of the Board of Ordnance, and was well aware that any attempts he might make to improve it would fall foul of financial stringency and the British reluctance to place too much military power in one office in peacetime. Nevertheless, to Wellington his duty was clear: he had served the country all his adult life and he must continue to do so.

If Wellington's tenure as Master General of the Ordnance was not marked by any radical changes in the constitutional position of that office, he did bend his considerable talents to improving conditions where he could. As there was no extra funding available, he applied good management practices to make a saving of £200,000 in the annual budget, and used some of this to give each soldier in barracks an iron bedstead. Previously, even in the tropics, four men had to share a wooden crib, which was uncomfortable, unhygienic and increasingly seen as demeaning. Within the Royal Artillery he ended the separate existence of the Corps of Artillery Drivers, absorbing them into the regiment proper, and decreed that all artillery recruits were to be dual trained as both gunners and drivers. From his Peninsular experience Wellington well knew the worth of the Royal Engineers. He did his best to increase the establishment of officers and men, but was able to achieve little, such was the post-war desire for financial retrenchment, with the regular army reduced to the minimum needed for overseas garrisons, the Volunteers disbanded and conscription for the Militia put into abeyance.

When the construction and maintenance of public buildings was placed under the Board of Ordnance, Wellington devised a simple, but effective, means of ensuring that the usual custom of defrauding the public purse by shoddy workmanship was discouraged. Every construction or repair costing more than £1000 was to have a plaque affixed to it, showing the original estimate, the actual cost, the dates of commencement and completion, and the names of the responsible official and the contractor. No one, felt the Duke, would wish their names to be associated with damp, incomplete or collapsing buildings.

As Master General of the Ordnance Wellington was the government's chief adviser on military affairs, and much of his time was spent in examining the defence of overseas colonies and in positioning troops around the country in case of insurrection. Wellington thought that insurrection, sparked by demands for reform of the franchise and economic decline, was a real possibility. The government was held in low esteem, and its stability was not enhanced by the death of King George III on 29 January 1820. Locked away in Windsor Castle, as he had been for many years, the King was still revered by most of his subjects, while his successor, the dissolute George IV, was regarded with contempt.[9] In the summer of 1819 Wellington thought his views on the parlous state of the nation had been proved right. On 16 August a crowd, variously estimated to have been between 40,000 and 100,000, gathered at St Peter's Fields, just outside Manchester, to hear 'Orator' Hunt, a leading radical, address them on the subject of parliamentary representation. Manchester, while now a major industrial centre with a large and growing population, was still represented in Parliament by one rotten borough, of a few hundred voters, in accordance with an electoral system which had not been revised to take population shift into account. The meeting was legal, but the local authorities feared violence and drafted in 400 special constables to keep order. The military commander in the north, Major General Sir John Byng, who had commanded the 2nd Guards Brigade at Waterloo, ordered the Manchester Yeoman Cavalry (a part-time force), to be available to support the constables, while the 15th Hussars (veterans of Waterloo) and the 31st Foot were stood by in case things became really unpleasant. As the law then stood, the military could only be used against civil commotion in England on the orders of a magistrate, who had first to read the Riot Act, and then give the crowd time to disperse, before formally asking the military to intervene. Once control had passed to the military commander on the spot, it was he, and he alone, who had responsibility for the situation.[10]

Accounts of the Battle of Peterloo, as it became known, are contradictory. What appears to have happened is that the magistrate panicked; ordered the arrest of Hunt; saw that the chances of unarmed constables getting anywhere near the speaker were remote; gabbled the Riot Act where nobody could possible hear it; and ordered the Yeomanry to assist the constables. Forty amateur horsemen, sabres drawn, began to push their way individually into the crowd. Very soon the yeoman lost contact with each other, and each was isolated in the dense crowd, whose members began to cheer, or jeer. No violence appears to have been used at this stage. Then, presumably thinking that the Yeomanry were about to be annihilated, the officer commanding the detachment of the 15th Hussars ordered his men to charge the crowd. It is relatively easy to disperse a crowd with cavalry bloodlessly, but there are two provisos: the crowd must have a route by which to escape; and the cavalry must use the flats of their sabres, rather than the edge or the point. In this case the Hussars had no experience of crowd control – ironically the charge was blown on a bugle used at Waterloo – and the result was pandemonium. Such a dense mass of people was unable to get out of the way quickly enough, and while the crowd had dissolved within ten minutes, eleven dead and several hundred wounded were left on the ground.

The way in which the meeting had been broken up gave the radicals more ammunition with which to attack the government, and unrest in the north spread. The situation was not helped by ministers, including Wellington, drawing up a memorandum for the Prince Regent congratulating the author-ities on their actions. Wellington thought that the action taken had been correct. While he considered that the magistrate was wrong to read the Riot Act when and how he did, he was adamant that the magistrate had to be supported; otherwise magistrates in other areas would simply do nothing. Wellington's popularity went down, and there was an abortive plan by one James Ings, a bankrupt butcher, to stab him as he walked across Green Park. Efforts to prosecute the ringleaders of the St Peter's Fields meeting for treason failed, and the best that the law could do was to imprison Hunt for two years. In November the government passed the 'Six Acts', which forbade drilling (quasi-military training) by civilians, imposed controls on the Press and banned 'seditious' public meetings. Despite the Duke's fears than a mass insurrection was just around the corner, unrest subsided, although this may have had more to do with an upturn in the economy than with the repressive effects of the Six Acts.

James Ings, who had intended to murder Wellington, but had changed his mind when his quarry had met Fitzroy Somerset in the park and continued to walk with him, was a member of the next threat to public order, the Cato Street Conspiracy - so called from the location of its members' meeting place. This was a plot, of almost childish naivety, to assassinate the entire Cabinet as they consumed their traditional dinner at the house of Lord Harrowby, Lord President of the Council, in Grovesnor Square, prior to the new Parliamentary session of 1820. The dinner was to be held on 23 February and the plotters intended to kill the Cabinet, seize public buildings and proclaim revolution. Even if the attempt had taken place as planned, desire for reform in the country fell far short of overturning the constitution, but the government was well aware of the plan. Wellington, thirsting for the fire and smoke that he had been denied for nearly five years, advised that ministers should smuggle pistols into the dinner, concealed in their despatch cases, and allow the plot to take its course. It was as well, however, that his more cautious colleagues did not follow his advice, for the conspirators intended to throw bombs through the windows as a prelude to entering the house with drawn swords. As it was, constables supported by troops surrounded the house in Cato Street and all the conspirators were arrested, either that day or the next. Tried for high treason, five were executed and their heads exhibited on Tower Bridge.

As the country reverted to a more peaceful state, Wellington continued to run the Board of Ordnance and, increasingly, to advise on matters well outside the military remit. He was the best-known figure in the government and the social lion of London. He now had two principal residences. The nation had bought him a country estate in July 1817, Stratfield Saye in Hampshire, purchased from Lord Rivers for slightly more than the £200,000 originally intended. It was not a great pile like Blenheim Palace, but then it did not cost the fortune in upkeep that the nation's last gift to a great general had. The Duchess loved it, and spent most of the rest of her life there. Wellington, ever interested in gadgets, installed steam-powered central heating, and one of the first ever examples of double-glazing. It was ideal for hunting, still the Duke's chief recreation, and from it he could discharge his new duties as Lord Lieutenant of Hampshire. Most of Wellington's time, however, had perforce to be spent in London, as Master General of the Ordnance and as a member of the Cabinet, and there he used his London home, Apsley House. Originally a modest red brick affair on Hyde Park Corner, Wellington purchased it from his brother, Marquess Wellesley, in

1817. Known thereafter as 'Number One, London', it was close to his offices and big enough for the increasing entertainment that fell to him. It could also house his treasures, including many of the paintings looted from King Joseph's wagon train after Vittoria. This was not a case of the scourge of plunderers turning plunderer himself; rather the restored King of Spain had made a gift of the paintings to Wellington as a mark of thanks for the Duke's part in the liberation of his country. In any case, Wellington had now no need of dubiously acquired wealth. The prize money for Waterloo had been distributed in June 1819, and Wellington's share was £60,000, two thirds of which he returned to the Treasury. Other generals got £1250 each, and so on down to subalterns who got £33. Sergeants received £9 and private soldiers £2 10s. (or about three months pay after deductions).

The difficulties between the new King and his wife, Caroline of Brunswick, inevitably involved Wellington, if only because everyone concerned wanted his advice. His only military involvement was when there was unrest in a battalion of the 3rd Guards, thought to be connected with the vociferous support for the Queen exhibited by the lower orders. It was hardly a mutiny, although called so at the time, but more an airing of grievances about low pay, bad food, cramped conditions and too little time off. The offending battalion was marched out of London and Wellington went to see them go, being disturbed by their failure to show the usual enthusiasm of troops when faced by their old commander. Wellington's view was that the trouble was caused by the Guards being drawn from the same low stratum of society as the rest of the army, and by the confusing plethora of channels of communication with Guards regiments, whereby the King, the Commander-in-Chief, the Colonel of the Regiment, and the Gold and Silver Sticks in waiting could all issue orders, many of them contradictory.

At one point the government considered appointing Wellington as Lord Lieutenant of Ireland, where agrarian unrest and clamour for Catholic Emancipation was gathering momentum. Wellington demurred: 'Take care least you let off your great gun against a sparrow', he said. Instead, Marquess Wellesley, who badly needed the money, went and promptly annoyed his brother (who had urged Liverpool to appoint him) and incensed the establishment by marrying a Roman Catholic. Wellington was upset because the girl was one of three American sisters to whom he had been particularly close, and the Anglo-Irish objected to a marriage ceremony carried out in Dublin Castle by a Catholic bishop in full regalia (illegal in England, but not in Ireland). The Marquess's views on Catholic Emancipation were now far more liberal than those of his brother, who still supported the removal of restrictions but was wary of proceeding too fast least this be seen as a sign of political weakness. Wellesley's sojourn as Viceroy of Ireland did allow him to redeem his debts, but he was unpopular with tradesmen, as he could not afford to live in the style of previous holders of the office; he could not move quickly enough on emancipation to satisfy the more extreme Catholics, while on one occasion he was attacked by a mob of Orangemen for being too sympathetic to the papists.

In May 1821 Napoleon Bonaparte died in exile in St Helena. Wellington had always respected his old adversary's military abilities, and often praised them. Left to Wellington alone, Napoleon would probably have been more kindly treated than by being imprisoned in a remote island in the Atlantic. Wellington's admiration for the ex-Emperor was somewhat muted when he heard the contents of his will – which left a bequest to a discharged French subaltern who had attempted to assassinate Wellington in Paris – and his opinions on Waterloo, which gave little credit to Wellington's army and a great deal to the Prussians.[11]

In August 1822 Wellington was in the Netherlands, carrying out an annual inspection of fortifications there, when he heard the news of the death of his long-time supporter and political friend, the Marquess of Londonderry (previously Lord Castlereagh, he had succeeded to his father's Irish title in 1821, but remained in the House of Commons). The previous year, on his way home from the House, Londonderry had been inveigled into a brothel by what appeared to be an attractive young girl but was in fact a homosexual transvestite. The entrapment had been set up by some of Londonderry's enemies, who had since been paying the mob to catcall him in the street. The matter had preyed on his mind and Londonderry committed suicide by cutting his throat. A replacement as Foreign Secretary was needed, but Wellington made it very clear that he was not interested. If his appointment was essential for the prosecution of national policy he would accept, he explained, but with great reluctance. He had no wish to become embroiled in party affairs. As Master General of the Ordnance he was of course in the Cabinet, but his post was such that he could distance himself from political wrangling and state his own opinions as a soldier. The next obvious choice was George Canning, who had a strong following in the Commons. Canning had resigned from the government over the Queen Caroline affair (he was alleged to have been one of her many lovers) and was about to depart for India as Governor-General. The King was initially reluctant to appoint Canning as Foreign Secretary, but was persuaded to do so by Wellington, something that the Duke would later regret.

The same year Wellington suffered the first setback in his health for many years. He attended a live firing demonstration of a new type of howitzer at Woolwich, stood too near to the firing point and was deafened in his left ear. Surgeons attempted to treat the ear with a caustic solution, botched the job and left the Duke feeling ill, dizzy, and with excruciating pains in his head.

For the first time in many years Wellington took to his bed. He recovered, largely by ignoring his doctors' advice, but the hearing in his left ear was permanently gone, and for the rest of his life he suffered from occasional fevers and giddy spells – which may have been exacerbated by malaria picked up in Flanders or India.

Although he had not yet recovered from his ear problems, Wellington's next major task was to attend the Congress of Verona later that year, 1822. There his major task was to press Foreign Secretary Canning's policy of encouraging the liberalisation of regimes in Europe, something that Wellington viewed with suspicion but which he accepted as government policy. In Spain the restored King, Ferdinand VII, was under pressure from radicals attempting to force him to accept a constitution. Wellington made it clear to France that Great Britain would not support an invasion of Spain to save the King from revolution. The next year the French invaded anyway, and British involvement was confined to sending troops to Portugal to protect that country from incursions by Spanish insurrectionists.

Still Lord Liverpool's government managed to stay in office, although increasingly there were those, both in government and in opposition, who thought Wellington was the man who, if made Prime Minister, could best hold the administration together. Wellington would have none of it: he was a soldier first and foremost and would not involve himself in factional politics. In 1824 he threatened to resign from the Cabinet (but was persuaded not to), over British policy towards the breakaway Spanish colonies in South America. In 1826 the Master General was in St Petersburg, attempting to persuade the Russians not to go to war with the Ottoman Empire over Greece. Despite the respect in which Wellington was held in Russia, the war happened the following year, but at least his intervention had bought time.

On 5 January 1827 the Duke of York died of dropsy, a condition where the body retains massive amounts of fluid and which leads to heart or liver failure. Now should have been the culmination of all that Wellington had worked for throughout his military career: he was the obvious choice as Commander-in-Chief. The King did, briefly, consider assuming the command himself, but, quickly realising that this would be totally unacceptable to both government and army, appointed Wellington. Wellington could have resigned as Master General of the Ordnance, and normally one man was not permitted to hold both posts, but the government was anxious to retain him in the Cabinet, particularly as he was seen as one of the few members of the government who had the complete confidence of the King. Wellington held both offices, although drawing the salary of only one. George IV did indeed hold 'dear Arthur' in the highest esteem – no one else could have persuaded him to have Canning in the Cabinet – but his admiration for the Duke's military virtues was often muddled. The King had convinced himself that it had been he, as Prince Regent in disguise, and not General von Bock, who had led the great cavalry charge at Salamanca, although he frequently changed the action's location to Waterloo. In his cups the King would often recount the tale at dinners when Wellington was present. 'Is that not so?' the King would shout to Wellington. 'I have often heard Your Majesty say so', was Wellington's tactful reply.

The army of which Wellington was now Commander-in-Chief was hardly an army at all, as if nothing had happened since 1793. Of the eighty-three battalions of line infantry existing in 1827, fifty-one were stationed overseas, five were on the high seas returning from or going to foreign stations, twenty-three were in Ireland and only four in Great Britain. There were not even enough troops available in the capital to give the Duke of York a military funeral. Wellington's first task was to resolve the debts of his predecessor, which were considerable and mainly revolved around a swarm of mistresses, current and previous. The Marquess of Londonderry, half brother of Wellington's old confidant Castlereagh, and, as Charles Stewart, the over-enthusiastic Adjutant General in the Peninsula until 1813, suggested that these be paid by a voluntary levy from all officers of the army. Wellington realised that, even if all the officers remaining on the active list agreed to pay, which they probably would not, the sum raised would be insufficient, and insisted that Parliament must foot the bill.

This period could have been a great opportunity for a root and branch reform of the British system of military administration. As the holder of both major military offices Wellington might, had he been minded, have removed the pettifogging restrictions and bureaucratic inefficiencies by which the army was managed and commanded, but on 11 April 1827, after only two months as Commander-in-Chief, Wellington resigned both his positions. Had he remained in office it is doubtful whether he would, or could, have done very much. Wellington was becoming increasingly convinced that the settlement of Vienna, of which he had been the prime architect, was the best possible solution for the shape of Europe, and that the British constitution, as it then stood, was as near perfect as it was possible to be. He had been away from England for many years: when he returned it was as the most eminent figure in the land, and he failed to realise that the old balance between landed and commercial interests had shifted, and that the emergence of an influential middle class and a new industrial working class would mean changes to the way the nation was governed. Given his increasing conservatism, he would have been loathe to make sweeping and fundamental changes in a military system which, for all its well-known faults, had enabled the British army to become, at least for a time, the finest in Europe.

Wellington's resignation was caused by what, from a distance of 180 years, seems a minor, even petty, upset. On 17 February 1827 the Prime Minister, Lord Liverpool, suffered a stroke, taking him out of public affairs.[12] There were those who wanted Wellington to be Prime Minister as well as Commander-in-Chief and Master General of the Ordnance. One man in England would not have held such power since Cromwell, but Wellington instantly removed himself from the running. He wanted to remain as a soldier and he would not mix soldiering with party politics. The search to find a successor to Liverpool went on, and eventually the King asked Canning to form an administration.

At six o'clock in the evening of 10 April 1827 Canning wrote to Wellington from the Foreign Office:

> My dear Duke of Wellington, The King has, at an audience from which I have just returned, been graciously pleased to signify to me His Majesty's commands to lay before His Majesty, with as little loss of time as possible, a plan of arrangements for the reconstruction of the Administration. In executing these commands it will be as much my own wish, as it is my duty to His Majesty, to adhere to the principles on which Lord Liverpool's government has so long acted together. I need not add how essentially the accomplishment must depend upon your Grace's continuing a member of the Cabinet. Ever, My dear Duke of Wellington, Your Grace's sincere and faithful servant, George Canning.

Wellington replied the same evening:

> My dear Mr Canning, I have received your letter of this evening, informing me that the King had desired you to lay before his Majesty a plan ... and that it was your wish to adhere to the principles on which Lord Liverpool's Government had so long acted together. I anxiously desire to be able to serve His Majesty, as I have done hitherto in his Cabinet, with the same colleagues. But before I can give an answer to your obliging proposition, I should wish to know who the person is whom you intend to propose to his Majesty as the head of the government? Ever, my dear Mr Canning, yours most sincerely, Wellington.[13]

Wellington knew perfectly well that, by long hallowed custom, the person to whom the King entrusted the formation of an administration would be its head, and on the following day Canning duly replied to the Duke:

> I believed it to be so generally understood that the King usually intrusts [sic] the formation of an Administration to the individual whom it is His Majesty's gracious intention to place at the head of it, that it did not occur to me, when I communicated to your Grace yesterday, the commands which I had just received from His Majesty, to add, that, in the present instance, His Majesty does not intend to depart from the usual course of proceeding on such occasions. I am sorry

to have delayed some hours this answer to your Grace's letter; but from the nature of the subject, I did not like to forward it without having previously submitted it (together with your Grace's letter) to His Majesty.[14]

Wellington was furious. He felt that he should have been consulted on the composition of the Cabinet, and that Canning's tone was impertinent. The implication that all Canning had said and done was with the King's approval was the last straw, and on the same day Wellington resigned both his military offices and, by extension, his Cabinet post. Despite Canning's assurances that policy would continue as before, he did not believe that to be possible; and if the principles which he had previously adhered to were abandoned – which he believed they would be – then conflict was inevitable and he could not remain in the Cabinet.

While the Cabinet post of Master General of the Ordnance was incompatible with refusal to serve in the government, Wellington need not have resigned as Commander-in-Chief. Speaking in the House of Lords, he explained:

The Commander-in-Chief must necessarily be daily in confidential relations with His Majesty on all points of the service. He must likewise be so with the person filling the situation now filled by the Right Honourable Gentleman [Canning, the Prime Minister]. Although the Commander-in-Chief has nothing to say as to the finance of the army, yet there are questions under discussion every day ... upon which the Right Honourable Gentleman cannot decide in a satisfactory manner, unless after reference to the Commander-in-Chief ... How was it possible for me to consider that I was likely to possess the Right Honourable Gentleman's confidence on any of these points, after receiving from him, in His Majesty's name, such a rebuke as was contained in his letter to me of the 11th?[15]

Wellington decamped to Stratfield Saye. William Beresford, Wellington's trusted subordinate in the Peninsula, was appointed Master General of the Ordnance, but the post of Commander-in-Chief was left vacant. Canning's administration was short-lived. On 8 August 1827 he died, aged fifty-seven, from what was said to be a cold (probably turned to pneumonia) caught at the Duke of York's funeral the previous January. Canning was succeeded by Viscount Goderich, and Wellington once more assumed the appointment of Commander-in-Chief. This tenure too was of short duration, but in the autumn of 1827 Wellington was able to scotch a further reduction in the army by bluntly stating that such a measure would increase unrest in the country, and make Ireland even more difficult to pacify. He also pointed out that with the recent developments in steam ships, military expeditions could be transported much more quickly than hitherto, and so troops must now be stationed in the English ports to guard against invasion.

It soon became evident that Goderich had a hopelessly divided Cabinet and was unable to command sufficient support in both Houses. The King now appealed to Wellington to form a government. Still reluctant to embroil himself in party matters, Wellington felt that it was his patriotic duty to try to meet the King's wishes: no one else seemed to be able to carry Parliament and the country with them, and so, on 9 January 1828, Wellington became Prime Minister. He tried to form a Cabinet that would carry out the King's business without too much regard to party. It was, of course, impossible, but he finally formed a government composed of Tories and Whigs, and proponents and opponents of Catholic Emancipation. Having formed his Cabinet, he was somewhat irritated to be told by it that he should resign as Commander-in-Chief. He had hoped to retain the military command but, having so often said that politics and soldiering did not mix, he was in a poor position to argue the case. He therefore resigned as Commander-in-Chief forthwith. He was replaced at Horse Guards by his old wartime divisional commander Rowland Hill.

After resigning as Commander-in-Chief on becoming Prime Minister in 1828, Wellington held no military command for fourteen years. It has to be admitted that as a Prime Minister he was not a success. He had worked with and for ministers for many years while a commander in the field; he understood how international relations were conducted; he had been an ambassador twice; he had negotiated on behalf of his government on many occasions; he had enormous stature in the country, was trusted by the King and was universally held to be motivated by the national, rather than personal, interest. Despite this, Wellington never understood, nor accepted, how governments worked internally. As a general he had long been accustomed to considering a situation, deciding how it should be resolved and giving orders that were obeyed. Even when – rarely - he discussed his plans with those under him, neither he, nor they, were ever in any doubt that it was for Wellington to decide what action was to be taken, and for them to carry it out. Subordinate officers had no constituencies to satisfy, no interests to placate. Wellington was accustomed to lead, while others followed, but this was not the way that politics, or politicians, worked. He saw no reason for every man to state his opinion, nor any need for long Cabinet discussions. His political colleagues resented his peremptory military manner, while he found their interminable intriguing and vacillation disloyal and time-wasting. Whether anyone else could have made a better fist of being Prime Minister at the time is questionable. Wellington had to deal with dissent over the Corn Laws, the repeal of the Test and Corporation Acts, Irish unrest, economic decline, a wave of mini revolutions in Europe, violence by agricultural workers and, continually, parliamentary reform.

Two major reforms that he did achieve were the formation of the London Metropolitan Police in 1829, and, at last, Catholic Emancipation - although he split the Tory Party and scandalised the King in so doing. Wellington's views on the whole question of restrictions on Catholics had not changed: he thought they were unfair and should be done away with, but at the same time he did not wish to appear to be giving way to Irish agitation, nor to harm the established interests. His approach, as to many other difficult matters with which he had to deal, was severely practical: better to give freely what would otherwise be taken in blood. Wellington finally managed to persuade the King and his parliamentary colleagues to accept the inevitable, and on 13 April 1829 Catholic Emancipation was passed by both Houses. Along the way Wellington, against all his professed strictures while in command of the army, fought a duel with the Earl of Winchelsea a few weeks before the Act was passed. Winchelsea, a rising political star of the Tory Party and a stout defender of Protestantism, wrote to King's College London withdrawing his subscription in protest against the Duke of Wellington's 'insidious designs for the infringement of our liberties and the introduction of Popery into every department of state'.[16] The letter was published in the newspapers and, when Winchelsea refused an apology, Wellington demanded satisfaction.[17] The two met at Battersea Fields at eight o'clock in the morning of 21 March 1829. Each was given a pistol and they faced each other from a distance of twelve paces. Wellington fired and missed, whereupon Winchelsea deloped – that is, fired his pistol into the air. Honour was satisfied. Wellington is said to have told the Secretary at War that he fired at Winchelsea's legs, but his target may have been fortunate, for Wellington was a notoriously bad shot.

It was the issue of parliamentary reform that led to the downfall of Wellington's government. He was not prepared to accept it, and in the general election of July 1830, which followed the death of George IV and the accession of his brother as King William IV, the government lost seats to pro-reform candidates. Despite the results of the election Wellington thought he could hold the line on reform. The King opened Parliament on 2 November 1830, and, after the speech from the throne, Earl Grey proposed an amendment, in which he criticised the recent emancipation of the Catholics, blaming the present unrest in Ireland upon it, and hoped that the government would bring forward measures for parliamentary reform. In reply, the Duke pointed out that it was not emancipation that had caused the present state of affairs in Ireland, but the opposition to it for so long. Turning to the subject of reform, Wellington made the speech that was to bring down his government:

> The representation of the people at present contains a large body of the property of the country, and in which the landed interest has a preponderating influence.

Under these circumstances, I am not prepared to bring forward any measure of the description alluded to by the noble Lord. And I am not only not prepared to bring forward any measure of this nature, but I will declare that, as far as I am concerned, as long as I hold any station in the government of the country, I shall always feel it my duty to resist such measures when proposed by others.[18]

On the evening of 15 November 1830 the government was defeated in the House of Commons on the civil list for the new reign. Wellington heard the news as he was dining with the Prince of Orange at Apsley House. Parliamentary reform was to be debated the following week, and if the government could not command a majority over the civil list, they could certainly not hope to achieve it over reform. Wellington resigned the next day.

The King now summoned Grey, who formed a coalition of Whigs, Canningites and a few ultra-Tories. On 1 March 1831 the government introduced its first Reform Bill. The debate lasted only two days and then passed its second reading by the narrowest of margins: 302 to 301. The Bill then went to the committee stage; but, when an amendment proposing that no change should be made to the total number of English and Welsh seats (the Bill proposed the abolition of fifty-seven) was carried by 299 votes to 291, the government decided upon a general election. During the election campaign the Duchess of Wellington died, on 24 April 1831. She had played little part in her husband's military life, but he mourned her nevertheless. His feelings for 'the mob' were not enhanced when the Lord Mayor of London ordered the capital to be illuminated in support of reform. Apsley House, with the body of the Duchess laid out inside, remained unlit, and the mob stoned the house. A blunderbuss fired from the roof drove them off. The election provided yet more members in support of reform and the second Reform Bill passed the Commons but was defeated in the Lords (with Wellington leading the opposition to it) on 8 October 1831. There was yet another stoning of Apsley House. The government tried again, but on 7 May 1832 the third Reform Bill was thrown out by the Lords.

There was now near anarchy: in the streets of London mobs attacked those they thought to be opposed to reform; in the country, houses were set on fire; all parties were divided and the King sent for Wellington. Could the Duke form a government which would command the support of the Commons and which could defuse the reform issue? The Duke could not, and on 15 May Grey was recalled. Wellington had never believed in committing himself to a battle which he knew he could not win. He agreed that, should the new government introduce a fourth Reform Bill, then he and his friends would abstain. This was a critical period, needing all Wellington's powers of persuasion as Leader of the Lords, but on 7 June 1832 the Great Reform Bill became law. Despite Wellington's remark that he never saw such a collection of bad hats in all his life, the new Parliament was not composed of red revolutionaries. The Whigs, with a fair sprinkling of radicals, won 320 seats, to the Conservatives' (as they were now increasingly called) 150. True, there were some odd characters in it, including William Cobbett and the boxer Tom Gully, but Orator Hunt had lost his seat, and the majority, while perhaps less aristocratic than the members of the old House, were hard-working moderates with no wish for violent constitutional change.

Wellington, out of office, was far from idle. He became Constable of the Tower of London in 1827; Lord Warden of the Cinque Ports in 1829; a governor of Charterhouse School and an Elder Brother of Trinity House in 1830; and Chancellor of Oxford University in 1834. Never prepared to regard any appointment as a sinecure, Wellington put much energy into the proper discharge of those offices, including the draining of the moat of the Tower, a project that had defeated previous incumbents for at least two centuries.

On 8 July 1834 Grey resigned as Prime Minister and was replaced by Lord Melbourne. Melbourne was unable to get government business through, and in November King William dismissed the Whigs and yet again sent for Wellington.[19] By now utterly disillusioned by high political office, Wellington refused to become Prime Minister himself, but agreed to act in a caretaker capacity until Sir Robert Peel could return from abroad. From 15 November until 9 December Wellington held no less than three seals: those of First Lord of the Treasury (Prime Minister), Foreign Secretary, Home Secretary and Colonial Secretary. On Peel's return and appointment to head the government Wellington remained as Foreign Secretary until April 1835 and then, on the fall of the Conservatives, became leader of the Opposition in the Lords. He held that position for the next six years, when he insisted on a bipartisan approach to all matters of policy: it was the public good and not party whim that must prevail. It was a difficult period, including the death of William IV and accession of Queen Victoria, the Chartist riots, the repeal of the Corn Laws and more problems in Ireland. Although without military office, Wellington was in constant touch, official and unofficial, with the army. The Commander-in-Chief, Hill; the successive Masters General of the Ordnance, James Kempt (1830-34), George Murray (1834-35 and 1841-46), Hussey Vivian (1835-41); and the Military Secretary, Fitzroy Somerset, all had served under the Duke. All had learned their trade by watching him and all deferred to him, whether he was in office or out of it.

Peel was again returned to office after the general election of 1841, and in 1842 Hill resigned as Commander-in-Chief. At the urging of the young Queen, and to the general delight of the army, Wellington was once more appointed to the supreme command. He immediately announced his intention of resigning from the Cabinet, partly because of his usual objection to mixing politics with soldiering, but also because he said he could not hear anything that was being said at Cabinet meetings. He was prevailed upon not to do so – his presence was considered essential – and he did remain in the Cabinet, without portfolio, until 1846. Wellington's advice was now sought as to a promotion to field marshal for Hill, on the grounds that he had been Commander-in-Chief for fourteen years. Wellington regretfully disagreed. The principle of seniority could not be deviated from: Hill was the nineteenth senior general in the army and if he were promoted then all the others would expect and demand it. Wellington admitted that he himself had been promoted to field marshal over the heads of half the generals in the army, but that was after the great victory of Vittoria, which could not possibly be taken as a precedent in this case. Hill retired as a general, but was advanced one step in the peerage as consolation. He died shortly afterwards.

Wellington was now seventy-two years of age and would be Commander-in-Chief until his death. He had become increasingly opposed to change, was permanently deaf in his left ear and was losing the use of his right. He still retained much of his old energy, despite the occasional bout of ill health, and it was largely due to his ability to persuade ministers and to galvanise what little army there was in England that the Chartist agitation of 1842 died down without major confrontation, although he was accused of overreacting at the time. His tenure as Commander-in-Chief was not entirely beneficial to the army. He changed little of the administrative machinery which governed the service, did little to improve barracks and did not carry forward the reforms in the promotion system begun by the Duke of York. He did nothing to resolve the anomalous relationship between the Horse Guards and the Board of Ordnance. That said, he was commanding during a period of relative peace, when once more no government wanted to spend money on the army. He did warn, constantly, repetitively and sometimes almost hysterically, that the army was too small, too ill-equipped, too badly paid and too tortuously controlled to meet its primary purpose: the defence of the Empire and of England itself. He increasingly saw threats to the safety of the realm that were, perhaps, not always there. Most of his protests fell on deaf ears, although he did manage to have the Militia removed from the control of the Home Office to that of the Commander-in-Chief, and obtained funding for the improvement of coastal defences, including the repair of Martello towers along the Kent coast in case of a French invasion (on a number of occasions during his tenure as Commander-in-Chief war with France was a real possibility). He was always ready to defend the army, specific regiments and individual officers against criticism in the press or in Parliament, and he always had an ear, and a sovereign, for a hard luck story from an old soldier or a military widow. He found it difficult, however, to believe that the army he had led in the

Peninsula all those years ago could ever be bettered. When he assumed the command-in-chief the army was still equipped with the smooth bore musket, Brown Bess, which had been the weapon of the British infantryman since before Marlborough, although the flintlock had been replaced by a percussion cap between 1839 and 1842. In 1845, when it was proposed to replace the Brown Bess with a rifled weapon using a minié ball, Wellington only reluctantly agreed, and then insisted that it must be a muzzle loader.[20] The technology to produce a breech loader existed, but that, thought the Duke, would only encourage soldiers to waste ammunition.

Contrary to what he had ordered and encouraged in the Peninsula, Wellington as Commander-in-Chief was not in favour of an expansion of schools for the training of non-commissioned officers and soldiers. He has been criticised for not abolishing purchase, but to be fair there was not the money to do so, and in any case, surprising though it may seem from a distance of a century and a half, it did work. The men who held commissions at regimental duty and at brigade and divisional level from 1809 onwards were exactly the same people who hold them now; the difference being that today they fill those posts after rigorous selection and intensive training – and at a much older age than the officers of Wellington's army.

Wellington's views on keeping order in the service did not waver. Shortly before he took over as Commander-in-Chief, he gave evidence to a commission established by Parliament to look into military discipline. Increasingly the public, and some officers of the army, felt that flogging was an outdated and demeaning punishment, which should be abolished. Some commanding officers had begun to use communal locking up, or solitary confinement, as a substitute. Wellington was unmoved. The whole point of flogging, he told the Commission, was not so much to punish the individual for what he had done but to act as a public example to other potential miscreants. He pointed out that in a battalion of the Coldstream Guards, whose commanding officer had implemented confinement rather than flogging, there were currently 100 men locked up, out of a battalion strength of 600. Flogging would have affected far fewer men, who would then have been available for duty. Under questioning, he agreed that in the French army no man could be struck or suffer corporal punishments, but felt that this could not be applied to the British army, which was 'taken entirely from the lowest order of society'.[21] The French army was filled by conscription, which produced a better class of man in the ranks, where the men of intelligence and good behaviour kept the others in check. In any case the French army was so large, compared to the British, that a loss of men by desertion or plundering could be borne. As a sting in the tail, the Duke pointed out that the French army inflicted the death penalty to a far greater degree than did the British.

The commission wondered whether an increased number of officers' commissions awarded, without purchase, to men in the ranks might improve the overall character of the British army by attracting a better class of recruit. The Duke doubted if it would. It was difficult enough, in the small peacetime army, to find places for all those coming out of Sandhurst: the number of commissions that could be given to men in the ranks would be too few to make much difference. Pressed on the subject of commissioned rankers generally, Wellington said that he had commissioned as many sergeants as he could while in the Peninsula, but that in general he did not have a high opinion of officers from that source:

> In truth they do not make good officers; it does not answer. They are brought into society to the manners of which they are unaccustomed; they cannot bear being at all heated with wine or liquor ... I think in general they are quarrelsome, they are addicted to quarrel a little in their cups, and they are not persons who can be borne in the society of the officers of the army; they are men of different manners altogether ... [they are] punctilious and uncomfortable. There are very few indeed that stop any time, or that ever rise beyond the subaltern ranks of the army.[22]

At the same inquiry Wellington did state his approval for an order of merit for the army, open to all ranks and with two classes: one for gallantry and another for good behaviour.[23] He was also of the opinion that stoppages of pay would be an effective punishment, although it would be a century and a quarter before this was implemented except in specific and very limited cases. All in all he stuck to his original opinion: the only way to keep miscreants in check and to protect the men of good behaviour was to retain public flogging.

Throughout Wellington's tenure as Commander-in-Chief the senior officers of the army were men who had served under him and who believed in him unquestionably, while the junior officers held him in awe. 'What would the Great Duke do?' was the question most often asked when a commander in some far-flung corner of the Empire was faced with a choice of operational decisions. In many ways this was good - the Duke was a master of the battlefield – but, because Wellington had never delegated, or educated his subordinates, or taken them into his confidence except rarely, it did stifle any original thought at a senior level. When the British army took the field in the Crimea, two years after Wellington died, the administration of the army was in a slough not seen since the last decade of the eighteenth century. Commanded by Fitzroy Somerset, now Lord Raglan, Wellington's old Adjutant General, who kept referring to the enemy as the French (he meant the Russians – the French were allies), its men went into battle dressed very much as they had been at Waterloo, but with a commissariat riddled with inefficiencies and corruption; an Ordnance service that barely worked at all; and a medical service that hardly existed. That they won great victories against near hopeless odds – stacked against them by their own government and the Horse Guards – was due to the fighting qualities of the ordinary soldier, pride in regiment, and the leadership of regimental officers. That, at least, was a Wellingtonian legacy that had not been frittered away.

As time went on old age began inexorably to take its toll, although the Duke would never admit it. Daily he would mount his horse at Apsley House and ride to Horse Guards. He would refuse to allow anyone to help him to dismount, although that became an increasingly dangerous procedure, and he would climb the stairs to his office. Often he would fall asleep, but his staff had been with him for so many years that they knew what his opinions were. Rather than wake him, they would take the papers away and make the decision in his name. When not needed in London, he spent more and more time at Walmer Castle, the official residence of the Warden of the Cinque Ports. He travelled on horseback or by coach, for, ever since he had witnessed William Huskisson, MP for Liverpool and a former President of the Board of Trade and Colonial Secretary, being killed by George Stevenson's *Rocket* in 1830, he had distrusted railways.

Wellington enjoyed Walmer, the bracing air, the military flavour of the castle, the genuine love and respect in which he was held; and it was there, at twenty-five minutes past three o'clock in the afternoon of Monday, 13 September 1852, at the age of eighty-two years and four months, that he died. He had not been ill; indeed he had continued to show his energy and love of entertaining and conversation until the end. The death certificate gives the cause of death as 'epilepsy', presumably because he had several convulsions in his last hours, but the real cause was surely old age and a lifetime of service in the public interest. Queen Victoria asked for a lock of his hair, and the whole nation mourned. His body lay in the room where he died for nearly two months, guarded by soldiers of the 95th Rifles, renamed at Wellington's request in 1816 the Rifle Brigade, while Parliament planned the greatest state funeral ever staged in the history of this nation. On 11 November the coffin was taken to Chelsea Hospital, where the Duke lay in state for two days. On 13 November 1852 Arthur Wellesley, duke and field marshal, was buried at St Paul's Cathedral, with all the civil and military pomp of a grieving Empire. It was truly the end of an era.

15

Epilogue

Wellington commanded far smaller bodies of men than did his principal opponents, but in the early days of the Peninsula it is amazing that he was able to keep an army in being at all. He joined the service when it was the resort of younger sons with no other prospects, placed in charge of men flogged into obedience. When he gave up his last field command, in 1818, he had, almost single-handedly, transformed the British army into a well-led, well-trained body that could, in his own words, 'beat any enemy that may be opposed to it'. The transformation from callow subaltern into commander of victorious armies was neither rapid nor without effort. In his first experience of active service, in Flanders in 1794-95, he showed sound common sense and some promise, very largely because so many others did not. Given his head by his brother in India, he learned by experience and by being placed in a situation where he had great responsibility for his age and rank. There, where everything from supplying his troops to devising tactics to counter numerous and well-armed enemies fighting in their own country had to be improvised, he showed that he had a mind untrammelled by received doctrine, and had a capacity to innovate and to adapt. India may have been regarded as a backwater of the military art, but it was service there that was the making of the field marshal.

In Portugal and Spain he never lost sight of fact that he commanded Britain's only army: its preservation was vital. He never fought an unnecessary battle and he never risked men's lives to no purpose. Popular he was not, but he was held in far greater respect by officers and men than any of his predecessors. Outwardly he was an austere, sometimes unfeeling, personality. He had given way to emotion once, at Seringapatam, and from then on he developed an inner control that rarely slipped. In some eyes he was an unenlightened commander, seemingly uninterested in welfare and relying on savage discipline to keep his men obedient to orders, but Wellington knew very well the character of the all-volunteer army that he commanded. It was not motivated by patriotism (the have-nots are rarely inspired by higher motives), nor by the low pay, nor by appeals to their better nature (many had none). In the place of those high-minded ideals he had to give them something else: a fierce pride in their race, a sense of professionalism, a feeling of belonging to the regimental family, and a dogged will to stick it out come what may. If Wellington did little to promote material comforts, he was well aware that sullen, diseased men of low morale would not fight. By hard, realistic training, by good administration, by forcing officers to do their duty, and by personal example, Wellington ensured that they would, and did, fight magnificently. Wellington had an unshakeable confidence in his own abilities; if he had doubts – and on occasions he had – they were never revealed except to his closest and most trusted friends. This confidence was contagious. Generals, field officers and soldiers began to realise that British military operations need not end in defeat and ignominious withdrawal. They could beat Mysoreans, Mahrattas, Frenchmen, and then go on to beat them again.

Almost alone amongst his contemporaries Wellington understood the importance of allies to a small British army fighting in unfamiliar territory. His wooing of the Hyderabad contingent, and his learning of the languages of the soldiers of the East India Company; his support for Beresford in the reformation of the Portuguese army, and his incorporation of Portuguese brigades into British formations; his understanding of the immense value of the Spanish guerrillas provided they were used appropriately; all these allowed him to achieve results out of all proportion to the assets at his disposal. Although not an intellectual, Wellington had a sharp brain: he calculated the effects of his own, his allies' and his enemies' actions, and then moved accordingly. He was rarely wrong. Wellington quickly realised the advantages, and the limitations, of skirmishers, proved in the short, sharp and economical actions of his light infantry in the Copenhagen affair, and he expanded the proportion of light infantry and rifles in his Peninsular army. If his siegecraft was untidy and expensive in lives, it was because time and the lack of equipment, and of trained men to use it, left him no option. Talavera and Waterloo were models of the defensive battle, Assaye and Salamanca examples of the seizing of a brief opportunity, and Vittoria a classic of the art of manoeuvre.

It is true that Wellington was biased towards those whom he considered gentlemen, and while he tolerated – even encouraged – the commissioning in war of those who were not, provided they had much needed ability, he had no great faith in them. He did advance the cause of those whom he regarded as fitting in to what he thought the army should be, but only if they met his exacting standards of competence. He was a master of the written word, and even today his despatches and letters are models of what good military writing should be: concise, clear, unambiguous and to the point. He had a well-developed sense of humour, although it was rarely displayed on formal occasions, except in sarcasm, which could on occasion be hurtful. He was less good at public speaking, and some of his speeches in the Lords – particularly as he got older – were rambling and repetitive, but his loss of hearing did not help. His long service in the field had made him worldly wise and sceptical – even cynical. He well understood the human failings of others, even if he did punish them severely, but he frequently pardoned sinners if their regiment had distinguished itself or if a man owned up to save the collective punishment of his comrades. He also appreciated the limitations of his subordinate commanders, using their talents and compensating for their weaknesses. He had a mastery of detail and was capable of prodigious amounts of work. Unlike modern generals, he effectively ran the whole army single-handed. He had an instinctive feel for strategy and tactics, and consistently applied those seemingly opposed principles of war: maintenance of momentum and economy of effort, being able to predict what his opponents would do and having the speed of reaction to take advantage of their mistakes. England had had few victories before Wellington. After him there was rarely a defeat.

In an age where self-interest was the norm and morality a middle-class aberration, Wellington's life shines out. From the day he achieved real responsibility by purchasing command of the 33rd Foot, what he did was motivated by what he called the public interest. He abhorred jobbery, placemen and importuners of undeserved favours. He never accepted a penny that was not lawfully his and the use of such patronage that was at his disposal was dispensed only to deserving recipients on strict grounds of merit.

It is a great pity that the Duke of York did not stand down in favour of Wellington in 1818, when the field marshal returned from commanding the army of occupation in France. Perhaps this was too much to expect; but if Wellington had been appointed Commander-in-Chief at that time, at the height of his vigour and with twenty years of almost continual active service just behind him, his unassailable prestige might have allowed him to force through a real reform of the army. Certainly no one else could have done so, but by 1842 it was too late. It took the next war, begun two years after the end of Wellington's ten-year tenure and his death, to spark a reform of the evils that had crept back into the army since Waterloo. Even so, it was a century after Waterloo before it was necessary for a British army to involve itself in major war on the Continent of Europe, and by then it could be considered as professional as that commanded by the Great Duke in 1814.

In the British army of today purchase and flogging have long gone and soldiers are far better paid. It has pensions, barracks and married quarters. Wellington would still recognise it, however, or at least its infantry. It is still largely composed of single battalion regiments, fiercely proud of their traditions and peculiarities; still officered in the most part by gentlemen; still all volunteers and still with drunkenness as the major cause of crime. He would recognise the sentries on his old office at Horse Guards; the Household Cavalry dressed in the uniforms in which they charged d'Erlon's corps at Waterloo; and the Guardsmen in the bearskins adopted in memory of their defeat of Napoleon's *Immortels*. The Great Duke would approve of the fact that the one offence amongst officers for which there is no appeal is the merest hint of lack of integrity, and that medals are awarded with (slightly) more generosity than he was able to persuade governments to agree to.

Today there is hardly a regiment of the British army that does not bear outward and visible sign of its connection with Wellington. Eagles on shoulders, titles, badges, battle honours, all bear witness to the enormous and lasting effect of this greatest of soldiers. All over the world British regiments celebrate the anniversaries of Assaye, Talavera, Salamanca and, of course, Waterloo. In this book I have attempted to examine the qualities that made Wellington great, how he commanded his army and how he fought his battles. I have also asked what it was that formed his character, and why he was the greatest general of his age and the greatest British general of any age.

Notes

Notes to Preface

1 Although there is a theory that the nickname dates from Wellington's installation of iron shutters on the windows of his London residence, Apsley House, after rioting sparked by reform agitation in 1831. Supporters of parliamentary reform placed lighted candles in their windows at night; Wellington's duchess had just died and her body lay in the darkened house (Wellington would not have lighted candles for reform anyway); the mob began to stone the house until they were persuaded to move on by one of the Duke's servants firing a blunderbuss from the roof.

Notes to Chapter 1: Ireland

1 For accounts of Wellington's birth and family antecedents see Elizabeth Longford, *Wellington: The Years of the Sword* (London, 1969); Philip Guedalla, *The Duke* (London, 1937); and Sir John Fortescue, *Wellington* (London, 1925).

2 For a discussion of Wellington's views on religion see Gregory Holyoake, *Wellington at Walmer* (Dover, 1996), pp. 105–6; Elizabeth Longford, *Wellington: Pillar of State* (London, 1972), pp. 119–120 and 300; Sir Charles Oman, *Wellington's Army, 1809–1814* (London, 1913), pp. 320–31.

3 The state of the army prior to Wellington's joining it is dealt with in David Ascoli, *A Companion to the British Army* (London, 1984); Richard Glover, *Peninsular Preparation* (Cambridge, 1983).

4 For a discussion of the Militia see Glover, *Peninsular Preparation*, pp. 225–29, 243, 249–52; Ascoli, *A Companion to the British* Army, pp. 37–38; Alan J. Guy (ed.), *The Road to Waterloo* (London, 1990), pp. 32–39 (Ian F.W. Beckett, 'The Militia and the King's Enemies, 1793–1815).

5 For the gradual implementation of standardised tactics see John Strawson, *Beggars in Red: The British Army, 1789–1889* (London, 1991), pp. 14–19; Glover, *Peninsular Preparation*, pp. 11–122.

6 Today both these officers would be major generals.

7 For the details of the purchase system see Glover, *Peninsular Preparation*, pp. 143–61; Oman, *Wellington's Army*, pp. 195–207; Tony Hayter (ed.), *An Eighteenth-Century Secretary at War* (London, 1988); pp. 175, 275, 328; Stuart Reid, *King George's Army* (London, 1995); pp. 10–17; Anthony Bruce, *The Purchase System in the British Army, 1660–1871* (London, 1984); Fortescue, *Wellington*, thinks that some of Arthur Wesley's early promotions and exchanges might have been free of purchase because the regiments had only recently been raised.

8 For details of mutinies in Highland regiments, see John Prebble, *Mutiny* (London, 1975), pp. 406–501.

9 For all Wellington's speeches in the Irish and imperial Parliaments, see John

Gurwood, *The Speeches of Field Marshal the Duke of Wellington in Parliament,* 2 vols (London, 1854).

Chapter 2: Early Days

1 For a brief summary of the American war see John Keegan, *Warpaths* (London, 1995), pp. 159–98; and for an account by one who was there, Ira D. Gruber (ed.), *John Peebles' American War* (Stroud, 1998).

2 Wellington's association with the 33rd is covered in the regimental publication *The History of The Duke of Wellington's Regiment (West Riding), 1702–1992* (Halifax, 1993).

3 For an account of the careers of the sons of George III, see Christopher Hibbert, *George III* (London, 1998), pp. 358–72.

4 John Gurwood, *The Speeches of Field Marshal the Duke of Wellington in Parliament,* 2 vols (London, 1854).

5 The Dukes of York and Richmond had actually fought a duel some years before. The Duke of Richmond received a large part of the blame for failing to produce a siege train on time and for the lack of all manner of stores, but as he had received little notice and as most of the equipment demanded was simply not in existence, he seems to have done his best.

6 Sources disagree as to the exact movements of the 33rd and of their commanding officer. Philip Guadalla, *The Duke* (London 1937); Arthur Bryant, *The Great Duke* (London 1971); and Elizabeth Longford, *Wellington: The Years of the Sword* (London, 1969), all relate how the 33rd did accompany the expedition when it recommenced its journey in December, that Wesley was with them and that the ship transporting them was one of a number which were again scattered by storms and blown back to the English coast, when the 33rd were disembarked and sent to Poole. Gurwood, in *Dispatches*, i, says that there was only one abortive attempt to sail and that Arthur Wesley and the 33rd were part of the force. As Wellington himself read Gurwood's *Dispatches* prior to publication, his account would seem to be the best evidence.

7 Richard Aldington, in his *Life of Wellington* (London, 1946), suggests that the promotion list was extended to include Wesley as compensation for his going to India and thus giving up any prospects of a career at home. As the previous brevet, that of 21 August 1795, was of the same order of magnitude – forty names – there is no reason to suppose that Wesley's promotion was other than by the normal advancement by seniority.

8 Wesley's library is analysed in detail by Guedalla, *The Duke,* who compares it with that of Napoleon.

9 For a description of the development of the East India Company's armies up to Wesley's arrival in India, see T.A. Heathcote, *The Military in British India* (Manchester, 1995), pp. 53–61.

10 The naval mutinies at Spithead and The Nore are described in Lawrence James, *Mutiny* (London, 1987).

Notes to Chapter 3: Learning the Trade

1 2nd Duke of Wellington (ed.), *Supplementary Despatches, Correspondence and Memoranda of the Duke of Wellington* (London, 1858–72), i, p. 187.

2 Ibid., i, p. 203.

3 Ibid., i, pp. 202–3.

4 Stapleton Cotton, later Field Marshal Viscount Combermere, was born in 1773 and commissioned in 1790. He fought in the Flanders expedition of 1793–94 and served as Wellington's cavalry commander in the Peninsula from 1810. He eventually returned to India as Commander-in-Chief and led the capture of Bhurtpore in 1826.

5 Many biographers deal only briefly with this incident, and the original sources are contradictory. Probably the best account is in Jac Weller, *Wellington in India* (London, 1972), pp. 61–65. Some correspondence, largely favourable to Wellington, is contained in *Supplementary Despatches*, i.

6 For the details of the assault see Weller, *Wellington in India*, pp. 70–81.

7 The casualty figures are from Fortescue, the historian of the British army, who considered that the very high number of enemy dead might be accounted for by the brutal method of execution (murder, to the British) meted out to nine men of the 33rd's grenadier company captured in the abortive night attack on the tope on 5 April. Some had been killed by having nails hammered into their skulls, the rest were strangled by Tippoo's 'strongmen'.

8 The usages of war in Europe allowed for a town under siege which had refused an offer to surrender once a breach had been made in its walls to be given up to plunder by the attackers. Wellesley considered this to be inappropriate in India, where the civil population had no say in military or political affairs.

9 *Supplementary Despatches*, i, pp. 419–21.

10 For a description of the characteristics of canister, see Philip Haythornthwaite, *Weapons and Equipment of the Napoleonic Wars* (Poole, 1979), pp. 60–61.

11 *Supplementary Despatches*, ii, pp. 165–68.

Notes to Chapter 4: Sepoy General

1 Richard Wellesley was now Marquess Wellesley and Earl of Mornington, both in the Irish peerage; but while his brother's letters to him were addressed to the Marquess Wellesley, the salutation remained 'Dear Mornington'.

2 Brigadier general was then an appointment, not a rank, and substantive promotion was from colonel to major general. There were a total of twenty-five officers on the list, and Wellesley was twenty-second.

3 A 'half caste' referred to someone of mixed British and Indian parentage. Today the expression is 'Anglo-Indian', but in the Wellesleys' time an Anglo-Indian was a Briton who lived in India.

4 2nd Duke of Wellington (ed.), *Supplementary Despatches, Correspondence and Memoranda of the Duke of Wellington* (London, 1858–72), iii, pp. 205–6.

5 Ibid., iii, p. 309.

6 The Peshwa was known by the British as Baje Rao. Rao is a Mahratta surname and *baje* means grandfather, but used as an honorific.

7 For the details of the Treaty of Bassein, and how it was arrived at, see Anthony S. Bennell, *The Making of Arthur Wellesley* (Mumbai, 1997), pp. 6–24.

8 Arrack meant any locally produced spirit. Here it was probably distilled from rice, although some scholars think it may have been a type of rum made from sugar cane.

In remote areas of India today arrack is distilled from rice, not sugar, despite the latter being plentiful. Wellesley's arrack was probably made from rice.

9 'Battery' is the modern term. The terms then in use were 'company' for field artillery and 'troop' for horse artillery. Horse artillery – sometimes referred to as 'galloper guns' – was now horse, rather than bullock, drawn because it had to be able to keep up with the cavalry.

10 J.W. Croker, *The Croker Papers* (London, 1884).

11 The Silladar system was one where soldiers joining provided their own horse and weapons, and in return received a higher rate of pay. Silladar cavalry, the self-provision of horse and weapon replaced by a sum of money for which the regiment provided horse and weapons, remained in the British Indian army until the outbreak of the First World War.

12 For a detailed description of the battle of Assaye, see Jac Weller, *Wellington in India* (London, 1972), pp. 170–94.

13 The battle of Argaum is described ibid., pp. 195–213.

14 For Wellesley's own estimate see Gurwood, *Dispatches*, iii, p. 7. Later authorities disagree and Weller, after a thorough examination of the fort in 1968, thinks that as many as 4000 may have escaped. See Weller, *Wellington in India*, p. 225. Even if Weller is right (and his argument is convincing), that still leaves 4000 Mahrattas dead, wounded or captured.

15 To put this into perspective, the infantry private soldier or sepoy carried around sixty-five pounds weight of arms and equipment, and the normal march rate, unencumbered by baggage or followers, was calculated at two miles per hour on reasonable going. Wellesley's march indicates a very high standard of physical fitness among the troops, and so it would today.

16 For the various addresses and valedictory letters, see Gurwood, *Dispatches,* iii, pp. 675–83.

17 Quoted in Anthony Brett-James, *Wellington at War* (London, 1961), pp. 121–22.

18 In 1801 the posts of Secretary for War (itself dating only from 1794) was combined with that of Secretary for the Colonies. Viscount Castlereagh (Marquess of Londonderry in the Irish peerage) was the third holder of the office, which he assumed in that year, 1805. The post of Secretary at War remained non-ministerial.

19 For a summary of the Duke of York's reforms see David Ascoli, *A Companion to the British Army* (Cambridge, 1988); for the duties of York as Commander-in-Chief and more details of his reforms, see Richard Glover, *Peninsular Preparation* (Cambridge, 1983), pp. 40–45 and 151–59.

Notes to Chapter 5: Vimeiro to Coruña

1 For a full account of Wellington's courtship and marriage see Joan Wilson, *A Soldier's Wife: Wellington's Marriage* (London, 1987).

2 Arthur's elder brother, born 1763, he assumed the additional surname of Pole after inheriting the estates of his cousin, William Pole of Ballyfin, Ireland. He served in the Royal Navy for a while and then followed a political career. He became 3rd Earl of Mornington in 1842 on the death of his eldest brother Richard, who had no legitimate (although many illegitimate) heirs.

3 If the regiment was not up to establishment then pay of the non-existent men went to the colonel. In the worst case it went into the colonel's pocket, in the best case it was

used to pay widows' pensions, and in most cases it was used to defray the costs that fell to the colonel.

4 John Gurwood, *Duke of Wellington's Speeches in Parliament,* 2 volumes (London, 1854), i, p. 6.

5 Ibid, p. 7.

6 Ibid, p. 8.

7 Ibid, p. 11.

8 By capturing the French West Indian islands the British created the French sugar beet industry. It is still a staple of French agriculture today, although the British have long since refrained from preventing French imports from the West Indies.

9 Mutiny was not unknown in the Company's armies. The previous serious one had been an officers' mutiny in 1766 when field allowances had been cut. The officers' case was not strengthened by a claim that, when in the field, each officer needed an allowance to cover thirty bottles of Madeira, thirty bottles of beer and fifteen bottles of arrack a month.

10 Quoted in Anthony Brett-James, *Wellington at War* (London, 1961), p. 126.

11 Ibid, p.127.

12 Royal Horse Artillery guns were horse-drawn and the crews were mounted, thus being able to keep up with the cavalry whom they existed to support. Foot artillery guns were also horse-drawn, but the crews marched. Horse artillery was necessarily of smaller calibre.

13 For the original correspondence and reports concerning the Copenhagen expedition, see Public Record Office, Kew, WO 1/188.

14 Home Popham was a fascinating character who had joined the Royal Navy in 1778 at the age of sixteen. Engaged in a bit of private merchant trading in 1793 when on half pay, he had his ship seized and cargo confiscated for carrying contraband and infringing the East India Company's monopoly on the Far East trade. In 1806, back in service, he was conveying Major General David Baird, who had left India in a huff, to the Cape when he persuaded the general to detach a battalion for a totally unauthorised foray to South America. He was court-martialled for this jape but received only a reprimand, which harmed his career not a jot. He would support Wellington along the Spanish coast during the Peninsular War.

15 Charles IV, described by Sir Charles Oman as a 'benign imbecile', had come to the throne in 1788. He allowed affairs of state to be managed by his Queen, Maria, and her lover Manuel Godoy, the chief minister. In March 1808 he abdicated in favour of his son, Ferdinand, and then withdrew his abdication. Spanish resistance was in the name of Ferdinand.

16 The camp is still there, titled Sir John Moore Barracks and presently occupied by that epitome of the skills of the rifleman, a Gurkha battalion.

17 Moore's journal, quoted in Roger Parkinson, *Moore of Corunna* (Abingdon, 1976).

18 John Gurwood, *Dispatches,* iv, p. 27.

19 Ibid., iv, pp. 65–76.

20 A Volunteer, in this sense, was a gentleman who could not afford to purchase a commission and who served in the ranks until an ensign's vacancy caused by death came up, which could be filled without purchase. Volunteers were legally private soldiers and stood in the ranks, but were often treated as officers when not on duty.

21 Parkinson, *Moore of Corunna.*

22 Moore's journal, quoted in Carola Oman, *Sir John Moore* (London, 1953).

23 For the evidence given before the court of inquiry into the Cintra affair, see Public Record Office, Kew, WO 1/415.

Notes to Chapter 6: Talavera

1 For Wellesley's parliamentary activities from 22 January to 28 March 1809, see John Gurwood, *The Speeches of the Duke of Wellington in Parliament*, 2 volumes (London, 1854), i, pp. 44–74.

2 For the full text of the memorandum see John Gurwood, *Dispatches* (London, 1837), ix, pp. 261–63.

3 Captured enemy ships, taken into British service, retained their original names.

4 For Wellesley's letters written on 24 April 1809, see Gurwood, *Dispatches* , iv, pp. 265–71.

5 For a full list of the various staff and civil departments, see the introduction to Gurwood, *The General Orders of Field Marshal the Duke of Wellington KG* (London, 1837). For how the various branches operated, see Michael Glover, *Wellington's Army* (London, 1977), pp.133–43.

6 Today a commander of an infantry brigade, depending on the role of his brigade, has between seven and twelve staff officers and a plethora of clerks as part of his headquarters. There is a signals squadron devoted entirely to communications, a whole regiment of artillery (eighteen guns), a squadron of transport, a medical unit and a detachment of military police. There would still be only three battalions of infantry supported by a squadron of (mechanised) cavalry.

7 For Wellesley's view of this extraordinary tale, see Gurwood, *Dispatches*, iv, pp. 273–75 and 337–40. Gurwood has deleted the names of the French officers involved, but the officer who originally brought the information to Wellesley was Colonel Argentan. Whatever the truth of the matter, nothing ever came of it and Wellesley does not seem to have placed much reliance on the information.

8 For the details of the Battle of Oporto, see Jac Weller, *Wellington in the Peninsula* (London, 1962; reprinted 1973), pp. 70–85.

9 Wellesley's letter to Castlereagh detailing the problems of indiscipline is in Gurwood, *Dispatches*, iv, pp. 432–36.

10 August Schaumann, *On the Road with Wellington* (London, 1924), p. 159. Schaumann, a Hanoverian, enlisted in the KGL as a commissary and moved round various KGL and British regiments during the war. His diary, translated from the German, gives a vivid and detailed description of the work and tribulations of the commissariat in the Peninsula.

11 Most authorities say that this happened a few days after Wellesley arrived in Portugal, in April 1809, but Gurwood, in *Selections from the General Orders and Dispatches of Field Marshal the Duke of Wellington* (London, 1851), says the appointment was made on 6 July 1809. As Gurwood was in the Peninsula at the time, and as he showed the draft of his book to the Duke before publication, he seems the best source. It is immaterial when the appointment was made: Wellesley and Beresford would have cooperated happily anyway.

12 After the defeat of James II in 1690 a large number of Irish soldiers fled Ireland. Many of them joined the armies of Spain, Austria or France, and their descendants served on. O'Donohue was one such. Sometimes spelt O'Donoju, he acted as a chief of staff

to Cuesta, as well as interpreter. Another officer of Irish descent on Cuesta's staff which whom Wellesley had dealings was Colonel O'Lalor.

13 For Wellesley's opinions as to the state of the Spanish army at this stage of the war, see Gurwood, *Dispatches*, v, pp. 82–90.

14 For the details of the Battle of Talavera see Jac Weller, *Wellington in the Peninsula*, pp. 86–107.

15 The casualty return is reproduced in Gurwood, *Dispatches*, iv, p. 538.

Notes to Chapter 7: The Defence of Portugal

1 There is disagreement amongst scholars as to the rate of fire, varying from four rounds a minute to two. Experiments carried out by this author in 1999, using a musket identical to those issued to Wellington's army, showed that the realistic rate is two rounds a minute, although well-drilled soldiers who could ignore the effects of fatigue and being shot at might manage three rounds a minute for a short period. The first minute of an engagement would produce three rounds, as the musket was already loaded when action commenced.

2 If the flank companies had been detached, as they often were, and the battalion was left with only eight companies, then it would form a square with two companies on each face.

3 For a detailed description of infantry tactics of the period see Michael Glover, *Wellington's Army* (Newton Abbot, 1977), pp. 45–60.

4 Wellington's title was chosen by his brother, William Wellesley-Pole; the Wellington was the Somerset village where the family was said to have once owned estates.

5 The two-day battle of Wagram gives a good example of the scale of European battles, fought with conscript armies whose size the British could never hope to emulate. The French, who won, had 46,000 casualties and lost twenty-one guns. The Austrians, who lost, had 40,000 casualties and lost twenty guns.

6 Like so many of Napoleons generals, Bernadotte had started his military life in the ranks of the Bourbon army, rising to the equivalent of sergeant major. He was a fervent revolutionary and had 'death to tyrants' tattooed on his arm. He became a marshal in 1804 and ended up as King Charles XIV of Sweden. The present Swedish royal family is descended from him.

7 John Gurwood, *Selections from the Dispatches and General Orders of FM the Duke of Wellington* (London, 1854), p. 287.

8 John Gurwood, *The Dispatches of Field Marshal the Duke of Wellington*, 12 volumes (London, 1837), iv, pp. 134–37.

9 Ibid., iv, pp. 221–22.

10 There were eighteen Royal Engineer officers employed at San Sebastian: eleven of them became casualties.

11 For the details of the Lines of Torres Vedras, and what can be seen there today, see Julian Paget, *Wellington's Peninsular War* (London, 1990), pp. 113–18.

12 Gurwood, *Dispatches*, iv, pp. 234–39.

13 Ibid., iv, pp. 232–34.

14 Ibid., iv, pp. 240–42.

15 Cathedrals and churches were regularly used as powder magazines, being often the

only buildings which had the space and weather proofing to house large quantities of delicate explosive.

16 Invented by Henry Shrapnel, an officer of the Royal Artillery, and taken into service in 1804, 'spherical case shot' – later known colloquially as shrapnel after its inventor – was a British secret weapon. The shell consisted of an iron case into which was packed musket balls and a bursting charge of black powder. A fuse was inserted into the shell which was then fired from an artillery piece in the normal way. If the gunners had calculated the length of fuse correctly, the shell burst in mid air scattering the target with one-ounce lead balls. It was particularly effective against massed troops in the open. The term shrapnel is still in use in the British army, but now refers to the splinters produced by a fragmenting shell, rather than the original lead balls.

17 For the details of the battle of Busaco, see Jac Weller, *Wellington in the Peninsula* (London, 1962; reprinted 1973), pp. 124–40.

Notes to Chapter 8: The Keys to the Kingdom

1 Flanker battalions were composite units made up of the flank companies (grenadier and light) of a number of regiments. Browne's battalion had six companies, two each from the 1/9th, 1/28th and 2/82nd foot. Barnard had eight companies, two from each of the 2nd 47th Foot and the 20th Portuguese Infantry and four of the 3/95th Rifles. They were high-grade troops.

2 The French eagles are often thought of as being equivalent to British colours, but whereas every British battalion (except rifles and composite battalions) had colours, only the first battalions of French regiments had eagles: they were therefore harder to capture. The one captured at Barrosa by the 87th Regiment from the French 8th Regiment of the Line, was presented to the Prince Regent and was eventually hung in the Royal Hospital Chelsea, until it disappeared in the 1850s, stolen, it was thought, by a disgruntled Frenchman. The men of the 87th, later the Royal Irish Fusiliers, wore a miniature eagle on their shoulder straps as a badge of honour. It is still incorporated in the uniform of their successors, the Royal Irish Regiment.

3 Henry Wellesley, who had married Charlotte in 1803, divorced her in 1810, and Paget then married her. Henry refused to acknowledge the paternity of Charlotte's youngest son, Gerald, born before her elopement with Paget, and the child was brought up by Wellington and his wife. Gerald entered the church and became the Dean of Windsor. Another Wellesley brother, the Rev. Gerald, had married Charlotte's sister Emily in 1802 (both were daughters of the 1st Earl Cadogan). The Cadogan issue were evidently fond of playing away, as Emily eloped in 1819.

4 The full despatch is in John Gurwood, *Dispatches of Field Marshal the Duke of Wellington*, 12 volumes (London, 1837), vii, pp. 528–34.

5 Ibid., vii, p. 542.

6 See Wellington's letter to Beresford, in ibid., vii, p. 547, and his letter to Lord Liverpool, ibid., pp. 565–67.

7 Portuguese mules were relatively small. By the 1970s a British army artillery mule purchased from Pakistan could carry 400 pounds twenty miles in a day.

8 John Gurwood, *Selections From the Dispatches and General Orders of Field Marshal the Duke of Wellington* (London, 1851), p. 454.

9 Ibid., p. 455.
10 Ibid., p. 468.
11 Ibid., p. 455.
12 Ibid., p. 417.
13 Ibid., pp. 519, 520.
14 Ibid., p. 541.
15 Ibid., p. 493.
16 Ibid., p. 457.
17 Ibid., p. 540.
18 Ibid., p. 579.
19 Ibid., p. 451.
20 Ibid., p. 470.
21 Ibid., p. 502.
22 Ibid., p. 510.
23 Ibid., p. 451.
24 A twenty-four pounder could penetrate twelve feet of packed earth. Some of the guns in Ciudad Rodrigo were thirty pounders.
25 The guns were too far away from the walls for canister to be effective.
26 For the technical details of siege artillery and its handling, I have relied on a lecture by Brigadier K.A. Timbers, Historical Secretary of the Royal Artillery Institute, delivered on 2 October 1996 and subsequently printed in the *Royal Artillery Historical Society Journal.*
27 Gurwood eventually became a lieutenant colonel and was the prodigious compiler of Wellington's despatches, general orders and speeches in Parliament. The job must have taken its toll, for he committed suicide in Brighton in 1845.
28 The argument between the 3rd Division and the Light Division as to who actually got into Ciudad Rodrigo first was still raging in the pages of the *Journal of Royal United Services Institute* over thirty years later, and continued as long as any of the participants were still alive.
29 Sir John Kincaid, *Adventures in the Rifle Brigade* (London, 1830; reprinted, 1909), p. 58.
30 Gurwood, *Dispatches*, viii, p. 549.
31 Gurwood, *Selections From the Dispatches and General Orders of the Duke of Wellington*, p. 569.
32 For the details of the siege and capture of Ciudad Rodrigo, see Frederick Myatt, *British Sieges of the Peninsular War* (London, 1987), pp. 47–77.
33 Windage was the difference between the diameter of the barrel and the diameter of the shot. The closer fitting the shot the more accurate the fire.
34 To be fair, naval gunnery was not over concerned with accuracy, the prevailing operating procedure being to get as close as possible to an enemy ship and then batter it to pieces with weight of shot. Berkeley did relent eventually and sent ten English eighteen pounders. Gauging was the process of applying two iron rings to each shot. The shot had to pass through the first ring – or it would not go into the barrel – and must not go through the second ring, or the windage would be too great.
35 Philippon was sent as a prisoner to Oswestry, Shropshire, where he broke his parole and, helped by a local girl and the postmaster of Rye, managed to get a smuggler to take him to France.

36 For the details of the siege and capture of Badajoz, see Ian Fletcher *In Hell Before Daylight* (Tunbridge Wells, 1984).

37 Gurwood, *Dispatches*, ix, p. 45.

Notes to Chapter 9: Into Spain

1 Fitzroy Somerset was the thirteenth child, and eighth and youngest son, of the 5th Duke of Somerset and was twenty-four years old in 1812. He had joined the 4th Light Dragoons in 1804, transferring to the infantry in 1808 on purchasing a captaincy in the 45th Foot. He had been with Wellington at Copenhagen, Rolica and Vimeiro and was appointed Military Secretary in January 1811.

2 He remained with Wellington throughout the war, losing an arm at Waterloo. The association continued and when Wellington became Commander-in-Chief of the British army for the first time in 1827, Somerset became Military Secretary, a post that he held until Wellington died in 1852. He was then appointed as Master General of the Ordnance and raised to the peerage as Baron Raglan. He was an ineffectual commander of the British army in the Crimea, although the shortcomings were by no means all his fault. Promoted to general and field marshal, he died in the Crimea in June 1855 (the only British field marshal ever to die on active service).

3 John Gurwood, *The Dispatches of Field Marshal the Duke of Wellington*, 12 volumes (London, 1837), ix, p. 47.

4 Related in Anthony Brett-James, *Wellington at War* (London, 1961), pp. 233-34.

5 Waterloo and El Alamein, to name but two.

6 Sir James McGrigor, *The Autobiography and Services of Sir James McGrigor, Bart, Late Director of the Army Medical Department* (London, 1816). Up to April 1812 McGrigor's brother-in-law was also at Wellington's headquarters, for in 1810 he had married the sister of Major Colquhoun Grant, one of Wellington's senior observing officers and detached for that purpose from his regiment, the 11th Foot. Unfortunately Grant was captured on the Portuguese frontier in April, so was no longer with the army.

7 Maximilien-Sébastien Foy had an English mother and regularly sent messengers to the British lines to obtain English newspapers, allegedly to check his investments in the London stock market, but probably as the most reliable means of finding out what the British were up to. His remarks on Wellington at Salamanca are in his journals, *Vie militaire du Général Foy* (Paris, 1900), quoted by Sir Charles Oman in *History of the Peninsular War* (London, n.d.; reprinted 1995).

8 Gurwood, *Dispatches*, ix, p. 378.

9 The author's opinion, based on a thorough examination of the breaches and approaches in 1998.

10 For the details of the siege of Burgos see Frederick Myatt, *British Sieges of the Peninsular War* (London, 1987).

11 John Gurwood, *Selections from the Dispatches and General Orders of Field Marshal the Duke of Wellington* (London 1851), pp. 637-38. Gurwood has the irritating habit of removing names and regimental numbers to avoid embarrassing the guilty, but the culprit here is probably the 1st Battalion 23rd Foot, the Royal Welch Fusiliers.

12 Gurwood, *Dispatches*, ix, pp. 582-85.

13 The same could be said of any British regular army, then or now.

14 Gurwood, *Dispatches*, ix, p. 226.

Notes to Chapter 10: The Year of Victory

1 John Gurwood, *The Dispatches of Field Marshal the Duke of Wellington*, 12 volumes (London, 1837), ix, p.591.

2 This system was formally adopted in 1856. It compares with the present system whereby a colonel wears a crown and two stars, a lieutenant colonel a crown and one star, a major a crown, a captain three stars, a lieutenant two stars and a second lieutenant (equivalent to ensign) one star.

3 Gurwood, *Dispatches*, x, p.19.

4 Ibid., ix, p. 587.

5 Ibid., ix, p. 573.

6 Ibid., ix, p. 592.

7 Ibid., ix, p. 585.

8 Ibid., x, p117.

9 The War of 1812, considered by Wellington to be one of the more pointless wars engaged in by Great Britain, came about because of American objections to the British blockade of Napoleonic Europe, which included the stopping and searching of neutral shipping. What particularly incensed the Americans was the British practice of pressing seaman from American ships who did not have papers proving they were American citizens (and were therefore assumed to be British). What American history books do not say, however, is that the French also stopped American ships. They did not press the seamen, who spoke no French, but they did impound the ships and the cargoes.

10 This conversation must have been misreported. The 4th Division was two miles away and the 6th were not yet on the field. The obvious division to support Picton was the Light Division.

11 The descendants of that cavalry regiment still have Joseph's silver pot, known colloquially as 'the Emperor', and on regimental guest nights it is filled with champagne and passed round the table.

12 Gurwood, *Dispatches*, x, p. 473.

13 Syphilis, rare in England except around the ports, could eventually kill, and there was no penicillin. Cures varied, usually involving the insertion of a potion up the penis (salts of mercury was one of the few cures that did work, but it was expensive). Then, as now, soldiers who contracted venereal diseases were forbidden alcohol for three weeks: not because alcohol has any effect on the cure but to prevent the man from getting drunk and contracting a further dose.

14 For the details of the battle of Vittoria see Ian Fletcher, *Vittoria 1813* (Oxford, 1998).

15 Gurwood, *Dispatches*, ix, p. 452.

16 2nd Duke of Wellington (ed.), *Supplementary Despatches of the Duke of Wellington*, 14 volumes (London, 1872), viii, p. 17.

17 Gurwood, *Dispatches*, x, p. 495.

Notes to Chapter 11: France

1 'Their detention … cannot have any influence on the conduct of the war'. John

Gurwood, *Dispatches of Field Marshal the Duke of Wellington* (London, 1837), 12 volumes, xi, p. 128.

2 Gurwood, *Selections from the Dispatches and General Orders of Field Marshal the Duke of Wellington* (London, 1851), p. 710.

3 The 71st (Glasgow Highlanders). To be fair, they had been ordered back by their new commanding officer, only just arrived from England to replace the previous CO killed at Vittoria, and were quickly rallied. The incident so shocked the saintly 'Daddy' Hill that he was said to have uttered an oath – for only the second time in the whole war!

4 At the conference of Chaumont, reconvened in spring 1814 after Napoleon rejected the offer of peace based on the status quo ante the war, the Coalition determined to recognise Louis XVIII as the legitimate ruler of France.

5 The French claimed it as a victory too, but although they had inflicted more casualties than they had taken, they were forced to abandon their position.

6 The *London Gazette* of 27 April 1814 is laudatory of Hay, but 'A Peninsular Brigadier' by Major General Frederick Robinson, also a brigade commander in the Peninsula, and edited by G.T. Atkinson, which appeared in the *Journal of the Society for Army Historical Research*, 34 (1956), is scathingly critical.

7 Like many British officers, and civilians too, Wellington regarded fighting the Americans as distasteful: they were, after all, but Englishmen abroad.

8 Some historians aver that the Congress was but the imposition of the old self-seeking conservatism, which only bottled up problems until they re-emerged in 1848. In rebuttal, nearly all the little revolutions of 1848 failed, and the Congress did establish a template for Europe which lasted until the First World War: only broken because in 1914 Austria ignored the requirement to consult other powers affected.

9 Gurwood, *Dispatches*, xii, p. 251.

10 Ibid., xii, p. 201.

Notes to Chapter 12: Napoleon's Return

1 Louis XVIII was the nephew of the executed Louis XVI, whose son, who would have been Louis XVII, had died in prison.

2 According to Christopher Kelly, *The Memorable Battle of Waterloo* (London, 1817), quoted in David Hamilton-Williams, *The Fall of Napoleon* (London, 1994), the official English translation said 'Napoleon Bonaparte has placed himself without the pale of civil and social relations; and that as an enemy and disturber of the tranquillity of the world he has rendered himself liable to public vengeance.' 'Without the pale etc' is hardly an accurate translation of *hors la loi*.

3 It is unlikely that Napoleon actually said his much-quoted words, 'soldiers of the 5th, will you fire on your Emperor?', but if he did it is improbable that anyone actually heard him, such was the noise of cheering and singing of the *Marseillaise*.

4 Ney was out of touch with recent emanations from the court, having departed to his country estate after a row with the Duc d'Angouleme, who had insulted his wife.

5 Although there had been lynchings of royalists and settlement of old scores by enraged civilians in a number of areas, including Paris.

6 John Gurwood, *Dispatches of Field Marshal the Duke of Wellington*, 12 volumes (London, 1837), xii, p. 289.

7 Ibid., xii, p. 291

8 Ibid., xii, p. 317.

9 Ibid., xii, p. 299.

10 Ibid., xii, p. 308.

11 Having fallen on hard times, she published her journal in 1825. Hoping to make more money by not publishing than by publishing, she is alleged to have contacted the Duke. 'Publish and be damned' was his famous reply.

12 For an account of Wellington's supposed affairs see Patrick Delaforce, *Wellington the Beau* (Moreton-in-Marsh, 1990). This is an enjoyable, gossipy read but is unsourced and cannot be more than supposition.

13 During the recent controversy (1999) which resulted in the British Army being forced to accept homosexuals in the ranks (objected to not on moral grounds but because of their possibly divisive influence in an organisation where peer-bonding is all-important), one civilian homosexual pressure group alleged that a whole list of great soldiers, from Caesar onwards and including Wellington, had been homosexuals. This is arrant nonsense, with very little to support it.

14 Brigadier Douglas Wickenden, consultant psychiatrist to the British Army, has suggested two explanations to the author. Given that Blücher was not insane, and all the evidence is that he was not, he may have been making allegorical reference to the difficulties of commanding the Prussian army in a foreign country, with constant interference from the King of Prussia. Another possibility is that he had an addiction to coffee, which can cause hallucinations of the type referred to. The British of the period tended to drink tea, the Europeans coffee. Due to the British blockade of continental Europe and British control of the tea trade, coffee was cheaper and easier to get. Blücher certainly consumed coffee in very large quantities.

15 Gurwood, *Dispatches*, xii, p. 348.

16 2nd Duke of Wellington (ed.), *Supplementary Despatches of the Duke of Wellington*, 14 volumes (London, 1863), x, p. 216

17 Gurwood, *Dispatches*, x, p. 390.

18 Note that this officer is always referred to as von Pirch I, to distinguish him from the other Major General von Pirch (II) who was a brigade commander in von Zieten's 1st Corps.

19 In German sources this officer is known by his full name of Bülow von Dennewitz, but he is (and was) always referred to by the British as von Bülow, or simply Bülow.

20 Hofschröer, in his two-volume *1815: The Waterloo Campaign* (London, 1998 and 1999), argues this point. Hofschröer's knowledge and understanding of the German sources, upon which he places much reliance, is impressive, and his work a great contribution to the study of the campaign, but this author at least, while accepting that the Prussian and German contribution has been given insufficient credit by British historians in the twentieth century, remains unconvinced as to any dereliction of duty or deliberate falsification on Wellington's part.

21 In fact the Prussians had more of the long-range twelve pounders than the French (two batteries per corps to the French one), but the Prussian artillery was less experienced and less well handled. Frederick the Great had little time for the artillery arm and refused to allow gentlemen to join it, an attitude that persisted in the German army until 1945.

22 Dörnberg was supposed to be commanding the cavalry at Mons, but when he realised that his original despatch to Wellington on the 15th had been misleading, he rode across to see the Commander-in-Chief to explain the situation personally.

23 He did suffer from what would now be termed clinical depression, brought on by overwork and Napoleon's insistence that he marry a member of the German nobility rather than his long-term mistress, so suicide, rather than murder, seems more likely.

24 Initially there had been a squadron of Silesian cavalry, but they had been recalled to their own army at Ligny.

25 John Gurwood, *The General Orders of Field Marshal the Duke of Wellington KG* (London, 1837), Introduction.

26 Much later, Wellington claimed that he was able to see the action at Ligny. It is not possible today, as trees have grown up and the ground has altered, but with a good telescope Wellington may have been able to see at least some of what was happening on the forward slopes.

27 Well accustomed to tactical retreats in the Peninsula, Wellington's withdrawal was similar to the doctrine still extant in the modern British army: by day thinning out is from the rear, by night from the front.

28 Both the 1st and 2nd Life Guards had been represented in the Peninsula, where they had done well, but some of their squadrons had stayed at home, only to be deployed for the 1815 campaign. This trooper, and his officer, had presumably spent the war years being reviewed in Hyde Park.

Notes to Chapter 13: Waterloo

1 In view of what happened to Bylandt's brigade later, I believe them to have been so detailed, but the sources are vague.

2 Many accounts, relying mainly on W. Siborne, *History of the Waterloo Campaign* (London, 1844), and H.T. Siborne, *Waterloo Letters* (London, 1891), say that Bylandt was left on the forward slope until attacked by d'Erlon's corps later in the day. This is simply not credible, given Wellington's need to conserve men, his invariable practice of sheltering his infantry where possible, and the fact that a brigade left forward would impede the artillery behind it. They may have been forward originally, possibly collecting their piquets, but were surely moved back as soon as the artillery bombardment started, or shortly afterwards. John Hussey, in a paper published in the *Newsletter of the British Commission for Military History* (May 2000), gives the most convincing explanation to date for what actually happened to Bylandt's brigade at Waterloo. I am grateful to him for permitting me to cite his conclusions.

3 Legend has it that two grenadiers of the Black Watch carried Picton to the rear, and that one of them stole his gold-rimmed spectacles. Without wishing to spoil a good story, this is unlikely. The 42nd were in Pack's brigade, a good 400 yards away from where Picton fell. The nearest Highlanders were the 79th.

4 Ensign Gronow of the Coldstream Guards, *Reminiscences* (London, 1862).

5 To be fair, the Prince probably took advice from Charles Alten, Ompteda's divisional commander, who had no excuse. The Prince survived, to become King William II of the Netherlands, and was a popular monarch. The famous *Butte de Lion* on the field of Waterloo was built in the 1820s on the spot where the Prince was wounded. Wellington, on seeing it while taking George IV on a battlefield tour, snapped 'they have spoiled my battlefield', and never returned.

6 There is dispute as which units of the Imperial Guard actually took part. The British Guards thought they were of the Old Guard, but it was probably the Middle Guard.

7 An experiment carried out on the ground by this author in 1992, using his own Gurkha soldiers partially blindfolded to replicate the smoke on the battlefield, showed that the lie of the land tended to pull soldiers over to their left, and the representative Imperial Guardsmen did emerge onto the ridge roughly where the real Guard did.

8 John Gurwood, *Dispatches of Field Marshal the Duke of Wellington*, 12 volumes (London, 1837), xii, p. 529.

9 In the modern British army tests have shown that four hours continuous sleep in each twenty-four is, with training, sufficient for a man to perform on continuous operations without degradation of capability.

10 The Opposition in Parliament, and many government supporters, felt that Napoleon was being shabbily treated, in that his detention on board ship without trial was illegal under English law. Eager to embarrass the government, some Opposition members persuaded Admiral Sir Richard Cochrane, under examination for failing to properly engage a French fleet, to apply for a writ of Habeas Corpus so that Napoleon could give evidence as to the state of the French navy at the time. This would have produced Napoleon in open court, when the legality of his detention could be examined.

Notes to Chapter 14: The Later Years

1 A stipulation still extant, although now the presentation is of a replica Napoleonic eagle, rather than of a tricolour.

2 John Gurwood, *Selections from the Dispatches and General Orders of Field Marshal the Duke of Wellington* (London, 1851), p. 886.

3 Ibid., p. 904.

4 Ibid., p. 886.

5 Ibid., p. 872.

6 Ibid., p. 895

7 Ibid., p. 887

8 General Henry Phipps, 1st Earl of Mulgrave, commanded the British troops at Toulon, when Thomas Graham first tried his hand at soldiering. In 1809 be became a general, and held various political offices, including Foreign Secretary (1805–6) and First Lord of the Admiralty (1807–10), before becoming Master General of the Ordnance in 1810.

9 There is still argument as to whether the King was insane – as his doctors thought – or whether he suffered from an inherited form of porphyria, which had many of the symptoms of insanity.

10 This is still the legal situation in Great Britain in regard to the use of the military to disperse crowds, although now the request must come from the magistrate to the senior officer of police and then to the military. There is separate legislation for Northern Ireland.

11 Clause 5 of Napoleon's will, translated into English, said: 'We bequeath 10,000 francs to the subaltern officer Cantillon, who has undergone a trial, upon the charge of having attempted to assassinate Lord Wellington, of which he was pronounced innocent [by a French court of Bonapartist sympathisers]. Cantillon had as much right to assassinate that oligarchist as the latter had to send me to perish upon the rock of St Helena ... ' Quoted in 'An Ex-Aide-de-Camp' [Lord William Pitt-Lennox], *Three Years with the Duke* (London, 1853).

12 He never recovered, and died in 1818.

13 John Gurwood, *The Speeches of the Duke of Wellington in Parliament*, 2 volumes (London, 1854), i, p. 123.

14 Ibid., p. 124.

15 Ibid., i, p. 123.

16 King's College was a royal foundation, and the Prime Minister was, ex officio, on its governing body.

17 *Standard* (newspaper), 16 March 1829.

18 Gurwood, *Speeches of the Duke of Wellington*, i, p. 388.

19 The King had refused to accept Melbourne's recommendation of Lord John Russell as Leader of the House of Commons.

20 The problem with any rifle was the time it took to load: the ball had to fit tightly so that the rifling in the barrel could impart the necessary spin, and so it had to be forced down the barrel. The minié system used a loose-fitting ball, which expanded to fit the barrel once the weapon was fired.

21 Gurwood, *Selections from the Dispatches and General Orders*, p. 923.

22 Ibid., p. 923.

23 This was never implemented, although in 1917 the most Excellent Order of the British Empire was introduced, with two divisions (civil and military) and five classes of the Order (KCBE, KBE, CBE, OBE and MBE) and the medal of the Order (BEM). The military division of order was admissible for officers and warrant officers, the medal for other ranks. Both civil and military divisions may be awarded to non-nationals. The Long Service and Good Conduct Medal had been introduced by King William IV, at Wellington's urging, in 1830. It was awarded to non-commissioned ranks for twenty-one years unblemished service in the infantry, eighteen in the cavalry. The qualifying period is now (2001) fifteen years for all arms.

Bibliography

Adjutant General's Office *Instructions for Training and Exercising Local Militia* (London, 1809).

Aldington, R., *Life of Wellington* (London, 1946).

Alford, Richard, *On the Word of Command* (Tunbridge Wells, 1990).

Anglesey, Marquess of, *One Leg* (London, 1961).

Ascoli, David, *A Companion to the British Army* (London, 1984).

Austin, Paul Britten, *1812: The Great Retreat* (London, 1996).

Barnett, Correlli, *Bonaparte* (London, 1978).

Beamish, N. Ludlow, *History of the King's German Legion*, 2 vols (Dallington, 1997).

Beatson, Major General F.C., *Wellington, the Crossing of the Gaves and the Battle of Orthez* (London, 1994).

Bell, Douglas, *Wellington's Officers* (London, 1938).

Bell, Sir George, *Soldier's Glory* (Tunbridge Wells, 1991).

Bennell, Anthony S. (ed.), *The Mahratta War Papers of Arthur Wellesley* (Stroud, 1998).

Blond, Georges, *La Grande Armée* (London, 1979).

Boutflower, Charles, *The Journal of an Army Surgeon during the Peninsular War* (Staplehurst, 1997).

Brett-James, Anthony, *Life in Wellington's Army* (London, 1992).

Brett-James, Anthony, *Wellington at War* (London, 1961).

Bryant, Sir Arthur, *The Great Duke* (London, 1971).

Buckley, Roger Norman (ed.), *The Napoleonic War Journal of Thomas Henry Browne* (London, 1987).

Bunbury, Sir Henry, *Narrative of Some Passages in the Great War with France* (London, 1927).

Chalfont, Lord (ed.), *Waterloo: Battle of Three Armies* (London, 1979).

Chandler, David G., *Dictionary of the Napoleonic Wars* (London, 1979).

Chandler, David G., *Military Maxims of Napoleon* (London, 1987).

Chandler, David G., *Napoleon's Marshals* (London, 1987).

Chandler, David G., *The Campaigns of Napoleon* (London, 1966).

Chandler, David G., *Waterloo: The Hundred Days* (London, 1980).

Chesney, Colonel Charles, *Waterloo Lectures* (London, 1997).

Connelly, Owen, *Blundering to Glory* (Wilmington, Delaware, 1987).

Cooper, John Spencer, *Rough Notes from Seven Campaigns* (Staplehurst, 1996).

Croker, John Wilson, *The Croker Papers*, 3 vols (London, 1884).

de Chair, Somerset (ed.), *Napoleon on Napoleon* (London, 1992).

Delaforce, Patrick *Wellington the Beau* (Gloucestershire, 1990).

Fitchett, W.F., *Wellington's Men* (London, 1900).

Fletcher, Ian, *Fields of Fire* (Staplehurst, 1994).

Fletcher, Ian, *In Hell before Daylight* (New York, 1984).

Fletcher, Ian (ed.), *The Peninsular War* (Staplehurst, 1998).

Fletcher, Ian, *Vittoria 1813* (Wellingborough, 1998).

Fletcher, Ian, and Poulter, Ross, *Gentlemen's Sons* (Tunbridge Wells, 1992).

Fortescue, Sir John, *The Campaign of Waterloo* (London, 1987).

Fortescue, Sir John, *Wellington* (London, 1925).

Fosten, Bryan, *Wellington's Infantry* (London, 1981).

Fosten, D.S.V. and B.K., *The Thin Red Line* (London, 1992).

Gash, Norman (ed.), *Wellington* (Manchester, 1990).

Gates, David, *The British Light Infantry Arm* (London, 1987).

Gates, David, *The Spanish Ulcer* (London, 1986).

Glover, Richard, *Peninsular Preparation* (Cambridge, 1983).

Glover, Michael, *Wellington's Army in the Peninsula* (London, 1977).

Grattan, William, *Adventures with the Connaught Rangers* (London, 1989).

Grehan, John, *The Lines of Torres Vedras* (Staplehurst, 2000).

Griffith, Paddy (ed.), *A History of the Peninsular War*, ix (London, 1999).

Griffith, Paddy (ed.), *Wellington Commander* (Chichester, 1986).

Gronow, Captain, *The Reminiscences and Recollections of Captain Gronow* (London, 1862).

Gruber, Ira D. (ed.), *John Peebles' American War, 1776-1782* (Stroud, 1998).

Guedalla, Philip, *The Duke* (London, 1937).

Gurwood, John, *Selections from the Dispatches and General Orders of Field Marshal the Duke of Wellington* (London, 1854).

Gurwood, John, *The Dispatches of Field Marshal the Duke of Wellington*, 12 vols (London, 1837).

Gurwood, John, *The General Orders of Field Marshal the Duke of Wellington* (London, 1837).

Gurwood, John, *The Speeches of the Duke of Wellington in Parliament*, 2 vols (London, 1854).

Guy, Alan J. (ed.), *The Road to Waterloo* (London, 1990).

Hamilton-Williams, David, *The Fall of Napoleon* (London, 1994).

Hamilton-Williams, David, *Waterloo: New Perspectives* (London, 1993).

Havard, Robert, *Wellington's Welsh General* (London, 1996).

Hayter, Tony (ed.), *An Eighteenth-Century Secretary at War* (London, 1998).

Haythornthwaite, Philip, *Die Hard* (London, 1996).

Haythornthwaite, Philip, *The Napoleonic Source Book* (London, 1990).

Haythornthwaite, Philip, *Weapons and Equipment of the Napoleonic Wars* (Poole, 1979).

Haythornthwaite, Philip, *Wellington's Specialist Troops* (London, 1998).

Haythornthwaite, Philip, *Who Was Who in the Napoleonic Wars* (London, 1998).

Heathcote, T.A., *The Military in British India* (Manchester, 1995).

Hendrickson, Kenneth E., *Making Saints: Religion and the Public Image of the British Army, 1809-1885* (London, 1998).

Herold, J. Christopher, *Bonaparte in Egypt* (London, 1963).

Hibbert, Christopher, *A Soldier of the 71st* (Gloucestershire, 1996).

Hibbert, Christopher, *George III: A Personal History* (London, 1998).

Hibbert, Christopher, *The Recollections of Rifleman Harris* (London, 1970).

Hibbert, Christopher, *Wellington: A Personal History* (London, 1997).

Hofschröer, Peter, *1815: The Waterloo Campaign. Quatre Bras and Ligny* (London, 1998).

Hofschröer, Peter, *1815: The Waterloo Campaign. The German Victory* (London, 1999).

Holyoake, Gregory, *Wellington at Walmer* (Dover, 1996).

Horne, Alistair, *How Far from Austerlitz?* (London, 1996).

Horward, Donald D., *Napoleon and Iberia* (London, 1984).

James, Lawrence, *Mutiny in the British and Commonwealth Forces, 1797-1956* (London, 1987).

Keegan, Sir John, *Warpaths* (London, 1995).

Kelly, W.H., *The Battle of Wavre and Grouchy's Retreat* (London, 1905).

Kincaid, Captain Sir John, *Adventures in the Rifle Brigade* (Glasgow, 1981).

Larpent, F.S., *The Private Journal of F.S. Larpent,* 3 vols (London, 1853).

Le Marchant, Denis, *Memoirs of Major General Le Marchant* (Staplehurst, 1997).

Lennox, Lord, *Three Years with the Duke* (London, 1853).

Liddell Hart, B.H. (ed.), *The Letters of Private Wheeler* (London, 1951).

Lloyd, Peter A., *The French are Coming: The Invasion Scare, 1803-1805* (Tunbridge Wells, 1991).

Longford, Elizabeth, *Wellington: The Years of the Sword* (London, 1969).

Longford, Elizabeth, *Wellington: Pillar of State* (London, 1972).

Maxwell, H. (ed.), *The Creevy Papers,* 2 vols (London, 1903).

Mercer, General Cavalié, *Journal of the Waterloo Campaign* (London, 1985).

Messenger, Charles, *History of the British Army* (Swindon, 1986).

Muffling, Baron von, *Memoirs* (London, 1997).

Myatt, Frederick, *British Sieges of the Peninsular War* (London, 1987).

Myatt, Frederick, *Peninsular General* (London, 1980).

Napier, W.E.P., *History of the War in the Peninsula,* 5 vols (London, 1992).

Nicolson, Nigel, *Napoleon: 1812* (London, 1985).

Oman, Carola, *Sir John Moore* (London, 1953).

Oman, Sir Charles, *History of the Peninsular War,* 8 vols (London, 1995).

Oman, Sir Charles, *Stories from the Napoleonic Wars* (Hertfordshire, 1987).

Oman, Sir Charles, *Wellington's Army, 1809-1814* (London, 1913).

O'Neil, Charles, *The Military Adventures of Charles O'Neil* (Staplehurst, 1997).

Page, Brigadier F.D.C., *Following the Drum: Women in Wellington's War* (London, 1986).

Page, Julia (ed.), *Intelligence Officer in the Peninsula* (Tunbridge Wells, 1986).

Paget, Julian, *Wellington's Peninsular War* (London, 1990).

Paget, Julian, and Saunders, D., *Hougoumont* (London, 1992).

Parkinson, Roger, *Moore of Corunna* (Abingdon, 1976).

Partridge, Richard, and Oliver, Michael, *Napoleonic Army Handbook* (London, 1999).

Perett, Bryan, *A Hawk at War* (Chippenham, 1986).

Petre, Loraine, *Napoleon's Last Campaign in Germany: 1813* (London, 1992).

Pivka, Otto von, *Armies of the Napoleonic Era* (Newton Abbot, 1979).

Prebble, John, *Mutiny* (London, 1975).

Rathbone, Julian, *Wellington's War* (London, 1984).

Regimental Council Duke of Wellington's Regiment, *The History of The Duke of Wellington's Regiment (West Riding)* (Halifax, 1993).

Reid, Stuart, *King George's Army* (London, 1995).

Robertson, Ian C., *Wellington at War in the Peninsula* (Barnsley, 2000).

Robinson, C.W., *Wellington's Campaigns, 1808-1815* (London, 1910).

Roper, Michael, *The Records of the War Office, 1660-1964* (London, 1998).

Schaumann, August, *On the Road with Wellington* (London, 1924).

Siborne, H.T., *Waterloo Letters* (London, 1993).

Siborne, W., *History of the Waterloo Campaign* (London, 1990).

Smith, Digby, *The Napoleonic Wars Data Book* (London, 1998).

Stanhope, Earl of, *Notes of Conversations with the Duke of Wellington* (London, 1888).

Strawson, John, *Beggars in Red: The British Army, 1789-1899* (London, 1991).

Thompson, J.M. (ed.), *Napoleon's Letters* (London, 1998).

Thompson, Neville, *Wellington after Waterloo* (London, 1996).

Thompson, W.F.K., *An Ensign in the Peninsular War* (London, 1981).

Tranie, J., and Carmigniani, J.C., *Napoleon's War in Spain* (London, 1982).

Uffindell, A., and Corum, M., *On the Fields of Glory* (London, 1996).

Watson, S.J., *By Command of the Emperor* (London, 1957).

Weller, Jac, *On Wellington* (London, 1998).

Weller, Jac, *Wellington at Waterloo* (London, 1992).

Weller, Jac, *Wellington in India* (London, 1972).

Weller, Jac, *Wellington in the Peninsula* (London, 1962).

Wellington, second Duke of (ed.), *Supplementary Despatches of the Duke of Wellington*, 14 vols (London, 1872).

Wellington, seventh Duke of, *Wellington and his Friends* (London, 1965).

Wilson, Joan, *A Soldier's Wife: Wellington's Marriage* (London, 1987).

Wooten, Geoffrey, *Waterloo 1815* (London, 1992).

Index